STUDIES IN IMPERIALISM

General editor: Andrew S. Thompson

Founding editor: John M. MacKenzie

When the 'Studies in Imperialism' series was founded by Professor John M. MacKenzie more than thirty years ago, emphasis was laid upon the conviction that 'imperialism as a cultural phenomenon had as significant an effect on the dominant as on the subordinate societies'. With well over a hundred titles now published, this remains the prime concern of the series. Cross-disciplinary work has indeed appeared covering the full spectrum of cultural phenomena, as well as examining aspects of gender and sex, frontiers and law, science and the environment, language and literature, migration and patriotic societies, and much else. Moreover, the series has always wished to present comparative work on European and American imperialism, and particularly welcomes the submission of books in these areas. The fascination with imperialism, in all its aspects, shows no sign of abating, and this series will continue to lead the way in encouraging the widest possible range of studies in the field. 'Studies in Imperialism' is fully organic in its development, always seeking to be at the cutting edge, responding to the latest interests of scholars and the needs of this ever-expanding area of scholarship.

Royals on tour

Manchester University Press

SELECTED TITLES AVAILABLE IN THE SERIES

WRITING IMPERIAL HISTORIES
ed. Andrew S. Thompson

EMPIRE OF SCHOLARS
Tamson Pietsch

HISTORY, HERITAGE AND COLONIALISM
Kynan Gentry

COUNTRY HOUSES AND THE BRITISH EMPIRE
Stephanie Barczewski

THE RELIC STATE
Pamila Gupta

WE ARE NO LONGER IN FRANCE
Allison Drew

THE SUPPRESSION OF THE ATLANTIC SLAVE TRADE
ed. Robert Burroughs and Richard Huzzey

HEROIC IMPERIALISTS IN AFRICA
Berny Sèbe

Royals on tour

POLITICS, PAGEANTRY AND COLONIALISM

Edited by
Robert Aldrich and Cindy McCreery

MANCHESTER UNIVERSITY PRESS

Copyright © Manchester University Press 2018

While copyright in the volume as a whole is vested in Manchester University Press, copyright in individual chapters belongs to their respective authors, and no chapter may be reproduced wholly or in part without the express permission in writing of both author and publisher.

Published by Manchester University Press
Oxford Road, Manchester M13 9PL
www.manchesteruniversitypress.co.uk

British Library Cataloguing-in-Publication Data
A catalogue record for this book is available from the British Library

ISBN 978 1 5261 0937 8 hardback
ISBN 978 1 5261 0938 5 paperback

First published 2018

The publisher has no responsibility for the persistence or accuracy of URLs for any external or third-party internet websites referred to in this book, and does not guarantee that any content on such websites is, or will remain, accurate or appropriate.

Typeset by Out of House Publishing

CONTENTS

List of figures—vii
Notes on contributors—ix
Acknowledgements—xi

1 Empire tours: royal travel between colonies and metropoles *Robert Aldrich and Cindy McCreery* — 1

2 Royal tour by proxy: the embassy of Sultan Alauddin of Aceh to the Netherlands, 1601–1603 *Jean Gelman Taylor* — 23

3 French imperial tours: Napoléon III and Eugénie in Algeria and beyond *Robert Aldrich* — 38

4 Something borrowed, something blue: Prince Alfred's precedent in overseas British royal tours, c. 1860–1925 *Cindy McCreery* — 56

5 Royalty, loyalism and citizenship in the nineteenth-century British settler empire *Charles V. Reed* — 80

6 The Maharaja of Gondal in Europe in 1883 *Caroline Keen* — 94

7 Performing monarchy: the Kaiser and Kaiserin's voyage to the Levant, 1898 *Matthew P. Fitzpatrick* — 110

8 Colonial kings in the metropole: the visits to France of King Sisowath (1906) and Emperor Khai Dinh (1922) *Robert Aldrich* — 125

9 Tensions of empire and monarchy: the African tour of the Portuguese crown prince in 1907 *Filipa Lowndes Vicente and Inês Vieira Gomes* — 146

10 Belgian royals on tour in the Congo, 1909–1960 *Guy Vanthemsche* — 169

11 Royal symbolism: Crown Prince Hirohito's tour to Europe in 1921 *Elise K. Tipton* — 191

12 The throne behind the power? Royal tours of 'Africa Italiana' under fascism *Mark Seymour* — 211

CONTENTS

13 Strained encounters: royal Indonesian visits to the Dutch court in the early twentieth century *Susie Protschky* 233

14 The 1947 royal tour in Smuts's Raj: South African Indian responses *Hilary Sapire* 250

Index—271

FIGURES

1.1 Portuguese Crown Prince Luís Filipe on tour with colonial authorities in Johannesburg, South Africa, 1907 (photograph by R.C.E. Missen, Museu-Biblioteca da Fundação Casa de Bragança. Vila Viçosa)   *page* 14

2.1 Prince Maurits receiving the ambassadors from the Sultan of Aceh, 1602 (Rijksmuseum, Amsterdam)   31

4.1 'Welcome, Sailor Prince', photograph of triumphal arch celebrating the arrival of H.R.H. Duke of Edinburgh to Emerald Hill, Melbourne, in 1867 (State Library of Victoria, Melbourne)   62

4.2 Julian Rossi Ashton, 'Our Sailor Princes', wood engraving of Princes Albert Victor and George aboard their ship. *Australasian Sketcher*, 7 May 1881 (State Library of Victoria, Melbourne)   63

6.1 HH Thakor Saheb Sir Bhawatsinghji Sagramji, Thakor of Gondal, photo Lafayette Portrait Studios, London, 1911 (© Victoria and Albert Museum, London)   97

8.1 'Visite de Khaï-Dinh', antique postcard of visit of Emperor Khai Dinh to Paris, 1922 (collection of Robert Aldrich)   131

8.2 'Sisowath à Paris', caricature of King Sisowath of Cambodia in Paris, cover of *L'Assiette au beurre*, 30 June 1906 (collection of Robert Aldrich)   134

9.1 Crown Prince Luís Filipe, photographed in Africa, 1907 (photograph by J. & M. Lazarus, Museu-Biblioteca da Fundação Casa de Bragança. Vila Viçosa)   147

9.2 African performance for Crown Prince Luís Filipe, Lourenço Marques, Mozambique, 1907 (photograph by J. & M. Lazarus, Museu-Biblioteca da Fundação Casa de Bragança. Vila Viçosa)   155

9.3 Africans and Portuguese officials, Lourenço Marques, Mozambique, 1907 (photograph by J. & M. Lazarus, Museu-Biblioteca da Fundação Casa de Bragança. Vila Viçosa)   156

10.1 King Baudouin in Kamina, Congo, 1955 (photograph by C. Lamote of Congopresse. Collection of Guy Vanthemsche)   182

11.1 Crown Prince Hirohito and King George V in the state carriage on the way to Buckingham Palace, 1921 (*Kōtaishi denka toō kinen: Renzoku kinsha daiehagaki hanshashinchō* (Tokyo: Ikubunsha, 1922), plate 30. Collection of Robert Aldrich)   200

11.2 Crown Prince Hirohito at Cambridge University on receiving an honorary doctorate, 1921 (*Kōtaishi denka toō kinen: Renzoku kinsha daiehagaki hanshashinchō* (Tokyo: Ikubunsha, 1922), plate 54. Collection of Robert Aldrich)   202

LIST OF FIGURES

12.1 King Victor Emmanuel III and Mussolini: 'The King-Emperor and the Founder of the Empire', *La Domenica del Corriere*, 16 March 1937 — 213

12.2 King Victor Emmanuel III in Eritrea, *La Domenica del Corriere*, 16 October 1932 (Biblioteca di Storia moderna et contemporanea, Rome) — 222

12.3 King Victor Emmanuel III elephant-hunting in Somalia, *La Domenica del Corriere*, 2 December 1934 (Biblioteca di Storia moderna et contemporanea, Rome) — 226

13.1 Tengku Latifah and Tengku Kalsun, daughters of the sultan of Langkat, offering orchids to Queen Wilhelmina on the occasion of the fortieth anniversary of her reign, Olympic Stadium, Amsterdam, 1938 (Sparnestad) — 238

13.2 Queen Wilhelmina receiving the sultan of Modjopait at Paleis Het Loo for the Scouts World Jamboree, 1937 (*Koningin Wilhelmina: Vertig jaren wijs beleid 1898–1938* (Amsterdam: De Telegraaf and H.J.W. Becht, 1938). Royal Collections, The Netherlands) — 239

13.3 Th.M. Schipper, portraits of (from left to right) the sultan of Langkat, two of his brothers, his son the crown prince and another son, and his wife, 1938 (Royal Collections, The Netherlands) — 246

CONTRIBUTORS

Robert Aldrich is Professor of European History at the University of Sydney, and the author of works on colonial history, including *Banished Potentates: Dethroning and Exiling Indigenous Monarchs under British and French Colonial Rule, 1815–1955*. With Cindy McCreery, he edited *Crowns and Colonies: European Monarchies and Overseas Empires*.

Matthew P. Fitzpatrick is Associate Professor in International History at Flinders University, Adelaide. He is the author of *Purging the Empire: Mass Expulsions in Germany, 1871–1914* and *Liberal Imperialism in Germany: Expansionism and Nationalism, 1848–1884*.

Inês Vieira Gomes is a PhD student at the Institute of Social Sciences of the University of Lisbon. Her thesis focuses on photographic archives and practices in the Portuguese African colonies between 1890 and 1940.

Caroline Keen holds a PhD from the School of Oriental and African Studies, University of London. She has published *Princely India and the British: Political Development and the Operation of Empire* and *An Imperial Crisis in British India: The Manipur Uprising of 1891*.

Cindy McCreery is Senior Lecturer in History at the University of Sydney. Her publications include *The Satirical Gaze: Prints of Women in Eighteenth-Century England*, as well as journal articles and book chapters on British and colonial cultural and naval history, including Prince Alfred as the first global British royal tourist (c.1867–71). With Robert Aldrich she co-edited *Crowns and Colonies: European Monarchies and Overseas Empires*.

Susie Protschky is Senior Lecturer in Modern History at Monash University, Melbourne. She is the author of *Images of the Tropics: Environment and Visual Culture in Colonial Indonesia* and the forthcoming *Photographic Subjects: Monarchy, Photography and the Dutch East Indies*. This chapter is an outcome of an Australian Research Council Postdoctoral Fellowship (DP1092615).

NOTES ON CONTRIBUTORS

Charles V. Reed is an Associate Professor of History at Elizabeth City State University in the United States. He is the author of *Royal Tourists, Colonial Subjects, and the Making of a British World, 1860–1911*. He is president-elect of H-Net, editor of H-Empire, and associate editor of *Itinerario*.

Hilary Sapire is Senior Lecturer in the Department of History, Classics and Archaeology at Birkbeck, University of London. She has published widely on twentieth-century South African history and is completing a book on royal visits to Southern Africa and the contested histories of loyalism. She is a former editor, and current member of the editorial board, of the *Journal of Southern African Studies*.

Mark Seymour is Associate Professor of History at the University of Otago, New Zealand. He is the author of *Debating Divorce in Italy: Marriage and the Making of Modern Italians* and co-editor of *Politica ed emozioni nella storia d'Italia*. He is co-editor of the journal *Modern Italy*.

Jean Gelman Taylor is Honorary Associate Professor of History at the University of New South Wales, Sydney. Her publications include *The Social World of Batavia: European and Eurasian in Colonial Indonesia* and *Indonesia: Peoples and Histories*.

Elise K. Tipton is Honorary Associate Professor of Japanese Studies at the University of Sydney. She is the author of *Modern Japan: A Social and Political History*. Her research focuses on the relationship between society and the state during the interwar years.

Guy Vanthemsche is Professor of Contemporary History at the Free University of Brussels. Among his most recent books is *Belgium and the Congo, 1880–1980*. He is a member of the Royal Academy of Overseas Sciences and the Secretary of the Royal Historical Commission of Belgium.

Filipa Lowndes Vicente is a researcher at the Institute of Social Sciences of the University of Lisbon. She is the author of *Orientalisms: India between Florence and Bombay, 1860–1900* and is currently preparing English editions of *Between Two Empires: British Travellers in Goa (1800–1940)* and *The Empire of Vision: Photography in the Portuguese Colonial Context (1860–1960)*, originally published in Portuguese.

ACKNOWLEDGEMENTS

We would like to acknowledge with gratitude funding from the School of Philosophical and Historical Inquiry (SOPHI) at the University of Sydney, which made possible a conference on royal tours held in 2015; several of the chapters in this volume have been developed from papers initially presented at that conference. Robert Aldrich also acknowledges a Discovery Grant from the Australian Research Council that has been invaluable in work on European and indigenous monarchies in the colonial age.

Our thanks go to the contributors to this volume, and to others who participated in our conference (some of whose work will appear in a special issue of the *Royal Studies Journal* on royal tours of British Dominions in the twentieth century), to Briony Neilson for her sterling work in putting together the manuscript, to Nicholas Keyzer for scanning several images reproduced here, to Trevor Matthews for preparing the index, to Bruce Baskerville for assistance in checking the page-proofs and to Emma Brennan at Manchester University Press for her encouragement with this and our other projects.

Robert Aldrich and Cindy McCreery

CHAPTER ONE

Empire tours: royal travel between colonies and metropoles

Robert Aldrich and Cindy McCreery

Royals have always been a peripatetic species. In the Ancient world, Hadrian spent more than half of his reign travelling the Roman empire, from Britain to the Black Sea to Egypt. When monarchs still led their forces into battle, as did St Louis during the Crusades and as did other medieval and early modern kings, travel to battlefields abroad was necessarily part of the 'job'. With great pageantry and festivity, 'royal entries' marked the arrival of sovereigns into the major cities of their own realms. Emperor Charles V travelled ceaselessly through his domains in the Iberian peninsula, Low Countries, Burgundy and central Europe. Queen Elizabeth I of England made royal 'progresses' from one town and estate to another, sometimes bankrupting her fortunate or unfortunate hosts. Tsar Peter the Great left imperial Russia, still an exotic, distant and, in Western eyes, near barbaric kingdom, for a 'grand embassy' that took him to Vienna, Amsterdam and London. Neither Charles nor Elizabeth, however, visited their possessions in the New World, nor did Peter make it to the far reaches of his continental empire.

Non-European royals travelled less extensively. Rulers of China, Japan, Korea and Vietnam traditionally remained immured in their forbidden cities, though Mughal rulers on the Indian subcontinent and Moroccan sultans, like early modern European counterparts, regularly moved the court around their territories, and Ottoman and Persian rulers made visits to neighbouring states. However, Hindu sovereigns faced the loss of caste purity if they crossed the 'black waters', until maharajas breached that interdiction in the second half of the nineteenth century.

A few non-Western royals travelled to Europe in the early modern period. Franciscan missionaries escorted two princes from Ceylon to Portugal at the end of the 1500s; the 'Black Prince', Dom João, took the name of the Portuguese king when he was baptised, and he had a church constructed on the outskirts of Lisbon. A French cleric accompanied Prince Nguyen Phuc Canh, son of the ruler of Vietnam, to France in 1787. The youthful prince was received by King Louis XVI, had his portrait painted and was the darling of the Versailles court, although hopes for an alliance between the two kingdoms and conversion of the Vietnamese dynasty to Christianity came to nought. In between those two visits, numerous 'princes' landed in Europe, though in a period when knowledge of distant countries was vague, and titles were far from standardised and often contested, almost any traveller might be gratified with a royal title. Pocahontas, the daughter of a Native American chief – converted to Christianity and married to an Englishman – arrived in London in 1606, and was paraded around by the Virginia Company as a princess of the Powhatan empire. Subsequent 'royal' visitors to Europe included four 'Indian Kings' who visited England in 1700, a 'Prince of Timor' who travelled to the Netherlands, Britain and Canada at mid-century, and the Polynesian 'princes' Aoutourou and Omai who returned to Europe with Louis-Antoine Bougainville and James Cook.[1]

In the nineteenth century, royals began to travel more frequently and more widely, thanks in part (as will be discussed) to innovations in transport. European monarchs met for 'summits' and called upon one another individually, as seen by the reciprocal visits of Queen Victoria and Prince Albert with Emperor Napoléon III and Empress Eugénie. Recreation, affairs of state and family visits by royals married into foreign courts – notably, the progeny of Queen Victoria and of King Christian IX of Denmark, the 'father-in-law of Europe' – kept royals on the move.[2] By the *fin de siècle*, so many monarchs and their family members passed through France that the government had appointed a full-time official to look after visiting royals.[3]

The presence of non-Western royals in Europe also became somewhat more frequent, their number including some, such as the famous Sikh maharaja Duleep Singh, who had been dethroned by the British but allowed to settle in Britain.[4] Among royal or 'semi-royal' visitors in the second half of the nineteenth century were the hereditary prime minister of Nepal, the shah of Persia, the Ottoman sultan, the sultan of Johore, the kings of Zululand, Hawai'i and Siam, and three rulers from Bechuanaland.[5] For wealthy maharajas, visits to Europe were becoming as significant as the 'Grand Tour' of the European continent had been for the eighteenth-century British elite.[6] In European capitals, spa towns and Mediterranean resorts, royals were far from uncommon, though they travelled and were accommodated in ways to which commoners were far from accustomed.

Writing the history of royal tours

Royal tours of the 1800s and early 1900s, and since, have created much documentation, perhaps the most obvious record contained in newspapers and magazines, newsreels and then radio and television broadcasts. Royals were (and are) celebrities, their every move shadowed by eager journalists. The press had a field day when royals came to visit, writers and readers fascinated with banquets, ribbon-cuttings and speeches, the clothing and jewellery sported by royals and tittle-tattle about their less public activities. Royal tours have also produced more official accounts by court chroniclers, often published in illustrated commemorative albums. First-person accounts range from diaries written by royals themselves – though these are sometimes closely safeguarded within royal archives, or have been lost – and by those who accompanied or came into contact with them.

Images constitute particularly important documentation. Image, after all, was a key ingredient in the popularity (or lack of it) of royal personages, with tours carefully arranged for maximum exposure of the visitors. The invention of photography, and development of cameras that could be used by amateurs – royals and others – made possible posed, official and informal shots. These provide not just portraits of individuals, but portrayals of the panoply of celebrations and decorations. How various groups are depicted, from royal parties to 'natives' and commoners, gives insight into social hierarchies and inter-communal relations, and to the changing ways in which tours were staged and received. They occasionally also give evidence of opposition to the royal presence.

The material culture of visits provides further sources. Tours generally involved gift exchange, from precious presentation objects offered to royals to ethnographic 'curios' (in the language of the colonial age), many of these artefacts are now housed in museums and royal collections. There are, as well, elaborately crafted proclamations, medals and awards, and more quotidian items, including in recent times the huge array of souvenirs that help market the monarchy.[7] Left behind in the places visited are buildings the royals opened, statues they unveiled, plaques erected in their honour, and various other public and private 'relics'.

Libraries, museums and private collections, and even landscapes, thus abound with evidence of royal tours. Archival documents provide details on their organisation and execution, budgets, transport, protocol, timetables, banquets and ceremonies, programmes for gala performances, and the often large cast of characters who accompanied royal visitors or who were involved in the caravans, as well as information on luggage, conveyances and travel requisites. Given the wealth of documents it is somewhat surprising that royal tours have until recently commanded relatively little scholarly attention, though the theme is now being addressed in various genres, including new books directed to general readers, among which royalty is a popular subject.[8] They also include full-scale volumes on tours of particular countries, representative among them Jane Connors's study of royal tours of Australia.[9] Tours to Canada, South Africa and other parts of the British empire have also been investigated by scholars such as Phillip A. Buckner, who argue that these visits played an important role in consolidating national as well as imperial identities.[10]

The literature encompasses studies that specifically situate visits in the context of the history and evolution of 'modern monarchy', international relations and cross-cultural encounters. A pioneering volume published by Johannes Paulmann in 2000 underlined the importance of face-to-face royal encounters in the nineteenth century, when crowned heads reigned in most European countries (and thought of themselves as a majestic 'internationale' bound by heredity, status and intermarriage). Paulmann demonstrated how royal encounters sent strong political signals and provoked diverse responses. He introduced perspectives on 'symbolic politics', and the way that visits represented a 'staging' or 'performance' of monarchies seeking legitimation in the face of growing democratisation, parliamentarianism and challenges to the established order. For the public, the visits were, he added, at the very least 'international variety shows', even when there existed underlying ambivalence about the institution of monarchy itself.[11] Paulmann's work has inspired much further research, especially in the field of cultural history, on the monarchs in Germany – thirty-three kings, princes and other royals reigned until their dynasties were all disestablished after 1918, leaving historians a plethora of case studies to investigate.[12]

Not surprisingly the British monarchy has attracted much attention, not least in the countless biographies of royals. Scholars who have contributed to the emergence of a 'new royal history', such as David Cannadine,[13] have reflected on the constitutional role of royalty, as well as its spectacle, in the 'invention of tradition' and the 'ornamentalist' connections between Britain and its empire. Several works have made royal tours a particular focus. Matthew Glencross's book on the state visits of Edward VII discusses the diplomatic significance of that monarch's travels within Europe.[14] Charles V. Reed's monograph on nineteenth- and early twentieth-century British royal tours of empire demonstrates the importance of travel in the performance of both monarchy and imperial identity. Miles Taylor's ongoing research points to the intimate links between Queen Victoria and India, where she sent several of her sons and grandsons on tour.[15] Sarah Carter and Maria Nugent's edited collection makes clear the importance of Victoria – occasionally incarnated by a touring prince – for Indigenous people such as Aboriginal people in Australia and Maori in New Zealand.[16] For the twentieth century, Philip Murphy's work on the British monarchy and empire has offered a detailed analysis of relations between the crown and colonies in the era of decolonisation, by which time royals were frequent travellers. Murphy has shown how members of the royal family (though never the Queen) were solicited and despatched to independence ceremonies around the empire, concluding with the presence of the Prince of Wales at the handover of Hong Kong to the People's Republic of China in 1997.[17] Ian Radforth's study of an earlier Prince of Wales in Canada and the United States in 1860, and volumes edited by Frank Lorenz Müller and Heidi Mehrkens on monarchs' heirs, show how succeeding Princes of Wales, and other sons of monarchs – often more frequent travellers than their reigning parents –were sent on 'missions' abroad. Their travels exemplified a brand of personal politics and imperial 'soft diplomacy' increasingly important (not least because of media coverage) from the late 1800s.[18] These works testify to the broad contexts and wide-ranging implications of tours, and their value for an understanding of the dynamics of domestic, international and colonial affairs.

The 'new imperial history', and trends in historical writing that have contributed to a renewal of studies of colonialism, make possible fresh outlooks on monarchy. Royal tourists were prime exemplars of particular races, classes and genders, illustrating three central themes in the new historiography. Contemporary approaches have emphasised that colonising and colonised countries must be considered in the same analytical field, and that links between various colonies are often as significant as those between colonies and metropoles. Tours by roving royals, often visiting multiple colonial sites during the course of their journeys, were manifest ways in which 'home' and 'abroad', mother-country and overseas possessions, occupy connected terrains. Many strategies taken from literary analysis, cultural studies, postmodernism and postcolonialism have been enveloped in the new colonial history. These have encouraged scholars to 'read' various sorts of texts, from printed materials to images, and to examine the reception of these texts, and royal tours provide a panorama of words and pictures. They have also pointed out the ways in which individuals and groups 'perform' the roles assigned to them or the ones they create for themselves, and a royal tour was, in a very real sense, a performance for both visitors and hosts. Discussion of transnational linkages and cultural hybridities extends to overseas journeys, where festivities surrounding royals included both European traditions and ones – e.g., ceremonies of greeting, song, dance, art and artisanry – from local societies. In short, general trends in historiography over the past several decades beneficially influence the way royal tours can now be studied (as the chapters in this volume testify), and research on such journeys also contributes original perspectives to the new imperial history.

European royals in the colonies

Our earlier edited volume on *Crowns and Colonies* identified many constitutional, personal and cultural ties between monarchies, states and subjects in colonial situations.[19] The present volume takes up the theme of royal tours, which figured in several chapters of that collection. Royal tours became, from the late 1800s, a primary strategy though which imperial paramountcy was projected in the colonies, feudatory obeisance to imperial authority was reflected, and mutual recognition between rulers of European nations and still independent overseas states was symbolised. The theme extends far beyond the British empire, and the cases contained here explore travels by continental European and British royals, and by Indigenous monarchs and their representatives as well. Comings and goings undertaken by sovereigns, their kin and their deputies moving between imperial centres and peripheries, and between Europe and Asia or Africa, offer a significant lens though which to view modern monarchy, cultural exchange, international relations, imperialism and decolonisation.

Visits by royals to the overseas possessions of their own and other countries, by vassal monarchs from protectorates to imperial metropoles, and by royals from countries hoping to stave off colonial takeover, we argue, were a vital, and largely new, aspect of high imperialism from the late 1800s to the mid-1900s. Tours expressed and promoted royal and imperial authority, though in some instances they revealed resistance against expansionist designs. They affirmed the legitimacy, status and privileges of dynasties, even those whose thrones had come under an onslaught by conquering armies and navies bent on annexing territory, proclaiming protectorates or 'opening' foreign countries to commerce and 'Western civilisation'. Tours developed a personal relationship between sovereign and colonial subjects: vice-regal officials, settlers, Indigenous peoples and diasporic migrants. They were intended to foster familiarity with distant places and cultures for populations back at home. They brought a sovereign, or kinsman of a sovereign, across the world, in flesh and blood, and put him on show in a theatre of pomp and ceremonial. Tours underlined the political role of dynasties and the might (and at times weakness) of their countries, but they also revealed and affirmed the emotional, mystical and spiritual character of the monarchy itself. The monarch (or a scion) stood at the apex of an entire political, social and cultural order, and that order, and not just the traveller alone, was on display.

For overseas territories where a 'protected' monarchy or princely dynasty had been retained, generally stripped of real power though perhaps still treated with deference, tours showed who was 'boss', and how the rights of a paramount ruler overrode those of 'underlords'. If an Indigenous monarchy had been abolished, tours emphasised how the imperial ruler had taken over the rights and privileges of a defunct dynasty: the imperial monarch as supreme military and political authority, arbiter of justice, patron of the arts, fount of honours. Tours showed off the might and majesty of monarchy. They testified to the unification of disparate territories into a single colony, and of varied colonies into a great empire. The tours aimed to procure the allegiance of the peoples over whom the monarch reigned, and his or her colonial government ruled, as well as opportunities to counter resistance, disloyalty and moves towards autonomy or independence. At the same time, somewhat paradoxically, they provided recognition and status for maharajas, sultans and other loyal Indigenous rulers who had kept their thrones after foreign takeover. Visits to historical and contemporary sites of cultural expression (most obviously, places of worship) acknowledged 'native' traditions but also indicated how they had been brought under the guardianship – or, to be more critical, how these traditions had been appropriated – by colonial masters.

The royal visitor was the central actor in a tour, but was surrounded by an entourage of other people and a store of paraphernalia that played essential roles. Ministers and government officials from the capital conferred with vice-regal authorities, representatives of settler populations, and elders and chiefs of 'native' peoples. Like the royals, they engaged in 'fact-finding' about natural resources, economic development, political and social issues. Journalists, who made up a significant contingent in many later tours, reported on ceremonies and speeches, gauged the reception given to the visitors, and wrote about curious sites and people they discovered. Military and naval officers – and especially the warships in which the royal party often travelled – proclaimed the firepower of the colonising country for conquest of new territories, 'pacification' of those over which flags had already been raised, and defence against enemies and rivals in the imperial scrambles. Ordinary sailors kept the fleet shipshape, and were deployed as muscled exemplars of the bravery and bravura of European manhood. Maids and valets ensured that royal personages were suitably caparisoned in the appropriate uniforms, medals and sashes, fashionable top-hats and frock-coats. In the visitor's voluminous baggage were packed not only countless changes of clothing and other travel needs, but gifts to be offered, decorations to be awarded, standards to be unfurled, portraits to be circulated. The ships (and trains) on which royals travelled served as mobile palaces, and the government houses and hotels in which they lodged became temporary courts. Not just a royal visitor, but the institution of monarchy had come to town.

An individual visit thus played on the emotional, cultural, 'spectacular' and mystical aura of the monarchy, and the show played itself out before various publics. The royal tourist was visiting kinsmen and compatriots bound by the 'crimson thread' of imperial bloodlines and heritage. There were also non-Europeans now bound, willingly or not, by imperial dominion and, in principle, the promises of the civilising mission. The royal's visit provided an opportunity to show off to the travelling party, and to the world, the achievements of empire-builders, to proclaim the loyalty but also to present the grievances of settler populations, and to exhibit 'native' peoples and cultures. Locals had an opportunity to advertise themselves, whether different Indigenous 'tribes' and ethnic communities, specific cities or provinces within a colony or colonial federation, various civic and voluntary associations, individual businesses or chambers of commerce and industry. A chance to present themselves (in a very real sense) to a royal, even for a brief moment, allowed a group to enhance its status, express its remonstrations, show off its accomplishments or simply mark out its place in a colonial society.

Some tours took on special significance. The visits of Emperor Napoléon III to Algeria were the first and only ones by a reigning French monarch, and 'first visits' by a royal, particularly a sovereign, enjoyed a particularly memorable status. In 1874 King Christian IX undertook the first visit by a Danish monarch to Iceland, marking the millennium of Danish settlement, but it was also the occasion to issue a new constitution for the island. The Delhi durbar of 1911 marked one of the most important moments in British rule of India, when King George V and Queen Mary were crowned emperor and empress, and received feudatory royals from throughout the subcontinent, the king of Bhutan and Shan princes from Burma. Never before or after did the Raj see such an imposing manifestation of British paramountcy and royal splendour.[20]

One royal visit could lead to others, often following a template established by initial visits, encompassing the same sights and festivities. Such visits became almost routine by the mid-twentieth century, but they still were potent moments in colonial and national histories – perhaps no more pointedly than when a visiting royal presided over a ceremony where a colony assumed its independence.

'Native' monarchs in imperial capitals

Tours by 'native' monarchs from Africa, Asia and Oceania presented, arguably, an even more complex scenario than those by Europeans. Rulers of still independent non-Western states who went to Europe were aiming to prevent the conquest of their countries by expanding colonial powers. Thus the Ottoman sultan, the Persian shah and the Siamese king were intent on affirming the sovereignty of their states, being treated as equals by fellow royals and the governments in Europe, and portraying themselves as competent and modernising rulers. If a country had already become a protectorate of a European state, a royal visit was generally intended – as was the case for Indian maharajas, Malay sultans and royals from French Indochina – to pledge the allegiance of a vassal sovereign to the paramount colonial power, and equally importantly, to affirm the status and residual powers of his dynasty.

Europeans viewed visitors from afar with great fascination, as well as with racialised stereotyping. Somewhat paradoxically, the 'native' princes gained credit for appearing exotic but were also expected to show themselves, in their behaviour and interests, to have become Europeanised (and thus 'civilised') gentlemen. This was a difficult balancing act, for instance, when a ruler with multiple wives visited a Christian country. European hospitality did not accord with certain taboos on food and drink – Muslim rulers generally did not drink alcohol, and one Indian prince insisted on shipping his own drinking water to Europe. Whether to wear 'native' or European clothing was always a question; the minders of the visiting Cambodian king in France suggested that crowds preferred for him to be dressed in Asian style. Social practices in which some visitors might have acceptably engaged at home – for instance, chewing betel-nut and expectorating the residue – hardly conformed to European etiquette.

Tours by non-Western royals always attracted great publicity, sometimes even more than the travels of European royals, but they achieved mixed outcomes. Two examples provide illustrations. Neil Parsons has studied one tour which scored considerable success, the 1895 visit to Britain by three 'kings' or 'chiefs' from Bechuanaland, over which London had declared a protectorate a decade earlier. The kings set out to argue against Cecil Rhodes's designs to annex Bechuanaland to the Cape Colony, exploit its mineral resources and use the territory to launch an attack on the Transvaal. Khama, Sebele and Bathoen were committed Christians – Sebele had been baptised by Dr David Livingstone – and were teetotallers. Nonconformist ministers organised their tour, and the Africans received rapturous welcomes in Nonconformist chapels and the meeting-halls of temperance unions. Queen Victoria graciously received the visitors, all attired in natty tailored suits, and presented Bibles. In part because of the warm reception, the government decided against annexation of Bechuanaland, and it remained a protectorate until the 1960s.[21]

Less successful was the European tour of Nasr Allah Khan, second son of the emir of Afghanistan, also in 1895. The emir hoped the tour would lead to closer direct diplomatic relations with Britain and thereby cut out the 'middle man' (the Government of India) and preserve the independence of a country in which Britain had regularly intervened since the mid-nineteenth century. According to a detailed Afghan account, the prince toured predictable sites, including the Tower of London ('the residence of the former shahs of England') and Buckingham Palace (where he 'took tea and fruit' as refreshments); he visited P&O ships, the Armstrong munitions factory, and manufacturing plants in London, Leeds, Birmingham, Liverpool and Newcastle. He was received by Queen Victoria, and attended the Ascot races with the Prince of Wales. But, according to European accounts, the prince looked bored throughout much of his tour, and compounded this error by outstaying his welcome. The day he left London for Paris, the *New York Times* printed the news under the headline 'At Last the Shahzada Goes Away'.[22]

In the absence of personal visits, rulers of non-Western countries often despatched embassies to Europe. The sultan of Morocco sent a delegation to Queen Elizabeth I in 1600 with proposals for a military alliance between the two countries (and Holland) against Spain. Though this did not eventuate, the visit to London and tour around England inaugurated a period of friendly relations, and may well have inspired Shakespeare's *The Merchant of Venice*, written six months after the embassy. In the early 1600s, an East Indian sultan was represented by a legation sent to Holland, a royal tour – as Jean Gelman Taylor suggests – 'by proxy'. In the 1680s, the king of Siam sent an embassy to Louis XIV, returning a visit by a delegation that the Sun King had sent to Siam. The Siamese carried a letter from their king, contained in a silver casket; the missive was a royal object, carried from ship to shore aboard a special barge. The Siamese delegates made obeisance to the letter and, so revered was it because of the royal provenance, that they objected when it was placed in a room on a lower floor than their own accommodation. Another grand Siamese embassy, to the court of Napoléon III almost two hundred years later, was followed by embassies from Burma and Japan in the 1870s. The ambassadors leading such delegations were personal representatives of their countries' monarchs, often bearing extravagant gifts (such as a jewel-encrusted girdle offered by the Burmese to Queen Victoria). The representatives of Asian monarchs were treated much as if they were royals: received in audience by the monarchs who hosted them, shown the sites, entertained at banquets and receptions, awarded decorations and given presents, and accorded honour guards and gun salutes.[23] Such embassies deserve further scholarly attention in the context of royal tours and in the history of monarchy.

Gender in royal travel

Royal tours can be 'read' in many different ways – for example, in terms of 'staging' and monarchical self-presentation, geopolitical significance and public reception. Gender represents another important aspect for consideration. Most of the royal tourists to and from colonies in the late 1800s and early 1900s were men. This is not surprising, since most monarchs were male – and the two most powerful queens, Victoria of Britain and Wilhelmina of the Netherlands, did not visit their overseas possessions. Rulership, in general, was considered a manly occupation, and in some countries, law and custom prohibited women from acceding to thrones. Many of the travelling 'heirs and spares' were military officers, a career reserved to men. Indeed, for the princes, overseas travel served as a rite of masculine passage, an opportunity to enjoy the camaraderie of sailors, officials and male colonists. Colonial travel also allowed them to escape the parental eye and avail themselves of high life and low life overseas. Most royal tours thus boasted a distinctly manly ethos, with such leisure pursuits as big-game hunting and outings to gentlemen's clubs and, on occasion, to bordellos.

Women, however, were not absent from royal travel. In the 1850s, for instance, Crown Prince Leopold of Belgium and his wife, Crown Princess Marie Henriette, went on a belated honeymoon to the Levant. The French Empress Eugénie accompanied her husband to Algeria in 1860, the new British monarch, George V, and his consort, Queen Mary, toured India together in 1911 and the Italian king and queen, Vittorio Emanuele III and Elena, went to Africa in the 1930s. Female royals even journeyed alone, as when the widowed former Empress Eugénie went to South Africa to see where her only son had been killed. Another ex-monarch, the unmarried Queen Ranavalona III of Madagascar, made regular visits to Paris and provincial spa towns (accompanied by an aunt and an orphaned great-niece she had adopted) after she was dethroned and exiled to Algeria in the late 1890s. Queen Emma of Hawai'i had gone to Britain and the United States in 1865, and the Indian Begum of Bhopal in 1863–1864 undertook a pilgrimage to the Muslim holy city of Mecca, accompanied by a retinue of a thousand people.[24]

Other women figured prominently in royal entourages. Particularly notable was a troupe of Khmer dancers, under the supervision of a princess, who journeyed with the Cambodian king to France in 1906, to the great delight of French audiences. Women in host countries were active as spectators, participants and organisers of levees, banquets, theatrical performances and religious services. Wives of vice-regal officials carried out duties as hosts and public figures. Females as eagerly as males vied with each other for invitations in the social whirl, and newspapers never failed to mention the women's elegant gowns and sparkling jewellery at the galas. The place of women in royal tours deserves further attention, especially as royal female travellers of the early twentieth century foreshadowed such celebrated later ones as Queen Elizabeth II and Diana, Princess of Wales.

Gender, of course, is not a question simply of men and women, but also of the ways that particular societies (and groups and individuals within them) think about masculinity and femininity. This becomes very evident in royal tours, where male royals were expected to wear uniforms bespeaking martial training and character, and pursue avocations that testified to courage, boldness, athletic prowess and fortitude. These European virtues were sometimes implicitly or explicitly contrasted with what was perceived as a certain effeminacy of Asian men clothed in flowing silks or skirt-like sarongs, bedecked with jewellery and supposedly prey to vice, or with Africans thought to possess unbridled lust, a sanguinary propensity to violence and a lack of 'civilised' behaviour. Similarly, royal women travellers were held to incarnate idealised European feminine traits of respectability, monogamy, domesticity and poise that distinguished them from the dubious morals and suspect deportment of 'native' women. Journalists' descriptions, royal tourists' reminiscences and images produced during tours reveal the 'performance' of gender in both public and private activities, and in perceptions of travellers and the various groups of 'natives', settlers and diasporic communities that received them.

The risks and rewards of royal tours

All was not smooth sailing for royal tourists. Travel, especially to distant destinations, was fraught with danger. There were the hazards to health and comfort during long voyages, different climates, unfamiliar food, contagious diseases and fatigue – the same problems faced by every traveller. Even royals were subject to the vagaries of weather, rough seas, missed connections, breakdowns in equipment and the need to rearrange schedules at the last moment (with consequent disappointment for those whose reception had been cancelled or whose town had been deleted from the itinerary). There was tedious protocol and the punishing schedules to which they were often subjected.

Security was a major concern, especially as anarchist terrorism and violent nationalism spread in the late 1800s and early 1900s. Several royals were victims while away from home: Empress 'Sisi' of Austria assassinated by an anarchist in Geneva in 1898, Archduke Franz Ferdinand and his wife Sophie felled in Sarajevo in 1914, and King Alexander I of Yugoslavia murdered in Marseille in 1934. (Among other kings assassinated in their home countries in the three decades after 1881 were the Russian tsar, the kings of Italy, Serbia and Greece, and the king and crown prince of Portugal. Republicans were not exempt, as shown with the murder of presidents of France and the United States.) Though attacks on travelling royals, in fact, were generally avoided, notable exceptions were an unsuccessful attempt to assassinate Prince Alfred, the son of Queen Victoria, by a would-be Irish nationalist in Sydney in 1868, and an attack on the Russian tsarevitch (the future Tsar Nicholas II) on a visit to Japan in 1891 (with the sabre wielded by the would-be assassin deflected by the cane of the quick acting Prince George of Greece and Denmark, the Russian's cousin and travel companion).

Tours were also threatened with disruption by political protests or marred with lapses of protocol. When one Indian maharaja turned his back on King George V at the Delhi durbar of 1911, the British press trumped up the minor incident into a case of heinous *lèse-majesté*. A durbar projected for King-Emperor George VI after he ascended the British throne in 1936 was aborted when the Indian National Congress called for a boycott, and diasporic Indians demanded the boycott of a royal visit to South Africa on the eve of Indian independence in 1947. Fractious debates in chancelleries and parliaments took place over the advisability of royal tours, for instance, on the first overseas trip made by a senior Japanese royal, the heir apparent and future Emperor Hirohito, in 1921. A visit to southern Africa by the Portuguese crown prince in 1907 could not stifle rising republicanism at home, and prevent the declaration of a republic in Portugal in 1910. (The South African, Japanese and Portuguese cases are discussed in chapters of this volume.)

Whenever a tour was planned, there was some concern that a royal might meddle in foreign policy matters better left to ministers and diplomats. The prolonged absence of a monarch or crown prince also posed a danger. There were questions about whether the traveller would 'perform' well and be appropriately received, and in the case of princes barely out of their teens, whether they had sufficient maturity and gravitas to carry out their duties. Faux pas, especially with journalists

1.1 Portuguese Crown Prince Luís Filipe on tour with colonial authorities in Johannesburg, South Africa, 1907

intent on good copy, could make them laughing-stocks and risk cordial relations with hosts. There were always fears that receptions overseas might be less than enthusiastic, or even hostile.

Partly because of risks and reservations, long-distance travel by European monarchs and other royals really emerged as a phenomenon only in the mid-1800s. There were, nevertheless, a few earlier exceptions. One pioneering royal traveller, already briefly mentioned, was the future King Leopold II of the Belgians. As heir to the throne, Leopold made several trips from the mid-1850s to the early 1860s around the Mediterranean, including visits to Ottoman Egypt, Palestine, Syria and Turkey, as well as to Italy, Spain, Portugal and Greece. In 1864–1865 he travelled even further, visiting Ceylon, India, Burma, Sumatra, Hong Kong and Canton. In public, Leopold's delicate health was often cited as the reason for his tours; in private his 'obsession to travel' was bemoaned by ministers and by his father, the king. But this obsession had a clear goal; in North Africa as well as in Asia, Leopold carefully studied the ways in which the British, French and Dutch governed their possessions, and he actively scouted out any opportunities for

Belgium to acquire colonies. These tours provided the background to Leopold's later acquisition of his own African empire, the Congo Free State.[25]

A number of developments favoured royal travel to faraway places after mid-century. Interest in 'exotic' overseas destinations increased dramatically, especially with newspaper articles, travelogues and memoirs written by explorers, as well as with national and international expositions held with regularity from the 1850s. Royals were not immune to the general wanderlust pervading Europe. Meanwhile, new types of transport made travel quicker, more comfortable and safer. The rise of steamships from the 1840s, the opening of the Suez Canal in 1869, and the spreading web of international railway and telegraph networks by the 1870s all made long-distance journeys more feasible and pleasant. Photography provided a novel avocation for travellers, new medicines served as prophylactics against tropical diseases, and a burgeoning infrastructure (such as hotels) accommodated tourists. By the last decade of the century royals, including non-Westerners, were travelling more regularly around their own regions and much further afield. Their long voyages were punctuated with stops en route. A journey between Europe and Asia indeed required refuelling stops – often in places such as Colombo and Aden – expanding the possibilities for official receptions, pilgrimages, recreation and 'fact-finding'. Before the age of air travel, such sea voyages were virtual international imperial 'progresses' from one colony to another.

The expansion of European colonial empires provided a strengthened imperative for royal tours. European royals considered visits to overseas territories as valuable and indeed necessary to affirm suzerainty over old and new dominions, and the growth of empires, of course, meant that there were more places to visit. Royals joined the increasing number of people going 'out' to the empire, as soldiers and sailors, colonial officials, merchants and missionaries. Some of these remained as settlers, but others served in postings of only a few years or less. Still others, including the ordinary tourists who ventured to colonial destinations as holiday-makers – such as those who joined the Thomas Cook tours begun in the 1870s – intended to spend only a short period abroad. Colonies were crossroads, the lists of arriving passengers in local newspapers ranging from impecunious migrants up to some of the wealthiest and most powerful people in society. Royals could not be left behind, both for their own edification and for reasons of state.

In an earlier age, colonialism was the work of charted companies such as the East India Company, nominally private enterprises under the aegis of the state. From the mid-nineteenth century (at least, in the case of Britain, after the Indian Uprising of 1857), colonialism was a national enterprise, demanding the support and participation of the whole body politic, with all enjoined to contribute to this great project. Yet colonialism never achieved unanimous support, even in Britain, and it was regularly denounced in some sectors for the corruption and enrichment of nabobs and profiteers, the vast cost in money and manpower, the uncertain benefits of taking over sometimes near inaccessible and barren lands, diversion of attention from social issues, overextension of national power, and the potential that colonial rivalries might ignite European wars. Promoters of empire had to strive continuously – through political lobbying, publications, exhibitions and other sorts of propaganda – to popularise colonies among the elite and the masses.

Royals were key agents in the campaign, their support for empire and their imperial forays tactics for galvanising public support. Royal tours, favourably reported in the press, provided an important weapon in the arsenal of propaganda, and royals enjoyed the power and celebrity that made them unparalleled and invaluable assets in efforts to gain and retain an empire. The advent of more extensive royal tours to the colonies coincided not only with imperial expansion, but also with more intense debate about the merits of empire (the critical views famously expressed in Dadabhai Naoroji's 1901 *Poverty and Un-British Rule in India*, and J.A. Hobson's *Imperialism*, published the following year). At the same time as marshalling support for empire at home, colonialists had to contest embryonic but fast-growing nationalism in the empire, seen with the increasing militancy of the Irish Home Rule movement, the growth of the Indian National Congress founded in 1885 and the setting up of the African National Congress in 1912; Marxist ideas were also beginning to circulate. Debates about empire were taking place at home, in other colonising states and overseas possessions. Royals, self-evidently, represented the institutions of monarchy and the empire; they generally also represented the forces of conservatism against radicalism, and order against revolution. A successful royal tour could thus do much to shore up the established order. For personal as well as political reasons, those of the royal traveller, the colonial lobby and the monarch's loyal subjects at home and abroad, it was worth the risks for them to go on tour, with the hope of reaping the rewards in buttressing the dynasty, the nation and the empire.

Despite the similarities of royal tours, specific objectives varied over the course of the 1800s and early 1900s. As noted, the future king of the Belgians undertook extensive travel to prospect for colonies. Napoléon III travelled to Algeria to reassure settlers of the monarch's ongoing commitment. Kaiser Wilhelm II, little interested in German colonialism, nonetheless went to the Ottoman empire to boost Germany's and the Hohenzollern dynasty's prestige on the international stage. Crown Prince Luís Filipe's voyage to Africa was intended to distract attention from the unpopularity of the monarchy at home in Portugal. The heir to the Japanese throne went to Europe to show off Japan as a modern country, great power in the concert of nations and legitimate colonial ruler of Taiwan and Korea. Specific goals and more generalised considerations thus mandated tours that were assertions of national power, imperial propaganda and personal adventure by royals. They were also great logistical undertakings.

Planning the tours and receiving the visitors

Royal travel evolved in organisation and arrangement, from the somewhat casual and slapdash arrangement, in the British case, of Prince Alfred's 1860s–1870s colonial tours to the professional and polished stage management of his great-nephew Edward's 1920s travels. In general, organisation improved over time, so that vague itineraries were replaced with precise timetables and choreographed programmes. Still, tours in the early twentieth century closely resembled the formal prototypes set by late nineteenth-century state visits within Europe.[26] This continuity is visible, for instance, in the pomp and circumstance of triumphal arches, loyal addresses, levees, balls, religious services, the evening illumination of buildings, firework displays, military reviews and the conferring of honours on local notables. Speeches, banquets, processions and receptions filled the schedule of every tour. There were visits to important historical sites, wonders of nature and infrastructure projects. On the programme as well were meetings with officials and colonists, 'native' representatives and leaders of diasporic populations.

Among key issues that tour organisers had to consider, beyond the central concern of security, was transport. Conveyances needed to move royals about as comfortably and safely as possible, and be grand enough to befit a monarch or prince. Royal conveyances differed, but there existed a noticeable link between royal travel and 'royal' navies. Many royals had a choice between travel in warships, their private yachts or commercial liners. The size and magnificence of vessels commonly increased over time, as national rivalries whetted public appetite for grandiose steamships and splendid private yachts. Royal vessels demonstrated the grandeur of the monarchy and the might of its military and merchant fleet. By 'showing the flag', the ships and royal passengers fulfilled a ceremonial and diplomatic mission. Later, royal air travel served as an advertisement for flagship national carriers.

Tours involved serious consideration of the government's priorities in international or colonial policy, which determined even such details as schedules, exacting deployment of security forces, officials and honour guards, and punctilious adherence to protocol. Indeed, protocol was a vital aspect of politics: the pomp of flags, anthems, gun salutes, medals and uniforms clearly indicated the status of visitors and hosts. The particular sites visited and ceremonies held had more to do with *raison d'état* than with visitors' personal proclivities, though royals occasionally managed to escape programmes and minders for improvised sorties, shopping, sport or excursions to 'pleasures quarters'.

If the visitors were the key actors in tours, audiences were integral, and the lack of large and sympathetic, indeed enthusiastic, receptions for a royal meant failure for a tour. Tours were meant to allow a sovereign's subjects (or the residents of an independent country) to see and applaud a royal figure in person. The near-religious persona of a sovereign or prince was what primarily distinguished the visit of a royal from that of a minister, governor, general or 'ordinary' human, no matter his or her stature. In some cultural traditions, as in North Africa and South Asia, indeed, the very sight of a sovereign could confer blessings upon an individual and community. European countries, even a republic like France, also continued to revere royals as icons and gawk at them as celebrities. It was essential that positive receptions – and glowing press reports – overwhelm negative comments or untoward incidents.

Many people, of course, remained largely unaware of or unconcerned by royal tours: those who lived far away from the places the travellers visited, subaltern populations whose lives were little touched by the upper echelons of the national and colonial state, and those who simply took little notice of public affairs. The vast majority of Indians, for example, lived an impossible distance from the site of the Delhi durbars, and most never saw newspapers where these festivities were chronicled (and were unable to read the reports in any case). In Europe and the colonies, some viewed royal tours with, at best, passing curiosity or puzzled bemusement. Nevertheless, the number of participants and spectators in tours, and those who read reports about visits, was substantial, and tours presented unique opportunities for expressions of support and enthusiasm, or hostility. The range of opportunities and responses is indeed what commands attention to royal tours.

Tours in the late nineteenth and early twentieth centuries provided templates for later and still more frequent travels by royals as well as other heads of state, particularly the presidents who increasingly replaced monarchs. The 'pomp and politics' of presidential visits, in fact, often closely followed models developed for princely travellers. In today's world, time and distance no longer present the challenges they once held. Jet planes ferry around monarchs and presidents, who fly in and out for sometimes just a few hours, and images of tours are instantaneously broadcast on television and streamed on the internet. Many heads of state, whether royal or republican, are global 'stars', and their travels, in addition to gaining wide media coverage, have considerable political significance and cultural interest. Yet issues around the security of visitors, the design of tours, the ceremonial and protocol, and the reception of travellers by press and public remain as pertinent as they were for the pioneering royal tourists well over a century ago.

The chapters in this volume provide case studies that illustrate multiple sources, methodological approaches and topics in the history of royal travel. Several concern individual tours, while other chapters compare royal travellers or follow a sequence of tours over a shorter or longer period. Three of the chapters focus on the British empire, while the rest look at travels to and from the Belgian, Dutch, French, German, Italian, Japanese and Portuguese empires, and touch on Europe, the Middle East, Africa, Asia and Australasia. Some consider reigning monarchs, others crown princes and members of royal families; the first chapter focuses on deputations and ceremonial gifts of royal tours 'by proxy'. They draw on sources encompassing memoirs and chronicles, press reports, writings inspired by travellers' experiences or provoked by their tours, and a variety of images (etchings, caricatures, photographs), radio broadcasts and film, and material artefacts.

These contributions develop themes introduced in the present chapter, such as the role of royal personalities and their hosts, the political contexts of visits, competing stakes in royal tours, and reactions in the public and press at home and abroad. They show the manifold responses of different individuals and groups, and in different colonies and provinces. The chapters look at the role of particular cohorts, including the military, civic leaders and ethnic communities; they point to questions of gender, age and education. These studies reveal the fragility of monarchical regimes and colonial overlordship that is apparent behind the pageantry and protocol deployed during these travels, and they also evidence the limitations of tours in achieving their core objectives. They identify specific ways in which monarchy and colonialism intertwined, and suggest many avenues for further research – on the travels of members of other dynasties, more recent royal and quasi-royal travel, and the material culture, legacy and memory of royal tours. In turn, the volume demonstrates the benefits of studies bringing together Europe with other parts of the world, and the significance of travel and tours (not just of the royal variety) in understanding transnational encounters. This book emphasises the role and significance of royal travels, from the mid-1800s to the mid-1900s, in transforming monarchies, colonial relations, international politics and cultural exchange.

Notes

1 Sagara Jayasinghe, *The Black Prince's Chapel: The Church Built by a Sinhalese Prince in Portugal* (Colombo: Vijitha Yapa Publications, 2014); Kate Fullagar, *The Savage Visit: New World People and Popular Imperial Culture in Britain, 1710–1795* (Berkeley: University of California Press, 2012); Jocelyn Hackworth-Jones, *Between Worlds: Voyages to Britain 1700–1850* (London: National Portrait Gallery, 2007); Frédéric Durand, *Balthazar: un prince de Timor en Chine, en Amérique et en Europe au XVIIe siècle* (Paris: Les Indes Savantes, 2015); Neil Rennie, *Far-Fetched Facts: The Literature of Travel and the Idea of the South Seas* (Oxford: Clarendon Press, 1998), 'Aoutourou and Omai', pp. 109–125.
2 See, e.g., Michael Nelson, *Queen Victoria and the Discovery of the Riviera* (New York: Tauris Parke, 2007).
3 Xavier Paoli, *Their Majesties as I Knew Them: Personal Reminiscences of the Kings and Queens of Europe* (New York: Sturgis & Walton, 1911), the memoirs of the 'kings' guardian'.
4 Robert Aldrich, *Banished Potentates: Dethroning and Exiling Indigenous Monarchs under British and French Colonial Rule* (Manchester: Manchester University Press, 2018); Michael Alexander and Sushila Anand, *Queen Victoria's Maharajah: Duleep Singh, 1838–93* (London: Weidenfeld & Nicolson, 1980); and, on the maharaja's formidable daughter, Anita Anand, *Sophia: Princess, Suffragette, Revolutionary* (London: Bloomsbury, 2015).
5 Mustafa Serdar Palabiyik, 'The Sultan, the Shah and the King in Europe: The Practice of Ottoman, Persian and Siamese Royal Travel and Travel Writing', *Journal of Asian History*, 50:2 (2016), 201–234; David Motadel, 'Qajar Shahs in Imperial Germany', *Past & Present*, 213:1 (2011), 191–235; A. Rahman Tang Abdullah, 'Sultan Abu Bakar's Foreign Guests and Travels Abroad, 1860s–1895: Fact and Fiction in Early Malay Historical Accounts', *Journal of the Malaysian Branch of the Royal Asiatic Society*, 84:300 (2010), 1–122; Robert Aldrich, 'France and the King of Siam: An Asian King's Visits to the Republican Capital', in Julie Kalman (ed.), *French History and Culture: Papers from the George Rudé Seminar*, Vol. 6 (2015) (H-France), www.hfrance.net/rude/rudevolvi/AldrichVol6.pdf; Bridget Theron, 'King Cetshwayo in Victorian England: A Cameo of Imperial Interaction', *South African Historical Journal*, 56 (2006), 60–87; Neil Parsons, *King Khama, Emperor Joe and the Great White Queen: Victorian Britain through African Eyes* (Chicago: University of Chicago Press, 1998); William N. Armstrong, *Around the World with a King* (New York: Frederick A. Stokes Co., 1904) (on King Kalakaua).
6 Rosie Llewellyn-Jones, 'Indian Travellers in Nineteenth Century England', *Indo-British Review*, 18:1 (1990), 137–141; Siobhan Lambert-Hurley, 'Out of India: The Journeys of the Begum of Bhopal, 1901–1930', in Tony Ballantyne and Antoinette Burton (eds), *Bodies in Contact: Rethinking Colonial Encounters in World History* (Durham, NC: Duke University Press, 2005), pp. 293–309; Amin Jaffer, 'Indian Princes and the West', in Anna Jackson and Amin Jaffer (eds), *Maharaja: The Splendour of India's Royal Courts* (London: V&A Publishing, 2009), pp. 194–227.
7 For example, Cele C. Otnes and Pauline Maclaran, *Royal Fever: The British Monarchy in Consumer Culture* (Berkeley: University of California Press, 2015).
8 *The Royal Tour: A Souvenir Album* (London: Royal Collection Publications, 2009).

9 Jane Connors, *Royal Visits to Australia* (Canberra: National Library of Australia, 2015). See also Arthur Bousfield and Garry Toffoli, *Royal Tours 1786–2010: Home to Canada* (Toronto: Dundum Press, 2010).
10 Ian Radforth, *Royal Spectacle: The 1860 Visit of the Prince of Wales to Canada and the United States* (Toronto: University of Toronto Press, 2004); Phillip Buckner, 'Casting Daylight upon Magic: Deconstructing the Royal Tour of 1901 to Canada', in Carl Bridge and Kent Fedorowich (eds), *The British World: Diaspora, Culture, Identity* (London: Frank Cass, 2003), pp. 158–189; Phillip Buckner, 'The Royal Tour of 1901 and the Construction of an Imperial Identity in South Africa', *South African Historical Journal*, 41:1 (1999), 324–348; Klaus Dodds, David Lambert and Bridget Robison, 'Loyalty and Royalty: Gibraltar, the 1953–54 Royal Tour and the Geopolitics of the Iberian Peninsula', *Twentieth-Century British History*, 18:3 (2007), 365–390; Jane Connors, 'The 1954 Royal Tour of Australia', *Australian Historical Studies*, 25:100 (1993), 371–382.
11 Johannes Paulmann, *Pomp und Politik: Monarchenbegegnungen in Europa zwischen Ancien Régime und Erstem Weltkrieg* (Paderborn: Schöningh Verlag, 2000).
12 Torsten Riotte, 'Nach "Pomp und Politik": Neuse Ansätze in der Historiographie zum regierenden Hochadel in 19. Jahrhundert', *Neue Politische Literatur*, 59 (2014), 209–228, which also provides a very useful bibliography.
13 David Cannadine, 'The Context, Performance and Meaning of Ritual: The British Monarchy and the "Invention of Tradition", c.1820–1977', in Eric Hobsbawm and Terence Ranger (eds), *The Invention of Tradition* (Cambridge: Cambridge University Press, 1983), pp. 101–164.
14 Charles V. Reed, *Royal Tourists, Colonial Subjects, and the Making of a British World, 1860–1911* (Manchester: Manchester University Press, 2016); Matthew Glencross, *The State Visits of Edward VII* (London: Palgrave Macmillan, 2015).
15 Miles Taylor, 'Queen Victoria and India, 1837–61', *Victorian Studies*, 46:2 (Winter 2004), 264–274.
16 Sarah Carter and Maria Nugent (eds), *Mistress of Everything: Queen Victoria in Indigenous Worlds* (Manchester: Manchester University Press, 2016).
17 Philip Murphy, *Monarchy and the End of Empire: The House of Windsor, the British Government, and the Post-War Commonwealth* (Oxford: Oxford University Press, 2013), pp. 82, 87.
18 Radforth, *Royal Spectacle*; Frank Lorenz Müller and Heidi Mehrkens, *Sons and Heirs: Succession and Political Culture in Nineteenth-Century Europe* (London: Palgrave Macmillan, 2016) and *Royal Heirs and the Uses of Soft Power in Nineteenth-Century Europe* (London: Palgrave Macmillan, 2016).
19 Robert Aldrich and Cindy McCreery (eds), *Crowns and Colonies: European Monarchies and Overseas Empires* (Manchester: Manchester University Press, 2016).
20 Julie F. Codell, *Power and Resistance: The Delhi Coronation Durbars* (Ahmedabad: Mapin Publishing, 2012); coronation durbars had been held in Delhi 1877 and 1903, but without the presence of the sovereign.
21 Neil Parsons, *King Khama*; 'Southern African Royalty and Delegates Visit Queen Victoria, 1882–95', in Carter and Nugent, *Mistress of Everything*, pp. 166–186.
22 *New York Times*, 4 September 1895, p. 5; Fayz Muhammad Katib Hazarah, *The History of Afghanistan*, ed. R.D. McChesney, Vol. 3 (Leiden: Brill, 2013), and Ludwig W. Aamec, 'Mission of an Afghan Prince to London: Nasrullah Khan's Visit to Britain as Reflected in the Press' (Occasional paper) (New York: The Afghanistan Forum, 1994).
23 Jerry Brotton, *This Orient Isle: Elizabethan England and the Islamic World* (London: Penguin, 2016), Introduction; Michael Smithies (ed.), *The Diary of Kosa Pan, Thai Ambassador to France, June–July 1868* (Chiang Mai: Silkworm Books, 1997); Xavier Salmon (ed.), *Le Siam à Fontainebleau. L'Ambassade du 27 juin 1861* (Paris: RMN, 2011); L.E. Baghawe, *Kinwun Ming-Gyi's London Diary: The First Mission of a Burmese Minister in Britain* (Bangkok: Orchid Press, 2006); Kume Kunitake, *Japan Rising: The Iwakura Embassy to the United States of America and*

Europe, 1871–1873, ed. Chushichi Tsuzuki and R. Jules Young (Cambridge: Cambridge University Press, 2009).
24 Siobhan Lambert-Hurley (ed.), *A Princess's Pilgrimage: Nawab Sikandar Begum's A Pilgrimage to Mecca* (Bloomington: Indiana University Press, 2008).
25 Carolus (Belgian Minister to Rome) to Baron Auguste Lambermont (Belgian Ministry of Foreign Affairs), 6 May 1863, AMAE Lambermont Papers, cited in Barbara Emerson, *Leopold of the Belgians: King of Colonialism* (London: Weidenfeld & Nicolson, 1979), p. 30; Emerson, *Leopold of the Belgians*, pp. 18–20, 30–32.
26 Glencross, *The State Visits of Edward VII*, pp. 9–11.

CHAPTER TWO

Royal tour by proxy: the embassy of Sultan Alauddin of Aceh to the Netherlands, 1601–1603

Jean Gelman Taylor

Royal tours are staged presentations of the crowned self before random or selected spectators. Elements of a tour may include public processions, uniformed retainers, honour guards, display of flags, levees or durbahs, religious ceremonies and gifts. The royal personage may travel in open carriage or closed litter, and in audiences may be elevated on a dais on public display or concealed by a curtain. Forms of obeisance mark concepts of royal personhood. Communication may be direct or through interpreters. We may question the timing and motivations for the tour, and what indices judge its success.

Here I examine how presentation is managed when ambassadors are sent in place of the royal personage. The ambassadors of this case study were appointed by Sultan Alauddin Riayat Shah Sayyid al-Mukammal of Aceh (r. 1589–1604).[1] Their mission was to stand in place of 'The Descendant of the Perfected One'[2] in dealings with Maurits of Orange-Nassau (in office 1585–1605). Maurits was also a placeholder, a *stadhouder* in Dutch; *stadhouders* were appointed officials who administered regions of the Low Countries for the Hapsburg kings. But, by 1602, when Aceh's ambassadors presented themselves, Maurits was placeholder for no monarch. The seven provinces united in the Republic of the Netherlands had renounced Spanish rule, and the *stadhouder* himself was leading the Republic's armed forces against Philip II of Spain. Aceh's ambassadors caught up with Maurits in his military headquarters at Fort Grave (in today's province of North Brabant). Subsequently they were conducted on a tour of the young republic before returning to Aceh.

This was the first embassy sent by a Southeast Asian king to Europe. The Sultanate of Aceh and the Republic of the Netherlands were pivots of global trade and communications. Aceh supplied pepper to the world. It was the terminus for trade routes from Indonesia's Spice

Islands; it sat astride sea routes to China and Japan. Its ships carried merchants, Islamic scholars and royal envoys to Indian Ocean and Red Sea ports. From the 1530s it had sporadic connections with the Ottoman sultan, symbolic head of the Islamic world. Low-lying territory and a network of major European rivers crossing it to the sea engendered a Dutch economy geared to water-borne commerce and manufacturing. The seaboard provinces hosted commercial companies that financed trade and navigation science, and outfitted fleets for long-distance voyages. In 1598 four Dutch ships sailed into Aceh's busy harbour. By 1600 Maurits had written to the sultan and by mid-1602 Alauddin's ambassadors had stepped ashore in the Netherlands. Pepper for guns and gunsmiths, and military alliance against Iberian power in Asia were topics of mutual import.

Primary sources for this first embassy from Southeast Asia are scant. They include correspondence between the States-General (the 'federal' body representing each province) and the private trading companies that formed into the United East Indies Company (VOC) in 1602. There are also two histories of the Dutch wars against Spain by chroniclers who were themselves present at the meeting between the ambassadors and Maurits. No documents from this historic mission survive in Aceh itself. Possibly they were lost, along with the sultanate's records of other important events, when the palace was destroyed by fire during the reign of Sultanah Nur al-Alam (r. 1675–1678).[3] Those known, contemporary Acehnese sources on the embassy lie in archives in the Netherlands. These include Sultan Alauddin's letter to Maurits, dated 24 August 1601.

Most of what is known of Aceh at this time is also from Europeans.[4] The first Dutch-Acehnese word list and sample dialogues, published in 1603, give a word picture of a cosmopolitan trading port.[5] The dialogues establish that Islamic formulaic expressions of greeting and piety were conventional usage in Aceh at the beginning of the seventeenth century. Illustrations of processions and entertainments in Aceh in the time of Sultan Iskandar Thani (r. 1637–1641), made by the British merchant-traveller Peter Mundy, suggest considerable royal wealth in elephants, retainers and soldiers.[6]

Background

There was a conjunction of interests between Maurits and Alauddin. Maurits's victories against the Iberians had given him control of major Dutch cities and coastal areas. Trading ventures to Indonesian harbour principalities convinced Maurits that, with Indonesian allies and profits from the Asian spice trade, the Dutch could defeat the Spanish and Portuguese in Asia too. Alauddin drew his wealth from cultivation and export of pepper. He controlled Aceh's harbour and navy, but Portuguese dominance in the Indian Ocean and ability to tax Muslim shippers sailing in the Straits of Malacca obstructed trading from Indonesia's spice emporia. Aceh was in a continual state of war against the Portuguese in the sixteenth century. Shortly after Alauddin seized power in Aceh, he bought a temporary end to hostilities by allowing the Portuguese to establish a settlement in his capital.

The first Dutch venture to buy pepper in Aceh failed. The sultan had offered a cargo of pepper if the Dutch ships would join in Aceh's proposed attack on the Sultanate of Johor. But, following disputes, Alauddin's navy had instead attacked the Dutch, seized their pepper and cash, killed sixty-eight of the crew, including Commander Cornelis de Houtman, and taken twenty-three prisoners. Maurits's initial contact with the sultan addressed three issues: guarantee of trade in good faith; release of the Dutch prisoners; and military alliance against the Portuguese.

Two men, two letters

Maurits wrote to Alauddin in Spanish on fine parchment edged with gold. The large salutation is in gold ink. The letter is dated 11 December 1600, and addresses Alauddin as Your Majesty. It bears two seals, Maurits's signature and the statement that the letter was written in his own hand at The Hague, seat of Holland's erstwhile Spanish overlords. These elements indicate the importance the *stadhouder*-captain attached to this testamentary representation of himself.[7] Aceh's politics of parade had it that presentation of this letter should be made in public. Wrapped in silk, the letter was raised to the sultan seated in a portable mini-throne room atop a white elephant, high above his nobles, crowds of onlookers and the Dutch. Accompanying the letter were gifts of 1,000 gold pieces of eight (Spanish dollars minted in Mexico), gilded weapons and fine, Venetian glass mirrors.

Aceh's sultans were accustomed to receiving ambassadors from Asian and Persian kings and to sending their own envoys on diplomatic missions. Ambassadors stood in for the royal person, and so they could negotiate with foreign kings. Maurits and his personal representatives roused apprehension, for he had signed his letter:

The hands of Your Majesty are kissed
By Your Servant
Maurice de Nassau

and described his representatives this way:

> I have given orders and full powers to those bringing this Letter, namely, to the four Captains, Cornelis Bastiaanse, Jan Tonneman, Matthijs Antonisse and Cornelis Adriaansz, and also to those commissioned for this business, whose names are: Gerard de Roy, Laurens Begger [Bicker], Jan Jacobsz and Nicolaas van der Lee.[8]

Asian kings were particularly sensitive to the presumption they should commune, not with royalty and aristocrats, but with commoners and merchant employees of a private trading company. The first Dutch embassy to the Japanese shogun in Edo in 1627 was even turned back without an audience or acceptance of the gifts offered because of this perceived slight by commoners presuming to negotiate as equals.[9] Dutch merchants at Asian courts very soon took to referring to Maurits, elected head of the Dutch Republic, as Prince and even King Maurits. The issue was to be resolved by building up the status and pomp of the VOC's chief officer in Batavia.[10] The governor-general of the Indies came to be perceived in Asian courts as quasi-royal. Java's sultans, for example, addressed him as 'Elder Brother'.

Maurits knew the Portuguese were telling Alauddin his merchants were pirates. 'They have told Your Majesty lies', he writes, and 'deceived you'. The letter continues that he has been informed of

> the warfare that the Portuguese are carrying on in Your Kingdom, on orders from the King of Spain, aiming to deprive the inhabitants of their freedom and to reduce them to their slaves, just as they attempted to do in our region for a period of more than thirty years. But God has not willed this. On the contrary, we have resisted them with the might of our arms, just as we are still doing. Wherefore, I beseech Your Majesty not to place any faith in the Portuguese.

Maurits guarantees that his letter bearers

> in my Name may work out with the Royal Personage of Your Majesty and His subjects what help He may need against His enemies, which, for this purpose, those named have been given orders and full authority.

Sultan Alauddin resolved to send his own representatives to Maurits to determine who and what he was dealing with. He placed his seal on Maurits's letter as evidence of royal perusal and sent it back with his ambassadors together with his own letter, written in Portuguese. The ambassadors requested Maurits affix his seal to Alauddin's letter so that they could return to Aceh with proof Maurits had read it and was satisfied with the contents. Consequently, while both the letters of Maurits and Alauddin have been preserved in the Netherlands, Alauddin's letter is a copy of the original.

Few of the many royal letters sent to European dignitaries by Indonesian sultans in the seventeenth century have survived. Sher Banu Khan notes that Dutch archives often preserve only translated copies of the main body of the letters, and omit or severely abbreviate the lengthy opening statements in which the sultan details his titles, wealth and might, because these were regarded as formulaic boasts.[11] To form a conception of the artistry of Aceh's scribes and illuminators, we have to turn to Annabel Teh Gallop's studies of royal letters from Aceh extant in British archives.[12] She calls them 'golden letters' because of the liberal use of gold leaf and ink. Royal letters are characterised by an elaborate headpiece, meandering patterns of flowers and tendrils framing the text, a long introductory section extolling the royal sender, a shorter body of content, and the sultan's seal.

Alauddin's seal is the oldest known extant seal from the Malay-Indonesian sultanates. In its centre is engraved in Arabic language and script: 'The Sultan Alauddin, son of Firman Shah.' Circling his name are the words: 'He who trusts in the King [Allah], who has chosen him to possess kingdoms and is pleased with him; may God perpetuate his glory and grant victory to his banner.'[13]

In his letter to Maurits, Alauddin expounds on how he understood himself – or wished to be understood:

> A King, shining like the sun at midday, and like the full moon; a King perfect as the North Star; a King who, when standing erect, gives shelter in his shadow to all his slaves; a King whose eyes sparkle like the morning star; a King who possesses a toothed elephant, red, coloured, black, white and speckled elephants; a King to whom God Almighty gives clothing for the elephants, decorated with gold and precious stones, plus a great number of war elephants with iron houses on their back, whose toes are covered with iron sheathes and have copper shoes; a King whom God Almighty gives horses with gold coverings with precious stones and emeralds, plus hundreds of war horses, splendidly equipped, from Arabia, Turkey, Cati & Balakki; a King who can show everything that God has created; a king whom Almighty God has placed to reign on the throne of Aceh over everything.[14]

Maurits's representatives in Aceh were ships' captains and merchants. The Islamic names of Alauddin's ambassadors signal they were members of Aceh's elite and close to the person of the sultan. Abdul Hamid, Alauddin's chief ambassador, was designated head of the embassy. Fellow envoys were Sri Muhammad, commander of Aceh's navy, and Mir Hasan, who shared a claimed lineage with the sultan. Their personal retinues and 'some Arab merchants' accompanied them. Participation by Arab merchants in the embassy indicates Aceh's links to international Islamic trade networks, the sultanate's principal commercial partners and determined competitors of the Portuguese.

Holding the important insider's role of interpreter was Léonard Werner. He had been a sailor on the first expedition to Aceh and a prisoner there since 1598. Like Frederik de Houtman, author of the *Dialogue and Dictionary*, Werner had spent his years in Aceh acquiring competence in Acehnese Malay. Alauddin's own interpreters knew Portuguese. No comparable word list and conversation exercises promoting a working knowledge of Dutch seem to have been produced by the Acehnese counterparts of Werner and De Houtman.

Voyage to the Netherlands

Aceh was a seafaring state in an archipelago of sea peoples. Boats were propelled by wind and manpower. Aceh regularly raided villages on the Malay Peninsula to acquire slaves as rowers for its ships and labourers on its pepper plantations. Captains sailed along segments of the Indian Ocean trade routes guided by knowledge of shorelines and promontories, winds, currents and night skies, without navigational instruments. They put in at ports along their route for trade and supplies. Indonesian sailors and ships, however, could not journey across vast expanses of open water. Consequently, Aceh's ambassadors to the Dutch Republic travelled by Dutch ship.

There is no record of the ambassadors' observations or reports upon their return to Aceh. For personal experience and an Acehnese perspective we have to substitute information on the circumstances of their six-and-a-half-months' journey to the Netherlands aboard one in the convoy of large, three-masted ships, designed and equipped for the long voyages between Europe and Asia.

These Dutch ships combined the functions of merchant vessel and battle ship. They were fitted with cannon. Captains had maps, compasses and instruments to plot position, calculate distances and sound depths of the seabed. On deck were two smaller vessels that could be launched on Asian shores to travel up rivers. Outward bound they brought large quantities of gold and silver bullion to finance the Asia trade. In the holds were stores of salted foods to feed the soldiers, sailors, merchants and specialists aboard. They carried tools, medical supplies and paper. Ships' captains had to be literate, keep navigation records, muster rolls, and make reports for the paper administration of a complex commercial company. Merchant commanders, appointed to conduct trade and diplomatic negotiations, had to write detailed descriptions of the places, peoples, religions, customs and resources, the statecraft and taxation systems they encountered in Asian ports and royal cities.

Aceh's harbour could not accommodate the bulky Dutch vessels, nor were there dock facilities there such as cranes for loading and unloading cargo. Dutch ships anchored in deep water, and relied on the services of small Indonesian boats to ferry goods and men between bay and land. It took around four months and many local porters to prepare consignments of goods and load a Dutch ship for the return journey to Europe.

Aceh's ambassadors were housed in cabins on the quarterdeck, alongside the ship's captain and senior merchants. Their retinues were assigned spaces in the cramped quarters for the crew and soldiers below. They sailed in a convoy that departed Aceh in December 1601. The long sea journey gave the ambassadors the opportunity to observe daily life in what was a floating Dutch village, and perhaps they informed themselves about the Dutch and their ambitions in conversation with officers and merchants. They had occasion also to observe Dutch naval fighting power, for the ship on which the ambassadors were travelling fired on a Portuguese galleon off St Helena in March 1602. The Dutch captured the ship's crew and a cargo estimated at half a million guilders.[15] The average sea journey took eight months, so this was reckoned a relatively quick voyage when the ship berthed in Middelburg, the major seaport of Zeeland, on 22 July 1602.

Royal tour by proxy

Alauddin's representatives arrived in the northern summer, but Abdul Hamid died within three weeks of disembarking on 9 August 1602. His status as placeholder for his sultan impressed on the Dutch authorities that state honours were due him and that he should be buried following Muslim rites. A great procession of mourners – officials and magistrates of Zeeland, twenty-five directors of the VOC and major ship owners – progressed through Middelburg's streets, led by Abdul Hamid's fellow envoys, who were dressed in black. The funeral took place within twenty-four hours of Abdul Hamid's death. He was placed on his right side in a coffin draped in black cloth, his sword placed atop it, and interred facing Mecca in the graveyard of St Peter's Church. Seventeenth-century Dutch theologians condemned Islam and its 'popes', but St Peter's clergy authorised Abdul Hamid's compatriots to recite Muslim prayers in Arabic on Christian grounds. Later the VOC had a tombstone laid over Abdul Hamid's grave, with an inscription in Latin. It managed in nine lines to name the deceased, list his sultan's titles, confer the dignity of 'Prince' on Maurits, publicise the fighting capacity and capture of booty by Dutch seamen, and advertise the benevolence of the Company's directors:

> Here lies buried
> Abdulhamid, head of the Embassy
> Of Sultan Alauddin Rajat Shah Lillolahe FelAlam
> Conveyed here
> By the most illustrious Prince Maurits
> With two Zeeland ships, which won booty from a Portuguese galleon.
> He was seventy-one years old, and died in 1602.
> Directors of the East Indies Company have
> Had this memorial erected.[16]

Sri Muhammad now headed the embassy, which left Middelburg on 1 September and made its way inland in quest of Maurits. The commander was camped, with 20,000 Dutch and English soldiers, around Grave, an important town on the Maas River and stronghold of Spanish forces. Since 20 July 1602 the armies had dug an extensive trench network around the town and defeated a Spanish army sent to relieve the besieged. Fort Grave had not yet surrendered when the embassy arrived on 4 September. Presentation of Alauddin's envoys therefore took place in alarming circumstances. Maurits sent his carriage with his master of horse and a company of riders to escort the ambassadors to a house prepared for their stay near the tents of the Dutch camp. After rest and refreshments, the ambassadorial party was received by Maurits, numerous members of the Dutch nobility, gentlemen and officers in the tent that was his military headquarters.

Eyewitnesses to this historic meeting paid particular attention to the clothing and formal manners of the ambassadors in addressing Maurits. In the account relayed by Wap 150 years after the embassy and in his commentary to Dutch readers, a contrast is set up between the Dutch Republic, the Spanish and the court of Alauddin. Wap quotes François Valentijn at length on the extravagance of Aceh's sultans – their dinner plates of gold, silk wall hangings, elephants and horses shod in gold and silver.[17] Aceh's ambassadors came representing a sultan of ostentatious opulence to '"Sultan Maurits"', writes Wap, here where every man was his own master, none were slaves, but free men who had been fighting the king of Spain for thirty years and were still rich.[18]

Wap's account draws on the Dutch historians Emanuel van Meteren (1535–1612) and Frederik van Vervou (1550–1621). Van Meteren had been born in Antwerp into a family of publishers who printed early English-language versions of the Bible for smuggling into England. He served in the 1580s as Consul for the Traders from the Low Countries in London, where he assisted refugee Protestants from

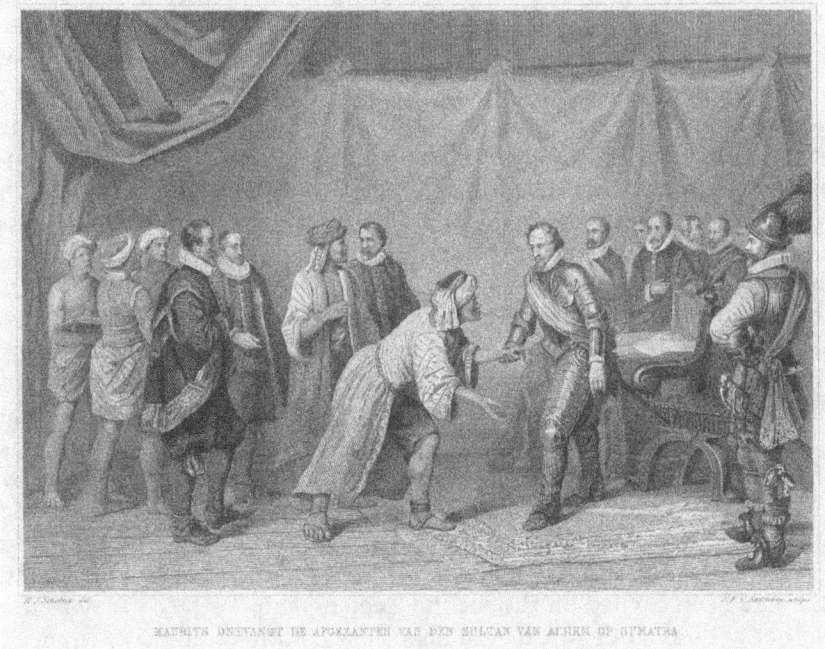

2.1 Prince Maurits receiving the ambassadors from the Sultan of Aceh, 1602

Spanish persecution. Van Meteren became the historian of the Dutch wars against Spain, was present with Maurits at important battles, and was a member of the entourage that received Aceh's ambassadors in Maurits's tent in September 1602.

Van Meteren's account of this historic meeting is in volume eight of his history of the Dutch wars, which was published in 1614.[19] Van Meteren understood history as chronicle. Each chapter is devoted to a single year, and gives the reader his judgement of the most significant events marking the period, together with background information or references to his own earlier writings where relevant. In the chapter for 1602 we find Van Meteren's account of the Acehnese embassy to the Netherlands. He gives the historical background: the first Zeeland voyage to Aceh, the Acehnese attack on the Dutch, the seizing of Frederik de Houtman, and the decision of Maurits to intervene as prelude to his description of the visit. Mostly it is a businesslike, straightforward narration. There is no 'exoticising' of the Asian visitors, or indeed any hint that such an embassy was an extraordinary event during the wars and politics of the Dutch Republic and Spain.

Van Meteren includes some revealing details – slight perhaps in themselves – that convey a more personal interest or perception. These details have not been included within the more accessible secondary sources of Wap, Van Dijk,[20] Mitrasing and Wassing-Visser. For example, Van Meteren wryly remarks that the Dutch action in firing on the Portuguese ship off St Helena and seizing its cargo must confirm for the envoys the truth of Portuguese allegations that the Dutch were pirates. From what may have been a personal confidence, he tells us that Sri Muhammad had fallen out of favour with Alauddin and this calamity had made him more willing to undertake the arduous voyage to an unknown land and a difficult mission. According to Van Meteren, it was the envoys who requested that Abdul Hamid be buried in St Peter's cemetery. He gives a telling detail in his account of the first meeting of the envoys with Maurits. Sri Muhammad moved through the large throng attending Maurits making *sembahs* (gestures of respect), then 'at last seeing the person [of Maurits], he tried to bow his head to [Maurits's] feet, except that the Prince prevented it, taking him by the arm'.[21]

The envoys presented Maurits with Alauddin's letter and a copy that had been carried on the second Zeeland ship in the convoy to the Netherlands as surety against mishap at sea. Both letters were wrapped in silver cloth. The envoys then presented Maurits with the sultan's gifts: a ring set with four large stones; a dagger in a sheath of gold and copper ornamented with rubies, wrapped in a silver cloth; a golden cup and saucer; a gold-plated silver pot containing two pounds of camphor; and a Malay-speaking parrot with a silver chain.[22] The dagger, in Indonesian conceptions, stood in for the royal person. Van Meteren relates its ceremonious presentation: Sri Muhammad raised the dagger high above his head before offering it to Maurits.

Heightening the ambassadors' interest in this audience on a battlefield was that Maurits himself was suffering from a head wound and he excused himself from accompanying the honour guard of twenty-five musketeers that escorted them back to their residence. During the audience Sri Muhammad requested permission to inspect the Dutch army. The following day Maurits sent his master of horse and courtiers on horses to accompany Sri Muhammad. This veteran of sea battles spent four hours studying the land forces commanded by Maurits. On 6 September sixteen trumpeters in full battle array fired salutes in their honour, and then both Sri Muhammad and Mir Hasan, accompanied by Counts Ernst Casimir of Nassau-Dietz and Willem Lodewijk van Nassau-Dillenburg, viewed the rows of large guns and other siege works encircling Grave. To mark the occasion the principal ambassador fired two of the cannon on the city. At midday they ate at Maurits's table with these two military commanders and members of the House of Nassau. Maurits was again not present because of his illness, but Van Meteren says he joined the ambassadors at an afternoon meeting where they discussed the wars the Dutch and Acehnese were fighting and captures of Iberian ships by both parties, and agreed on a treaty of friendship, trade and alliance against the Portuguese.

The other eyewitness was Frederik van Vervou, a Frisian nobleman. As logistics officer for Willem Lodewijk, Maurits's cousin, brother-in-law and co-military strategist in the war against Spain, Van Vervou was in the inner circle. He set down in diary entries over the years 1568 to 1620 information on the army and on military actions, epidemics ravaging the Netherlands, the weather, controversies in the Reformed Church, and international events, including the Aceh embassy to the Netherlands. His memoirs were not published until a century later.[23]

Van Vervou explains the embassy as arising from Alauddin's desire to understand where his interest lay between the Portuguese and the Dutch. His account of the meeting with Maurits covers the same elements as Van Meteren's, and he contributes his own significant details. Vervou describes the 'Sumatrans' as having the same skin colour as Arabs and being dressed in long robes with a dagger at the hip. He says Maurits and Lodewijk received them with real warmth. Van Vervou conversed with the ambassadors through Werner, and recounts that they refused to eat chicken or any other meat, and would only eat the meat of animals they themselves had slaughtered and prepared. (Van Vervou probably means that the ambassadors' Indonesian attendants did the slaughtering and cooking.) He does not make reference to *halal* laws, but this detail informs us of the determination and ability of the ambassadors to adhere to Islamic dietary laws in remote Protestant Holland.

The political discussions were accomplished in three days, and on 7 September the ambassadors left in Maurits's carriage with an escort of mounted trumpeters for their tour of the provinces comprising the Republic at that time. The siege of Grave was lifted on 20 September, but there was no apparent need for Maurits to meet with the ambassadors again. Van Meteren and Van Vervou remained with Maurits and Lodewijk, so we do not have personal information from them about the tour, which was conducted by carriage, boat and, in winter, by sled. The itinerary, devised and paid for by the VOC, took the ambassadors through cities that had ancient histories of municipal rights. They were commercial, processing and manufacturing centres, and had fought hard battles and undergone long sieges in the previous two decades to be freed from Spanish rule.

The Acehnese had gained their first impressions in Middelburg, an important seaport and trade centre, wrested from Spanish control after a two-year siege in 1574. A map from 1652[24] shows Middelburg as a walled city with defensive redoubts, surrounded by a moat. Its population, when the ambassadors stayed there, was around 20,000.[25] Their journey to Grave took them through Dordrecht, a major stapling town and education centre, and site of the first secret meetings to organise the revolt against Spain. On leaving Grave the ambassadors journeyed to Nijmegen, Culemborg and to Utrecht, a major religious centre and independent archbishopric until its incorporation into the Dutch Republic. The tour returned to the coast and ended in Amsterdam, which was the most important city of the Republic and seat of the central administration of the VOC. In 1602 its population was around 60,000. Van Vervou comments that the plague had subsided there by the time the ambassadors arrived, noting that at its height 750 people were dying every week. Perhaps the ambassadors visited the world's first stock exchange, which had opened in Amsterdam in 1602. The conclusion of their sojourn in the Netherlands was dependent on the winds. On 18 December 1603 they embarked to travel in a convoy of thirteen ships to Aceh.

The ambassadors had much to report. They had met 'Prince' Maurits; they had negotiated a treaty of trade and alliance against the Portuguese. They had toured the Dutch Republic, seen its shipbuilding, arms manufacturing, processing of raw materials, dairy industry, and mills for grain, timber and paper. Wap says they returned to spread Dutch fame and argue that friendship with the Dutch was superior to slavery under the Iberians.[26] But to whom were they to recount what they had seen and learned? Sultan Alauddin was now deposed and dead, allegedly poisoned by his oldest son. Aceh was about to be plunged into another period of turmoil – civil war between rival claimants to the throne, depositions and assassinations, such as had characterised most of the sultanate's history in the sixteenth century.

The VOC had evidently held great hopes for riches from Aceh's pepper. Three contracts were reached with Aceh's rulers between 1600 and 1607, but with the rise of absolutism under Sultan Iskandar Muda (r. 1607–1636) the easy relations anticipated never took root. In 1641 the Dutch expelled the Portuguese from Malacca. This had been the goal of Aceh's sultans for a century, but it was done without them. Wap's book on the embassy was published in 1862. Aceh was still an independent sultanate, but it was no longer of interest to Wap.[27] His short history of the embassy was conceived as a tribute to the heroes of wars against Spain, rather than a history of Dutch–Indonesian relations.

Closing observations

In Aceh, Sultan Alauddin's proposal of a partnership between sovereign states has entered mythology, forged during decades of armed resistance to Indonesia's central government. The Dutch staged a commemoration of this singular embassy in 1978 to signal a more positive relationship with their former colony. St Peter's Church had fallen into ruins in the nineteenth century and its old graves were lost. Acehnese and Dutch representatives again came together at the (rebuilt) St Peter's. There a plaque was unveiled in Abdul Hamid's memory and a positive moment in Indonesian–Dutch relations recalled.

No other embassy was sent from Aceh to the Netherlands. Aceh's sultans were not cut off from the rest of the world, but it was the practice of Islamic states to send embassies with letters and gifts only when a specific issue needed resolution. Alauddin was prepared to wait three years for news from Istanbul or Mecca or from Grave, but now further relations between Aceh and the Dutch were conducted in nearby Batavia. After 1661 the Dutch closed their commercial quarters in Aceh.

Alauddin did not himself tour the Netherlands. He was already elderly, said to have been ninety-five years old when he died. Local conditions could not permit his absence. He had won his throne by deposing his predecessor and killing men of the merchant elite who were kingmakers in the sultanate. Alauddin mounted instead a royal tour by proxy in which he was embodied – and concealed – in his gifts and in the humbler persons of his placeholders. Ordinary Dutch citizens saw Alauddin's envoys and their honour guard ride through their cities and villages; burgomasters and VOC dignitaries hosted them in their slow progress through the provinces. But the history of this cross-cultural encounter remains unbalanced for there are no accounts of it from Sri Muhammad or Mir Hasan.

How did the ambassadors' reception in a military camp by an aristocracy of army captains and landholders, with whom they could only communicate through an interpreter, equate with their understanding of kingship? Were they disappointed by men in armour who rejected excessive flatteries, or did they appreciate the less formal protocol compared with their own court? How did their tour of a country emerging through warfare crystallise their understanding of the Netherlands and of the potential of the Dutch in Southeast Asia? Did they hope to foster new developments in industry, shipbuilding or military strategy in Aceh based on their observations in the Netherlands? Seemingly their return excited no peculiar interest in Aceh's new ruling elite. We cannot know how the ambassadors' impressions of Maurits compared with their imagining of 'Sultan Rum', head of the Ottomans and the other great signifier in Aceh's view of the world.

Notes

1 Aceh is at the northern tip of Sumatra in the Indonesian archipelago. It was incorporated into the Netherlands East Indies in 1903 and has been a province of Indonesia since its declaration of independence from the Netherlands in 1945.
2 The prestigious title Sayyid al-Mukammal states the sultan's claim to being of the same tribe as Muhammad.
3 Ingrid Sarosa Mitrasing, 'The Age of Aceh and the Evolution of Kingship 1599–1641' (PhD dissertation, Leiden University, 2011), p. 9.
4 Anthony Reid, *Witnesses to Sumatra: A Travellers' Anthology* (Kuala Lumpur: Oxford University Press, 1995).
5 Denys Lombard (ed.), *Le 'Spraeck ende Woord-Boek' de Frederick de Houtman* (Paris: École Française d'Extrême-Orient, 1970).
6 *The Travels of Peter Mundy in Europe and Asia, 1608–1667*, Vol. III, 1634–1637 (Cambridge: Hakluyt Society, 1919).
7 A photograph of the letter is in Rita Wassing-Visser, *Royal Gifts from Indonesia: Historical Bonds with the House of Orange-Nassau (1600–1938)* (Zwolle: Waanders, 1995), p. 29, fig. 7.
8 The original Spanish text is given in Dutch translation by Dr Johannes Jacobus Franciscus Wap in his *Het gezantschap van den sultaan van Achin 1602 aan Prins Maurits van Nassau en Oud-Nederlandscbe republiek* (Delft: J.H. Molenbroek, 1862), pp. 14–16. The translation into English is mine.
9 Adam Clulow, *The Company and the Shogun: The Dutch Encounter with Tokugawa Japan* (New York: Columbia University Press, 2014).
10 Batavia (present-day Jakarta) on Java's northwest coast was the headquarters of VOC operations in Asia.
11 Sher Banu A. Latiff Khan, 'Rule behind the Silk Curtain: The Sultanahs of Aceh 1641–1699' (PhD dissertation, University of London, 2009), p. 27.
12 Annabel Teh Gallop with Bernard Arps, *Golden Letters: Writing Traditions of Indonesia/Surat Emas: Budaya Tulis di Indonesia* (London: British Library/Jakarta: Yayasan Lontar, 1991); Gallop, 'Gold, Silver and Lapis Lazuli: Royal Letters from Aceh in the 17th Century', paper presented at the First International Conference of Aceh and Indian Ocean Studies, 24–27 February 2007; and Gallop, 'Seventeenth-Century Indonesian Letters in the Public Record Office', *Indonesia and the Malay World*, 31:91 (2003), 412–439. See also Mark Durie, 'Poetry and Worship: Manuscripts from Aceh', in Ann Kumar and John H. McGlynn (eds), *Illuminations: The Writing Traditions of Indonesia* (Jakarta: The Lontar Foundation, 1996), pp. 79–100.
13 Annabel Teh Gallop, 'Ottoman Influences in the Seal of Sultan Alauddin Riayat Syah of Aceh (r.1589–1604)', *Indonesia and the Malay World*, 32:93 (2004), 187. The seal's design suggests a craftsman with some knowledge of the iconography of Ottoman seals.
14 Wap, *Gezantschap*, pp. 19–20.
15 Ibid., p. 18.
16 My translation of Wap's Dutch-language translation from the original Latin, *ibid.*, p. 19.
17 Ibid., pp. 20–21. Valentijn (1666–1727) was a minister for the Dutch Reformed Church in eastern Indonesia. He made translations of the Bible into Malay and, on repatriation, compiled a vast encyclopaedia of information and social history of the region, containing many engravings and maps. It was published as *Oud en nieuw Oost-Indiën* in several volumes between 1724 and 1726.
18 Ibid., p. 22.

19 Emanuel van Meteren, *Historie der Neder-landscher ende haerder na-buren oorlogen ende geschiedenissen, tot den iare M. VI.c XII* (Gorinchem: Wed. Van Nicolaas Goetzee, Ordinaris Stads-Drukkeres, 1614), pp. 128–144. His history was republished in 1764 and digitised by the University of Ghent in 2009.
20 Cees van Dijk, '1600–1898: Utusan, Budak, Seorang Pelukis, dan Beberapa Siswa', in Harry A. Poeze (ed.), *Di Negeri Penjajah: Orang Indonesia di Negeri Belanda 1600–1950* (Jakarta: Gramedia, 2008), pp. 1–24.
21 Van Meteren, *Historie*, p. 143.
22 Mitrasing, 'Age of Aceh', p. 88. The sultan had sent two parrots, but one died during the sea voyage. According to Wap the sultan also sent Maurits a special lance by another of the ships in the convoy, *Gezantschap*, p. 27.
23 Van Vervou's diaries were published by the Frisian Society in 1841 as *Enige gedenckvveerdige geschiedenissen tot narichtinge der nakomelingen, sommarischer wijze beschreven, 1568–1610*. They were republished by Graddy Boven as *Gedenkwaardige geschiedenissen: Avonturen van hofmeester Frederik van Vervou in dienst van stadhouder Willem Lodewijk* (Soesterberg: Aspekt, 2012).
24 In Willem en Joan Blaeu, *Toneel der steden*, 1652, University of Groningen.
25 Population figures for the cities on the ambassadors' tour are in Piet Lourens and Jan Lucassen, *Inwonertallen van Nederlandse steden ca. 1300–1800* (Amsterdam: Netherlands Economic History Archive, 1997). Dordrecht had a population of around 18,000; Utrecht's was 30,000.
26 Wap, *Gezantschap*, p. 22.
27 Eleven years after the book's publication, the Dutch invaded Aceh. After a lengthy period of guerrilla war, they abolished the sultanate in 1901 and sent Aceh's last sultan into exile in Java.

CHAPTER THREE

French imperial tours: Napoléon III and Eugénie in Algeria and beyond

Robert Aldrich

'The visit of a Sovereign is always a great favour. That of Your Majesty is more than a favour, it is an act of generosity, and gratefulness is one of the Algerian virtues', intoned the mayor of Algiers, in presenting the keys of the city to Emperor Napoléon III when he landed in the North African port on 3 May 1865.[1] It was the emperor's second and more substantial visit to France's most significant overseas territory – this 'new France', as Napoléon sometimes called Algeria; an extensive tour by the emperor and Empress Eugénie five years earlier had been abbreviated to only three days because of the grave illness of the empress' beloved sister and the couple's speedy return to Europe.

These were the only colonial tours made by a French monarch either in the *ancien régime* or after the Revolution.[2] With the definitive establishment of a republic following the disastrous Franco-Prussian War of 1870–1871, which brought about the demise of the Second Empire, France had no more kings or emperors to visit an expanding colonial realm that became the second largest overseas empire of European states. Presidents and other senior officials visited France's possessions, paying their respects to indigenous sovereigns in protectorates – the bey of Tunis, emperor of Vietnam, kings of Cambodia and Laos, even the kingly chiefs of tiny Pacific islands. But such journeys were no longer royal tours. Though voyages by republicans displayed a great deal of pageantry, they could not draw on the mystique of a monarch, even one like Napoléon III who had gained the throne by *coup d'état*. As representatives of a secular regime they could not invoke the benediction of the church and an alliance between throne and altar as did the emperor. Neither could they directly draw on the legacy of Napoléon I. During the visits of *Napoléon le petit* (as critics satirised him), orators evoked his uncle's occupation of Egypt in 1798 and heralded the revival of imperial and

French grandeur under the Bonapartist heir. Republican visitors had to replace that mythology with one wound around the ideals of the Revolution, though liberty, equality and fraternity were not principles enacted in colonial situations.

This chapter examines the tours of Napoléon (and, on his first visit, Empress Eugénie) to Algeria, setting them in the context, first, of the emperor's energetic colonial and international policies and, second and briefly, in relation to other travels of the imperial couple and their son, the prince imperial (also named Napoléon). It shows the variety of journeys undertaken by members of royal families, including ones deposed from their thrones. It demonstrates the way in which experiences and impressions during a tour, such as Napoléon's brief first visit to Algeria, contributed to the formulation of policy, and how that second tour both revealed and obscured conflicts inherent in colonialism. Napoléon III did not just reign, he ruled, and the tours of a near dictatorial monarch had particularly potent significance.

From exile to emperor

Charles-Louis Napoléon Bonaparte was born in Paris in 1808, son of Napoléon I's brother Louis, king of Holland from 1806 to 1810, and Hortense de Beauharnais, the daughter (by her first marriage) of Napoléon's first empress, Joséphine. When Louis lost his throne, his family went into exile. Charles-Louis, or Louis-Napoléon as he was called, became head of the Bonapartist house and claimant to the French imperial throne after the death of Napoléon's son (nominally Napoléon II). Louis-Napoléon spent his early life in Switzerland and Germany, before settling in Britain, developing a familiarity and esteem for the country that he retained throughout his life. In 1836, he made an amateurish and failed attempt to invade France, but lack of success forced him back to Britain; a second attempt at gaining power, in 1840, led to his imprisonment in France, though he managed to escape. Amidst the manoeuvrings, Napoléon travelled to Brazil and the United States; these journeys to America and through Europe were the sorts of 'tours' common among dethroned and itinerant former rulers.[3]

The 1848 revolution provided another opening for Louis-Napoléon, who seized the opportunity to return to France. Promising stability and *grandeur*, as his uncle had once done, he secured election as president of a newly declared republic. In 1851, he engineered a *coup d'état* that saw him being proclaimed, 'by the Grace of God and the will of the Nation', Emperor of the French. Two years later he married a young and beautiful Spanish noblewoman, Eugénie de Montijo, who gave birth to their only child in 1856. All three were fated to spend much time in travel and to ending their lives in overseas exile.

Napoléon exercised strong-arm rule as head of state. He also established a glittering court modelled on that of the first Napoléon. The imperial eagle again became a national symbol, a song based on the exploits of a Crusader, *En partant pour la Syrie*, became the imperial anthem, and the palaces of Napoléon and his elegant empress sparkled under the new gas-lights.[4] Napoléon fared badly with historians after his overthrow, but writers now assess his regime as a time of extraordinary change. The French economy boomed, aided by a free trade treaty with Britain signed in 1860. A railway network was completed, and French technological prowess was harnessed in the project of Ferdinand de Lesseps to build a canal across the isthmus of Suez. Napoléon's prefect of police, Baron Haussmann, redesigned Paris in one of the largest programmes of urban renewal ever undertaken, giving Paris its broad boulevards, imposing squares and grandiose new buildings.[5] The rebuilt city intentionally reflected the wished-for majesty of the dynasty (and the wide boulevards not coincidentally made it impossible, authorities hoped, for revolutionary protestors to erect barricades). Napoléon also initiated a more outward-looking and aggressive foreign and colonial policy, though it produced a mixed set of successes and failures.

Grandeur and empire

A cornerstone of Napoléon's international policy was collaboration with Britain, both diplomatically and commercially, and the state visit of the emperor and empress to London in 1855, followed almost immediately by a visit to France by Queen Victoria and Albert, the Prince Consort, the first by a British monarch since the reign of Henry VI, sealed the informal alliance. Indeed, the couples became extremely close. Victoria was little less than enamoured of the emperor (despite her earlier support for the Orleanist dynasty that Napoléon had displaced), and Eugénie's beauty and charm seduced both of the British royals. For their part, the French couple treated Victoria as a senior and something of a mentor; although relations cooled later in the 1850s because of disagreements on policy in Italy, the friendship remained firm. Victoria arguably felt closer to Eugénie – especially after the death of Prince Albert, Napoléon III and the prince imperial – than to anyone outside her family, a tie renewed by letters and frequent visits until Victoria's death.[6]

Napoléon III's global ambitions, which created rivalry as well as cooperation with Britain, were nearly as unbounded as those of Napoléon I, and he did not hesitate to use French military might in overseas interventions.⁷ French troops participated alongside the British and other allies in the Crimean War in the mid-1850s. The emperor had wanted to lead the soldiers in Russia himself, but Eugénie feared fighting and disease, and one of the reasons Victoria invited the French couple to Britain was to persuade him not to travel to the Russian theatre. In the late 1850s, the emperor sent French soldiers to Italy to fight the Austrians in the period of the Risorgimento, an intervention that earned the cession of Nice and Savoy to France from the king of Piedmont. Then the French and the British fought together in the Second Anglo-Chinese War, a conflict that saw the sacking at British instigation of the Summer Palace of the Chinese emperor in Beijing, and the shipping back to France of much booty for Eugénie's 'Musée Chinois' at the palace of Fontainebleau.⁸ There, in 1861, the imperial couple received emissaries from the Siamese King Mongkut; the ambassadorial tour popularised Siam among a European audience, testified to Napoléon's aspirations for expanded influence in the Far East and added to Eugénie's collection of Asian treasures.⁹ A more ill-fated undertaking was Napoléon's patronage in the proclamation of the Austrian emperor's brother as Emperor Maximilian of Mexico. In the face of violent opposition to the new regime, Napoléon withdrew the troops he had despatched to Mexico and the rebels executed the would-be emperor. Back on the continent, Napoléon viewed with concern the ominously rising power of Prussia and its victories over Denmark in 1864 and Austria two years later.

When Napoléon III took the throne, France's overseas domains amounted to a mere fragment of the colonies of the *ancien régime*. France claimed only tiny Saint-Pierre and Miquelon off the coast of Newfoundland as a remnant of its North American empire. Martinique and Guadeloupe in the Caribbean remained French, though the days when they had thrived from slavery and sugar were fading into the past. Guiana in South America was considered little more than a malarial purgatory. France maintained scattered enclaves in India and Réunion Island in the Indian Ocean, but its trading posts on the western coast of Africa held considerably more promise for future expansion.

The Restoration (1815–1830) saw little effort to create a new overseas empire, and little wherewithal to do so. Only in early 1830 did a major intervention occur, when King Charles X sent a fleet to take over Algiers, a tardy riposte to an earlier slight to a French representative and a desperate attempt to preserve the Bourbon dynasty from mounting opposition. Gunboat diplomacy did not save the king, who was overturned in a revolution in June of the same year, but it did lay the foundations for France's North African empire and its most important settler colony. Under King Louis-Philippe, during the July

Monarchy (1830–1848), the French extended their control throughout Algeria with the defeat (and exile) of Abd el-Kader, the most powerful native commander. Elsewhere, the objective of the July Monarchy was not conquest of continental holdings but acquisition of coastal ports, or preferably islands, such as Mayotte in the Indian Ocean and Tahiti in the South Pacific, that would provide harbours and provisions for the merchant and military fleets.

Under Napoléon III, France's empire grew, though not yet to the great dimensions it would reach under his republican successors. In 1853, France took over New Caledonia, both as future penal colony and a commercial and military base in the southwestern Pacific; policy-makers and businessmen already eyed trade with China and the possible construction of a canal between the Atlantic and the Pacific. France was eager as well for a beachhead in Southeast Asia, where Britain, the Netherlands and Spain boasted flourishing colonies, and in 1859 the navy landed troops in the southern part of Vietnam. Using the classic techniques of military strength, political coercion and promises of future amicable relations, the French forced the emperor of Annam to cede provinces around Saigon that the French turned into the colony of Cochinchina. In 1863, France made neighbouring Cambodia a protectorate after its king sought assistance in the midst of domestic strife and fears of Siamese aggression. (After the end of the Second Empire, the French would also take over Annam and Tonkin – central and northern Vietnam – and Laos.) Meanwhile, the French took Obock, on the Horn of Africa, the heart of the future colony of Djibouti, in 1862. In the early 1860s, France also intervened in Syria in its self-assigned role as protector of Levantine Christians, who were faced with massacres by Muslims; France's old foe, Abd el-Kader, now living in Syria – after having been released from detention in a Loire-Valley chateau by Napoléon III – saved many Christians from death. Rumours circulated that France hoped for a Middle Eastern colony, perhaps with Abd el-Kader as nominal ruler under French paramountcy, though France in fact did not gain territory there (under League of Nations mandates) until after the First World War. Under Napoléon, France's colonial territory nevertheless tripled in size, to encompass a population of five million. Throughout the empire, Napoléon promoted economic development and public works projects, with the French quarter of even tiny Pondichéry in India designed along the lines of Haussmann's Paris.[10]

Napoléon and Eugénie's interest in the wider world was manifest, from Eugénie's collection of Asian 'curios' to Napoléon's release of Abd el-Kader, from the reception accorded the Siamese ambassadors to overseas wars and the conquest of new colonial territories. Strengthened by the plans for industrial and urban modernisation, growing trade and geopolitical advantage, and with his military machine firing – literally and figuratively – in various directions, Napoléon espoused great ambitions for French influence in the Americas, Africa, the Middle East, Asia and Oceania. Despite the Mexican fiasco, he had scored triumphs – the *exposition universelle* held in Paris in 1867, and Empress Eugénie's presence as chief guest at the opening of the Suez Canal two years later, represented the apogee of the Second Empire.[11] At this moment of international success, Napoléon little foresaw that his declaration of war against Prussia in 1870 would lead to disaster: a humiliating defeat of France, the ignominious capture of the emperor at Sedan, the declaration of a provisional government at home (and ultimately establishment of the Third Republic), a Prussian siege that nearly starved Paris, and the revolutionary Paris Commune and its repression. The ousted imperial family was left from 1871 to spend the remainder of their lives in exile. Before that reversal, however, Napoléon and his policy-makers devoted much attention to the colonies. Algeria, not surprisingly, occupied pride of place in imperial and imperialist endeavours.

Napoléon and Algeria

Although by the time Napoléon III mounted the throne, France had claimed dominion over Algeria for more than two decades, many issues concerning *Algérie française* remained unresolved. (Indeed, some remained so throughout France's imperium, which lasted until the end of the Franco-Algerian War in 1962.) Should Algeria be administered by military or civilian authorities? Should there be direct government from Paris, or should power be devolved onto assemblies of settlers or even indigenous Algerians? How could the reluctant French be encouraged to try their fortunes as settlers across the Mediterranean? Should the primary actors, and beneficiaries, of colonisation be the indigenous populations? What should be the place of native Berbers, Arabs, Jews and nomads in a French-ruled Algeria? Should or could 'natives' be assimilated into European society; could they be 'civilised', as nineteenth-century writers did not hesitate to ask?[12]

Lack of space precludes detailed discussion of Napoléon's policies in Algeria, but several points are useful to underline. Although before his accession to power Louis-Napoléon displayed little interest in colonialism, he nevertheless remained the legatee of his uncle's international aspirations. As prince-president then emperor, he held ultimate authority over France's possessions; the empire became a source of personal pride, an expression of French *grandeur* and a laboratory for experimentation with political, economic and social theories. His views were much influenced by ideas associated with the utopian socialist Saint-Simon, transmitted, in the case of Algeria, by Ismaÿl Urbain, a Frenchman who had converted to Islam, married an Algerian and served as a near constant companion to the emperor during his 1865 tour; on Algerian policy, no one had Napoléon's ear as did Urbain.[13] Saint-Simon and his disciples preached the reconciliation of capital with labour, the beneficence of industrialisation and agrarian innovation, and the advantages of marshalling new technological processes for modernisation and progress, symbolised by canal-building. More controversially, many Saint-Simonians thought that colonisation, though warranted, should aim primarily at the well-being of the colonised, a view summed up in the title of Urbain's *Algérie pour les Algériens*.

Napoléon had considered having himself crowned in 1852 as 'King of Algiers' as well as Emperor of the French, but he invested limited effort in Algeria during the first years of his rule. Napoléon's journey to Algeria in 1860 introduced the country to him and moulded his policy.[14] After visiting the newly acquired Savoy and Nice, Napoléon and Eugénie landed in Algiers on 17 September, and began a round of engagements with welcomes by the governor-general and mayor, and a service at the cathedral. Urbain had also organised a grand fantasia, a display of 10,000 Arab horsemen engaged in manoeuvres and jousts. The exhibition much impressed Napoléon, as did the Arabs whom he met – they rather than *colons*, the European settlers, commanded his interest – and they inspired what critics saw as Arabophilia. Napoléon soon named his first cousin Prince Jérôme to a newly established civilian post of Minister for Algeria and the Colonies. The prince seemed more sympathetic to settler interests than had military administrators, but within less than a year, the position was abolished, and colonial administration reverted to military authorities, whose relations with settler populations continued to be strained.

A reception for Algerian dignitaries in the imperial palace at Compiègne in 1861 did little to counter the view that Napoléon was more concerned with Arabs than with settlers. The emperor and Urbain remained in regular contact, and Urbain's *Algérie pour les Algériens* and another volume (published under a nom de plume and in fact commissioned by Napoléon) infuriated colonists. A letter from Napoléon to the new governor-general, which the emperor allowed to be published in 1863, drew on Urbain's ideas. Napoléon stated that, from the outset, the French had promised to respect the religion and property of Algerians; he did not condone colonists' demands for alienation of Arab land and confinement of native Algerians into American

Indian-style reservations. What was now crucial was 'to convince the Arabs that we have not come to Algeria to oppress and despoil them, but to bring them the benefits of civilisation'. Algerians must be reconciled with French rule, and he argued that there were room and resources enough for both indigenous and settler populations. Repeating a phrase used earlier, Napoléon continued: 'Algeria is not a colony properly so called, but an Arab kingdom. The *indigènes* as well as the *colons* have an equal right to my protection and I am just as much Emperor of the Arabs as Emperor of the French.'[15] What exactly an 'Arab kingdom' would be was never spelled out, though the idea was still periodically revived that Napoléon would create an Algerian throne, that the young prince imperial would be given an Algerian crown, or that Abd el-Kader would be brought from Syria to become king; none of the options eventuated because of opposition among officials in Paris and settlers in Algeria.

When Napoléon decided to make a second tour of Algeria in 1865, his views were well established. The respectful, indeed obsequious speeches of *colons* during his stay belied their discontent with his reputed Arabophilia and with the continuation of military administration. Their words and displays of patriotic productivity clearly had as an objective convincing the emperor of the benefits of settlement and the priority of settler over native Algerian interests.[16]

Napoléon's 1860 and 1865 visits, thus, were not just ceremonial tours by a figurehead sovereign to an overseas domain, but occasions for an authoritarian ruler to see first-hand his most important colonial possession and to impress on the indigenous and settler populations his visions of Algeria under the French flag.[17] For the second tour, Napoléon left Eugénie in France, where she had rather unusually been named as regent for his five-week absence. He arrived in Algiers on 3 May 1865, and returned to Toulon on 9 June, having travelled over 3,000 kilometres in Algeria. He journeyed to the major cities of Algiers, Oran and Constantine, and to many smaller towns, as well as the picturesque desert oasis of Biskra and the aptly named Fort-Napoléon; the imperial party, travelling by carriage, horseback or railway, often also stopped at isolated French settlements. Napoléon managed to see a significant cross-section of the Algerian landscape and society. As with most royal tours, this one was carefully orchestrated with busy schedules, countless receptions and much speechifying. Many of the emperor's contacts were formal and formulaic – including the deferential remarks welcoming him at every locality – and his contacts were largely with the elite. Though on a few occasions Napoléon rode out on his own, accompanied only by several aides and soldiers, and engaged in conversations with ordinary settlers and Algerians, he was normally accompanied by the governor-general, Marshal Patrice MacMahon (a future president of the Third Republic), and senior military officials, as well as Urbain.

Everywhere huge crowds of both Europeans and Algerians, according to reports, greeted the emperor with wild ovations; perhaps even those suspicious about his policies could not contain the excitement of seeing their sovereign. At each stop, a local dignitary gave a speech (in general, mercifully short) extolling the glories of the emperor and the benefits of French rule, and inevitably concluding with 'Vive l'empereur!' and similar acclamations of the empress and prince imperial. Only occasionally did orators stray into political territory, as when a director of one chamber of commerce called for the abolition of duties on Algerian products entering France and pleaded for greater stimulation to immigration.[18]

Each location Napoléon visited was festooned with banners and *arcs de triomphe*, many decorated with or made entirely of local products – cork, oranges, dates, cotton and wool – that illustrated the fertility of the soil and the entrepreneurship of settlers. Communities also put together country fair-style displays of their best products. Even individuals decorated their houses and set up stands, which the 'august visitor' often 'deigned' (as accounts always put it) to pause to admire. One settler family presented him with bottles of their wine, another farmer gave him a bunch of giant asparagus. Young girls always came forward to offer bouquets, one child winning a kiss when she asked the emperor to convey a posy to the prince imperial. The emperor was touched when he came upon a stele erected by a settler with a plaque inscribed 'The Emperor dined here'. Such gestures provided personal expressions of allegiance and pride, and they also 'played well' among the visitors and, no doubt, for readers of the metropolitan press, which ran detailed coverage of the tour. Napoléon's paternalistic attentions meanwhile burnished his reputation among *colons* and Algerians.

Napoléon tirelessly visited farms and public buildings, as well as projects such as a dam. He went to Algiers' public library and museum, which was filled with Roman antiquities from Algeria – the French often argued that they were restoring European and Christian rule to a region usurped by Arabs and Turks. He spent several hours at the city's botanical garden, admiring Australian gum trees and other plants that scientists were trying to acclimatise. At the botanical gardens and elsewhere, the emphasis was on the resources of Algeria and the profits, commercial and other, that it could bring to France. Napoléon's sojourn thus was not that of a holidaying tourist but a working monarch.

There was recreation for the busy emperor, though he remained 'on duty' even at social occasions. Entertainments represented an important part of royal tours, occasions of sociability between ruler and subjects, and opportunities for a colony to show itself off. In 1865, Napoléon enjoyed another Arab fantasia, and European culture was also on show. The imperial party took in a performance of *Rigoletto* by an Italian opera company, and went to a performance by a Spanish theatre troupe. Soon after Napoléon's arrival, a grand ball was held at the Mustapha Palace on the heights of Algiers. In the evening, ships in the harbour and key buildings in the city (including mosques) were specially illuminated, the scene described as one straight out of fairy-tales. The great and good, including selected Arab notables, gathered for the arrival of the emperor, *la maréchale* MacMahon on his arm. Late in the evening supper was served, tables laden with Algerian specialities or those inspired by local products including such treats as 'porcupine garnished with antelope kidneys', boiled ostrich eggs, gazelle cutlets and pomegranate jelly, along with 'Arab pastries'. Napoléon stayed at the ball until well after midnight, watching the fireworks set off around the city, and other guests danced until dawn.

Most of Napoléon's quotidian duties, predictably, involved Europeans, who numbered about 200,000 amidst a population of three million indigenous people. His engagements included receptions by settler groups, and audiences with representatives of municipal councils, chambers of commerce, agricultural associations and mutual aid societies. Some 80,000 of the Europeans were migrants from Spain, Italy and Malta, and their communities, as a sign of allegiance, also built triumphal arches and raised banners inscribed with salutations in their native languages. The Italians celebrated Napoleon's armies' victories against Austria in the Italian peninsula, and the Spaniards, particularly in the largely Spanish-settled city of Oran, showed particular enthusiasm because of the origins of the empress. Napoléon also met with German and Swiss migrants to Algeria. Many of the Europeans were hoping to be naturalised as French citizens (which did occur under the Third Republic), and *Algérianiste* writers would soon propagate the idea of a new (white) Algerian race blending together the qualities of migrants from across southern Europe.

Napoléon, whose regime professed its Catholic faith, made a particular effort to see representatives of the different faiths. He attended a *Te Deum* at the Algiers cathedral, and went to mass on Sundays; he made a prolonged visit to a Trappist monastery and visited a Protestant church. Contacts with the Jewish community were very important, as the 37,000 Jews in Algeria were regarded as supporters of the French regime. Napoléon had several meetings with Jewish leaders, who alluded with gratitude to the emancipation of France's Jews under Napoléon I. They spoke with pride of Jewish contributions to commerce in Algeria, but also discreetly raised issues about institutional discrimination they still perceived, and one rabbi expressed hopes for the granting of French citizenship to Algerian Jews.[19]

Napoléon also came into official contact with foreign delegations. The Italians had sent a small fleet of warships to Algeria to coincide with his tour, and their commander welcomed the emperor aboard the flagship. Like the Italian *colons* in Algeria, he recalled Napoléon's role in the war against the Austrians and relayed greetings from the king of Italy. Napoléon received two delegations from independent North African countries, Tunisia and Morocco, both fated to be taken over as French protectorates (in 1881 and 1911, respectively). The sultan of Morocco sent emissaries, and the bey of Tunis despatched his brother to meet the emperor.[20]

Exercising a ruler's prerogative for amnesty and providing charity from his coffers constituted important expressions of monarchical rights and munificence at home and in the colonies. Napoléon dispensed numerous monetary gifts to charitable associations, and occasionally slipped a few coins to children or beggars. At one stop, Arabs from the Flitta tribe besieged his cortege, pleading for release of fellow tribesmen incarcerated following a rebellion, and to their delight, Napoléon proclaimed an amnesty.[21] On another occasion, the mother of an imprisoned Algerian flung herself at his feet, and Napoléon similarly ordered the release of her son.

Napoléon's engagement with Algerians, and the culture of Algeria, thus became an important part of his tour. Indigenous peoples were nonetheless left in no doubt about French attitudes, as Napoléon's proclamations warned them of the consequences of insurrection and affirmed French supremacy. Speeches given by Frenchmen spoke openly of the supposed pacification of the natives, and the necessity of submission to the French. They made passing reference to the value of the native Algerians, though as 'auxiliaries' to French colonisation or as labour.

Whether because of Napoléon's personal interests and wishes, Urbain's influence or simply as a strategic and public relations exercise, tour organisers made certain that Napoléon had meetings with Muslims. He toured the city's mosques (although one of the grandest had been razed in the early years of French colonisation). He pinned a decoration on an Arab man hailed for loyalty to the French cause. He visited a school for Arab children; the Algerian student chosen to make a no doubt scripted speech said that 'it is Your Majesty who has brought us to this college in order to initiate us into the benefits of civilisation; it is you who have wrenched us from the shameful dangers of ignorance'. After the fantasia, Arabs ceremonially presented dishes of couscous and other foods to the emperor, and there were Arab musicians in an orchestra that played for him. Arab dignitaries were presented as Napoléon visited provincial centres, and (as mentioned) were invited to the grand ball in Algiers; he also invited native leaders to dine, the chefs presumably taking account of Muslim dietary restrictions.

Napoléon issued three imperial proclamations, and these are worthy of some consideration. The first, a brief statement to 'the inhabitants of Algeria', presented on the day of his arrival, spoke of the emperor's desire during his tour to 'know for myself your interests, second your efforts, [and] assure you that the protection of the metropole will never be lacking'. He immediately added: 'For long you have struggled with energy against two redoubtable obstacles: virgin nature and a warlike people; but better days are coming.' The twin foes of *nature vierge* and *peuple guerrier* appeared a perhaps not inaccurate description of the challenges of a seemingly inhospitable landscape and climate, and of a population that had resisted conquest, words that comforted *colons* and assured them of Napoléon's sympathy. The phrases also clearly betrayed European ideas about North Africa (and the colonised world in general). The emperor promised that French businesses would develop Algeria 'by their industry and their capital', a good Saint-Simonian pronouncement, and that the Arabs 'contained and enlightened about our benevolent intentions, will no longer be able to trouble the tranquillity of the country'. He concluded:

> Have faith in the future; attach yourselves to this land that you labour, like a new fatherland, and treat the Arabs, among whom you must live, as compatriots.
>
> We must be the masters, because we are the most civilised; we must be generous because we are the strongest. Let us without cease justify the glorious acts of one of my predecessors who, thirty-five years ago planted on the soil of Africa, the flag of France and the cross, set up the sign of civilisation, the symbol of peace and charity.[22]

The words succinctly reflected the link between throne and altar, appropriated the actions of King Charles X, and affirmed France as synonymous with civilisation.

Two days later there followed a proclamation to 'the Arab people'. It began with an orthodox statement of the takeover of Algeria by a country that 'did not come to destroy the nationality of its people, but, on the contrary, to emancipate the people from centuries-long oppression': France had freed Berbers, Arabs and Jews from Turkish tyranny. The Algerians had contested French conquest, but 'far be it from me the thought to make that a crime', said Napoléon – perhaps with Abd el-Kader in mind – 'rather I honour the warrior dignity' that inspired them. Napoléon then drew an explicit and rather surprising parallel between the Algerian resistance and the way that the ancient Gauls had resisted the 'foreign invasion' by the Romans: 'The vanquished Gauls assimilated themselves with the victorious Romans, and from that forced union between the contrary virtues of two opposed civilisations, with time was born this French nationality that, in its turn, spread its ideas around the whole world.' The French presence in Algeria would provide for the 'regeneration' of the Arab people, and he cited a verse from the Quran saying that God gives power to those whom he chooses. Napoléon promised to honour the Arab chiefs, respect the people's religion, increase their well-being, and more and more allow them to participate in the administration of the country and the 'benefits of civilisation'.

All of this was on condition that 'you respect those who represent my authority'. He thanked Algerians who had submitted to French rule, warned those who had not, evoked the glories of the French army in Crimea, Italy, China and Mexico (and the service of Algerian soldiers with them), and concluded with another Quranic verse stating that the one whom God directs is well directed. The proclamation thereby drew up a contract for French colonisation. It preached French might, but also the promise of reconciliation, respect and prosperity. Exactly what the emperor meant in practice remained vague – how much 'participation' would the Arabs be accorded in administration and when? A basic assumption, that France brought civilisation and its benefits, was clearly affirmed as were ethnocentric stereotypes about Arabs, though it is noteworthy that Napoléon went out of his way to make reassuring remarks.

That all the Algerians, even with the cheering for the visiting sovereign, accepted the tenets of his pronouncement, and shared such a roseate vision of a future under the French, is unlikely.[23] However, that they hoped to obtain concessions following his tour is fully believable, as is indicated by the speeches and petitions in which Algerian notables pledged loyalty and sought to counter beliefs about their opposition. Clearly some had cast their lots with the French. At another level, the very presence of the 'sultan of the sultans' (as he was sometimes called) may have promised advantages. One French reporter following the tour noted that for Algerians the very sight of a monarch brought good luck not only to those who gazed upon him but their families and communities, hence the great effort, and occasional jostling, to catch a glimpse of the emperor. In this perspective, the sight of the supreme ruler per se rather than Napoléon himself brought blessings upon his subjects.[24]

Napoléon's third proclamation, just before his departure from Algeria, was directed to the French army in Africa. He hailed their heroism and battlefield success, and said, rather sanguinely, that 'never in your ranks did anger survive the struggle; among you [there is] no hatred for a vanquished enemy, no desire to enrich yourselves from his assets; you are the first to extend to the wayward Arabs a friendly hand'. He spoke of Africa as a 'great school for the education of the soldier; he has here acquired those virile virtues which are the glory of armies'.[25] The words were not particularly original, but underscored the role of colonies as a source of revivification for the French as well as for the Algerians.

The years immediately following Napoléon's second visit, while seeing settlers further rooted in Algeria, did not bring the peace and prosperity that his tour had predicted. Nor did they resolve questions about governance and the place of the Arabs in the French possession. Soon after his return to Paris, Napoléon received Abd el-Kader and decorated him with the Legion of Honour, another sign of favour to reconciled Arabs. Napoléon tried to implement Saint-Simonian inspired policies for Algeria and to respond to certain requests made during his tour; in 1865 Algerian Arabs and Jews were given French nationality (though not citizenship and the right to vote), and the following year legislation allowed Arabs to sit on municipal councils. The *colons* were hardly enthusiastic, but they had other problems to face. A plague of locusts wreaked havoc in 1866, there was an earthquake at the beginning of the following year, then outbreaks of cholera and typhus. By 1868, Algeria may have lost 17 per cent of its population.

In 1870, discontent in Algeria festered while Napoléon set off on his ill-fated war against the Prussians. After the emperor was captured, a decree of the provisional government, the *Décret Crémieux*, made Algeria's Jews into French citizens. The naturalisation of the Jews, French capitulation to the Prussians and the end of the Second Empire emboldened resistance, and a revolt by Algerian troops broadened into a general insurrection of around a third of the Algerian population in 1871. The military put down the 'Mokrani rebellion' (named about one of its leaders), and deported 2,000 rebels to New Caledonia. The optimistic sentiments pronounced by the emperor and his hosts a few years earlier must now have rung hollow, and it would fall to the Third Republic, which abjured the monarchy if it did not fully disavow the emperor's foreign and colonial policy, to confront the problems of *Algérie française*.

The imperial family's travels

Napoléon's tours of Algeria may be set not only within the context of colonial developments but also within the wider itineraries of the imperial family.[26] These ranged from regular movements around various residences – Paris, Fontainebleau, Compiègne, Biarritz – and tours of the French provinces to their enforced sojourns abroad, primarily in Britain, before Napoléon came to power and after he was overturned.[27] Indeed, the ex-emperor died in Britain in 1873; Eugénie died on a visit to Spain in 1920. During almost half a century, as dethroned empress and widow, Eugénie had developed a passion for travel around Europe (sometimes on her own yacht); at the age of eighty-two, she even visited Ceylon.[28] Her most poignant journey was to another British colony, South Africa, in memory of her son.

For the heir to Napoléon I and Napoléon III, a military vocation and need to exhibit bravery on the battlefield were a birthright and obligation. The prince imperial, known as Napoléon IV to Bonapartists, completed training at the British military academy in Woolwich. In 1878, he asked to join Austrian soldiers sent to the Balkans, but the Habsburg emperor declined; as a consolation, the prince embarked on a tour of Scandinavia, where he was received by royals and military brass. When his British regiment was deployed to South Africa in 1879 to fight the Zulus, the prince expressed his desire to serve with his comrades. Although Eugénie was strongly opposed, the prince used his influence to press his case. Finally, with Queen Victoria's approval, it was decided that he could join the regiment, but as a uniformed observer not as a combatant. A tearful Eugénie farewelled her son, and his letters testified to joy at heading for the battlefield and fascination for the African landscape. The prince, however, would not return alive, as he was killed in an engagement with the Zulus.[29]

Eugénie determined to make a pilgrimage to the site of her son's death. Her entourage were hesitant because of the hazards of such a journey for the grieving empress, and her friend Queen Victoria counselled against the trip. Eugénie was as insistent as her son had been, and the queen offered to provide funding and place British officials in her service. In Cape Town, Eugénie was received by the governor, and in Durban, she stayed in the very rooms her son had occupied. Then began an almost month-long expedition, by train and carriage, to the place where he had fallen. Eugénie spent the entire night coinciding with the first anniversary of the prince's death in prayer at the site, where Victoria had ordered a cross be raised and inscribed in tribute to a man killed 'with his face to the foe'. Eugénie noticed or imagined Zulus on the crest of the nearby hill and mystically felt the prince with her. She returned to Britain via St Helena, where she toured Longwood, Napoléon I's residence in exile.[30]

In her long life, Eugénie saw and played a part in the evolution of European monarchy, the expansion of colonial empires, and the growing popularity and new technologies of travel. The rise and fall of Napoléon III, the extension of a French empire over which he reigned and which his republican successors were left to rule, and the intertwined destinies of the Bonapartist pretender and British troops conquering new lands for their queen illustrate the twists and turns of nineteenth-century history. Touring made it possible for royals (including deposed monarchs) such as the French imperial family to witness momentous events and tectonic transformations on site across Europe, in the Americas, Algeria and South Africa, and South Asia. Regular long-distance travel, still limited when Napoleon was striving to become emperor, by the time of the death of his widow had assuredly become pleasure, vocation, political obligation and duty for members of reigning royal families, and consolation and necessity for those who had lost their thrones.

Notes

1 *Voyage de S.M. Napoléon III en Algérie* (Algiers: Bastide, 1865), pp. 248, 10. This volume, which contains a detailed account of the emperor's travels, as well as verbatim reproductions of his proclamations and speeches in his honour and paraphrased renditions of his own comments, has provided the major primary source on his voyage. The editorial comments and preface are signed only as an unidentified 'F', who appears to have accompanied the imperial party. I have also used *Voyage de l'Empereur Napoléon III en Algérie*, an extract from the journal of the commander of the ship *Solférino*, published in the *Revue Maritime et Coloniale* in October 1865, in the collection of the Bibliothèque Nationale de France, Paris. Florian Pharaon, *Voyage en Algérie de Sa Majesté III* (Paris: Henri Plon, 1865) provides a chronology, proclamations and speeches, and drawings by A. Darjou.
2 However, several of King Louis-Philippe's sons – the Ducs d'Orléans, d'Aumale, de Nemours and de Joinville – served in Algeria in the 1830s and 1840s, and the Duc d'Aumale was governor-general of Algeria from 1847 to 1848.
3 Roger D. Price, *Napoleon III and the Second Empire* (London: Routledge, 1997), provides a succinct historiographical introduction. On Eugénie, see Desmond Seward, *Eugénie: The Empress and Her Empire* (London: The History Press, 2004). In French, there are biographies by Pierre Milza, *Napoléon III* (Paris: Perin, 2004); and Jean des Cars, *Eugénie, la dernière impératrice* (Paris: Perrin, 2000). For Napoléon's overseas policy, chapter 18 of Milza's book provides a fine overview.
4 Guy Cogeval, Yves Badetz, Paul Perrin and Marie-Paule Vial (eds), *Spectaculaire Second Empire* (Paris: Musée d'Orsay and Éditions Skira, 2016).
5 See Stephane Kirkland, *Paris Reborn: Napoleon III, Baron Haussmann, and the Quest to Build a Modern City* (London: Picador, 2012).
6 Theo Aronson, *Queen Victoria and the Bonapartes* (London: Thistle Publishing, 2014) documents the friendship between the British and French royals.
7 Yves Bruley, *La Diplomatie du Sphinx: Napoléon III et sa politique internationale* (Paris: Éditions CLD, 2015) is the most recent treatment.

8 Xavier Salmon and Vincent Droguet (eds), *Le Musée chinois de l'Impératrice Eugénie* (Paris: Artlys, 2011).
9 Xavier Salmon (ed.), *Le Siam à Fontainebleau: l'ambassade du 27 juin 1861* (Paris: RMN – Grand Palais, 2011); on French policy towards Siam, Nigel J. Brailey, *Imperial Amnesia: Britain, France and 'the Question of Siam'* (Dordrecht: Republic of Letters, 2009).
10 Emmanuelle Guenot, 'Napoleon III and France's Colonial Expansion: National Grandeur, Territorial Conquests and Colonial Embellishment, 1852–70', in Robert Aldrich and Cindy McCreery (eds), *Crowns and Colonies: European Monarchies and Overseas Empires* (Manchester: Manchester University Press, 2016), pp. 211–226.
11 On the exposition, Paul Greenhalgh, *Fair World: A History of World's Fairs and Exposition from London to Shanghai, 1851–2010* (Newbury: Papadakis, 2011). On the canal, including Eugénie's presence at the opening, Zachary Karabell, *Parting the Desert: The Creation of the Suez Canal* (London: John Murray, 2003), and Roberto Morra di Lavriano, *Journal de Voyage en Égypte – Inauguration du Canal de Suez* (Paris: Gründ, 1977).
12 Martin Evans and John Philipps, *Algeria: Anger of the Dispossessed* (New Haven: Yale University Press, 2011).
13 Pamela Pilbeam, *Saint-Simonians in Nineteenth-Century France* (London: Palgrave Macmillan, 2014), esp. chapter 6. On Urbain, Michel Levallois, *Ismaÿl Urbain: Royaume arabe ou Algérie franco-musulmane? 1848–1870* (Paris: Riveneuve Éditions, 2012).
14 See, in particular, Levallois, *Ismaÿl Urbain*, pp. 251–254.
15 The letter is reproduced in Jean Martin, *L'Empire renaissant, 1789–1871* (Paris: Denoël, 1987), pp. 386–388.
16 Bonapartism and its heritage for colonialism in Algeria is analysed by Jennifer E. Sessions, *By Sword and Plow: France and the Conquest of Algeria* (Ithaca: Cornell University Press, 2011). Georges Spillmann, *Napoléon III et le royaume arabe d'Algérie* (Paris: ASOM, 1975), and Annie Rey-Goldzeiguer, *Le Royaume arabe: la politique algérienne de Napoléon III, 1861–1870* (Algiers: Société nationale d'édition, 1977) look at policy under his reign. Recent contributions on Algerian colonisation in this period include Gavin Murray-Miller, 'A Conflicted Sense of Nationality: Napoléon III's Arab Kingdom and the Paradoxes of French Multiculturalism', *French Colonial History*, 15 (2004), 1–38; and David Todd, 'Transnational Projects of Empire in France, c. 1815–c. 1870', *Modern Intellectual History*, 12:2 (2015), 265–293.
17 The fullest discussion of the imperial tours of Algeria is René Pillorget, 'Les Deux Voyages de Napoléon III en Algérie (1860 et 1865)', *Napoléonia*, No. 21, based on a lecture delivered in 1987. Online at www.napoleon.org/histoire-des-2-empires/articles/les-deux-voyages-de-napoleon-iii-en-algerie-1860-et-1865, accessed 5 May 2017.
18 *Voyage de Napoléon III*, p. 283.
19 *Ibid.*, pp. 163–164, 292–296.
20 On the Italian fleet, *ibid.*, pp. 245–250, on the Moroccan delegation, pp. 191–193, and on the Tunisian delegation, pp. 348–352.
21 *Ibid.*, pp. 227–228.
22 *Ibid.*, pp. 27–28.
23 *Ibid.*, pp. 38–41.
24 *Ibid.*, p. 222, quoting an unnamed writer in the *Moniteur du soir*.
25 *Ibid.*, pp. 354–356.
26 See Charles-Éloi Vial, *Les Derniers feux de la monarchie: La cour au siècle des revolutions, 1789–1870* (Paris: Perrin, 2016), pp. 499–510.
27 Examples of accounts include Louis Le Bondidier, *Napoléon III et Eugénie aux Pyrénées* (Pau: Mont Hélios, 2015); F. Laurent, *Voyage de Sa Majesté Napoléon III Empereur des Français dans les départements de l'Est, du Centre et du Midi de la France* (Nîmes: Lacour/Rediviva, 1989, the re-issue of an undated contemporary account); and C.L. Cormont, *Voyage de Leurs Majestés Impériales en Auvergne* (Nîmes: C. Lacour, 2005 [1862]).

28 Marie de Larminat de Garnier Des Garets, *L'Impératrice Eugénie en exil: la mort de Napoléon III et du Prince Impérial, 1870–1880* (Clermont-Ferrand: Paleo, 2009 [1929]).
29 Ian Knight, *With His Face to the Foe: The Life and Death of Louis Napoléon, the Prince Imperial, Zululand 1879* (Stroud: Spellmount, 2001). See also Eric Pradelles, *Le Prince impérial, Napoléon IV: Correspondance inédite, intime et politique* (Aix-en-Provence: Éditions Mémoire et documents, 2013).
30 John Laband, 'An Empress in Zululand: The Pilgrimage in 1880 by the Empress Eugénie to the Site of the Death of Her Son, the Prince Imperial of France', *Natalia*, 30 (2000), 45–57.

CHAPTER FOUR

Something borrowed, something blue: Prince Alfred's precedent in overseas British royal tours, c. 1860–1925

Cindy McCreery

When the young British princes Albert Victor and George visited Australia in 1881, they and their hosts recalled another royal tour and another royal tourist. Visiting a new grammar school in Brisbane, 'they were told how their uncle, the Duke of Edinburgh, had laid the foundation-stone of the old Prince Alfred Grammar School, within sight, and now vacated'.[1] Alfred was in many ways the first British royal to tour major parts of the British empire and wider world, and this chapter argues that his 1860s and 1870s journeys provided an important precedent for the more famous British princely tours that followed. Like the old grammar school, Alfred's precedent is a historical subject 'within sight, and now vacated'. As in 1881, a tour guide is needed.

Prince Alfred Ernest Albert, Duke of Edinburgh (1844–1900) remains a surprisingly shadowy historical figure.[2] The second son of Queen Victoria and Prince Albert, Alfred served as a career officer in the Royal Navy (1858–1893), rising to the highest rank of Admiral of the Fleet. In 1893 he succeeded his Uncle Ernst (Prince Albert's elder brother) as Duke of Saxe Coburg Gotha in Germany. Alfred was thus a prominent British naval officer as well as European royal. His death in 1900 (a year before his mother), long absences from Britain and status as a 'spare' rather than 'heir' to the British throne partly explain his relative obscurity. Today, Alfred is often confused with other princely relations bearing similar names: Albert (father), Albert Edward (elder brother) and Albert Victor (nephew). Where identified correctly, Alfred is often reduced to a brief mention in his more famous relatives' biographies.[3] Yet, during his lifetime and into the twentieth century Alfred and his travels remained well-known within Europe, the British empire – and beyond. Through private photograph albums, correspondence and conversations, Alfred's tours were kept alive for the royal family, court and others.[4] Shortly after Alfred returned with rapturous accounts of his 1869 visit to Hawai'i, for example, the press allegedly reported that his elder brother 'declared that if he ever made a long cruise his first visit would be to these islands'. Over ten years later, in 1881, when the Hawai'ian King Kalakaua visited London, members of the British royal circle repeated Alfred's favourable impressions. Queen Victoria, for instance, remarked to Kalakaua that the islands must be very beautiful 'for the Duke often spoke of them'.[5]

Alfred provided a template for later royal tours in three ways. First, he pioneered a new relationship with the Royal Navy as a training institution for British princes and a source of royal mentors and companions. Second, his lengthy visits to Britain's southern settler colonies as well as India paved the way for similarly ambitious global tours. Finally, Alfred's tours cultivated a range of trusted support staff (from governors, tutors and chaplains to physicians and local guides, artists, equerries, bodyguards and personal friends), many of whom fulfilled similar roles in subsequent tours and/or stayed on as permanent staff of the royal family. In turn, local audiences welcomed later royal tours with many of the same entertainments, mottoes and even decorations used for Alfred.

With the partial exception of the tour of the Duke and Duchess of Cornwall and York in 1901 (the first major international tour by a British royal couple, which set a new trend for tours by married royals), nineteenth- and early twentieth-century British royal tours borrowed generously, though not necessarily consciously, from Alfred's template.[6] The point is not that later royal tourists always recognised Alfred as their model – they often didn't – but rather that Alfred pioneered, mostly through trial and error, naval tours, itineraries and programmes which suited the needs of the young British princes and the diverse global audiences who increasingly expected, even demanded, their visits. In turn, Alfred's tours drew upon the eighteenth-century tradition of educating young noblemen by sending them on a 'Grand Tour' to view Europe's cultural treasures. Just as these Grand Tours soon developed a core itinerary, so, in many ways, later royal tourists followed in Alfred's footsteps, visiting many of the same cities, sights and, theoretically, learning the same lessons about how to behave as a prince. But as with the Brisbane grammar school, later royal tourists were usually viewed as a more modern, up-to-date version of the original. For all the deference paid to the past, each new royal tour was supposedly more memorable than the last, particularly when the latest royal tourist was an heir rather than a 'spare'. Alfred's tours were increasingly forgotten.

British princely tours from the 1860s to 1925 often involved remarkably ambitious journeys that contrast sharply with the relatively modest patterns of earlier royal travel.[7] Aside from regular visits to royal residences like Osborne (Isle of Wight) and Balmoral (Scotland) as well the continent, including, in the latter years of her reign, winter health trips to the Riviera, Queen Victoria preferred to remain at home in Windsor, especially following the death there of Prince Albert in December 1861.[8] Ironically, the queen's determination not to travel far made the princes' travel to the expanding British empire and beyond all the more necessary. But Victoria remained anxious about and at times hostile to their travel. This royal mother and grandmother frequently expressed concern for the princes' safety and health both aboard ship and on distant shores; conversely she resented unnecessary and possibly morally harmful absences from home and family in Britain.[9] The enormous cost and pomp of the tours incensed a growing chorus of republican critics at home and abroad, expressed in frequent editorials in London's republican *Reynolds's Newspaper*, as well as in some Indian newspapers.[10] Despite criticism and foreboding, the tours continued and indeed proliferated. Along with government ministers and officials, Queen Victoria increasingly recognised the value of these royal tours in boosting the reputation of the individual prince, the royal family, nation and empire.[11] By the twentieth century, overseas tours by younger royals became a key part of the public performance of the monarchy; this extended to attending ceremonies in former colonies marking the end of formal empire.[12]

There was no overarching 'master plan' for British royal tours, but rather an ad hoc exchange of correspondence concerning prospective travel between the royal family, Admiralty, prime minister, Colonial Office, Foreign Office, colonial governors, foreign governments as well as personal friends and advisors of the princes.[13] There were multiple, overlapping reasons for the tours, and the immediate needs as well as the expectations of individual princes influenced the decision of when and where to travel overseas. Disputes, delays and difficulties were common, and the final version of a tour often bore little resemblance to its original plan. Yet while each journey was planned separately, and for particular ends, together these tours constituted a symbolic response to decisive trends in British foreign, colonial and military policy. In particular, they relate to the military reforms and budget cuts which shifted responsibility for colonial defence largely to the settler colonies.[14] The resulting withdrawal of imperial troops and warships was deeply unpopular with settlers, and princely visits, especially aboard imperial naval vessels, appealed to many, though by no means all, parties in the colonies as well as in Britain.[15] Royal tours provided, at least in theory, evidence that Britain, and in particular its royal family, had not forgotten the empire. What was implicit in the nineteenth century became explicit in the twentieth century, especially after the Boer and First World Wars, when princes were sent to thank the dominions for their enormous war contribution.

The current volume demonstrates the importance of viewing royal tours within a larger comparative framework. By revisiting Alfred's tours, we can better understand the larger pattern of British and indeed European royal tours more generally. We can also trace the ways in which tours contributed to the relationship between monarchy and empire, as well as to the preparation of royals – both heirs and spares – for their future duties.[16]

Alfred was in many ways the first major British royal tourist.[17] His youthful naval tours of the Mediterranean and West Indies (1858–1860) and especially South Africa and West Africa (1860) influenced the subsequent naval tours of his teenage nephews Albert Victor and George aboard HMS *Bacchante* in 1879–1882. Alfred's global tours on HMS *Galatea* (1867–1871) further refined the template of British princely tours, shaping the journeys of his brother Albert Edward and grand-nephew Edward.

The origins of the British royal tour

Alfred, too, followed in his predecessors' footsteps. Just as Australian newspapers compared the visit of Albert Victor and George in 1881 with that of Alfred, so too in 1868 they compared Alfred's naval service with that of his great-uncle William IV.[18] William served as a sea-going naval officer in his youth; this experience was thought to provide him with a greater understanding of ordinary subjects, and greatly added to his later popularity as king. But this naval duty did not involve any royal tour of the colonies. William visited North America in his naval capacity during wartime and perhaps understandably, given the unpopularity of his father George III during the 1776–1783 American War of Independence, no attempt then was made to show him off as a model 'sailor prince'.[19] It was also too early in the development of royal tours as publicity exercises. William served in the navy to learn, not to shore up support for the crown. Less than a century later, the relationship between the royal family and Royal Navy – and the colonies – had changed markedly.

From the early nineteenth century, the notion of the dutiful sailor prince gained wide purchase and became a powerful advertisement for the continuing relevance of the British royal family to distant colonial societies, particularly those dependent on the navy for the protection

Table 4.1 Overseas tours by British royals c. 1858–1927[a]

Royal figure	Vessel	Year	Destination(s)
Major overseas tours by British princes, 1858–1921 with major destinations in **bold**			
Alfred (1844–1900)	HMS *Euryalus*	1858	Caribbean
*Alfred	HMS *Euryalus*	1859	Mediterranean
	HMS *Euryalus*	1860	Rio de Janeiro, **South Africa** and Sierra Leone
Albert Edward, Prince of Wales (later Edward VII) (1842–1910)	HMS *Hero*	1860	**Canada** and the **United States**
Albert Edward	HMS *Osborne*	1862	**Egypt, Palestine, Syria, Lebanon, Turkey** and **Greece**
*Alfred, Duke of Edinburgh	HMS *Galatea*	1867–1871	**South Africa, Australia, Pacific Islands, New Zealand, Japan, China,** Singapore, Malaysia, **India**, Mauritius, South America
[Minor Tour] Albert Edward and Alexandra, Princess of Wales	HMS *Ariadne*	1869	**Egypt, Constantinople, Crimea, Greece**
*Albert Edward	HMS *Serapis*	1875–1876	Greece, Egypt, Aden, **India, Ceylon** (Sri Lanka), Malta, Gibraltar, Spain, Portugal
*Albert Victor (later Duke of Clarence and Avondale) (1863–1892) and George (later Duke of Cornwall and York, Prince of Wales, and then George V) (1865–1936)	HMS *Bacchante*	1879–1882	Falkland Islands, **South Africa, Australia, China, Japan,** Fiji, Singapore, **Ceylon,** Aden, Egypt, Palestine, **Greece**
Albert Victor	SS *Oceana* (returned on SS *Assam*)	1889–1890	India, Burma and Egypt
[Minor Tour] George, Prince of Wales	HMS *Indomitable*	1908	Canada

*Edward, Prince of Wales (later Edward VIII) (1894–1972)	HMS *Renown* (II)	1919	Canada and the United States
		1920	West Indies, San Diego, Honolulu, Australia and New Zealand
		1921–1922	Mediterranean, Suez, Aden, India, Burma, Ceylon, Federated Malay States, Singapore, Hong Kong, Japan, Manila, Labuan, Brunei
	HMS *Repulse*	1925	West Africa, South Africa and South America

Major tours by British princes and their wives, 1901–1927

George, Duke of Cornwall and York and Mary, Duchess of Cornwall and York	HMS *Ophir*	1901	Australia, New Zealand, South Africa and Canada
George, Prince of Wales and Mary, Princess of Wales	HMS *Renown* (I)	1905–1906	India and Burma
George V and Queen Mary	HMS *Medina*	1911	India
Albert, Duke of York (later George VI) and Elizabeth, Duchess of York (later Queen Elizabeth)	HMS *Renown* (II)	1927	Fiji, New Zealand, Australia and Mauritius

Notes

[a] Some information is drawn from John Fabb, *Royal Tours of the British Empire 1860–1927* (London: B.T. Batsford, 1989); and Alan Major, *Royal Yachts* (Stroud: Amberley, 2011).

* refers to tours discussed in detail in this chapter.

of maritime trade. When fifteen-year-old Alfred visited Sierra Leone in 1860 as a midshipman aboard HMS *Euryalus*, the colony's Legislative Council expressed its pleasure 'in seeing in the person of Your Royal Highness, a Prince of the Royal family of England engaged in the service of the State. This pleasure is enhanced by the fact that it is [to] the British Navy we are indebted for the security which trade enjoys on this Coast'.[20] Such comments were repeated throughout Alfred's 1860 and 1867–1871 voyages, on illuminated transparencies, banners, triumphal arches as well as in newspaper editorials.[21] Alfred's tours may have inspired another trend in British royal tours: the recycling of decorations, particularly those welcoming 'our Sailor Prince/s' (Figures 4.1 and 4.2). In the twentieth century, royal tours might emphasise the individual personality of the prince, but in the nineteenth century one sailor prince was welcomed much like another. Naval training was not unique to British princes – nineteenth- and early twentieth-century German, Danish and Greek princes also increasingly received a naval education, and proved similarly popular with their respective publics.[22]

4.1 'Welcome, Sailor Prince', photograph of triumphal arch celebrating the arrival of H.R.H. Duke of Edinburgh to Emerald Hill, Melbourne, in 1867

SOMETHING BORROWED, SOMETHING BLUE

4.2 Julian Rossi Ashton, 'Our Sailor Princes', wood engraving of Princes Albert Victor and George aboard their ship. *Australasian Sketcher*, 7 May 1881

In the navy

In some ways the nineteenth-century royal family's practice of sending sons into the armed forces followed earlier royal precedents (like William IV) as well as the custom of aristocratic and gentry families. The usual inheritance pattern gave the eldest son the family title and estate, with younger sons despatched to the army, navy and Church to pursue a career. But the decision to send Alfred into the navy also reflected the particular ambitions of his parents, especially his father Prince Albert.

While his brother Ernst, the reigning Duke of Saxe Coburg Gotha, wished his heir to become familiar with his German territory, Prince Albert preferred that Alfred first follow his own inclination and serve in the British navy. Albert saw naval training as beneficial to both the individual and the nation, and he also increasingly emphasised the important role which his eldest sons could play in boosting the empire's loyalty to Britain via princely visits to the colonies.[23] While Albert Edward's 1860 tour to the United States and Canada received more press attention, Alfred's contemporaneous visit to Sierra Leone and South Africa probably had more influence in shaping subsequent tours along naval lines.[24] Certainly Alfred's appearance as a hard-working junior officer, who did not let his enthusiastic royal welcome go to his head, captured South African colonists' imagination.[25]

Such pleasing reports encouraged the royal family to use the navy more extensively for princely training. Alfred's elder brother Albert Edward sent both his own sons into the Royal Navy as adolescents.[26] Moreover he expressed a keen interest in the service and often wore his honorary naval uniform in photographs taken with his brother and sons. Not only did Albert Victor and George receive similar naval instruction but an extensive tour, which combined the training elements of Alfred's 1860 tour with the global reach of his 1867–1871 voyages, was organised for them in 1879–1882. In turn George sent three of his own five sons into the navy.[27] Like their father and great-uncle, the two elder princes (the future Edward VIII and George VI) both developed strong bonds with the navy, which arguably became their substitute family. Had they produced sons, it seems likely that they too would have received naval training.[28] By the twentieth century, naval training of British princes had thus moved from the occasional to the expected. Alfred was the forgotten pioneer of British princes wearing navy 'blue'.

From royals in the navy to naval royal tours

Numerous parallels between Albert Victor and George's 1879–1882 royal tour and those of Alfred in 1860 and 1867–1871 have so far gone largely unnoticed. In all three tours the princes travelled as naval officers in training, not passengers. This ostensibly provided valuable experience for them as well as publicity to colonists.[29] Images of apparently hard-working princes played well in societies like Australia, which prided themselves on their egalitarian ethos, but which nevertheless delighted in the honour conferred by a royal visit.[30] Numerous engravings and photographs circulated in Australia of Albert Victor and George in naval uniform, or alternatively, in work clothes visiting a gold mine; several recall earlier photographs of Alfred in similar poses and locations.[31]

Naval service was also intended to protect the princes from moral harm, shielding them from unfavourable publicity as well as shaping their behaviour. Royal anxiety about the many temptations London offered to adolescent and young adult males as well as particular concern about individual physical and mental development partly motivated many of the tours, and shaped both their timing and length. In the 1860s and early 1870s Queen Victoria became increasingly keen to keep Alfred away from London and the decadent influence of his elder brother Albert Edward; hence the several extensions made to the *Galatea* voyages.[32] Conversely, in 1879 a lengthy voyage with his more lively younger brother George was viewed as beneficial for the apparently listless Albert Victor, while in 1889 a solo trip to India was deemed useful.[33]

Beyond royal parents and grandparents, these royal tours owed much to the paternal advice and practical arrangements provided by two senior naval officers who acted *in loco parentis*. Admiral Sir Henry Keppel advised Alfred and his brother Albert Edward on their 1860s and 1870s voyages, and mentored Alfred as well as Albert Edward's sons in their naval careers. After his death in 1904, Queen Alexandra spoke for the whole royal family when she farewelled 'my beloved "Little Admiral"'.[34] Alexander Milne was the naval officer who accompanied Albert Edward to Canada and the United States in 1860, a visit Albert Edward recalled to him affectionately some thirty years later.[35] In late 1861, Milne personally broke the news of Prince Albert's sudden death to young Alfred, then serving under him in North America. For decades, Milne served the princes by securing from the Admiralty the right ships, officers, promotions and itineraries for their travels.[36]

Keppel and Milne formed part of a much more extensive linkage between the Royal Navy and royal family. On the *Euryalus* and *Bacchante* tours, the young princes were placed under the authority of experienced captains who enjoyed the confidence and patronage of the royal family. On Alfred's 1860 cruise Captain John W. Tarleton, whose previous ship was stationed near the queen's residence Osborne on the Isle of Wight 'for saluting purposes during the visit of Grand Duke Constantine of Russia' and who had been Alfred's commanding officer since 1858 aboard HMS *Euryalus*, continued in this role. On the 1879–1882 *Bacchante* cruise Albert Victor and George joined Captain

Lord Charles Scott, who had previously travelled in China with Alfred and had also served as a lieutenant in the royal yacht *Victoria and Albert*.[37] The admiral in charge of the detached squadron (*Bacchante* travelled as part of a squadron of five warships) Richard Meade, Earl of Clanwilliam, had earlier served as aide-de-camp to Queen Victoria. In turn the success of these royal cruises further advanced these officers' already successful careers: Tarleton reached the rank of Second Naval Lord while Scott ended his career with the highly prestigious post of Commander-in-Chief, Portsmouth.[38] Even more impressively, Keppel, Milne and Clanwilliam reached the highest rank of Admiral of the Fleet (one also attained by Alfred, and, in an honorary capacity, Albert Edward). While Milne, in particular, clearly deserved this honour, royal patronage proved crucial for career progression in a peacetime navy top-heavy with officers.[39] The choice of these individuals in turn signalled the ongoing connections between the royal family and aristocratic families with long naval pedigrees such as the Keppels. Thus naval royal tours were peppered with aristocrats who served as shipboard officers and/or aides-de-camp, equerries or private companions to the princes.[40]

In addition to Tarleton, Scott and Clanwilliam, who played a fatherly role on these cruises, the young princes were also supervised by military governors and chaplains appointed by the royal family: in 1860 Major John Cowell and the Rev. William Lake Onslow and in 1879–1882 the Rev. John Neale Dalton.[41] These governors benefited from the success of the tours: Cowell held the senior royal post of 'Master of the Household' from 1866 until his death in 1894; Onslow followed Alfred to his new ship HMS *St George* in 1861 and was later appointed Rector of Sandringham and Chaplain in Ordinary to the Prince of Wales (Albert Edward); while Dalton was appointed governor to Albert Victor at Trinity College, Cambridge and later held the plum position of Canon at St George's Chapel, Windsor.[42] Perhaps most significantly, these individuals shaped their young charges both during and after their travels. Onslow remained on close terms with the royal family; an 1874 sketch shows the young Albert Victor and George snowballing him.[43] So important was Dalton to George, meanwhile, that he brought him along on his and his wife Princess Mary's voyage to Australia (the first major 'married' royal tour) in 1901.[44] Such gratitude boosted these individuals' careers, and reinforced to the royal family and the general public the importance of providing the princes with appropriate moral guardianship on their long journeys away from home.

As they grew older, however, princes often saw the tours as opportunities to demonstrate their independence from family members and chaperones. While Alfred was accompanied by a chaplain, the

Rev. John Milner, on the first (1867–1868) *Galatea* tour, Milner seems to have viewed his main duty as recording the voyage for posterity in an official and discreet tour volume.[45] In Australia, Alfred was criticised for his lax attitude to punctuality and apparent boredom; Melbourne's *Age* newspaper noted that a mentor would have been useful.[46] In fact, Alfred did have a chaperone of sorts: Frederick Standish, Melbourne's chief of police, who took Alfred to a high-class brothel during his 1868 visit and welcomed him back to the city in 1869.[47] On this second visit Alfred also took the precaution of hiring a bodyguard, Detective John Christie, who accompanied him to New Zealand. Christie's hard work and discretion were rewarded thirty-two years later when he was handpicked to guard George and Mary on their 1901 Australian and New Zealand tour.[48] Alfred also relied heavily on the advice of Henry Keppel, now the admiral in charge of the China Station, whilst in Asian waters, but he resisted the suggestion that a senior official accompany him to India.[49] Similarly, Alfred's elder brother Albert Edward made clear his objection to travelling to India with a chaperone, and despite his mother's attempt to vet his companions he managed to include numerous young men with lively reputations.[50]

Subsequent journeys by teenage princes continued to involve specially appointed guardians, for example, Dalton, or at least the watchful eye of a colonial governor. But no longer were older princes permitted the relative freedom that Alfred and Albert Edward had enjoyed in the 1860s and 1870s. Global telegraph networks, mass market newspapers, steamships, and the Suez Canal facilitated 'instant' news and thus increased public awareness of and indeed expectations of tours as impressive spectacles. In turn, the tours' organisation became much more polished and professional and with a conscious focus on presenting an image of a hard-working, responsible prince to a global public. Alfred's somewhat haphazard schedule was replaced with a more structured, precise itinerary designed to show the princes off to best advantage, which mirrors the broader improvement in the performance of British royal ritual from the late 1870s.[51] Where Alfred travelled indirectly to India using (mostly) sail power aboard HMS *Galatea*, five years later Albert Edward travelled via steamship and more directly, thanks to the recent opening of the Suez Canal. While Alfred arrived in India late, Albert Edward was early. And while Edward may have rivalled his uncle Alfred in partying with like-minded young people on his 1919–1925 overseas tours, unlike Alfred, in Australia and New Zealand at least, no one could fault Edward's public displays of energy, enthusiasm and overall attention to duty.[52] These early tours anticipate the vernacularisation of the British royal family in the tours of the late twentieth and early twenty-first centuries, where successive royals demonstrate both their humility and their 'ordinariness' – but also their work discipline – to approving and ever watchful global fans.[53]

In short, Alfred's ad hoc, hastily and, by later standards, casually arranged travels proved successful enough to inspire longer, better organised and more professionally run as well as closely scrutinised tours. These visits were crafted to publicise, and indeed to celebrate, Britain's global maritime dominance – in trade as well as naval power. While there were some inland components, much of this travel was sea-based and the tours involved lengthy ocean crossings. Here the princes focused on their naval training and were inducted into maritime traditions such as the festive 'crossing the line' ceremony at the Equator. They also visited commercially valuable seaports.[54]

Voyages by young princes involved a mix of preparatory naval training (some of it at home in British waters) and general education as well as sightseeing. The teenage Alfred, Albert Victor and George began with preliminary tours to the Mediterranean, which included visits to classical ruins, familiar to generations of young British aristocrats following the well-trodden path of the 'Grand Tour'.[55] There was also time to visit other royals, some of whom, like the Danish-born George I, King of the Hellenes, were members of their own extended family. To an extent, these naval cruises resembled the private cruises increasingly made by European royals in the Mediterranean and Baltic seas to visit royal relatives; for instance, Queen Alexandra and her extended family's cruises to Denmark in the summertime.[56] On the other hand, the princes' tours took place aboard serving warships, and some attention was paid to British naval history. The album commemorating the *Bacchante*'s visit to the West Indies includes a photograph of the statue in Spanish Town, Jamaica, of Admiral George Brydges Rodney, the British victor of the celebrated 1782 Battle of the Saintes which 'saved' the valuable sugar colony from the French.[57] Yet the major focal point of this and the other global tours were the ports of both the settler colonies and other up-and-coming nations. If the young princes were intended to learn from sites made famous by classical history – or more recent naval warfare as in the West Indies – they were also expected to learn from places further afield which promised future glory for Britons. In turn, princely visits to such wealthy and influential societies as Australia, South Africa, Japan and even China came to be seen as valuable diplomatic missions, which enhanced Britain's global prestige.[58]

Like the successive Mediterranean and West Indies tours, there is a remarkable overlap in the global itineraries. On his *Galatea* tours Alfred visited the major British colonies of the southern hemisphere – Australia, New Zealand and South Africa – as well as India, South

America, China and Japan – all of which (except New Zealand and India by the *Bacchante*) were subsequently visited, albeit in a different order, on the *Bacchante* as well as the *Renown* and *Repulse* voyages.[59] While successive tours of British colonies would naturally cover much of the same ground (especially given the preference for the healthy, wealthy and large settler colonies which arguably gave royal tourists the most bang for their buck), later tours also copied *how* Alfred travelled. In particular, Alfred set an important precedent through his use of prominent warships.[60]

Warships as royal tourists

The wooden auxiliary steam frigate HMS *Galatea*, launched in 1859, was an impressive-looking vessel, and colonial reports often noted that she was the largest warship yet seen in local waters.[61] Great attention was paid her and thousands of colonists flocked to her 'visiting' days in Sydney and other Australian ports. This was part of a wider process of late nineteenth-century colonial engagement with visiting warships. This was not unique. While foreign navies wanted to make their presence felt, especially within the ever-more commercially valuable Asia-Pacific region, the British were keen to appease colonial opinion angry at the staged withdrawal of military forces.[62] Naval royal tours provided an extra-special version of 'flying the flag' voyages to colonial audiences, reassuring them that the Royal Navy, and indeed the royal family, had not forgotten them.[63] The *Galatea* tour fits within this rubric, as does the *Bacchante*, which involved not merely one impressive warship, but five.

The French, German, Russian, US as well as Japanese navies made similar voyages, partly to show off their increasingly large and powerful warships and partly to prospect for suitable colonies, particularly among the islands of Oceania.[64] The 'royal naval arms race' accelerated in the early twentieth century. As nations vied to build bigger and more powerful warships, princes turned to these vessels for their overseas tours, which further enhanced their own status as naval officers. Thus in 1919–1925 Edward travelled on the powerful *Renown* and then her sister ship *Repulse*, the fastest major warships in the world when built in 1916, on journeys to thank colonists for their huge contribution to the allied war effort.[65] These ships need to be recognised as celebrities in their own right. Numerous official publications commemorated the visits of the vessels and their officers as much as the royal tourists.[66] As with HMS *Vanguard*, the biggest, fastest and also last British battleship, which brought the royal family to South Africa in 1947, these earlier naval vessels communicated British naval might to their viewers, as well as nostalgia for a time when British warships were permanently stationed in colonial ports.[67]

Just as the vessels the princes travelled on were important, so too were their destinations. Beyond the British empire, Japan, China and the South American republics brought the royal tourists face-to-face with some of Britain's most promising new trade partners, and gave them a glimpse of ancient empires transforming, albeit unevenly, into modern nations. Visits to the settler colonies emphasised local wealth, but they also resembled precious homecomings, providing opportunities for long-lost kin to meet.[68] In keeping with this emphasis on family, reports often mentioned previous royal visitors or, at least, the monarch. Sometimes, as in Brisbane in 1881, or South Africa in 1947, Alfred's precedent was remembered, but often, and particularly in India, he was forgotten completely, at least in press accounts.[69] Within the royal family and Royal Navy in Britain, Alfred was harder to ignore. On 6 August 1879, the day Albert Victor and George embarked HMS *Bacchante* at Cowes, the ship gaily displayed 'masthead flags in honour of the Duke of Edinburgh's birthday'.[70] Uncle Alfred joined his brother Albert Edward and other royals to farewell the young princes on their overseas tour. When the princes returned to Britain, they and their shipmates posed for photographs on the deck of the *Bacchante* with their proud father and their mentor Admiral Henry Keppel.[71] On this occasion Alfred was absent, but his example continued to shape princely naval tours.

In turn, the visits were seen to benefit the young princes. Much emphasis was placed on their keen desire to learn and the value of such tours for their future royal roles.[72] But there was a distinction. While the *Euryalus* and *Bacchante* tours emphasised the educational benefits to the princes, the *Galatea*, *Serapis* and *Renown* and *Repulse* tours focused on presenting these princes to colonists as mature adults.[73]

Passages to India

This emphasis on mature princes can be seen especially with the Indian tours. Alfred's 1869–1870 visit started a tradition, usually thought to begin with Albert Edward in 1875–1876, of grown British princes visiting India. These tours differed from both the long-range naval tours by adolescent princes as well as the (usually) briefer royal visits to other destinations.[74] The emphasis here was not on the Royal Navy; rather the links between Indian princes and the British royal family, with a particular emphasis on princely hospitality via 'royal' sports like tiger hunting. These tours asserted broad Indian support for British rule as well as Britain's ongoing commitment to India, an objective that became more important – if harder to sustain – in later tours.[75] Indian tours involved much careful planning. Alfred's trip was no exception, involving considerable discussion between Queen Victoria, Prime Minister Benjamin Disraeli, Viceroy of India Lord Mayo and the Prince of Wales Albert Edward, among many others. Perhaps with an eye to his own future visit, Albert Edward emphasised the importance of Alfred travelling in style: 'As no son of *any* sovereign has been in India before – he will have to travel in great pomp, or it may not have a beneficial effect in India.'[76]

Thus, in India HMS *Galatea* was largely forgotten while Alfred's splendid land tour gained public attention.[77] So too Albert Edward's transport to and from the subcontinent on HMS *Serapis* (a troopship converted for the royal voyage) or even Edward's on the famous warship HMS *Renown* received much less press coverage than their magnificent progresses ashore.[78] But naval officers, especially the princes' aristocratic friends, continued to play an important role in India as on other royal tours. Just as Albert Edward followed Alfred in including the fun-loving expert hunter Lord Charles Beresford in his party, the elder brother followed his younger brother in appointing the eminent doctor Joseph Fayrer as his personal physician.[79] While the order of the itinerary varied from Alfred's, later royal visits similarly involved much criss-crossing of the subcontinent by train, including most of the destinations of the first. Alfred's ceremonial as well as private meetings with Indian princes were repeated by his successors, and indeed there developed a particularly close association, with many return visits, between certain Indian princely families such as the maharajas of Jaipur and the British royal family. In addition to visits to palaces and the exchange of royal gifts (a source of anxiety for Alfred's tour planners as much as Albert Edward's), particular attention was paid to hunting expeditions.[80] Tiger hunting held special prestige, and beginning with Alfred the rulers of Nepal in particular grew adept at hosting hunts for visiting British royals for diplomatic gain.[81] Alfred also initiated visits to sights commemorating the 1857 Mutiny and its British victims. So too 'native entertainments' were provided for Alfred and his successors.[82] But perhaps the most influential event was the investiture of Alfred as a Knight of the Order of the Star of India at a ceremony involving Indian princes as well as the British Viceroy. While certainly much more modest than the famous coronation durbars of 1877, 1903 and 1911 (and a proposed imperial durbar during Alfred's tour had been cancelled due to cost and concerns about local criticism), it did employ some of the same features, for example the Viceroy's durbar tent. By emphasising Indian princes' fealty to Queen Victoria via the figure of the Viceroy, Alfred's investiture played a role, since forgotten, in the 'invention of tradition'.[83]

As well as employing some of the same companions, specialists, royal hosts, hunting trips, visits to Mutiny sights and durbar ceremonies, later royal tourists followed Alfred's example in India by commissioning private as well as official records. Photographs for the use of the royal family provided souvenirs of the tour, and, in the case of Albert Edward, the ship on which he travelled.[84] Like Alfred, Albert Edward's Indian trip was commemorated in a special public exhibition held after his return to Britain. This displayed some of the many magnificent gifts acquired overseas, as well as watercolours by the artists who accompanied the prince. These exhibitions opened first at South Kensington in London and then toured throughout the United Kingdom and, in the case of Albert Edward's tour, also went to Paris.[85] Perhaps most importantly for communicating news of the tours within the royal family, Alfred wrote brief – while his assistants wrote long – descriptive letters home to Queen Victoria and his siblings, including Albert Edward, some of which were then circulated more broadly.[86] More attention should be paid to how these diverse objects, letters and photograph albums, many of which graced royal residences for many years where they were seen by multiple family members, influenced royal attitudes to India and the empire, as well as to touring itself.[87] Finally, private conversations and direct observation would have also encouraged royal travel. Family members frequently farewelled and/or welcomed home royal travellers from their overseas tours in person, which gave them ample opportunity to inspect the ship, meet the travelling companions, and, perhaps, start planning their own future journey.[88] Albert Edward almost certainly had Alfred's tour in mind when he planned his own, more splendid India tour in 1875–1876, yet this connection remains underexplored.

While Alfred's precedent was clearly important in shaping the Indian as well as other royal tours, it was not followed either blindly or exactly. Local as well as metropolitan circumstances shaped later tours. Thus, Alfred did not visit Burma on his tour of India, but, following the annexation of Upper Burma by Britain in 1885, it was added to the itinerary of subsequent royal tourists to the subcontinent. Moreover, while Alfred may have provided the 'precedent', it was always the heir (here his elder brother Albert Edward) who took 'precedence'. In India, as elsewhere, locals were finely attuned to the distinctions between the heir and a 'spare'. While Albert Edward participated in many of the same activities as Alfred, his position as heir to the throne was acknowledged through, for example, the provision of finer gifts as well as more elaborate ceremonies. Unlike Alfred, who was accompanied by no journalists and whose tour received uneven coverage in the British press, Albert Edward took along the distinguished correspondent William Howard Russell, and this and later royal tours of India were closely covered in British newspapers, including the illustrated press.[89] This, too, may explain why it was Albert Edward's visit to India that was so often remembered as the first British royal visit. Where Alfred's visit was recalled, it was usually compared less favourably with that of his elder brother.[90] In part this may reflect the elder brother's greater charm as well, perhaps, as more thoughtful planning (thanks to the experience of Alfred's tour) and certainly the much greater press coverage. But it may also reflect the desire to pay the heir to the throne – and thus the monarch – the greater compliment. Forgetting Alfred's tour reinforced the significance of the heir's. Subsequent tours emphasised the special connection between the Prince of Wales (heir to the throne), the monarch (who from 1877 was also Empress/Emperor of India) and the continuation of British rule in India.[91] Alfred's pioneering royal tour to India of 1869–1870 was thus forgotten in most subsequent tour accounts and (at least publicly) by most later royal visitors – and scholars.

Conclusion

Twelve years after Albert Victor and George were reminded of their Uncle Alfred's first royal visit to Australia, another event stirred royal memories. In 1893, George, now Duke of York, married Princess Mary of Teck in St James's Palace, London. The mood was poignant; Albert Victor, George's elder brother, the original bridegroom for Mary, had died suddenly of influenza a year earlier. The 'spare' was now the heir – and the husband. While George's favourite travelling companion was unavoidably absent, the presence of other veterans reminded both him and onlookers of the important role royal tours played in the lives of princes, their family, friends and royal and naval personnel. Those pioneering tourists, George's father Albert Edward, Prince of Wales and his brother Alfred, Duke of Edinburgh, now accompanied George on his journey to the altar in their role as the two official 'supporters' of the bridegroom. Alfred's former governor Major Cowell, as well as George and Albert Victor's old tutor Canon Dalton played prominent roles in the ceremony. Among the numerous naval officers invited were Admiral the Earl of Clanwilliam (head of the Detached Squadron during the *Bacchante* tour) and Rear-Admiral Lord Charles Scott, captain of HMS *Bacchante* itself. Admiral of the Fleet Sir Henry Keppel was only one of several Keppels present; his son Lt. Colin Keppel and daughter-in-law attended Alfred's wife the

Duchess of Edinburgh, while his nephew Derek served as equerry to the bridegroom. Admiral Milne and Lord Charles Beresford were absent, but Milne's son Captain Milne and Beresford's younger brother Lord Marcus (who ran Albert Edward's stables) both attended. Another link with royal tours was provided through the presence of several Indian rulers, who by this date were becoming regular fixtures at royal ceremonies in London.[92] The bridegroom, the future George V, would become closely associated with the empire, and in particular India, through a series of spectacular royal tours with his bride between 1901 and 1911. But the earlier British royal tours, which had shaped the lives and careers of so many in St James's Chapel that day, also deserve attention, not least for their link with Alfred.

Forgetting Alfred's role in shaping later British royal tours is part of a wider phenomenon of forgetting younger princes, especially those who spent much of their careers abroad, either in military, naval or government service or through their marriage into other European royal houses. Whether on tour or at home, the spare was usually less memorable than the heir, though as the example of both George V and George VI demonstrated, the spare could unexpectedly become the heir – and/or the monarch.

Alfred's tours were remembered, at least privately, by later princes and tour planners, however. All copied Alfred in using the journey to both train princes and show them off to the world on increasingly long and global journeys, especially around the British empire. To do this the Royal Navy, governors and mentors, and a close group of male companions were all employed. Naval training and educational 'Grand Tours' were emphasised for younger princes, while the tours of adult princes were increasingly presented to the empire and the world as proof of the British monarchy's ongoing concern for its colonies, former colonies and other states. Royal tours varied in their character and reception, and much depended on the individual personality of the princes, their status as spares or heirs, as well as the particular local contexts of the visit. Still the tradition at least partly invented by Alfred proved to be a strong and enduring one. Alfred thus deserves to be remembered as the first major British royal tourist, from whom later princes borrowed 'something blue'.

Notes

1 L.J. Byrne, *Visit of the Detached Squadron with their Royal Highnesses Prince Edward and Prince George of Wales to Brisbane, from 16th to 20th August, 1881* (Brisbane: J.C. Beal, 1881), p. 28.
2 Charles V. Reed, who does give some attention to Alfred's tours, notes that 'Alfred has received surprisingly little attention from scholars'; *Royal Tourists, Colonial*

Subjects and the Making of a British World, 1860–1911 (Manchester: Manchester University Press, 2016), p. 15, n. 47.

3 Alfred receives very limited coverage in biographies of his mother and elder brother, e.g. A.N. Wilson, *Victoria: A Life* (London: Penguin, 2014); Julia Baird, *Queen Victoria* (Sydney: Allen & Unwin, 2016); Christopher Hibbert, *Edward VII: The Last Victorian King* (New York: Palgrave Macmillan, 2007); Giles St. Aubyn, *Edward VII: Prince and King* (London: Collins, 1979). The fullest account remains J. van der Kiste and B. Jordaan, *Dearest Affie ... Alfred, Duke of Edinburgh: Queen Victoria's Second Son 1844–1900* (Gloucester: Alan Sutton Publishing, 1984); for the Australia tour see Brian McKinlay, *The First Royal Tour* (Adelaide: Rigby, 1970) and Cindy McCreery, 'Two Victorias? Prince Alfred, Queen Victoria and Melbourne, 1867–68', in Robert Aldrich and Cindy McCreery (eds), *Crowns and Colonies: European Monarchies and Overseas Empires* (Manchester: Manchester University Press, 2016), pp. 51–76.

4 See the albums of the 1860 *Euryalus* (Royal Collections Identification Number (hereafter RCIN) 2917614) and 1867–1868 *Galatea* (RCIN 2372036) tours in the Royal Photographs Collection, Windsor.

5 William N. Armstrong, *Around the World with a King* (New York: Frederick A. Stokes, 1904), pp. 215, 224.

6 For the more private tour of Albert Edward and his wife Alexandra to the Mediterranean and Middle East in 1869; see Sophie Gordon, 'Travels with a Camera: The Prince of Wales, Photography and the Mobile Court', in Frank Lorenz Müller and Heidi Mehrkens (eds), *Sons and Heirs: Succession and Political Culture in Nineteenth-Century Europe* (Basingstoke: Palgrave Macmillan, 2016), pp. 92–108, esp. p. 101.

7 The pioneering royal tours of George IV in 1821–1822 were restricted to Britain, Ireland and Hanover; see Christopher Hibbert, 'George IV (1762–1830)', *Oxford Dictionary of National Biography*. Hereafter I use '*ODNB*' to refer to relevant individual biographies.

8 Michael Nelson, *Queen Victoria and the Discovery of the Riviera* (London: I.B. Tauris, 2001).

9 Hibbert, *Edward VII*, pp. 129, 182–184; Andrew Cook, *Prince Eddy: The King Britain Never Had* (Stroud: The History Press, 2006), pp. 70–71.

10 Hibbert, *Edward VII*, pp. 130–131; Chandrika Kaul, 'Monarchical Display and the Politics of Empire: Princes of Wales and India 1870s–1920s', *Twentieth Century British History*, 17:4 (2006), 464–488.

11 E.g. Queen Victoria to George Duke of Cambridge, 18 January 1867, RA VIC/ADDA15/1021. I gratefully acknowledge the permission of Her Majesty Queen Elizabeth II to make use of material from the Royal Archives.

12 Philip Murphy, *Monarchy and the End of Empire: The House of Windsor, the British Government, and the Post-War Commonwealth* (Oxford: Oxford University Press, 2013).

13 E.g. Albert Edward to Queen Victoria, 20 January 1867, RA VIC/ADDA3/76.

14 Jeffrey Grey, *A Military History of Australia* (Cambridge: Cambridge University Press, 1990), pp. 24–25; John F. Beeler, *British Naval Policy in the Gladstone-Disraeli Era, 1866–1880* (Stanford: Stanford University Press, 1997), pp. 34–37, 78–79.

15 See Reed, *Royal Tourists*, chapters 3 and 4, as well as his chapter in this volume (Chapter 5).

16 The role of tours in royal education remains unexplored; e.g. Peter Gordon and Denis Lawton, *Royal Education: Past, Present, and Future* (London: Frank Cass, 1999; 2nd edn, Routledge, 2003).

17 Richard Price calls Alfred's 1860 tour of Africa 'the invention of the Royal Tour'; *Making Empire: Colonial Encounters and the Creation of Imperial Rule in Nineteenth-Century Africa* (Cambridge: Cambridge University Press, 2008), p. 336; see also pp. 346–351.

18 *Sydney Morning Herald*, 22 January 1868, p. 4.

19 *ODNB*.

20 *The African*, Freetown, 19 October 1860. Clipping in Royal Archives.

21 John Milner and Oswald Brierly, *The Cruise of H.M.S. Galatea, Captain H.R.H. the Duke of Edinburgh, K.G., in 1867–1868* (London: W.H. Allen and Co., 1869), p. 48; Anita Callaway, *Visual Ephemera: Theatrical Art in Nineteenth-Century Australia* (Sydney: UNSW Press, 2000), p. 41.
22 Miriam Magdalena Schneider, The 'Sailor Prince' in the Age of Empire: Creating a Monarchical Brand in Nineteenth-Century Europe (London: Palgrave Macmillan, 2017).
23 Albert to Lord Palmerston, 14 August 1860, and Albert to Lord Hardwicke, 24 July 1858; quoted in Theodore Martin, *The Life of His Royal Highness The Prince Consort* (London: Smith, Elder & Co., 1882), p. 29; Albert to Baron Stockmar, 27 April 1860, quoted in *ibid.*, pp. 15–16; Miles Taylor, 'Prince Albert and the British Empire', *Prinz Albert – Ein Wettiner in Gorssbritannien/Prince Albert – A Wettin in Britain*, ed. Franz Bosbach and John R. Davis (Munich: K.G. Saur, 2004), pp. 75–82.
24 For the Canadian tour see Ian Radforth, *Royal Spectacle: The 1860 Visit of the Prince of Wales to Canada and the United States* (Toronto: University of Toronto Press, 2004).
25 *The Progress of His Royal Highness Prince Alfred Ernest Albert through the Cape ... 1860* (Cape Town: Saul Solomon, 1861), p. 29.
26 Albert Victor and George. Alfred's only son, also called Alfred (1874–1899), heir to the dukedom of Saxe-Coburg and Gotha, received German military training, but died young; Wilson, *Victoria*, p. 562; *ODNB*.
27 The future Edward VIII, George VI and the Duke of Kent. The latter switched to the Air Force in the Second World War. George V's third son, Henry Duke of Gloucester, had a long career in the Army while the youngest son Prince John died young; *ODNB*.
28 While George VI's daughters Elizabeth and Margaret did not serve in the Navy, Elizabeth's sons Charles and Andrew did.
29 Dalton stresses this point in the preface to *The Cruise of H.M.S. 'Bacchante', 1879–1882. The Private Journals, Letters and Note-books of Prince Albert Victor and Prince George of Wales, with additions by John N. Dalton* (London: Macmillan and Co., 1886), Vol. 1, pp. ix–x.
30 E.g. 'Our Sailor Princes' (Fig. 4.2).
31 E.g. 'H.R.H. the Duke of Edinburgh and suite in mining costume after descending the Band of Hope Gold Mine, Ballarat', Roberts Bros., albumen silver photograph c. 1867 (State Library of Victoria), http://handle/slv.vic.gov.au/10381/68019, accessed 1 June 2017; and 'The Princes and suite at Ballarat', albumen George Willetts, silver albumen photograph, 1881 (State Library of Victoria), http://handle.slv.vic.gov.au/10381/52793, accessed 1 June 2017.
32 Alfred to Queen Victoria, 16 January 1870, RA VIC/ADDA20/1305; 5 April 1870, RA VIC/ADDA20/1314.
33 Cook, *Prince Eddy*, pp. 70–71, 150. In 1930 Edward took his younger brother George (Duke of Kent) on his tour of South America, partly to keep him away from malign influences in London; *ODNB*.
34 Vivian Stuart, *The Beloved Little Admiral: The Life and Times of Admiral the Hon. Sir Henry Keppel* (London: Robert Hale, 1967), p. 253.
35 Milne Letters Re: Royal Family (1861–1893), National Maritime Museum, Greenwich, MLN/167.
36 Albert Edward to Milne, 19 March 1876, NMM MLN/167.
37 'Biography of John Walter Tarleton R.N.', William Loney RN naval history website, www.pdavis.nl, accessed 5 May 2017; *ODNB*; Alfred to Queen Victoria, 3 October 1869, RA VIC/ADDA20/1296.
38 *ODNB*.
39 Andrew Gordon, *The Rules of the Game: Jutland and British Naval Command* (Annapolis: U.S. Naval Institute Press 1996), esp. pp. 215–224; A.P. McGowan, *Royal Yachts* (London: National Maritime Museum 1953; 3rd edn 1977), p. 7.
40 Henry Keppel, his son Colin and other members of the Keppel family served the royal family as naval officers, advisers, courtiers, hunting companions, friends, and

in the case of their relation by marriage Alice Keppel, lover; Stuart, *Beloved Little Admiral*; ODNB.
41 Lindsay, *Royal Household*, p. 78.
42 *Ibid.*, p. 26.
43 Col. Sir William James Colville, 'Revd William Lake Onslow with Prince Albert Victor and Prince George', 24–31 December 1874, RCIN 928378, www.royalcollection.org.uk/collection, accessed 1 June 2017.
44 ODNB.
45 Rev. John Milner and Oswald Brierly, *The Cruise of H.M.S. Galatea, Captain H.R.H. The Duke of Edinburgh, K.G. in 1867–1868* (London: W.H. Allen, 1869).
46 *Age*, 6 January 1868, p. 4.
47 McCreery, 'Two Victorias?', pp. 66–68, 71.
48 Alfred to Queen Victoria, 5 April 1870, RA VIC/ADDA20/1314; John Lahey, *'Damn You, John Christie!': The Public Life of Australia's Sherlock Holmes* (Melbourne: State Library of Victoria, 1993), pp. 41–44, 218–219.
49 Disraeli to Queen Victoria, 21 September 1868, RA VIC/MAIN/A/37/52.
50 Hibbert, *Edward VII*, p. 130.
51 David Cannadine, 'The Context, Performance and Meaning of Ritual: The British Monarchy and the "Invention of Tradition," c. 1820–1977', in E.J. Hobsbawm and T. Ranger (eds), *The Invention of Tradition* (Cambridge: Cambridge University Press, 1983), p. 120.
52 Privately Edward was prone to periods of depression which were compounded by his separation from his lover and confidante Freda Dudley Ward, and in India his growing despair at British policy; Philip Ziegler, *King Edward VIII: The Official Biography* (London: Collins, 1990), p. 140.
53 These tours may also be seen as a form of monarchical 'soft power'; Frank Lorenz Müller, '"Winning their Trust and Affection": Royal Heirs and the Uses of Soft Power in Nineteenth-Century Europe', in Frank Lorenz Müller and Heidi Mehrkens (eds), *Royal Heirs and the Uses of Soft Power in Nineteenth-Century Europe* (Basingstoke: Palgrave Macmillan, 2016), pp. 1–19.
54 E.g. Victor E. Marsden, *Crossing the Line with His Royal Highness the Prince of Wales ... in H.M.S. 'Renown', Friday–Saturday, April 16–17, 1920* (Sydney: Angus & Robertson, 1920).
55 *Cruise of ... Bacchante*, Vol. 1.
56 Reginald Crabtree, *Royal Yachts of Europe from the Seventeenth to Twentieth Century* (Newton Abbot: David & Charles, 1975); Alan Major, *Royal Yachts* (Stroud: Amberley, 2011).
57 'Rodney's Statue before Removal, Spanish Town, Jamaica c.1880', albumen print, RCIN 2580553, www.royalcollection.org.uk/collection, accessed 5 May 2017.
58 *Cruise of ... Bacchante*, Vol. 1, p. x.
59 See Table 4.1.
60 As early as 1861 HMS *St George*, which took Alfred on naval service to North America, was praised as an impressive warship; see *Illustrated London News*, 29 January 1861.
61 Cindy McCreery, 'A British Prince and a Transnational Life: Alfred, Duke of Edinburgh's Visit to Australia, 1867–8', in Desley Deacon, Penny Russell and Angela Woollacott (eds), *Transnational Ties: Australian Lives in the World* (Canberra: ANU E-press, 2008), pp. 57–74.
62 Cindy McCreery, 'Neighbourly Relations: Nineteenth-Century Western Navies' Interactions in the Asia Pacific Region', in Robert Aldrich and Kirsten McKenzie (eds), *The Routledge History of Western Empires* (London: Routledge, 2014), pp. 194–207.
63 There were also non-royal Detached Squadron visits to colonies in this period; see the table provided at www.pdavis.nl/Flying.htm, accessed 5 May 2017.
64 McCreery, 'Neighbourly Relations', pp. 194–207.
65 Even in the background of a photograph (of Freetown in 1925) the *Renown* looks impressive; see Hilary Sapire, 'Ambiguities of Loyalism: The Prince of Wales in India

and Africa, 1921–2 and 25', *History Workshop Journal*, 73 (July 2011), Fig. 1. This point could be extended to other royal tourists; for example, the warships employed by the Crown Prince of Japan to travel to Europe in 1922; see Chapter 11 in this volume.

66 For example, *H.M.S. 'Renown' and Ships of the Royal Australian Navy: With Lists of Their Officers* (Melbourne: Government Printer, 1920).
67 Dr Kai Easton is currently researching the *Vanguard*'s visit to South Africa.
68 Cindy McCreery, 'Rude Interruption: Colonial Manners, Gender and Prince Alfred's Visit to New South Wales, 1868', *Forum for Modern Language Studies*: A Special Issue 'Interrupted Itineraries: The Unexpected in European Travel Narratives', ed. David Culpin and Michael Titlestad, 49:4 (2013), 437–456.
69 'Album of photographs presented to George VI as a memento of the Royal Visit of Prince Alfred in 1860', 1947, RCIN 2371923, www.royalcollection.org.uk/collection, accessed 5 May 2017.
70 *Cruise of ... Bacchante*, Vol. 1, p. 44.
71 'Portsmouth, 3 May 1880', albumen print, RCIN 2580599, www.royalcollection.org.uk/collection, accessed 5 May 2017.
72 See, for example, *Cruise of ... Bacchante*, Vol. 1, p. viii.
73 Albert Victor's tour of India reflected his position as a young adult who was believed to need continual supervision; Cook, *Prince Eddy*, pp. 191–194, 204–208, 211–212.
74 It was also distinct from tours of India by married royals, starting with George and Mary in 1905–1906 and culminating in their famous 1911 tour – the first imperial tour by a British reigning monarch.
75 The Indian tours of Albert Edward and Edward have received scholarly attention, although the link with Alfred is barely mentioned; Hibbert, *Edward VII*, p. 135; Kaul, 'Monarchical Display'; H. Hazel Hahn, 'Indian Princes, Dancing Girls and Tigers: The Prince of Wales's Tour of India and Ceylon, 1875–1876', *Postcolonial Studies*, 12:2 (2009), 173–192; Sapire, 'Ambiguities of Loyalism', pp. 37–59; Ruth Brimacombe, 'The Imperial Avatar in the Imagined Landscape: The Virtual Dynamics of the Prince of Wales's Tour of India in 1875–6', in Veronica Alfano and Andrew Stauffer (eds), *Virtual Victorians: Networks, Connections, Technologies* (Basingstoke: Palgrave Macmillan, 2015), pp. 189–214; Milinda Banerjee, 'Ocular Sovereignty, Acclamatory Rulership and Political Communication: Visits of Princes of Wales to Bengal', in Müller and Mehrkens, *Soft Power*, pp. 81–100; Gordon, 'Travels with a Camera', pp. 102–105.
76 Albert Edward to Queen Victoria, 22 July 1868, RA VIC/MAIN/Z/449/16.
77 The *Galatea* does not seem to have hosted many 'visiting days' in India, perhaps because Indians (other than princes) were less welcome aboard than white settlers. Alfred's tour was covered, sporadically, in *The Times* and *Illustrated London News* as well as in local newspapers such as the *Madras Mail*.
78 Likewise, relatively little attention was given to Albert Victor's 1889–1890 voyages; outbound on SS *Oceana* and home via SS *Assam*; Cook, *Prince Eddy*, pp. 190, 212.
79 In turn, Fayrer published an account of both visits; the title gives precedence to the Prince of Wales; *Notes on the Visits to India of their Royal Highnesses the Prince of Wales and the Duke of Edinburgh, 1870–1875–6* (London, 1879).
80 Duke of Argyll to Lord Mayo, 13 October 1869, Photo Eur 466, f125 (British Library); Hibbert, *Edward VII*, p. 131.
81 *In the Oudh and Nepal Forests: A Letter from India* (Edinburgh, 1870).
82 *The Times*, 18 January 1870; Alfred to Queen Victoria, 30 April 1870, RA VIC/ADDA20/1316; *The Times*, 22 January 1870.
83 *The Times*, 31 January 1870; N.A.C., *The Prince in Calcutta; or Memorials of H.R.H. the Duke of Edinburgh's Visit in December 1869* (Calcutta, 1870), pp. 95–110; Julie F. Codell, 'Photography and the Delhi Coronation Durbars, 1877, 1903, 1911', in Julie F. Codell (ed.), *Power and Resistance: The Delhi Coronation Durbars* (Ahmedabad: Mapin Publishing, 2012); Bernard S. Cohn, 'Representing Authority in Victorian India', in Eric Hobsbawm and Terence Ranger (eds), *The Invention of Tradition* (Cambridge: Cambridge University Press, 1983), pp. 165–209.

84 Loose photographs of Alfred's Indian tour are in the Veste Coburg in Germany; 'HMS *Serapis*, 1875–1876' album, Calcutta: Westfield & Co., RCIN 2583966; 'Duke of Clarence and Avondale in India 1889–90' album, RCIN 2702104, www.royalcollection.org.uk/collection, accessed 1 June 2017.
85 *A Guide to the Works of Art and Science, collected by Captain His Royal Highness The Duke of Edinburgh, K.G. During his Five-Years' Cruise Round the World in H.M.S. 'Galatea.' (1867–1871) and lent for exhibition in The South Kensington Museum. February, 1872* (London: John Strangeways, 3rd edn, 1872); Gordon, 'Travels with a Camera', p. 103.
86 For example, Alfred to Queen Victoria, 9 January 1870, RA VIC/ADDA20/1304; Alfred to Queen Victoria, 5 March 1870, RA VIC/ADDA20/1311.
87 E.g. the photograph album of Alfred's first *Galatea* tour (1867–1868), now in Windsor, bears bookplates from the royal libraries of both Coburg and Sandringham.
88 Crown Princess to Queen Victoria, 2 November 1868, *Your Dear Letter*, p. 210; F. H. Poore, 12 May 1876, RMM 1976/462 11/13/074 Poore and Grimston *Letters and Diary* 1869–1883.
89 Hahn, 'Indian Princes', p. 174.
90 Albert Grey, quoted in Hibbert, *Edward VII*, p. 135.
91 Thus subsequent tours of India by 'spares' such as the Duke of Connaught (1903, 1921) were viewed as proxies for the presence of the Prince of Wales or sovereign. So too, scholars have focused on the visits to India by Princes of Wales; see Kaul, 'Monarchical Display'; Hahn, 'Indian Princes'; Sapire, 'Ambiguities of Loyalism' and Banerjee, 'Ocular Sovereignty'.
92 *Supplement to the London Gazette of Tuesday, the 18th of July. Wed. July 19. 1893*, reprinted in Lindsay, *Royal Household*, pp. 249–273.

CHAPTER FIVE

Royalty, loyalism and citizenship in the nineteenth-century British settler empire

Charles V. Reed

On 12 March 1868, Prince Alfred was shot in the back with a pistol at Clontarf, on the north shore of Sydney Harbour in New South Wales, by an Irishman named Henry James O'Farrell, in a Fenian-inspired assassination attempt.[1] Months earlier, three Fenians, who became known as the Manchester Martyrs, had been executed in Britain for killing a policeman. The assassination plot aroused trepidation across the British world that an empire-wide Fenian conspiracy was underway, a fear best illustrated by the draconian Treason Felony Act passed by the Parliament of New South Wales six days after the attack and modelled on the English Act of 1848.[2] Without question, ethnic and sectarian tensions informed the political, social and cultural discourses of the nineteenth-century colonies of settlement, as the outburst of anti-Irish rhetoric and violence in the aftermath of O'Farrell's act demonstrates. During Alfred's visit, Irish Catholics in Melbourne had rallied outside of the Protestant Hall, evoking the Battle of the Boyne in illuminations projected onto the façade of the building.[3] However, the Sydney Catholic newspaper *Freeman's Journal*, fearing that an Irishman would soon be revealed as the shooter, affirmed that, if such were the case, 'Irishmen must bow their heads in sorrow, and confess that the greatest reproach which has ever been cast on them, the deepest shame that has ever been coupled with the name of our people, has been attached to us here in the country where we have been so free and prosperous'.[4] The assassination attempt was condemned by Irish communities across Australia and the empire.

Curiously enough, even O'Farrell's commitment to republicanism appears questionable, and in interviews he advocated a future for the Irish within the British empire. Excerpts from his diary and the transcript of an interview with the Colonial Secretary of New South Wales, Henry Parkes, were published in 1868 as *Fenian Revelations: The Confessions of O'Farrell Who Attempted to Assassinate the Duke* of *Edinburgh*.[5] During his confession, O'Farrell claimed that he was part of a Fenian cell in Sydney ordered from England to assassinate the prince.[6] While he condemned the execution of the Manchester Martyrs and damned England, he also expressed little sorrow in having failed, indicating that he 'rather liked' the duke and had voted against the plan to kill him in the first place.[7] When Parkes interrogated him on his political beliefs, O'Farrell advocated not an independent republic of Ireland but a united republic of the British empire.[8] He conveyed concern that the prince would be in grave danger should he steam on to New Zealand, only for the purposes of 'a few more addresses'.[9] While perhaps an extreme example, O'Farrell's apparent loyalty to the empire, despite his hatred of the English and the monarchy, complicates more traditional narratives of ethnic and sectarian conflict in the British world.

In the last decade, historians of empire have increasingly turned their attention to the British colonies of settlement, in a project aimed at reassessing the role of Britishness and imperial identities in the political, cultural and social worlds of colonial settlers. For these scholars, the colonial societies of the British world were neither mere extensions of metropolitan society nor foreordained nation-states, but transnational cultural spaces that were informed both by local circumstances and contingencies and by a political, cultural, social and historical relationship with Britain and the British diaspora. In this context, British national identity must not be understood as a set of ideas and beliefs packed in a suitcase and carried to 'Greater Britain', but a competing collection of identities made in and of the imperial experience.[10] Britishness was a 'composite, rather than exclusive, form of identity', which was appropriated and adapted, made and remade by British and non-British colonial subjects around the world.[11]

Through the royal tours by Queen Victoria's children and grandchildren, colonial officials in Britain and abroad sought to make real the emergent mythology of imperial monarchy and the justice-giving Great Queen and thus to bind Britain's colonial empire more closely to the 'motherland'. While these visits were unevenly reported in Britain, they were celebrated and remembered in the colonies of settlement as founding moments in burgeoning imperial and local narratives of belonging. In the empire, the narrative of the royal tour was taken up and remade by the colonial press and by social elites as a means of developing local mythologies of order and belonging.[12] They, and the colonial subjects who challenged and contested their elite-constructed mythologies, interpreted the royal tour through a lens of Britishness and imperial citizenship, through which they demanded British liberty as their endowed rights as citizen-subjects. In this context, what it meant to be a Natalian Briton or an Auckland Briton, or to be a British South African or a New Zealander, was shaped and informed by class cooperation and conflict, social status and identity, ethnic and cultural heritage, local politics, and cultural and economic contact with a larger world.[13]

While non-British and non-English 'outsiders' did on occasion use the royal tour as a site of ethnic and sectarian contestation – where Canadian Catholics protested against the participation of Orangemen in 1860, for instance – they overwhelmingly used the moment to appeal for inclusion in a national-imperial community and to petition for the rights as citizen-subjects of a British world.[14] As Donal Lowry has demonstrated, empire loyalism was a crucial means by which ethnic 'outsiders' participated in imperial culture.[15] Imperial citizenship and even Britishness were embraced by non-English and non-British subjects of the queen. In Canada, Lowry argues, ethnic outsiders could and did feel an intense and personal loyalty to the monarchy and the empire on par with their Anglo-Protestant compatriots. In fact, the 'personal nature of monarchy, vertically acknowledged', was better suited to the political assimilation of French Canadians, indigenous Canadians, Jews and other 'non-British' peoples than a republic by 'avoid[ing] the controversies of what it meant to be a Canadian, Australian, or New Zealander'.[16] Just as *respectables* of colour professed their loyalty and Britishness, a significant number of non-British settlers – Dutch-speaking Boers, South Asians, Germans and Chinese, among others – professed loyalty to the queen and the empire, thus challenging more exclusive and ethnicity-bound visions of imperial citizenship. Scottish, Irish and Welsh settlers, who lived in and served the empire in disproportionate numbers relative to their populations in the British Isles, often claimed ownership of and citizenship within the British empire, despite their history of conflict with an English core at home. While ideas about imperial citizenship, and even Britishness, among non-British and non-English settlers did not replace or displace other identities, they were far more robust and significant than the historiography of the past has suggested.[17] As Lowry argues, such outsiders in fact played less of a role in opposition to the monarchy than has been suggested; in the case of Canada, anti-monarchy agitators were as likely or more likely to be Anglo-Protestant than Irish Catholic.

Much recent and important work has identified the investment and contribution to the British imperial project by the Scottish, Welsh and Irish who administered, fought for, evangelised in and settled the British empire. Aled Jones and Bill Jones, for instance, argue that scholars of Welsh history have, until recently, avoided any prolonged discussion of Welsh empire building because of 'an unease with ... participation in, or, to borrow from an Irish parallel, of "collaboration" with, British imperial expansion'.[18] While the Scots, Welsh and Irish, in particular, had complicated pasts vis-à-vis the English 'core' at home, they actively participated in British overseas commerce and colonisation, often simultaneously claiming both British (or imperial) and Celtic identities.

John MacKenzie's enlightening work on the Scots of South Africa contends that 'migrants retained not only an awareness of layered or multiple identities, but also in many cases a sense of plural domicile'.[19] In the context of the Irish, Donal McCracken has appealed to nationalist contestation of the South African War, even 'pro-Boer fever', across the cultural networks of the Irish diaspora as evidence of shared anti-colonial sentiment that connected not only Irish men and women to their kin across the globe but also the 'colonized' Irish and Boers to the causes of the other.[20] While this work importantly contributes to the histories of identity and ethnicity in the British empire – in the face of a micro-industry of Celtic heritage and genealogy publishing – it often risks overestimating the role of homelands and diasporas at the cost of British and imperial identities.

As O'Farrell's testimony demonstrates, notions of belonging in the British empire were multiple, overlapping and often conflicted. A settler might simultaneously imagine his community as Irish, local and imperial – not to mention as encompassing other political and social worlds. The community of empire was an important, if an oft neglected, category of belonging for many people who lived on the towns of and frontiers of the southern British empire, regardless of their ethnicity. For the most part, nineteenth-century incarnations of imperial citizenship were not defined along the lines of racial difference – thought they did at times appeal to a civilisational difference (e.g. civilised versus savage). Ethnic differences, too, informed the political and social worlds of the nineteenth-century colonies of settlement, but not in the way imagined by the political rhetoric of the day or by the teleology of later nationalist historiography. The point here is not that notions of imperial community were uncomplicated, or even dominant, but that they did inform the way that nineteenth-century colonial subjects thought about their political and social universes – and themselves.

The Cape Dutch (1860 and 1901)

The ethnic rivalry between the British and the Boers is one of the major narratives of South African and British imperial history. The brief discussion in this chapter about the 'Cape Dutch' and *De Zuid-Afrikaan* does not intend to uproot this traditional narrative completely, but rather to interrogate and problematise it. Despite the mythology of the Great Trek, whereby the nascent Afrikaner nation abandoned the British Cape Colony for parts east and north, many Dutch-speaking people, often dismissed as the 'Anglicised' Cape Dutch, stayed in the Western Cape.[21] While they outnumbered English-speaking Capetonians, they developed and sustained connections with British commerce and the British government. Moreover, trekking Boers shared their animosity towards the British government at Cape Town with many English-speaking frontier settlers of the Eastern Cape. The British and the Dutch shared deeply embedded cultural, social and political associations, which were more likely an element of everyday life in South Africa than the more obvious sentiments of hostility and opposition.

Was the *Graham's Town Journal* correct to wonder, in 1860, if some 'higher feeling than mere vulgar curiosity' brought the Dutch-speaking farmer from his home 'miles away' to wait along the roadside to see Prince Alfred go by?[22] During the 1887 jubilee-year celebrations, the Afrikaner Bond, the political party that claimed to represent the interest of Dutch-speaking British subjects in the Cape, professed, 'We assure you humbly and respectfully [of] our true loyalty to your throne, and we feel proud that in the great British Empire there are not more loyal subjects than those we represent'.[23] During royal visits to South Africa during both 'Anglo-Boer' wars (1880–1881 and 1899–1902), princes visited prisoner-of-war camps, where captured Boers claimed no animosity towards the British monarchy or the British empire, only towards specific individuals and policies seeking to deny them their rights. Dutch-speaking British subjects, particularly those of the Western Cape who were more assimilated into an imperial culture, could object to the practices of British rule yet embrace the British monarch and a co-ownership of the empire itself. In a sense, the invention of Afrikanerdom during the late nineteenth and the twentieth centuries was as much a response to the cultural potency of a British loyalism as it was a function of opposition to British injustices.

Founded in 1830, the Cape Town newspaper *De Zuid-Afrikaan*, published in English and Dutch (a fairly typical practice across the empire), 'represented … a Dutch-Afrikaner bourgeoisie, many with commercial and business interests, but with few direct ties to Britain. They were attuned to the feelings of the mass of older colonists, sympathetic to their sentiments on race and class relations, resentful of the more established British mercantile elite, and increasingly antagonistic to its humanitarian relations'.[24] The politics of the *Zuid-Afrikaan* fiercely opposed the influence of liberal-humanitarians in Britain and Cape Town on the policies of British rule, particularly relationships between masters and slaves/servants, focusing most of its ire on John Fairbairn's *South African Commercial Advertiser*.[25] The newspaper represented a liberalism that differed significantly from the politics of the *voortrekkers* to the north and east. While the politics of the Cape Dutch were largely transcended by the more conservative nationalism that we might associate with Afrikanerdom by the end of the century, the comparatively liberal political tradition associated with them did not die out completely. In fact, a British policy of white conciliation in the aftermath of the South African War, or Second-Anglo Boer War (1899–1902), brought many Dutch-speaking South Afrikaners to the fold of empire and monarchy.

As an 1878 editorial reflects, loyalism – despite developing antagonisms between British and Boer – was extremely important to the identity and sense of legitimacy of the Cape Afrikaners, as described by Hermann Giliomee:

> *De Zuid-Afrikaan* declared that the Afrikaners wanted no '"republican freedom, equality and fraternity" ... If aggrieved, they said: "Let us send a petition to the Queen."' If ever they formed a republic it would be along the lines of the white oligarchies in the southern states of the United States of America. It is striking that there is no reference here to the Boer republics. The colonial Afrikaners identified themselves with their kinsmen across the Orange River, but put the Cape's interests first and rarely hid their sense of superiority over the northern Afrikaners.[26]

While the *Zuid-Afrikaan* arguably had as much to do with the creation of an Afrikaner identity as its trekking neighbours and frequently opposed the injustices of British political and cultural domination, it imagined the future of the Dutch-speaking communities of South Africa in the British empire and under a British monarch.

Expressions of loyalty to Queen Victoria and the British empire by the *Zuid-Afrikaan* were not uncomplicated, of course. The fact that these identities were complicated and often conflicted does not mean that pronouncements of loyalty to Queen Victoria were disingenuous. The *Zuid-Afrikaan* described the 'natural' feelings of loyalty and interest in Alfred's visit:

> [The loyalty] of the Dutchman is of a more sedate, and perhaps a more faithful character [than the French], not so readily transferred from one object to another; but the loyalty of the Englishman springs directly from the heart, because it has its root in his nationality ... what is loyalty at the Cape? The British-born colonist may share the loyalty of his more favoured countryman who lives in the land of his forefathers; but even he cannot help feeling that, as a colonist, he is not all together what he would have been at home: even with his best intentions he cannot fully

> sympathize with those among whom he has cast his lot. And what shall we say of the descendants of those whose parents lived under the Dutch flag, and of the alien [e.g. Africans], destitute of political privileges, that stranger that lives in our gates, – can they be expected to be loyal? All but the aliens enjoy equality of rights with the English, and owe a debt of gratitude to the Queen, for the liberal constitution so recently granted to this colony ... so we can feel for our gracious Sovereign,- and it is but natural that we should share to some extent the enthusiasm of our English-fellow [sic] colonists at a time when this colony in honoured by a visit of one of the Royal Family.[27]

While they certainly did not imagine themselves as Dutch-speaking Britons, the editors of *Zuid-Afrikaan*, a rather specific sub-set of a larger non-British population, articulated a vision whereby Dutch settlement could be reconciled in the British empire, using a language that appealed to their loyalty to the Great Queen and the British liberty that she had bestowed upon them.

While the *Zuid-Afrikaan* commemorated the arrival of Prince Alfred and the return of Sir George Grey to South Africa in 1860, carefully reporting their movements and the celebrations across South Africa, the editors also challenged the excesses of the visit and proposed the royal tour as an opportunity to reform the government of the Cape. The editors complained of the 'great stir and bustle, and a vast deal of extravagance pretending to be demonstrations of loyalty', through the course of which 'some persons [will] have made themselves ridiculous and others contemptible'.[28] At the same time, they hoped the royal presence and the arrival of Grey would change the political landscape of the Cape, for Grey to serve the interests of Capetonian settlers and not his 'constituents' at home and to make better policy decisions than his predecessors.[29] Like their counterparts in the Eastern Cape, they suggested that a railway would benefit the colony far more than a breakwater (the inauguration of which was the crowning achievement of Alfred's visit), but they agreed that its construction should move forward without delay. The editors also complained that expenditure by the Cape government far outpaced revenue and that the costs of the breakwater and the royal visit ought to be more carefully considered. These opinions were far from seditious; they shared much in common with the editorial pages of other papers. They reflected a rather profound pro-British loyalism, albeit one that refused to be subservient to the interests of an English-speaking majority or an imperial government in London.

The compatibility between non-British colonial subjects and imperial citizenship and loyalty are perhaps best illustrated in the paper's commentary on immigration policy in the Cape Colony. As

Cape Town awaited the arrival of Prince Alfred, the *Zuid-Afrikaan* challenged the stance of the *Cape Argus* on immigration to South Africa, namely its opposition to bringing German settlers to the Cape.[30] According to the *Zuid-Afrikaan*, 'the slightest allusion to the relative value of anything not directly imported from the United Kingdom is resented as a monstrous offence'.[31] In challenging the 'insularity' of the *Argus*, the editors of the paper presented an elaborate defence of German immigration, including shared Anglo-Saxon origins, the contributions of Prince Albert to Great Britain, and the easy assimilation of Germans into other cultures. In other words, they argued that non-British subjects could be productive and loyal citizens of a British-dominated society.

When the Duke and Duchess of Cornwall and York visited southern Africa in 1901, the British colonies and the Afrikaner republics were in the middle of an embarrassing and bloody imperial war. It is extremely difficult to discern how Dutch-speaking South Africans perceived the British and the British empire at this time through the haze of constructed mythologies. The emerging story of Afrikaner nationalism focused on a long history of conflict with the British, from whom the *voortrekkers* fled during the 1830s and against whom the Boer republics fought for their liberty during the two Anglo-Boer Wars. In English-language works, the dominant narrative highlighted the contrasts between British liberty and Boer despotism, as demonstrated by the progress of British civilisation at the Cape and the protection of indigenous peoples by the colonial government. A corollary to this mythology, popularised in the English-speaking press during the royal tour, held that most Boers were naturally loyal to the British monarchy but that they were led by demagogic political leaders into conflict with the British:

> The Boers ... even in their bitterest moments, always had a deep respect for the late Queen, and we believe that when there is created that spirit of brotherly feeling and sympathy which mutual interests are bound to bring about, [they] will transfer the regard they had for Queen Victoria to her descendants.[32]

While this pronouncement was, to some degree, war propaganda, it also reflected at least a grain of truth; many Dutch-speaking settlers were not inherently hostile to British rule in southern Africa. They shared much in common with the frontier settlers of the Eastern Cape, who maintained a suspicious and hostile attitude towards the colonial government at Cape Town and the imperial government in London. Cape Afrikaner loyalty was informed by political contingencies, and the Jameson Raid, the imperial politics of the High Commissioner of the Cape, Alfred Milner, as well as the current war itself did much to erode their support of empire.[33] Although their claims to Britishness were fragile and inconstant, Dutch-speaking South Africans did employ British political traditions and the language of Britishness in a way that has been underplayed by historians.

Irish Catholics in New Zealand (1901)

Dunedin's Roman Catholic newspaper *The New Zealand Tablet* was a cultural product of the Irish diaspora. It printed original content and re-published stories from Irish newspapers and Catholic publications around the world – from Ireland, America and Australia – participating in a global conversation about Irish Catholic politics and identity.[34] Between 1858 and 1901, the Irish-born population of New Zealand had expanded exponentially, from 4,554 to 43,534 (excluding Northern Ireland). Heather McNamara argues that the *Tablet*, 'like many other Irish diaspora journals, self-consciously identified itself within the history of Irish nationalist newspaper publishing, and conceived of its work for the Irish national cause [as] a continuation of that tradition'.[35] At the same time, the newspaper simultaneously imagined the place of the Irish in an imperial community, reporting 'Intercolonial' news about Irish Catholics from across the empire. Despite outright hostility towards 'disloyal' Catholics by the mainstream settler press in New Zealand, particularly in the context of Irish nationalism and the politics of Irish Home Rule, the editor of the *Tablet*, Henry William Cleary (1898–1901), framed his paper's reception of the visit by the Duke and Duchess of Cornwall and York around a discourse of imperial loyalism that he understood as antithetical neither to his Irish nationalism nor his Catholicism.

The *Tablet* offered detailed and elaborate reports on the progress of the royal visit through New Zealand. In most of the reports, Cleary generally focused on the intensity of colonial loyalty to the British monarchy, rather than using the visit as an opportunity to shed light on the plight of Irish Catholics in the empire. He understood that Irish Catholic loyalty to the king and the empire might be misunderstood by outsiders:

> To foreigners unacquainted with the story of British colonisation, the extraordinary enthusiasm of the preparations and demonstrations in these far outskirts of the Empire in connection with the royal visit must be a riddle indeed. Its secret lies partly in the personal worth and high popularity of the British Sovereigns of the present generation, but chiefly in the wise and statesmanlike extension of free representative institutions ... Endowed with liberal Constitutions, the various colonies

of the Australasian group were permitted to work out their own destinies, each in its own way. The result has been the growth of unexampled rapidity, peace, prosperity, equal laws, and that contentment which is the best safeguard of the existing order.[36]

The fact that most of Cleary's descriptions of the royal tour were virtually indistinguishable from those of the mainstream settler press perhaps reflects both the generous application of quotations and details lifted from other sources, which was endemic to nineteenth-century print culture, and a rhetorical strategy by the editors of the *Tablet* to emphasise and normalise Irish Catholic loyalty to king and empire. More importantly, however, the language of the *Tablet* represented an understanding of community and citizenship that concurrently expressed loyalty to the pope in Rome, an Irish nation, the British monarchy and the British empire – without the confusions and complexities of modern identity politics. These notions of belonging were not articulated in the absence of knowledge about the cruelty and violence of British rule in Ireland, but rather with a profound understanding of them.

At the same time, Cleary used his newspaper to educate the Irish Catholics of New Zealand on the importance of loyalty, and to highlight Catholic participation in the ceremonies of the visit as well as their engagement in the South African War, which provided the backdrop for the 1901 royal tour. In describing the recent history of the relationship between the British royal family and Irish Catholics, he explained to readers:

> The late Queen Victoria was the first actual British constitutional sovereign. At an important period in the history of European monarchies she popularised British royalty by her personal virtues and her prudent regard for the limitations of her office ... Whatever his defects or limitations, Edward VII ... deserves the good-will of Irish people for the liberality of his personal views on questions ultimately affecting their national wellbeing; of Catholics, for his marked evidences of good-will toward our ecclesiastics and ecclesiastical institutions; and of all friends of civil liberty for the stern and uncompromising manner in which ... he publicly declined ... association with or countenance of the dark-lantern fanatics of the Orange lodge. The Duke and Duchess of York – the future King and Queen – are as yet little past the portals of their public life. They have to make their own mark in their own way. But all the traditions surrounding them are in their favour, and we bespeak them a right royal welcome on our shores.[37]

The newspaper highlighted the role of Catholics in royal rituals, reproducing in full the addresses given on behalf of the Catholics of the Dioceses of Dunedin and Wellington as well as describing the appearance of 'his Lordship Right Rev. Dr. Lenihan in his beautiful purple robes, and the Very Rev. Father Benedict, O.P., in his snow-white habit, [who] were, amidst the sombre [sic] black of the entire assemblage, the two most striking figures present'.[38] Lists of names carefully accounted for Catholic clergy who participated in the royal tour. While Cleary's loyalism obviously did not represent the viewpoints of all Irish Catholics in New Zealand, the message he sought to project was clear – that Irish Catholics were loyal citizens of New Zealand and subjects of the king.

Despite this projection of Irish Catholic loyalism, Cleary identified his paper with Irish nationalism and called attention to British injustices towards the Irish. In fact, he appealed to a reciprocal relationship between the British Crown and its Irish Catholic subjects, whereby loyal Irish Catholics were owed the rights of imperial citizenship. The paper made a point to note that a crowded Catholic mass celebrated by Father Joseph Cooney at the Lyttelton Pro-Cathedral was attended by colonial troops in town for the military display.[39] While underscoring Catholic service to the imperial war effort, the *Tablet* did not ignore the injustices experienced by Irish Catholics under British rule, going as far as to compare the 1857 and 1886 Belfast 'Orange riots', described not as 'haphazard collisions of excited mobs with "innards" loaded with bad whiskey and brains aflame with sectarian hate', but as genuine civil wars, with the South African war.[40] In 1886, they argued, appealing to evidence from the Royal Commission of Inquiry, 'the results achieved by the mob-energy surpass those of many a "great battle" of the South African war. At least 32 lives (chiefly of Catholics) were lost – even women shot in the streets'.[41] While Irish Catholics served *their* empire in South Africa, the British government allowed their kinsmen and women to be mowed down in the streets, like Boers or Bushmen. In using such rhetoric, the editors of the *Tablet* demonstrated the depths of Irish Catholic loyalty – but also its limits.[42]

Cleary also identified another betrayal by the British, an affront to loyal Catholic subjects, in Edward VII's coronation oath, for which they demanded an apology from the Duke of Cornwall and York. The coronation oath, last administered to Queen Victoria in 1838, required the new king to denounce the Holy Eucharist and devotion to the Virgin Mary as idolatry, which some observers claimed Edward read in a quiet voice with his head bowed.[43] The Catholic and Protestant press together, the *Tablet* declared, called for 'the removal therefrom of words which are as heartless an outrage upon the feelings of the King as they are upon those of his Catholic subjects ... The same end can be secured without utilising a direct insult; and certainly to declare ... that the use of Mass is "superstitious and idolatrous" is to insult the whole body of Catholics'.[44] Bishop Michael Verdon of Lyttelton exulted in his address that the government was working to remove language offensive to 'eleven millions of his faithful Catholic subjects' from the coronation oath and wished that 'every part of the Empire may enjoy an unbroken era of peace, prosperity, wise and equal laws'.[45] In expressing their loyalty to the Duke and Duchess of Cornwall and York, the Irish Catholic settlers, as represented by the *New Zealand Tablet*, sought peace and justice for themselves and their homeland *within* the British empire, not outside of it.

There are, of course, many other stories of 'outsider' loyalty to the monarchy and the empire that cannot be covered in a short chapter – the Chinese triumphal arches that welcomed Alfred to New Zealand in the 1870s, the response of Gandhi and a South Asian community to royal visits to South Africa in the early 1900s, and so on.[46] Of course, these communities were largely excluded from imperial-colonial communities and the national ones that emerged from them. During the twentieth century, whiteness came to define community in the settler empire and ethnic, sectarian and racial conflict became vital to the politics of empire. But none of this was a foregone conclusion during the nineteenth century, particularly to those who actually lived in the political, social and cultural worlds of empire. The 'imperial factor', as it has been called, need not only characterise the role of metropolitan politics and culture on colonial cultures but the ways in which diverse communities across the empire appealed to belonging – and even citizenship – in a community of empire. In the cases of the Cape Dutch and the Irish Catholics of New Zealand, so-called 'outsiders' were themselves the authors of imperial culture and citizenship.

Notes

1 Whether or not O'Farrell was actually a Fenian remains unclear. The Colonial Secretary of New South Wales at the time, Henry Parkes, who doubled as a police detective during the investigation, remained convinced, thirty years later, that O'Farrell was of sound mind. Henry Parkes, *Fifty Years in the Making of Australian History* (London: Longmans, Green & Co., 1892), pp. 190–211.
2 John Manning Ward (ed.), *The State and the People: Australian Federation and Nation-Making, 1870–1901* (Leichhardt, NSW: Federation Press, 2001), p. 16.
3 Malcolm Campbell, 'A "Successful Experiment" No More: The Intensification of Religious Bigotry in Eastern Australia, 1865–1885', *Humanities Research*, 12:1 (2005), 67–78.
4 Cited in *ibid.*, p. 70.
5 *Fenian Revelations: The Confessions of O'Farrell who Attempted to Assassinate the Duke of Edinburgh* (London: G. Slater, 1868).
6 *Ibid.*, p. 5.
7 *Ibid.*, pp. 3, 13. He told Parkes that the Fenians did not target the Prince of Wales because he was 'useful to the cause – the Republican cause, because he disgraces loyalty ... He is turning England against royalty'.

8 *Ibid.*, pp. 12–15.
9 *Ibid.*, pp. 9–10, 24. 'Perhaps he wants to make up a million exactly, or a legion, 10,000; he has received a stream now from all parts of the colony ... Will he take them all home with him? Will the *Galatea* hold them all? I think he ought to set fire to the lot and take the ashes of them all home.'
10 Krishan Kumar, *The Making of English National Identity* (Cambridge: Cambridge University Press, 2003); Robert J.C. Young, *The Idea of English Ethnicity* (Malden: Blackwell, 2008).
11 Saul Dubow, 'How British Was the British World? The Case of South Africa', *Journal of Imperial and Commonwealth History*, 37:1 (2009), 1–27.
12 See Benedict Anderson, *Imagined Communities: Reflections on the Origin and Spread of Nationalism* (New York: Verso, 1983); Alan Lester, *Imperial Networks: Creating Identities in Nineteenth Century South Africa and Britain* (New York: Routledge, 2001); Jane McRae, '"Ki nga pito e wha o te ao nei" (To the Four Corners of This World): Maori Publishing and Writing for Nineteenth-Century Maori-Language Newspapers', in Sabrina Alcorn Baron, Eric N. Lindquist and Eleanor F. Shevlin (eds), *Agent of Change: Print Culture Studies after Elizabeth L. Eisenstein* (Amherst: University of Massachusetts Press, 2007), pp. 287–300. For a fuller treatment of the royal tour and settler cultures, see chapter 3 of my *Royal Tourists, Colonial Subjects, and the Making of a British World, 1860–1911* (Manchester: Manchester University Press, 2016).
13 Richard Jebb, *Studies in Colonial Nationalism* (London: Edward Arnold, 1905); Douglas Cole, 'The Problem of "Nationalism" and "Imperialism" in British Settlement Colonies', *Journal of British Studies*, 10 (1971), 160–182. For a fuller treatment of royal tours and British settler communities, see chapter 3 of Reed, *Royal Tourists*.
14 Ian Radforth, *Royal Spectacle: The 1860 Visit of the Prince of Wales to Canada and the United States* (Toronto: University of Toronto Press, 2004), p. 170.
15 Donal Lowry, 'The Crown, Empire Loyalism and the Assimilation of Non-British White Subjects in the British World: An Argument Against "Ethnic Determinism"', *The Journal of Imperial and Commonwealth History*, 31 (2003), 96–120; see also Donal Lowry, '"These Colonies are Practically Democratic Republics": Republicanism in the British Colonies of Settlement in the Long Nineteenth Century', in David Nash and Antony Taylor (eds), *Republicanism in Victorian Society* (Gloucester: Sutton, 2000), pp. 125–139.
16 Lowry, 'The Crown', p. 99.
17 John MacKenzie, *The Scots in South Africa: Ethnicity, Identity, Gender and Race 1772–1914* (New York: Palgrave, 2007); Aled Jones and Bill Jones, 'The Welsh World and the British Empire, c. 1851–1939: An Exploration', in Carl Bridge and Kent Fedorowich (eds), *The British World: Diaspora, Culture, and Identity* (New York: F. Cass, 2003), pp. 57–81.
18 Jones and Jones, 'The Welsh World and the British Empire', p. 58; Aled Jones, 'The Other Internationalism? Missionary Activity and Welsh Nonconformist Perceptions of the World in the Nineteenth and Twentieth Centuries', in Charlotte Williams, Neil Evans and Paul O'Leary (eds), *A Tolerant Nation? Exploring Ethnic Diversity in Wales* (Cardiff: University of Wales Press, 2003), pp. 49–60. Also see Philip Constable, 'Scottish Missionaries, "Protestant Hinduism" and the Scottish Sense of Empire in Nineteenth- and Early Twentieth-Century India', *Scottish Historical Review*, 86 (2007), 278–313.
19 John MacKenzie, *The Scots in South Africa: Ethnicity, Identity, Gender and Race 1772–1914* (New York: Palgrave, 2007), p. 7. Also see Stuart Allen, *Thin Red Line: Empire and the Scots, 1600–2000* (Edinburgh: NMSE Publishing, 2006); Edward Spiers, *The Scottish Soldier and Empire, 1854–1902* (Edinburgh: Edinburgh University Press, 2006).
20 Donal McCracken, *Forgotten Protest: Ireland and the Anglo-Boer War* (Belfast: Ulster Historical Foundation, 2003).

21 It is also important to note that Dutch-speaking farmers developed a republican tradition and began trekking out of the colonial core at Cape Town long before the British arrived – in opposition to the Dutch East India Company (VOC).
22 *Graham's Town Journal*, 15 August 1860.
23 Quoted in Hermann Giliomee, *The Afrikaners: Biography of a People* (Charlottesville: University of Virginia Press, 2003), p. 225.
24 Timothy Keegan, *Colonial South Africa and the Origins of the Racial Order* (Charlottesville: University of Virginia Press, 1997), p. 106.
25 *Ibid.*, pp. 105–106; Giliomee, *Afrikaners*, p. 112.
26 Giliomee, *Afrikaners*, p. 225.
27 *De Zuid-Afrikaan*, 6 August 1860.
28 *De Zuid-Afrikaan*, 9 July 1860.
29 *Ibid.*
30 *De Zuid-Afrikaan*, 16 July 1860.
31 *Ibid.*
32 *Natal Mercury*, 16 August 1901.
33 Mordechai Tamarkin, 'The Cape Afrikaners and the British Empire from the Jameson Raid to the South African War', in Donal Lowry (ed.), *The South African War Reappraised* (Manchester: Manchester University Press, 2000), pp. 121–139.
34 Heather McNamara, 'The New Zealand Tablet and the Irish Catholic Press Worldwide, 1898–1923', *New Zealand Journal of History*, 37:2 (2003), 153–170.
35 *Ibid.*, p. 155.
36 *New Zealand Tablet*, 13 June 1901.
37 *New Zealand Tablet*, 21 March 1901.
38 *New Zealand Tablet*, 27 June 1901.
39 *New Zealand Tablet*, 4 July 1901.
40 *New Zealand Tablet*, 20 June 1901.
41 *Ibid.*
42 The newspaper was critical of the war effort, though couching its opposition not in 'pro-Boerism' but in the cost of lives as well as money to the British taxpayer.
43 *New Zealand Tablet*, 6 June 1901.
44 *Ibid.*
45 *New Zealand Tablet*, 27 June 1901.
46 For the latter, see Chapter 14 in this volume.

CHAPTER SIX

The Maharaja of Gondal in Europe in 1883

Caroline Keen

Under the Raj, the relationship between the British and the Indian states, which comprised two-fifths of the territory of the subcontinent and about one-fifth of its population, was never straightforward. The states were on the one hand early feudal territories, the traditional rule of whose indigenous 'kings and queens' was co-opted to legitimate imperialism in the second half of the nineteenth century. On the other hand they were potential sites of 'good government', which by definition was modern and could be used equally to justify the colonial presence. To maximise the full political potential of the Indian rulers, it proved necessary to maintain a subtle balance between the old and the new. Under the conciliatory tone adopted after the 1857 Mutiny, princely loyalty was secured through honours, titles, money and territories distributed lavishly in a series of vice-regal durbars and similar ceremonies. In addition, from the 1870s special educational facilities for young princes and members of the nobility were set up, such as Rajkumar College in Rajkot, Mayo College in Ajmer, Aitchison College in Lahore and Daly College in Indore. These establishments were intended to act as a countermeasure to the British education in secondary schools and colleges across the cities and towns of British India, such as Presidency College in Calcutta and Elphinstone College in Bombay, the curricula of which reflected the career hopes of students rather than national needs and that increasingly fostered anti-imperialist feeling. At the same time princely initiatives in the areas of education, health, infrastructure, irrigation and communication were welcomed as the work of 'model states' that reinforced the position of individual rulers as sovereign entities.[1]

As the result of exposure to Western ideas fostered not only by princely colleges, but also by members of the Political Department of the Government of India attached to princely states, a growing wave of Indian royalty and nobility arrived in Europe in the second half of the nineteenth century, to the great delight of Queen Victoria, who after her accession as Empress of India developed a passion for all things Indian (employing Indian servants and her notorious Indian Munshi or secretary, Abdul Karim). The Court and Social pages of *The Times* listed many announcements of the arrival and departure of visiting maharajas (many of whom chose to educate their children in England, most notable among them the Gaekwar of Baroda, the Maharajas of Cooch Behar, Gwalior and Bikaner, the Thakur Sahibs of Morvi and Gondal, and the Rao of Cutch). They were by no means the first royal visitors. In exile were Princess Gouramma, daughter of the ex-Raja of Coorg, who was christened at the age of thirteen in the private chapel of Buckingham Palace in 1852 and remained in Britain for the rest of her short life,[2] and Maharaja Duleep Singh, son of Ranjit Singh, the 'Lion of the Punjab', who arrived in Britain in 1854 and whose financial challenges led him to Russia and Paris before his death in 1893.[3]

The Indian and Colonial Exhibition of 1886 undoubtedly paved the way for a more general interest in India, despite newspaper criticism of the expense of sending exhibits to Britain which India could ill afford; the lavish Jaipur, Bombay, Punjab and other Indian courts drew over five million visitors in the several months the exhibition was open to the public.[4] During the following decade, the lavish celebrations in honour of Queen Victoria's Gold and Diamond Jubilees in 1887 and 1897 proved the main attraction for visiting Indian royalty in the late nineteenth century, and maharajas, nawabs and assorted members of the Indian aristocracy gave the great imperial occasions an exotic tinge which was captured by the popular press.[5] Thereafter, during the first half of the twentieth century – and of the greatest significance not only to Indian royalty but also to Indian soldiers and prominent Indian politicians – were the coronations of Edward VII in 1902 (attended by the Maharajas of Jaipur, Bikaner, Idar, Gwalior, Kolhapur and Cooch Behar),[6] George V in 1911,[7] and George VI in 1937,[8] at which the jewels of the Indian princes were said to rival in splendour those of the imperial regalia.

Indian princes were also involved in the First World War, notably the Maharaja of Bikaner, who was delegated to the Imperial War Cabinet, and the rulers played a major role at the Round Table Conferences held in London in 1930 and 1931 to determine India's future. In the sporting arena, among other contests which linked Britain and India, the shared passion for cricket was enlivened in Britain by the most famous Indian player of his time, the Jam Saheb of Nawanagar, Ranjitsinhji, and later his nephew, Duleepsinhji, as well as the Nawab of Pataudi. However as the twentieth century progressed, pleasure tended to be the principal purpose of foreign travel as Europe increasingly became a playground encouraging Indian royalty to indulge in conspicuous consumption of luxury items and, as the Viceroy, Lord Curzon, observed, to 'acquire ideas and tastes which are incompatible with subsequent residence in a Native State'.[9] This was not a purely British point of view. At the start of the century Suniti Devi, the Maharani of Cooch Behar, whose sons were at Eton, also recognised the shortcomings of exposure to European life. The young princes returned to India speaking French and Greek, but not Sanskrit, Urdu or Bengali, and no longer fluent in the local dialect of Cooch Behar.[10]

One young prince who was present in Britain at some of the most glittering events of the late nineteenth century was the Thakur Sahib (hereditary ruler) Bhagvatsinh (1865–1944), a Rajput who ruled Gondal state from 1884 until his death and assumed the title of Maharaja in 1888. Gondal, a land-locked territory in the bowl-shaped peninsula of Kathiawar on the northwestern coast of India, bordered the principalities of Rajkot and Junagadh in the Saurashtra region. The state was consolidated in the middle of the eighteenth century, when the Rajput Kumbhoji II forged alliances with the Muslim Nawab of Junagadh and the Maratha Gaekwad of Baroda. In 1864 the current ruler, Sagramji II, married Monghiba, the daughter of Rana Sartanjee of Minapur, and a year later Monghiba gave birth to their eldest son, Bhagvatsinh. When Sagramji died in 1869, the Kathiawar Agency of the British Political Department oversaw the administration through the political agent stationed at Gondal, Captain A.M. Phillips, until Bhagvatsinh came of age in 1884 and was able to assume full powers. Against his mother's wishes, Captain Phillips sent her eight-year-old son to Rajkumar College from 1873 to 1882; he proved an impressive pupil and was placed in an individual class by the principal, Chester Macnaghten. However later in life Bhagvatsinh publicly criticised a princely education that focused upon sport and the acquisition of language skills to the detriment of academic input. In his view an ability to speak English with a good accent and to excel at cricket and polo did not make an individual fit to rule a state and he regretted that Rajkumar had failed to provide him with a knowledge of world politics, history and global economics.[11]

The British political agent wished Bhagvatsinh to postpone marriage, but his mother prevailed and, while still a student at Rajkumar, the sixteen-year-old prince married four women in a quadruple ceremony in June 1881. In 1882, when her son finished his schooling, Monghiba expected him to return to assume full control of Gondal. However the British considered that at seventeen Bhagvatsinh was not prepared for such responsibilities and would benefit greatly from foreign travel. In

THE MAHARAJA OF GONDAL IN EUROPE IN 1883

6.1 HH Thakor Saheb Sir Bhawatsinghji Sagramji, Thakor of Gondal, photo Lafayette Portrait Studios, London, 1911

the 1880s a guided tour of Europe was seen by many British officials as an integral part of a princely education in order to expose future rulers to a 'superior' culture and to remind them of their position in the imperial hierarchy (although Macnaghten himself doubted the benefits of exposure to British life in that it had 'an unhappy tendency to detach Indian minds from all their old anchors'[12]). Such a tour proved particularly popular with the ex-students of the princely colleges who, having been weaned off palace life in the confines of a boarding school, were not fazed by the prospect of leaving Indian shores. It was hoped that in the healthy surroundings of Britain mental and moral qualities might be expanded. To this end Bhagvatsinh was to be accompanied by Major (later Lieutenant-Colonel) George Hancock of the Kathiawar Political Department to provide suitable supervision.

During his six-month tour, which was extraordinary in its breadth and diversity, the Thakur Sahib kept a detailed journal of his experiences in which he reflects with much frankness on various cultural, economic and political issues.[13] With the exception of the less eloquent diaries of Rajaram II, Raja of Kolhapur,[14] who travelled to Europe in 1870, and Jagatjit Singh, Maharaja of Kapurthala, who published his travelogue in 1895,[15] such accounts of Indian royalty abroad are virtually non-existent before the twentieth century. However other South Asians, for the most part urban elites such as 'anglicised' teachers, journalists and lawyers (including Mohandas Karamchand Gandhi[16]), who tended to express moderate nationalist views, were also travelling to Britain in the late nineteenth century and recording new insights and changing political views. As Antoinette Burton has suggested, 'their narratives provide historical evidence of how imperial power was staged at home, and how it would be interrogated by "natives"'.[17] Like Bhagvatsinh, these privileged Indian authors advocated the educational value of travel and took on the role of teacher for Indian readers. For some the literary use of a travelogue provided an opportunity to make criticisms which would have been censored had they written openly political diatribes.

Bhagvatsinh's journal gives an insight into his thoughts at an early age on government and society, and reveals the influence of his Rajkumar College education in its aim to produce a new multi-faceted breed of ruler who was prepared to act as a force for progress.[18] Colouring his observations is a well-developed snobbery which seems likely to be a product of the Thakur Sahib's adoption of British upper-class arrogance in the public school atmosphere of Rajkumar (although it also inflected the comments of urban elite fellow travellers, such as Behramji Malabari,[19] the prominent Parsi social reformer, journalist and poet, and Jhinda Ram,[20] a pleader in the Chief Court of the Punjab, both of whom tended to disassociate themselves from the 'masses' in Europe). Macnaghten appears to have encouraged his students to participate in the empire as partners rather than loyal servants of the British, and indeed during the Raj on a social if not political level there was much 'aristocratic' bonding across racial lines between individual Indian princes and the most elevated imperial administrators, based on a shared recognition of social status.[21] However, Bhagvatsinh also expresses remarkably liberal views, suggesting that, despite his criticism of the narrow Rajkumar curriculum (consisting of English, vernacular and classical languages, mathematics, geography and science), he was undoubtedly influenced by the efforts of Macnaghten to impart to his students a strong sense of values, ethics and responsibility.[22]

Bhagvatsinh left Gondal (without his wives) on 16 April 1883 and in Bombay embarked upon the SS *Cathay*, 'a floating hamlet' with 'all the comforts and conveniences of a land life'. South Asian travel narratives of the period suggest that much the same path was travelled from the subcontinent to Europe and individual descriptions of particular sights and discussions of issues were often similar. Like Malabari, who followed a corresponding route in 1890, the Thakur Sahib was unimpressed with the Suez Canal and, despite appreciating that it was 'one of the greatest monuments of modern engineering work', described the passage as 'extremely tedious, and the steamer moves not faster than a snail'. Port Said, with its diverse mix of French, Russian, Turkish, Greek and Egyptian occupants, also lacked his approval, looking 'very dirty and dreary', and it was with much relief that he reached Malta on 12 May; Valletta struck him 'for the first time as something different from an Oriental city' with well-paved, clean streets and a very handsome Opera House where he heard, although failed to understand, *La Traviata*.[23]

After a violent crossing of the Bay of Biscay, Bhagvatsinh and his party (the members of which are never identified, although he mentions 'Jemadar Ali', an Arab servant, who accompanied him personally on various outings) set foot 'on the renowned country which it was my long cherished desire to see'. Speeding up to London, the Thakur Sahib was most impressed by the efficiency of the operation of the railway and the fact that 'Everybody appears to be doing his own work, and the word "business" seems as if it were stamped on his face. No idlers are to be found lounging about the place and interfering with other people's duties'. As he walked through the shopping area of Bond Street and the Burlington Arcade, many people appeared to notice the prince's exotic Indian dress. He declared that it would have given him 'great amusement to hear their criticisms', although their approval or disapproval mattered little, inasmuch as 'in matters of dress every individual has his own idiosyncrasies, to which he is partial'.[24]

Despite his amazement at the size of the city, Bhagvatsinh expressed his undoubted preference for the country, 'For the town, though the metropolis of the British Empire, is very smoky and sooty ... This, combined with the unceasing din and rattle that fill one's ears all day long, is likely to confuse a stranger used to a more quiet life'. Commenting on the streets in the vicinity of the Thames Tunnel, he observed, 'I was labouring under the impression that of all the cities of the world London, the metropolis of the vast English empire, must not only be a charming place to live in, but that its lanes and by-lanes must be entirely free of filth. The results of my personal observation, however, have been disappointing'.[25] Malabari agreed and was thankful that, however poor India was, it did not experience the level of poverty he had seen in parts of the East End of London, Glasgow and other congested cities, where 'Thousands drag out a miserable existence, embittered by disease from which death, too long delayed, is the only relief ... And side by side with such heart-rending scenes of misery, one sees gorgeously dressed luxury flaunting in the streets'.[26] As with other South Asian travellers, the glaring inequality between rich and poor came as a considerable shock and highlighted the difference between the real Britain and the Britain which had been portrayed in India. As Julie Codell suggests, 'such realities called into question British claims of superiority and Enlightenment idealism; poverty was Britain's Achilles heel'.[27]

For the formal reception of the Indian princes in Britain, a political aide-de-camp, O.J. Burne, had been appointed in 1872. His task was to make arrangements for their presentation at court, their attendance at naval and military reviews and other public spectacles, and their inspection of Britain's arsenals, dockyards and centres of industry, all illustrating Britain's imperial power and wealth.[28] The Thakur Sahib's visit was a fine example of such all-encompassing orchestration. Early in his visit he travelled to Epsom races in the royal train with the Prince of Wales to see the Derby, accompanied by the Thakur Sahib of the state of Morvi, a fellow prince of the Saurashtra region. Other outings included a dazzling reception at the Foreign Office, where the galleries and staircase were 'thronged with notables in full-dress costumes', and a Royal Levee at St James's Palace. Bhagvatsinh also attended Admiralty House to view Trooping the Colour, a state ball at Buckingham Palace and a 'wonderfully done' performance of *Much Ado about Nothing* at the Lyceum Theatre featuring Henry Irving and Ellen Terry. However, distancing himself from frivolous pursuits, he claimed to attend the theatre more as ethnographer than spectator, with the object of obtaining insight into the social life of English people. In his opinion, a good play 'should try to represent on the stage what we see in every-day life, in a pleasing and instructive manner. For good moral plays are, in my opinion, the best reforming agencies'.[29]

Meeting up again with fellow scions of Indian royalty, Bhagvatsinh travelled to Cambridge University, where he had a guided tour of the colleges and visited Dajiraj, the young Thakur Sahib of Wadhwan state in Saurashtra, an old school friend who was, like himself, 'a bird of passage in the country'. He expressed his 'intense delight in meeting a fellow-countryman ... there is always something in the similarity of language, dress, or even the very mode of thinking that draws minds towards each other'.[30] Nevertheless it is evident that, although later in his reign Bhagvatsinh sought and received advice from Indian middle-class reformers, his first trip to Europe did not involve socialising with Indians of an inferior rank. This disdain worked both ways. Malabari, who ironically held many similar views to Bhagvatsinh on late-Victorian British culture and Western mores, savagely attacked '"Indian princes" drinking in the doubtful admiration which the London mob knows how and on whom to bestow'.[31]

From Cambridge, 'surrounded by a mathematical atmosphere which was too hard for my lungs to breathe!' the Thakur Sahib progressed to Oxford University for Commemoration Day, when he witnessed honorary degrees being conferred upon 'distinguished persons'.[32] The Chancellor was constantly interrupted in his opening speech by students shouting from the galleries, much surprising Bhagvatsinh in that 'Such turbulent behaviour of disciples towards their preceptors would be past all belief in India, where something like divine respect is paid to the Gurus by their pupils'. Despite the prince's dismissal of the education at Rajkumar, an interest in science had clearly been forged at the college, and he was intrigued to spend a morning in the company of Dr Henry Wentworth Acland, Regius Professor of Medicine, who showed the party around the laboratories attached to Oxford University, 'fitted up with every convenience for learning each branch of scientific research'.[33] It was the belief of many educated South Asians that, with the help of Britain, India could achieve significant technological and scientific advances. Romesh Chunder Dutt, the economic historian and Indian civil servant, in his 1896 travel account expressed his hope that before long India would 'take her place among the nations of the earth in manufacturing industry and commercial enterprise'.[34]

During the month of June Bhagvatsinh was at Ascot races for the Gold Cup and in central London he visited the Albert Memorial in Kensington, the British Museum and Madame Tussaud's waxworks, and travelled to the relocation of the 1851 Great Exhibition's Crystal Palace, where he saw ivory-turning, ribbon-making and other sorts of production and was 'weighed, electrified, and had the capacity of our lungs tested'.[35] In addition the party was invited to a concert at Buckingham Palace to hear some of the best singers of the day.

Bhagvatsinh particularly liked one piece which resembled Indian music, as it was 'more ancient, more scientific and more complete as a science. The European music is something like a pen and ink sketch, exhibiting only broad outlines, while a native Rag [raga] is like a complete picture, showing the minutest shades and colours to perfection'.[36] He was also entertained at a fancy-dress ball, where he was 'at a loss to understand why so much time, money and ingenuity should be wasted on the sartorial art for the sake of the ephemeral delight of an evening', neatly reversing Government of India critiques of the extravagances of Indian royalty.[37]

Bhagvatsinh travelled by train to see the Arsenal at 'extremely filthy and dirty' Woolwich and after a short trip on the River Thames, 'which in point of length is only a streamlet when compared to the Ganges or the Indus', was shown 'some most enormous guns, the shot and shell for which were almost as big as I am!' He was also instructed in the manufacture of ammunition, gun carriages and other equipment for both military and naval warfare, which to him demonstrated 'the power and might of England. Every accessory of war is here turned out regardless of expense'.[38] Malabari, by contrast, was less impressed by displays of military prowess during his visit to Britain, declaring that 'The War Office may deny this; but it is no secret for the unhappy taxpayer that England, and all Europe, for that matter, is being crushed under the weight of military expenditure'.[39] Even more scathingly, Ram identified Britain's progress with 'all the ingenious scientific contrivances for improving the instruments of death'.[40]

In July Bhagvatsinh travelled to Scotland, where he visited the Edinburgh Royal Infirmary. He was 'much struck by the efficiency of the arrangements' for more than seven hundred 'inmates' and eighty doctors, and was later shown around the medical school of Edinburgh University by Sir Alexander Grant, the Principal,[41] expressing his desire (later to be fulfilled) to become a medical student himself. He and his party were taken to Holyrood Palace and the Castle, and subsequently travelled to the city of Glasgow, seeing the impressive shipbuilding yards of John Elder and Co. where more than 6,000 workmen were employed.[42] The Thakur Sahib's subsequent stay in Scotland was a huge success, prompting him to comment that 'Scotland is a place for learning and quiet pursuits of life; and England a place of restless activity and commercial enterprise'.[43]

Such enterprise was evident when, crossing the country to Liverpool, the prince was taken to a factory involved in the manufacture of woollen cloth, from the cleaning of raw wool to the production of the finest material. Aware that raw wool was imported into Britain in great quantity from his own country, Bhagvatsinh expressed his wish that such material might be produced in India, where labour was very cheap. Until Indian fabrics were able to compete fairly with their foreign rivals the Government of India should 'put some prohibitive duties on foreign imports', as 'the introduction of a free trade policy in India, at a time when her glorious industries are helplessly swept away by the gushing torrents of foreign goods produced in more favourable circumstances, is not fair'.[44] Although their paths did not cross in Britain in 1883, in focusing upon the drain of wealth from India into Britain, the young prince was expressing the concerns also felt by Dadabhai Naoroji, the Parsi political and social leader who became the first British Indian Member of Parliament in 1892 and was later a great influence upon and friend of Bhagvatsinh. Ram also deplored the inequality of trade with India, declaring of Britain that 'Commerce, commerce alone has made this noble nation, the wealthiest nation in the world ... Commerce, commerce alone, has put India full of millions under the British yoke'.[45]

When Bhagvatsinh returned to London, he received the 'great honour' of a call down to Osborne on the Isle of Wight to see Queen Victoria who, although in India was known only by her name and her pictures, nevertheless received 'thousands of blessings ... daily showered on her by my countrymen'. He much enjoyed his audience, declaring that 'she has an exceedingly kind face, and is smaller than most English ladies'. Fittingly, although with no royal presence, the prince subsequently visited Windsor Castle, 'a stately Palace, very beautifully situated on the Thames, and ... full of interesting relics of great value'.[46] However, after much reading around the subject of monarchy, he observed, in the light of the absolutism of Indian royalty, his puzzlement that in his opinion the crown exercised very little power under the current British constitution. Moreover, whereas a dynastic Indian ruler was the 'mother and father' of his people, the bizarre idea of an absentee imperial figurehead out of touch with a vast number of her subjects was not agreeable to the tradition-bound people of India (as indeed it was not agreeable to many Britons) in that 'The people are proverbially loyal, but the vast number of the ignorant mass do not know who their sovereign is. The viceroys and governors come and go like meteors, and they leave the people in still greater bewilderment ... how advantageous it would be, both for India and England, if the Queen-Empress were to remove her residence from Windsor to Bombay or Calcutta'.[47]

Summing up his opinion of Britain as he neared his departure date, Bhagvatsinh declared that 'Perseverance, enterprise, energy and industry are the cardinal features of Englishmen ... There is a grand intellectual race, and every one tries to outrun the other'.[48] Some 'usages of society' might well be adopted in India, such as giving more liberty to women, 'though not quite to the extent to which an English lady is privileged to enjoy it'. He could see no good reason why women should be 'confined within the four walls of their house and not allowed to go out without being veiled ... and oppressed by their mothers-in-law and sisters-in-law', as was the case in India. Jagatjit Singh, Maharaja of Kapurthala, was similarly impressed by the freedom of women in Britain, which was 'naturally a source of wonder to an Oriental ... this liberty is in no sense abused by the weaker sex, now long accustomed to self-reliance, which induces self respect'.[49] In addition, like Malabari who lobbied hard both in Britain and India to change the practice of child marriage and the prohibition of widow remarriage existing in India, the Thakur Sahib believed that 'the system of infant marriages' in his homeland should be condemned and was also 'happy to note that the English people do not favour polygamy'. With more than a passing nod to Indian independence, he considered with many of his fellow travellers that his country should be adequately represented in the British Parliament or granted 'a Parliament of her own on the basis and principles of the English Parliament' and some of the highest posts in India should be given to 'the deserving children of the soil', as was the case under Mughal rule. Finally, it was 'a grave political blunder to hurt the religious sensibilities of an alien people by permitting the killing of cows'.[50]

Leaving Britain, the European stage of Bhagvatsinh's tour began in Paris, where the people appeared to be less energetic than the British and 'idling about their work' due to 'epicurean habits'. In his opinion, 'An extravagant love of luxury has an enervating influence on nations as well as individuals. It has hastened the fall of many a flourishing kingdom ... I am afraid France, and also England, to some extent, are drifting towards this danger'.[51] Nevertheless the Thakur Sahib greatly enjoyed the paintings at the Louvre, the Arc de Triomphe and the Bois de Boulogne, and much admired Paris by night, commenting that 'The long lines of lamps shining ... with the brilliant illuminations of the shops, give the whole city the appearance of a continual "Divali"'.[52] In Switzerland he was agreeably surprised to notice that 'the electric telegraph extends to almost all the villages', but much regretted the Swiss system of government, 'carried on by a Federal Republic, consisting of two councils, the members of which are elected by the people', which seemed to him 'incapable of evoking that sincere and healthy spirit of loyalty from the inmost recesses of the people's hearts which a born and "anointed" king can do'. Unsurprisingly, the teaching at Rajkumar College did not countenance the ideas of James Mill on the removal of 'despotic' princely rule in favour of representative (albeit British) government,[53] and Bhagvatsinh was firmly of the opinion that 'those votaries of "Liberty, equality, and fraternity", who are carried astray by the disloyal wind of republicanism, will have to revert to the old form after bitter experience'.[54] Bhagvatsinh was not alone among Indian visitors in holding such views. Even the nationalist Malabari doubted the benefits to Europe of a republican form of government and saw the need for at least a symbol of royalty for the people, 'to be kept in good condition, perhaps in a glass house, and worshipped once or twice a year' and overseen by clever politicians 'to see that this symbol is made harmless'.[55]

The Thakur Sahib's impressions of Italy were mixed. In Venice the young prince found the idea of people conducting their business by waterways 'very pleasant', although the 'water smells horribly in the smaller streets' and the party was plagued by mosquitoes.[56] Florence was a great deal more appealing and during his short visit to the city he drove to the spot where a fellow Indian prince, the Raja of Kolhapur, had been cremated after falling ill during a trip to Europe in 1870, and where a 'handsome monument' in his memory had been erected. In Rome Bhagvatsinh visited the Vatican and was accorded an audience with Pope Leo XIII. A whirlwind tour of the ancient sites made him acutely conscious that the city had passed though 'many vicissitudes of fortune, and the signs of her past greatness are discernible everywhere'.[57] His fellow Indian visitor Ram agreed that the city was in 'ruin, ruin, ruin' and no longer 'Mistress of the World'.[58] In focusing upon the transient nature of imperial rule, and in particular the rule of the Roman empire with which the Victorians liked to compare themselves,[59] there was the unspoken belief that India would eventually be liberated from British control.

At Brindisi on 28 October a somewhat world-weary Bhagvatsinh boarded the *Tanjore* for home. As he approached Bombay, he summed up his impressions of the 'felicitous dream' that had been his foreign journey. The people of Europe undeniably set a good example in that 'Everybody tries to earn his maintenance by honest work, to which he is attached with a fondness well worth imitating. They are strong in physique, and consequently have great courage and enterprise, which tend to make a nation great. Invention is the order of the day'. However, such a drive tended to be focused upon the insatiable pursuit of 'increasing animal comforts' whereas Indians were accustomed 'to think less of the present life, and more of the life to come, in which they have an unshaken belief, and hence it is that they are not progressive in the modern sense of the word'.[60] The young prince felt most strongly that Indians should 'cultivate their faculties, which are lying dormant for want of exertion'. In his opinion, 'My tour has convinced me that we are living in the age of science. Europe is making great advances in field of science. It abounds in numerous technical schools and colleges of science, which enable thousands of young man to take independent stations in life. It is all the more essential that India should be overspread with such institutions ... and thereby make the country once more flourishing'. Moreover, by using 'the latent energy of the country lying idle in oblivion', Britain's hand would be strengthened rather than weakened.[61]

On his return from Europe in 1883, moving from the fine Naulakha Palace which had been built for his ancestors in the seventeenth century and eschewing the vast expense of a new establishment, Bhagvatsinh installed himself in the modern 'Huzur Bungalow', constructed in the 1870s as the residence of the British officer who administered the state early in his minority, Major H.L. Nutt. The publication of his diary in 1886 with its 'fluent and readable style' received a wide positive reception with favourable reviews in *The Indian Statesman*, *The Indian Spectator* and *The Times of India*, and, in Britain, in the *Dundee Advertiser*, *The Asiatic Quarterly Review*, *The New Review* and *The Sunday Review*.[62] In the course of the following decades, the Thakur Sahib returned to Britain not only for social occasions but also, quite possibly influenced by his first visit to its medical department in 1883, to attend the University of Edinburgh for three years, graduating in medicine in 1895 and becoming a Fellow of the Royal College of Physicians of Edinburgh. His three sons completed their education in Scotland, one as a doctor and two as engineers, and were later placed in separate charge of the state medical services, the state roads and the state railways of Gondal. The enthusiasm for many of the improvements that Bhagvatsinh carried out in Gondal prior to his death in 1944 had clearly been fired by his first trip to Europe. He reformed the administration, developed state resources, built schools, colleges and hospitals, and provided free compulsory education through university for both men and women; he also championed women's rights more generally. Undoubtedly influenced by British technological progress and the modernity of British manufacturing, he created technical schools for engineers and training facilities for labourers. He built dams and irrigation networks, overhauled sewage, plumbing and rail systems, and installed equipment for telegraphs, telephone cables and electricity. He published the first dictionary of Gujarati as well as a Gujarati encyclopaedia, the *Bhagavadgomanal*. Three years after Bhagvatsinh's death, at the independence of India in 1947, his son, Bhorajji, signed the Instrument of Accession to the Indian Union and Gondal was integrated into the newly created Saurashtra State before becoming part of the state of Gujarat in 1960.

The Thakur Sahib was not unique in his progressive attitude. The region of Kathiawar and its neighbouring states spawned a number of liberal-thinking princes during the period, such as the Gaekwar of Baroda and the Thakur Sahib of Bhavnagar, both of whom were frequent visitors to Europe; far from failing to keep pace with social developments, they became highly supportive of middle-class reformers in India and took on board their values. Like many of their fellow travellers from the Indian urban elites, these princes appear to have developed a form of moderate nationalism, believing in ideas of British civilisation, education and progress while arguing for administrative and constitutional reform. However, although they may have admired European practices and adopted many of them, they undoubtedly did not regard themselves as second-class citizens. Whereas the British took the view that politically they were superior partners in an unequal relationship between Britain and princely India, the Indian rulers saw matters differently. They were well aware that in order to exist they needed the British, but every ruler, major or minor, was proud of his lineage, his past and the fact that he still ruled a kingdom, and he disliked interference by outsiders (notably the over-zealous political officer) in his business of state. As far as was possible Bhagvatsinh succeeded in deflecting the intrusion of Government of India officials. Partly as a result of the widening of his horizons in 1883 and his later travels in Europe, the Thakur Sahib's reputation as an 'enlightened' and highly capable prince earned him considerable respect with the British administration and to some extent gave him the autonomy under British rule which he desired, preventing any incursions on his sovereignty in the name of maladministration and enhancing his monarchical authority.

Notes

1 For more general works on the princely states, see Caroline Keen, *Princely India and the British: Political Development and the Operation of Empire* (London: I.B. Tauris, 2012); Barbara Ramusack, *The Indian Princes and their States* (Cambridge: Cambridge University Press, 2004); and Robin Jeffrey (ed.), *People, Princes and Paramount Power: Society and Politics in the Indian Princely States* (New Delhi: Oxford University Press, 1979).
2 *The Illustrated London News*, 17 July 1852. See also C.P. Belliappa, *Victoria Gowraama: The Lost Princess of Coorg* (Kolkata: Rupa, 2009).
3 Obituary in *The Graphic*, 28 October 1893. See also Michael Alexander and Sushila Anand, *Queen Victoria's Maharajah, Duleep Singh, 1838–93* (London: Weidenfeld & Nicolson, 2001); and Anita Anand, *Sophia: Princess, Suffragette, Revolutionary* (London: Bloomsbury, 2015). On an earlier highly controversial Anglo-Indian exile, see Michael H. Fisher, *The Inordinately Strange Life of Dyce Sombre* (London: Hurst Publishers, 2014).

4 See Saloni Mathur, *India by Design: Colonial History and Cultural Display* (Berkeley: University of California Press, 2007).
5 Extracts from 'Queen's Journal', 29 and 30 June 1887, in G.E. Buckle (ed.), *Letters of Queen Victoria, 3rd Series, Vol. 1* (London: John Murray, 1930). *The Illustrated London News*, 10 July 1897.
6 *The Illustrated London News*, 12 July 1902; *The Times*, 11 August 1902.
7 *The Illustrated London News* and *The Times*, 24 June 1911.
8 *The Times*, 11 May 1937.
9 Curzon to St. John Brodrick, 2 February 1905, Curzon Collection F111, Vol. 164, Asian and African Studies, British Library. See Amin Jaffer, 'Indian Princes and the West', in Anna Jackson (ed.), *Maharaja: The Splendour of India's Royal Courts* (London: V&A, 2009), pp. 194–226.
10 Lucy Moore, *Maharanis* (London, 2004), p. 113. See also the autobiography of Sunity Devi's much-travelled granddaughter: Gayatri Devi and Santha Rama Rau, *A Princess Remembers: The Memoirs of the Maharani of Jaipur* (Philadelphia: Lippincott, 1976).
11 Nihal Singh, *Shree Bhagvat Sinhjee, the Maker of Modern Gondal* (Gondal: Golden Jubilee Committee, 1934), pp. 356–357. See also Bhavsinhji, H.H. Maharaja of Bhavnagar, *Forty Years of the Rajkumar College: An Account of the Origin and Progress of the Rajkumar College, Rajkot, 1870–1910* (London: Hazel, Watson and Viney, 1911).
12 Chester Macnaghten, *Common Thoughts on Serious Subjects; Being Addresses to the Elder Kumars of the Rajkumar College, Kathiawar* (London: John Murray, 1896), p. xxxv.
13 Bhagvat Sinh Jee, Thakore Saheb of Gondal, *Journal of a Visit to England in 1883* (Bombay: Education Society's Press, Byculla, 1886) also http://storage.lib.uchicago.edu/pres/2008/pres2008-0333.pdf, accessed 5 May 2017.
14 E.W. West (ed.), *Diary of the Late Rajah of Kolhapoor during his Visit to Europe in 1870* (London: Smith Elder, 1872).
15 Jagatjit Singh of Kapurthala, *My Travels in Europe and America 1893* (London: G. Routledge, 1895).
16 See Mohandas K. Gandhi, *An Autobiography; or the Story of My Experiments with Truth* (Ahmedabad: Navajivan Publishing House, 1990).
17 Antoinette Burton, *At the Heart of the Empire: Indians and the Colonial Encounter in Late-Victorian Britain* (Los Angeles: University of California Press, 1998), pp. 127–146. See also Rosie Llewellyn-Jones, 'Indian Travellers in Nineteenth Century England', *Indo-British Review*, 18:1 (1990), 137–141.
18 Satradu Sen, *Disciplined Natives: Race, Freedom and Confinement in Colonial India* (Delhi: Primus Books, 2012), pp. 107–131.
19 Behramji M. Malabari, *The Indian Eye on English Life or Rambles of a Pilgrim Reformer* (Bombay: Apollo, 1893), pp. 129–130.
20 Jhinda Ram, *My Trip to Europe* (Lahore: Mufid I-Am, 1893), pp. 8, 1.
21 David Cannadine, *Ornamentalism: How the British saw their Empire* (Oxford: Oxford University Press, 2001), pp. 10, 41–57.
22 See Macnaghten, *Common Thoughts*.
23 Bhagvat Sinh Jee, *Journal of a Visit to England in 1883*, pp. 21–23.
24 *Ibid.*, pp. 27–28.
25 *Ibid.*, pp. 30, 99.
26 Malabari, *Indian Eye*, pp. 85–87.
27 Julie Codell, 'Transposing Travel Narrative: Irony, Ethnography, and the Guest Discourse in Indian Travel Writing', in Pallavi Rastogi and Jocelyn Fenton Stitt (eds), *Before Windrush: Recovering an Asian and Black Literary Heritage within Britain* (Newcastle: Cambridge Scholars Publishing, 2008), p. 91.
28 Govt. to O.J. Burne, Political ADC, 12 October 1872, IOR L/PS/3/352, Asian and African Studies, British Library.
29 Bhagvat Sinh Jee, *Journal of a Visit to England in 1883*, pp. 32–46, 167.
30 *Ibid.*, p. 68.

31 Malabari, *Indian Eye*, p. 240.
32 Bhagvat Sinh Jee, *Journal of a Visit to England in 1883*, p. 61.
33 *Ibid.*, pp. 62–64.
34 Romesh Chunder Dutt, *Three Years in Europe* (Calcutta: S.K. Lahiri and Co., 1896), p. 46.
35 Bhagvat Sinh Jee, *Journal of a Visit to England in 1883*, pp. 52–57.
36 *Ibid.*, p. 79.
37 *Ibid.*, p. 96.
38 *Ibid.*, pp. 72–73.
39 Malabari, *Indian Eye*, p. 124.
40 Ram, *My Trip to Europe*, p. 60.
41 Vice-Chancellor of Bombay University from 1863 to 1865.
42 Bhagvat Sinh Jee, *Journal of a Visit to England in 1883*, p. 110.
43 *Ibid.*, p. 117.
44 *Ibid.*, p. 122.
45 Ram, *My Trip to Europe*, p. 82.
46 Bhagvat Sinh Jee, *Journal of a Visit to England in 1883*, pp. 145–146.
47 *Ibid.*, p. 163.
48 *Ibid.*, p. 170.
49 Jagatjit Singh, *My Travels*, pp. 42–43.
50 Bhagvat Sinh Jee, *Journal of a Visit to England in 1883*, pp. 170–180.
51 *Ibid.*, p. 183.
52 Hindu 'festival of lights'. *Ibid.*, p. 187.
53 Macnaghten, *Common Thoughts*, pp. xxviii, xxxiv, xxxviii, 97, 192. E. Stokes, *The English Utilitarians and India* (Oxford: Oxford University Press, 1959), pp. 56, 146.
54 Bhagvat Sinh Jee, *Journal of a Visit to England in 1883*, p. 221.
55 Malabari, *Indian Eye*, pp. 136–137.
56 Bhagvat Sinh Jee, *Journal of a Visit to England in 1883*, p. 227.
57 *Ibid.*, p. 232.
58 Ram, *My Trip to Europe*, p. 123.
59 See https://victorianist.wordpress.com/2015/08/31/primus-inter-pares-ancient-rome-and-the-victorians, accessed 5 May 2017.
60 Bhagvat Sinh Jee, *Journal of a Visit to England in 1883*, pp. 244–245.
61 *Ibid.*, pp. 177, 247–249.
62 Singh, *Shree Bhagvat Sinhjee*, pp. 118–121.

CHAPTER SEVEN

Performing monarchy: the Kaiser and Kaiserin's voyage to the Levant, 1898

Matthew P. Fitzpatrick

Despite his reputation as the driving force behind Germany's pre-1914 push for empire, Kaiser Wilhelm II never visited any of Germany's colonies. He did, however, visit the Ottoman empire three times: in 1889, 1898 and 1917. On the second of these trips, in autumn 1898, he and Empress Augusta Victoria ventured well beyond Constantinople during a pilgrimage to the chief sites of the Holy Land. The occasion of the tour was the opening and dedication of the Church of Christ the Redeemer, built on land in Jerusalem given to the Kaiser's father, the then Crown Prince Friedrich Wilhelm, by Sultan Abdülaziz in 1869.

The royal party set out on their *Orientreise* (journey to the Orient) from the palace in Potsdam on 11 October 1898. Leaving Venice on the royal yacht, the *Hohenzollern*, on 13 October 1898, they sailed for five days to reach Constantinople, where they spent several days (including the Kaiserin's birthday) as Sultan Abdülhamid II's personal guests. The German royals left Constantinople late on 22 October for Haifa and Jaffa, before journeying on to Jerusalem, arriving there on the 29 October. On 30 October there was a visit to the Church of the Nativity in Bethlehem, prior to the dedication of the Church of the Redeemer in Jerusalem on 31 October. They stayed in and around Jerusalem until 3 November, after which they travelled north via Beirut (5–6 November) to Damascus, where they stayed between 7 and 9 November. On 11 November, the Kaiser visited the ruins of Baalbek, which impressed him so much that he decided to pay for them to be systematically excavated,[1] before returning to Beirut for a leisurely sea voyage home. The royal tour ended with their arrival back in Berlin on 26 November, just in time for the Kaiser to reopen the Reichstag on 6 December 1898.[2]

Rather than by the German Foreign Office, the voyage was organised by the British travel agency Thomas Cook. Yet, despite this gesture towards private travel, the unprecedented pomp and ceremony of the trip made it quite clear that Wilhelm II was not travelling incognito, but as the German emperor. Moving the royal procession across the Ottoman empire required an army of workers to both prepare for its arrival and cater to the needs of the German royals while they were there. The official party had its own baggage train trailing it, consisting of 1,430 horses and pack animals, 116 coaches and wagons, 800 muleteers and 290 servants.[3] The Kaiser even commissioned bespoke tropical uniforms for the occasion,[4] a source of great mirth among those dragooned into accompanying the royal pair until the Palestinian heat made them glad for such vanities. The official party was also shadowed by two naval vessels and two steam liners filled with well-heeled tourists timing their pilgrimages to coincide with the royal visit, a tour hastily organised by the disgruntled German travel firm Carl Stangen, which swallowed its indignation to organise the shadow tour upon finding out that the royals had chosen a British firm over a German one to organise the royal trip.[5] The total cost of the royal voyage on the German side was an astronomical 1,263,967 Marks.[6] On the Ottoman side, not only did the Sultan spend heavily to improve the roads and the appearance of the cities along the route, he also built a new wharf at Haifa so the Kaiser's luxury yacht could berth there.[7] In a stunning act of archaeological vandalism that horrified the Kaiser, the sultan also commissioned the tearing down of a centuries-old wall abutting Jerusalem's Jaffa Gate to allow Wilhelm II and his entourage to enter the city in procession.[8]

Recently, Monika Wienfert has argued that during the nineteenth century 'many European monarchies can be said to have functioned rather successfully as national symbols and as means of effecting a national integration of peoples that were still, in many ways, heterogeneous'.[9] To some extent, this was evident in the royal pair's voyage to the Holy Lands, which was the occasion of symbolically important acts of gift-giving when the Kaiser formally gave over holy sites to both Protestant and Catholic Germans. Nonetheless, beyond the uniforms, the high-minded talk of solemn pilgrimages, and the spectacle of festive summitry that brought together two emperors from the East and the West, views of the actual significance of the voyage among the German public were decidedly mixed, ranging from seeing it as an ostentatious display of piety by the leader of Germany's Protestant Church to deriding it as yet another expensive royal junket of no political importance. The court diarist Baroness Hildegard von Spitzemberg could only hope that it would proceed without scandal and would not be marred by one of the Kaiser's characteristic gaffes.[10] In the Reichstag, the Kaiser's tour met with a stormy debate (led by the Social Democrats) over his attempt to have the government pay the expenses of the ministers and their entourage who were his (in many cases reluctant) travelling companions. It took a vigorous and highly exaggerated defence of the diplomatic work undertaken during the royal visit before the Reichstag reluctantly agreed to contribute to the costs.[11]

If the Kaiser had difficulty convincing Germans that his voyage was important to the interests of the state, external observers were far more ready to ascribe political importance to the voyage, viewing it as a direct expression of German foreign policy. Russian Pan-Slavists, the Vatican, Theodor Herzl and the Zionist movement, German colonists in Palestine and the Ottoman sultan, as well as various European governments, all sought to divine the underlying political significance of this royal visit. As this chapter argues, what most alarmed other European powers were the rumours circulating that the Kaiser would use the royal visit to Jerusalem to announce some type of German protectorate in Palestine, an announcement that would presage the long-feared general European war to settle the division of the ostensibly 'sick man of Europe'.

What these fears show is that, in the year between the announcement of the voyage and the tour itself, the Kaiser's capacity to alter the course of German foreign policy unilaterally was consistently overestimated outside of Germany. Confusing the synecdochic phrase 'the Kaiser's foreign policy' with the actual sovereign prerogative of Wilhelm II, European governments and the press of the 1890s (in contradistinction to the German government and press) mistook the extent of the monarch's autocratic power, a view that has lingered in some recent accounts of the *Kaiserreich* which have positioned the Kaiser as the architect of an expansive new *Weltpolitik* with a new Eastern focus.[12] In fact, not only was Wilhelm II unable to direct German foreign policy, but the 'Eastern question' had been a pressing issue for German diplomacy since at least the Herzegovina Crisis of 1875.[13] Beyond that, the Kaiser's visit to the Ottoman empire had been preceded by that of his father, Friedrich III, in 1869, when he had received as a gift from the sultan the highly prized religious site in Jerusalem that Wilhelm II was now visiting.[14]

If the Kaiser did not discover the Orient for Germany, his visit certainly suggested his personal affinity with both the Ottoman empire and its sultan, a development that worried all of Europe. As the following makes clear, however, there was a pronounced gap between the visit's public display of an all-powerful monarch and the consistent disappointment of the Kaiser's eccentric plans for his trip. The slight gains won for Germany from the royal visit to the Holy Land were the product not of royal intervention, but of the careful planning of Chancellor Chlodwig zu Hohenlohe-Schillingsfürst, the Foreign Secretary Bernhard von Bülow and the Foreign Office, particularly the ambassador to Constantinople, Adolf Marschall von Bieberstein. All paid careful attention to the limitations on the Kaiser's capacity to act autonomously imposed by German popular opinion, the Reichstag and the European balance of power. Despite the pageantry of opening the Protestant church in Jerusalem, all of the Eastern plans harboured by the Kaiser prior to the voyage were uniformly unsuccessful, while those towards which he professed indifference or unease were most successful, courtesy of the quiet, behind-the-scenes work executed by others.

The international context of the royal visit

One of the reasons that the Kaiser's trip came under such close scrutiny from the Great Powers was that it came so soon after the Germans' pointed official silence on the question of the Armenian massacres of 1894–1896.[15] Seemingly in defiance of the rest of Europe, the Kaiser was very public in his determination to visit the 'Red Sultan'. As British press commentators admitted, however, overlooking Turkish massacres despite Europe-wide condemnation was a practice not unknown to Europe, given that the British had similarly put their own Ottoman policy before the interests of the Bulgarians massacred in 1876. It was, Britain's *Daily Telegraph* suggested, *Realpolitik* imperatives that had ostensibly driven Germany's 'moral support' for the sultan against the other powers; that support, the paper argued, had afforded Germany 'immense material advantages within the Ottoman Empire'.[16] The cloud of the Armenian massacres persisted throughout the Kaiser's tour, however, with German officials fearing that Armenian protestors might seek to disrupt the visit. The presence of Armenian clerics alongside the Kaiser at key shrines in the Holy Land was also seen as a potential embarrassment to the sultan.[17]

Moreover, with problems flaring up in Crete in 1898, Wilhelm II's visit was also seen by some, particularly the French, as lending support to Ottoman 'intransigence' concerning the status of the island. Russia too sought to pressure the Kaiser into accepting their version of a European 'concert' position towards Crete, a stance that amounted to dismantling the remnants of Ottoman sovereignty there.[18] Following the lead of his ambassador in Constantinople and Chancellor Hohenlohe, and Germany's long established principle of supporting the sovereignty of the Sultan and the integrity of the Ottoman empire, the Kaiser quietly protested against Russian attempts to pressure the Sultan to evacuate Crete *tout de suite*, viewing it as tantamount to leaving Muslims on the island vulnerable to being massacred by its Christian population.[19] Once Germany's misgivings on the issue of the latest Cretan violence had been registered, however, the issue did not publicly follow the Kaiser to Jerusalem.

Creating even greater political headaches was the Kaiser's decision in March of 1898 to add a side-trip to Egypt to his itinerary. Were it to have gone ahead, it would have been the first visit by a head of state to Egypt since the beginning of the British occupation in 1882. To France and Russia, this appeared as a public confirmation by Germany of British claims there – a particularly divisive stance to make during the Anglo-French race for the Sudan that would climax with the Fashoda incident (which overlapped with the Kaiser's voyage). Unsurprisingly, the British press made clear their support for Wilhelm II's visit to Egypt, with the *Times* welcoming 'the presence of a friendly Monarch who has energy to see and intelligence to appreciate the fruits of the great reformation that has been effected'.[20] Equally unsurprisingly, this seeming normalisation of the British occupation of Egypt by a reigning monarch alarmed the French and Russian press, with critical articles in *L'Éclair* and *Le Figaro*, while *Novoye Vremya* argued that 'by accepting English hospitality the Kaiser has placed himself on the side of those who have damaged the Berlin Treaty'.[21] In the end, however, a plot by Italian anarchists to assassinate the Kaiser while he was in Egypt was uncovered in late September 1898.[22] Given the very recent assassination of the Austrian Empress Elisabeth by an Italian anarchist, the Kaiser agreed to skip the Egyptian leg of his voyage, on the twin pretexts of the seriousness of the Fashoda Incident,[23] and the need to return home to Germany to open the new Reichstag.[24]

Religious motives for the royal visit

Concrete plans for the royal visit to the Holy Land first emerged with an August 1897 letter from the chair of the High Council of the Protestant Church in Prussia, Friedrich Wilhelm Barkhausen, to Bülow, asking him to inform the Kaiser that the Church of the Redeemer was ready to be officially opened.[25] Upon its announcement, the plan for the Kaiser to open the church during a visit to the Ottoman empire was discussed in a lengthy article in the *Berliner Neueste Nachrichten* that pondered the trip's possible real 'political meaning'. Twelve months before the voyage, the paper speculated that the plans should be read through the lens of anti-French sentiment, as a signal that Germany was asserting its right to protect its own Catholic and Lutheran citizens in Palestine without recourse to the French, who continued to claim a traditional right to represent and protect non-Orthodox Christians in the Holy Land.[26]

This was not welcome news for the French, and the Paris press expressed fears for France's historic primacy in the Holy Land.[27] The Kaiser's trip was portrayed as yet another anti-French foreign policy provocation, directly aimed at diminishing French influence with the Porte and replacing it with German hegemony. *Le Matin* argued forthrightly that the Kaiser's visit 'directly threatens our secular authority in the Christian Levant',[28] while *Le Soleil* expressed concern that Wilhelm II would be given Syrian coastal territory as a colony by the sultan.[29] So worried were the French about the erosion of their influence in the Levant they would send high-ranking officials from the War Ministry and the Foreign Ministry to observe the Kaiser's progress and public pronouncements whilst in the Ottoman empire.[30]

In Russia, which also saw itself as the traditional protector of Christians in the Levant, the concerns over the status quo in the Ottoman empire were similar. The Tsarist organ *Novoye Vremya* even suggested Russo-French cooperation to stifle not just nascent German power in the region but also to mount 'resistance to any no doubt existing secret agreement between Germany, Turkey, and the Vatican'.[31] In London, an even more outlandish report of a German/Vatican conspiracy was published in the *Daily Chronicle*, which cited an ostensibly German source to argue that the Kaiser would leverage his influence over the sultan to 'hand Jerusalem over as a solemn gift to the Pope'.[32]

Somewhat more sober in its analysis of the balance of Christian power in the Levant, *The Times* in London pointed to the effect the voyage might have on the nationalist consciousness of German Catholics if the royal visit saw the Kaiser affirm the rights of the German empire to protect their interests in Palestine without reference to France's historical protectorate rights. With German Catholics having been alienated by the anti-Catholic *Kulturkampf*, which had systematically disadvantaged them since 1872, a strong statement in favour of German Catholic rights in Palestine, the paper reasoned, might assist with the process of encouraging them back into the nationalist fold.[33] This assessment was not too far off the mark. The effects of a royal visit to Jerusalem on German Catholics were certainly being considered by the German Foreign Office, which feared any further alienation of them after the *Kulturkampf*. Accordingly, the very dramaturgy of the royal visit was managed with a close eye to the Orthodox/Catholic contest for control over the sites of worship in Palestine, and careful plans for the Kaiser's visit to the Church of the Nativity in Bethlehem were made. At this site, even deciding which door to use in entering the church would be read as a sign of Germany's attitude towards the competing Orthodox and Latin claims to supremacy there:

> If the entrance through the Franciscan Church of St Catherine is taken, the Orthodox clerics will be thrust into the background, while it is also likely the case that initial entry through the Orthodox-occupied basilica will see the Latins overshadowed. Whether one is to be preferred over the other can only be decided on political grounds, on which it might be advisable to give the Foreign Office the opportunity to offer advice.[34]

With domestic relations with German Catholics in mind, the German Foreign Office advised that in all doubtful situations, Catholic clerics should receive priority over Orthodox ones.[35]

Secular motives for the royal visit

Beyond its religious significance, there were strong concerns that the Kaiser's visit to Palestine would see a disruptive commercial or colonial announcement that would upset the delicate balance between the powers in the Ottoman empire. In August 1898, Germany's ambassador in St Petersburg, Hugo von Radolin, reminded the German Chancellor of Russia's strident position that any major colonial announcement in favour of Germany in Asiatic Turkey would put the Sultan in a difficult position vis-à-vis Russia. Hohenlohe ensured that the Kaiser too received this message.[36] In particular, Radolin pointed to the intransigent stance of Vissarion Komarov's pan-Slavists, who had also warned the Tsar against allowing Germany to seek an outlet to the Persian Gulf, which they argued would 'directly threaten the interior of Russia itself'.[37] Seeking to smooth the waters, the Kaiser wrote directly to the Tsar, in the August 1898 instalment of the Willy/Nicky correspondence, to deny any such political motives and to admonish the press and politicians of Europe for indulging in wild speculation regarding a visit he assured the Tsar was a pious pilgrimage:

> I am most astonished at the amount of bosh and blarney that is being ventilated in the newspapers of Europe about my visit to Jerusalem! It is most discouraging to note that the sentiment of real faith, which propels a Christian to seek the Country in which our Saviour lived and suffered, is nearly quite extinct in the so-called better classes of the XIXth Century, so that they must explain the Pilgrimage forcibly by Political motives.[38]

Despite the Kaiser's protestations of innocence, however, Tsarist sources in Russia remained unmoved, flatly stating that if Germany received territorial concessions from the Sultan, so too should Russia and France.[39]

The idea that the Kaiser was actively seeking a colonial possession in Asiatic Turkey was similarly mooted in the English press. While *The Times* argued that the Russians need not be afraid that he was going to declare himself Lord Paramount of all Asiatic Turkey,[40] the *Daily Chronicle* confidently pronounced that it was all but inevitable that the royal visit would offer the Kaiser the opportunity to assist Germany in reaching imperial parity with the other European powers in the region.[41] In rather more alarmist terms, *The Spectator* insisted that the Kaiser's trip to Jerusalem was a sign of a German plan for complete mastery over Asia Minor and the first step towards attempting to make Constantinople German. This plan, the paper warned, would plunge Europe into a war for Ottoman territory, with Russia and France on one side and Germany on the other.[42] Such alarmist claims were scorned by the *Pall Mall Gazette*, which did not dispute Germany's imperialist intentions, but predicted instead a more subtle, long-term implementation of the Kaiser's ostensibly imperial vision for the region. Wilhelm II's tour, it was argued, was at heart a 'strategic walk', sizing up Ottoman territory for future reference so as to get a sense of the realities and opportunities there.[43] The *Daily News* supported this view, arguing that, although 'there can be little doubt that he has ideas in his mind for the extension of German influence in the East', the Kaiser's aims were far more gradualist than a rushed and dramatic announcement of a Palestinian colony.[44]

Such speculation raises the question of whether there were actually any plans for the Kaiser to further the colonial or commercial penetration of the Ottoman empire. Many recent accounts assume that, even if there was not a plan for wholesale colonisation, then at least vigorous lobbying for a German-controlled Baghdad railway was undertaken, as a Trojan horse for German commercial control of Asia Minor. The British were certainly aware that the project's financier, Georg von Siemens, and the Kaiser would be in the same place at the same time and surmised that this was no accident.[45] But was there marked progress on the Baghdad railway contract as a result of the Kaiser's direct intervention during his visit?

For some historians, such as Klaus Polkehn, it is beyond question that during his voyage, 'Wilhelm II was ... the highest lobbyist for German capital'.[46] According to Polkehn, the Kaiser was indispensable to negotiations, because only summit diplomacy between two monarchs could prevail. The narrative here is a simple one: 'the Kaiser and the Sultan opened the terminal station at Haydarpasha. And the Sultan gave the Baghdad Railway concession to Germany'.[47] For John Röhl, too, 'it was with some justification' that the Kaiser viewed the Baghdad railway as 'My railway!'[48]

Two things are to be said here. First, what Polkehn does not mention is that, while the long-negotiated but relatively minor concession to the Haydarpasha Port was formally granted to the German-financed Anatolian Railway Company upon the occasion of the Kaiser's visit, more than another year of grinding diplomacy was needed before Georg von Siemens' Deutsche Bank (not 'Germany') would be granted a preliminary agreement – and this occurred only after the bank had loaned the Ottoman empire 3.5 million Marks.[49] Second, the idea that the Kaiser was the careful architect of all this is quite false. While the royal visit may have assisted in improving the atmospherics surrounding negotiations, and the Kaiser presided over a short ceremony in Constantinople to award Siemens a minor German honour,[50] it was Ambassador Marschall, Chancellor Hohenlohe and Foreign Secretary Bülow who had been closely coordinating their actions since April 1898 in support of those mounting a bid for the Baghdad railway contract.[51] It was Bülow who met with Siemens during their time in Constantinople; not only was the Kaiser not involved in the negotiations, but when asked point blank by Bülow to intervene on behalf of Siemens, the Kaiser refused, citing strict instructions from the Prussian Finance Minister Johannes von Miquel that he was not to do so.[52] The push for the building of the Baghdad railway was driven by the combined energies of German capital and the Bülow-led Foreign Office, and not by the Kaiser.

Beyond the trade-related infiltration of Asia Minor desired by those hoping to win infrastructure contracts, the German Templer colonists of Palestine also hoped that the Kaiser's voyage to Palestine would add impetus to their own endeavours. The Templers had moved gradually away from their millenarian beginnings as a radical group migrating to the Holy Land in preparation for the Second Coming towards a more recognisable form of settler colonialism,[53] and they welcomed the opportunity to garner royal support for plans to enlarge their Palestinian colonies. Having petitioned the Kaiser for an audience where they could present him with a proposal,[54] they were delighted when a meeting with him was arranged,[55] and expectations in Germany of the Templers' role as a colonial Trojan horse in Palestine were heightened.[56] Upon arriving in Palestine, however, the Kaiser was deliberately evasive about the type of support Germany might offer the Templers. Absolutely no mention of state assistance in expanding the colonies (much less adopting them as German state colonies) was made in his multiple speeches directed towards the Templers.[57] Instead, the Kaiser informed them that, as German citizens, the Templers had the right to expect nothing more than the protection the German state offered all of its citizens abroad. With this, the Pan-German dreams and expectations held for the Templer colonies fell to earth.[58]

It was, however, not merely German imperialists who had sought and expected the Kaiser's intercession with the Sultan to bring about a royally sanctioned protectorate in Palestine. Theodor Herzl, the intellectual leader of Europe's Zionist movement, had also enlisted the assistance of the Kaiser for his plans for a Jewish colony there. Despite the Kaiser's seeming enthusiasm for Zionism, however, he was no more in a position to demand that the Sultan sacrifice Palestine to a consortium of Zionists than he was to demand territory be ceded to Germany's Templers. While in a September 1898 letter Wilhelm II had declared that 'I am convinced that the settlement of the Holy Land through the capital-rich and hard-working nation of Israel will benefit the former quickly with unimaginable blossoming and blessings',[59] this enthusiasm carried absolutely no weight in the real world.

Herzl, however, was greatly encouraged by the seeming seriousness of the Kaiser's commitment to Zionist colonialism, labouring under the misapprehension that the Kaiser enjoyed untrammelled freedom in directing German (and indeed Ottoman) foreign policy. When Herzl met the real representatives of German state power, namely Foreign Secretary Bülow and Chancellor Hohenlohe, however, they made it abundantly clear that they were unimpressed by his colonial plans for Palestine. Having met the two without the Kaiser present on 9 October 1898, Herzl was left to wonder how their attitude could be so 'depressingly cool' when the Kaiser was so positively engaged. In a moment of political clarity, Herzl wondered whether convincing the Kaiser might not be enough to ensure success.[60] Nonetheless, Herzl allowed himself to be misled again by Wilhelm II when he met with him on 18 October, and promised support for a Zionist chartered company under German protection. Again, however, as soon as the Kaiser had left them, Bülow flatly informed Herzl that 'the Turks are currently unfavourably disposed' towards a German-Jewish colony in Palestine.[61]

Bülow was right, and Herzl was deeply disappointed with his 2 November audience with the Kaiser in Jerusalem, where the Kaiser stiffly rebuffed him.[62] The Kaiser's comments to the European press that day were even more depressing for Herzl. Having met the Zionist delegation, the Kaiser said, he would only support endeavours 'that were aimed at improving the agriculture of Palestine so as to maximise the benefit to the Turkish Empire, with full respect for the sovereignty of the Sultan'. Colonial plans of all stripes for Palestine were now off the table. This reversal in the fortunes of his plans for a Jewish colony under German protection, Herzl surmised, was the work of Foreign

Secretary Bülow.[63] This was largely true, but Herzl had been mistaken to assume that the Kaiser held any real responsibility for German foreign policy. Palestine had never been the Kaiser's to offer, as the Sultan had made abundantly clear to the Kaiser.[64]

In direct contrast to the Kaiser's somewhat reckless support for Zionism, he was far more sceptical about Bülow's plan to assist German Catholics in acquiring an (admittedly small) piece of vacant land in Jerusalem, long coveted by the French – a site known as *Dormitio Sanctae Mariae Virginis*, reputed to be the place where the Virgin Mary had lived and died – upon which they could build a chapel.[65] Pushed by Bülow to approach the Sultan as a mediator for the purchase of the vacant land on the behalf of German Catholics, the Kaiser doubtfully agreed, on the proviso that 'the Mohammedans have absolutely nothing against it, otherwise under no circumstances'.[66]

Along with Ambassador Marschall, the Foreign Secretary pushed through his plan to support the German Catholic Association in Jerusalem and to prick French pretensions by showing German Catholics and the Catholic Centre Party in the Reichstag that, unlike the French, the German state could secure their spiritual and material interests in the Holy Land. Marschall asked the Sultan to purchase the land so that it might be then given as a gift to the Kaiser, who in turn would give the land to the German Catholic Association in Jerusalem, much as his father had done in 1869 for Prussian Protestants.[67] Carefully orchestrated by the experts of the Foreign Office rather than through the Kaiser's disastrous style of personal politics that had doomed the Zionist and Templers' bids for territory, the Sultan assented, and on 31 October, the formal transfer of the highly coveted holy site to German Catholics was made in a ceremony attended by the Kaiser and his retinue, the Catholic Patriarch of Jerusalem, the leadership of the German hospice, and German Franciscans, along with a large number of Ottoman officials. Having opened a Protestant church in the Holy Land, thanks to Bülow's plan the Kaiser was also able to offer German Catholics a site in Jerusalem that they too could call their own.

Conclusion

With the Church of the Redeemer formally opened and new sacred ground transferred to the custodianship of German Catholics, royal support for the two main faiths of Germany in the Holy Land had been clearly demonstrated. And yet, far from deepening his Christian faith, the Kaiser left Jerusalem far more impressed with Islam than with the squabbling factions of Christianity he had championed. This was evinced not only in his Damascus proclamation of global friendship for the world's 300 million Muslims – a speech that sent a shiver down the imperial spine of Britain, which ruled over many of those Muslims around the world – but also in his letter to the Tsar from Damascus, in which he professed his preference for the Ottoman empire's Muslims over its Christians and Jews:

> My personal feeling in leaving the Holy City was that I felt profoundly ashamed before the Moslems and that if I had come there without any Religion at all I certainly would have turned Mahommetan! ... I return home with feelings of great disillusion.[68]

Disillusioned with his slight successes, the rest of Europe nonetheless breathed a sigh of relief once the Kaiser returned to Germany.[69] Yet, whether in the case of the plans for the expansion of Jewish or German colonies in the area, the fate of the Berlin-to-Baghdad railway, or the symbolic politics associated with the French and Russian claims to primacy in Jerusalem, the focus on the Kaiser as the locus of German state power was entirely mistaken. As Herzl's Zionists and the Templers learnt, the Kaiser's enthusiasm for a foreign policy outcome was no sure guide to actual German foreign policy. Wilhelm II's trip to the Levant saw him open a Protestant church and accept a small plot of land for a Catholic church in Jerusalem. Despite having convinced eager colonial lobbyists and alarmed European powers that he had the power to establish colonies in Palestine under German protection, the Kaiser was in fact unable to choose for himself which door to use when entering a church without deferring to the Foreign Office.

Notes

1 Thomas Scheffler, 'The Kaiser in Baalbek: Tourism, Archaeology, and the Politics of Imagination', in Hélène Sader, Thomas Scheffler and Angelika Neuwirth (eds), *Baalbek: Image and Monument 1898–1998* (Beirut: Orient-Institut der Deutschen Morgenländischen Gesellschaft, 1998), pp. 15–16.
2 For the details of the itinerary and events of each day of the tour, see Ernst von Mirbach, *Die Reise des Kaisers und der Kaiserin nach Palästina* (Berlin: Ernst Siegfried Mittler und Sohn, 1899).
3 Obituary of James Cook, *Frankfurter Zeitung*, in Geheimes Staatsarchiv Preußischer Kulturbesitz (hereafter GStAPK), BPH Rep113 Nr 1099 Acta betreffend Orient-Reise 1898, pp. 224–225.
4 For the 23 August 1898 order of two tropics uniforms for each participant, see GStAPK BPH Rep 113 Nr 1094 Acta betreffend Orient-Reise 1898, p. 23. For the army's refusal to pay for them and demand that the Kaiser pay for them himself, see BPH Rep 113 Nr 1095 Acta betreffend Orientreise 1898, p. 163.
5 For the strained correspondence between Carl Stangen and the palace, see GStAPK BPH Rep 113 Nr 1099 Acta betreffend Orient-Reise 1898, pp. 84–103. See also Thomas Benner, *Die Strahlen der Krone. Die religiöse Dimension des Kaisertums unter Wilhelm II vor dem Hintergrund der Orientreise 1898* (Marburg: Tectum Verlag, 2001), pp. 234–236.

6 GStAPK BPH Rep 113 Nr 1103 Acta betreffend Orientreise 1898, p. 2. See too GStAPK BPH Rep 113 Nr 1097 Acta betreffend Orient-Reise, Jerusalem 1898, BPH Rep 113 Nr 1095 Acta betreffend Orientreise 1898, BPH Rep 113 Nr 1092 1898 Acta betreffend Orient-Reise 1898.
7 GStAPK BPH Rep 113 Nr 1092 1898 Acta betreffend Orient-Reise 1898, p. 257.
8 *Le Gaulois*, 26 September 1898, Politisches Archiv des Auswärtigen Amts (hereafter PAAA) IA Preussen 1 (Personalia) Nr1 Nr 4v R3730–3 Vol. 5, p. 241; Tischendorf to Eulenburg 19 September 1898, GStAPK BPH Rep 113 Nr 1092 1898 Acta betreffend Orient-Reise 1898, pp. 179–180.
9 Monika Wienfort, 'Dynastic Heritage and Bourgeois Morals: Monarchy and Family in the Nineteenth Century', in F.L. Müller and H. Mehrkens (eds), *Royal Heirs and the Uses of Soft Power in Nineteenth-Century Europe* (London: Palgrave, 2016), p. 164.
10 Rudolf Vierhaus (ed.), *Das Tagebuch der Baronin Spitzemberg* (Göttingen: Vandenhoeck & Ruprecht, 1976), pp. 370–371.
11 Paul Singer, *Verhandlungen des Deutschen Reichstags* (hereafter *VdR*), 22 March 1900, p. 4896.
12 See Klaus Jaschinski, 'Des Kaisers Reise in den Vorderen Orient 1898, ihr historischer Platz und ihre Dimensionen', in Klaus Jaschinski and Julius Waldschinski (eds), *Des Kaisers Reise in den Orient 1898* (Berlin: Trafo Verlag, 2002), p. 19; Sean McMeekin, *The Berlin-Baghdad Express: The Ottoman Empire and Germany's Bid for World Power* (Cambridge, MA: Harvard University Press, 2010), p. 11; Francesco Cerasani, 'Imperialism of Kaiser Wilhelm II: Perspectives and Historiography of German Südpolitik', in Antonello Biagini and Giovanna Motta (eds), *Empires and Nations from the Eighteenth Century to the Twentieth Century*, Vol. 2 (Newcastle: Cambridge Scholars Press, 2014), p. 30. For the Kaiser as a 'strong' monarch, see John Röhl, *Wilhelm II: Into the Abyss of War and Exile 1900–1941* (Cambridge: Cambridge University Press, 2014).
13 Friedrich Scherer, *Adler und Halbmond. Bismarck und der Orient, 1878–1890* (Paderborn: Ferdinand Schöningh, 2001), p. xii.
14 Frank Lorenz Müller, *Our Fritz: Emperor Frederick III and the Political Culture of Imperial Germany* (Cambridge, MA: Harvard University Press, 2011), p. 111.
15 Margaret Lavinia Anderson, 'A Responsibility to Protest? The Public, the Powers and the Armenians in the Era of Abdülhamit II', *Journal of Genocide Research*, 17:3 (2015), 259–283.
16 Benner, *Die Strahlen der Krone*, pp. 159–165; Abdel-Raouf Sinno, 'The Emperor's Visit to the East as Reflected in Contemporary Arabic Journalism', in Sader *et al.*, *Baalbek: Image and Monument 1898–1998*, pp. 115–116. See also 'Berlin and Constantinople', *The Spectator*, 22 October 1898, in PAAA IA Preussen 1 (Personalia) Nr 1 Nr 4v R3732-2 Vol. 7, p. 71; *The Daily Telegraph*, 11 October 1898, PAAA IA – Preussen 1 (Personalia) Nr 1 Nr 4v R 3731–3 Vol. 6, p. 222.
17 See GStAPK BPH Rep 113 Nr 1092 1898 Acta betreffend Orient-Reise 1898, p. 178, Consul in Sinaia to Chancellor Hohenlohe, 5 October 1898, in PAAA IA – Preussen 1 (Personalia) Nr 1 Nr 4v R 3731–2 Vol. 6, p. 108.
18 PAAA IA – Preussen 1 (Personalia) Nr 1 Nr 4v R 3731–3 Vol. 6, p. 193. See also *Pall Mall Gazette*, 6 October 1898, in PAAA IA – Preussen 1 (Personalia) Nr 1 Nr 4v R 3731–2 Vol. 6, p. 137.
19 See Ambassador Marschall to Chancellor Hohenlohe, 13 September 1898, Ambassador Radolin to Hohenlohe, 4 October 1898 (both with the Kaiser's approving margin comments) in Johannes Lepsius, Albrecht Mendelssohn Bartholdy and Friedrich Thimme (eds), *Die Grosse Politik der Europäischen Kabinette 1871–1914*, Vol. 12 (2) (Berlin: Deutsche Verlagsgesellschaft für Politik und Geschichte, 1924), pp. 498–501, 505–507. Kaiser Wilhelm II to Tsar Nicholas II, 20 October 1898, in Isaac Don Levine (ed.), *Letters From the Kaiser to the Czar* (New York: Frederick A Stokes, 1920), pp. 55–59.
20 *The Times*, 16 June 1898, in PAAA R3729-2 Vol. 4 Reise Seiner Majestät des Kaisers nach Athen und Konstantinopel, pp. 167–168.

21 Below to Hohenlohe 27 Aug 1898, in PAAA IA – Preussen I (Personalia) Nr 1 Nr 4v R3730-1 Vol. 5, pp. 70–79; *St Petersburger Zeitung* quoting *Novoye Vremya*, 23.8.1898, in PAAA IA – Preussen I (Personalia) Nr 1 Nr 4v R3730-1 Vol. 5, p. 44.
22 Bernhard von Bülow, *Denkwürdigkeiten*, Vol. I (Berlin: Ullstein Verlag, 1930), p. 242.
23 Kaiser to Marschall, 7 October 1898, in PAAA IA – Preussen 1 (Personalia) Nr 1 Nr 4v R 3731–2 Vol. 6, p. 110.
24 Foreign Office to Ministry of the Interior, 23 September 1898, in PAAA IHA Rep 77 Tit 96 Nr 2 Adh 1 Vol. 1 Orientreise 1898, p. 15; Bülow to the Kaiser, 7 October 1898 IA – Preussen 1 (Personalia) Nr 1 Nr 4v R 3731–1 Vol. 6, pp. 77–82.
25 Barkhausen to Bülow, 27 August 1897 in PAAA R3729–1 Vol. 4 Reise Seiner Majestät des Kaisers nach Athen und Konstantinopel, pp. 37–39.
26 For the German, French and Vatican diplomatic manoeuvring over the French Protectorate, see Lepsius *et al.*, *Die Grosse Politik*, pp. 589–638.
27 Münster to Chancellor Hohenlohe Paris, 10 June 1898 in PAAA R3729–2 Vol. 4 Reise Seiner Majestät des Kaisers nach Athen und Konstantinopel, p. 156; IA – Preussen 1 (Personalia) Nr 1 Nr 4v R 3731–3 Vol. 6, p. 237. See also Benner, *Die Strahlen der Krone*, pp. 189–195.
28 *Le Matin*, 17 October 1898, in PAAA IA – Preussen 1 (Personalia) Nr 1 Nr 4v R 3731–3 Vol. 6, p. 241.
29 Article in *Le Soleil*, 24 August 1898 in PAAA IA – Preussen I (Personalia) Nr 1 Nr 4v R3730-1 Vol. 5, p. 75.
30 Eulenberg to Bülow 11 October 1898 in PAAA IA – Preussen 1 (Personalia) Nr 1 Nr 4v R 3731–2 Vol. 6, p. 184.
31 *St Petersburger Zeitung* 5 July 1898 reporting on *Novoye Vremya* in PAAA R3729–2 Vol. 4 Reise Seiner Majestät des Kaisers nach Athen und Konstantinopel, p. 181.
32 *The Daily Chronicle*, 6 October 1898, in PAAA IA – Preussen 1 (Personalia) Nr 1 Nr 4v R 3731–2 Vol. 6, p. 135.
33 *The Times*, 8 October 1898, in PAAA IA – Preussen 1 (Personalia) Nr 1 Nr 4v R 3731–2 Vol. 6, pp. 148–149.
34 Barkhausen to Eulenburg, 20 September 1898, GStAPK BPH Rep 113 Nr 1092 1898 Acta betreffend Orient-Reise 1898, pp. 164–165.
35 Auswärtiges Amt (Derenthal) to Eulenburg 28 September 1898, in GStAPK BPH Rep 113 Nr 1092 1898 Acta betreffend Orient-Reise 1898, p. 207.
36 Radolin in St Petersburg to Hohenlohe 27 August 1898, IA – Preussen I (Personalia) Nr 1 Nr 4v R3730-1 Vol. 5, p. 91.
37 Radolin in St Petersburg to Chancellor Hohenlohe 1 Juli 1898 in PAAA R3729–2 Vol. 4 Reise Seiner Majestät des Kaisers nach Athen und Konstantinopel, p. 173.
38 Kaiser to Tsar 18 August 1898, in Isaac Don Levine (ed.), *Letters From the Kaiser to the Czar* (New York: Frederick A. Stokes, 1920), p. 53.
39 *St Petersburger Zeitung*, 20 October 1898 IA Preussen 1 (Personalia) Nr 1 Nr 4v R3732-2 Vol. 7, p. 99.
40 *The Times*, 8 October 1898, in PAAA IA – Preussen 1 (Personalia) Nr 1 Nr 4v R 3731–2 Vol. 6, pp. 148–149.
41 *Daily Chronicle*, 13 October 1898, PAAA IA – Preussen 1 (Personalia) Nr 1 Nr 4v R 3731–3 Vol. 6, p. 228.
42 *The Spectator*, 20 August 1898, clipped in Hatzfeldt to Foreign Office 21 August 1898 in PAAA IA – Preussen I (Personalia) Nr 1 Nr 4v R3730-1 Vol. 5, pp. 45–55. See also *The Spectator*, 22 October 1898, PAAA IA Preussen 1 (Personalia) Nr 1 Nr 4v R3732-2 Vol. 7, p. 71.
43 *Pall Mall Gazette*, 18 August 1898, in PAAA IA – Preussen I (Personalia) Nr 1 Nr 4v R3730-1 Vol. 5, pp. 53–54.
44 *The Daily News*, 8 October 1898, in PAAA IA – Preussen 1 (Personalia) Nr 1 Nr 4v R 3731–2 Vol. 6, p. 153.
45 *National-Zeitung*, 20 October 1898, in PAAA IA – Preussen 1 (Personalia) Nr 1 Nr 4v R 3731–3 Vol. 6, p. 269.
46 Klaus Polkehn, 'Wilhelm II in Konstaninopel. Der politische Startschuß zum Bau der Bagdadbahn', in Jaschinski and Waldschmidt, *Des Kaisers Reise in den Orient 1898*, p. 62.

47 *Ibid.*, p. 70. For a useful corrective to this, see Florian Krobb, '"Welch unbebautes und riesengroßes Feld": Turkey as Colonial Space in German World War I Writings', *German Studies Review*, 37:1 (2014), 1–18.
48 Röhl, *Wilhelm II*, p. 73.
49 Murat Özyüksel, *The Hejaz Railway and the Ottoman Empire: Modernity, Industrialisation and Ottoman Decline* (London: I.B. Tauris, 2014), pp. 23–24.
50 PAAA IA – Preussen I (Personalia) Nr 1 Nr 4v R3732-1 Vol. 7, p. 18.
51 Jonathon McMurray, *Distant Ties: Germany, the Ottoman Empire, and the Construction of the Baghdad Railway* (Westport: Praeger, 2001), pp. 30–31.
52 Karl Helfferich, *Georg von Siemens. Ein Lebensbild aus Deutschlands großer Zeit*, Vol. 3 (Berlin: Springer, 1923), pp. 87–88; Bernhard von Bülow, *Denkwürdigkeiten*, Vol. 1, p. 253.
53 Matthew P. Fitzpatrick and Felicity Jensz, 'Between Heaven and Earth: The German Templer Colonies in Palestine', in Andrekos Varnava (ed.), *Imperial Expectations and Realities: El Dorados, Utopias and Dystopias* (Manchester: Manchester University Press, 2015), pp. 144–165.
54 Letter to Kaiser's Ober-Hofmarshallamt from Chr Hoffmann, Vorsteher der Templegemeinde Jerusalem July 1898, in GStAPK BPH Rep113 Nr 1098. Acta betreffend Orient-Reise Jerusalem, 1898, p. 102. See also Alex Carmel and Ejal Jakob Eisler, *Der Kaiser reist ins Heilige Land: Die Palästinareise Wilhelms II. 1898* (Stuttgart: Kohlhammer, 1999), p. 52.
55 Reply from Wilhelmshohe 7 August 1898, in GStAPK BPH Rep113 Nr 1098. Acta betreffend Orient-Reise Jerusalem, 1898, p. 103.
56 See, for example, *National Zeitung*, 3 July 1898.
57 'Die Kaisertage in Palästina', *Die Warte*, 1 December 1898, in Alex Carmel, *Palästina-Chronik 1883–1914. Deutsche Zeitungsberichte von der ersten jüdischen Einwanderungswelle bis zum Ersten Weltkrieg* (Langenau-Ulm: Armin Vaas, 1983), pp. 206–208; 'Die Kaisertage in Palästina (Fortsetzung II)', *Die Warte*, 8 December 1898, in Carmel, *Palästina-Chronik 1883–1914*, pp. 213–214.
58 *Norddeutsche Allgemeine Zeitung*, 3 November 1898; also reproduced in the Templer periodical, *Die Warte*, see: 'Die Kaisertage in Palästina (Fortsetzung II)', *Die Warte*, 8 December 1898, in Carmel, *Palästina-Chronik 1883–1914*, pp. 213–214.
59 Kaiser, 29 September 1898, as cited in Benner, *Die Strahlen der Krone*, p. 219.
60 Theodor Herzl, *Tagebücher*, Vol. II (Berlin: Jüdischer Verlag, 1923), pp. 160–164. See also Benner, *Die Strahlen der Krone*, pp. 224–225.
61 Herzl, *Tagebücher*, Vol. II, pp. 183–199.
62 *Ibid.*, pp. 222–226.
63 *Ibid.*, pp. 237–238. See also Anon., *Das deutsche Kaiserpaar im heiligen Lande im Herbst 1898* (Berlin: Ernst Siegfried Mittler und Sohn, 1899), pp. 287–288.
64 John Röhl, *Wilhelm II. Der Aufbau der persönlichen Monarchie 1888–1900* (Munich: Beck Verlag, 2001), p. 1057.
65 Naci Yorulmaz, *Arming the Sultan: German Arms Trade and Personal Diplomacy in the Ottoman Empire Before World War I* (London: I.B. Tauris, 2014), pp. 135–137.
66 Benner, *Die Strahlen der Krone*, p. 200.
67 Anon., *Das deutsche Kaiserpaar im Heiligen Lande*, pp. 261–262. For Bülow and Marschall's careful management of the issue of German Catholics in Palestine in the interests of German foreign policy, see Benner, *Die Strahlen der Krone*, pp. 190–205.
68 Kaiser to Tsar, 9 November 1898 in Levine, *Letters From the Kaiser to the Czar*, p. 61.
69 See, for example, Ambassador Marshall's admission that 'the Palestine voyage has been exceptionally uncomfortable for Russia'. Marschall to Holstein, 30 December 1898, in N. Rich and M.H. Fisher (eds), *Die Geheime Papiere Friedrich von Holsteins, IV: Briefwechsel* (Göttingen: Musterschmidt Verlag, 1963), p. 91.

CHAPTER EIGHT

Colonial kings in the metropole: the visits to France of King Sisowath (1906) and Emperor Khai Dinh (1922)

Robert Aldrich

Reigning European monarchs and more junior royals were regular visitors to France in the early decades of the twentieth century. Non-European royals, however, were less frequently seen because of the distance their travels entailed, cultural prohibitions on monarchs leaving 'forbidden cities' or parlous relations between France and their realms. The visit to Europe of King Chulalongkorn (Rama V) in 1897 was the first by a reigning monarch from the Far East.[1] Politicians, the press and the public flocked to see the King of Siam, the *paparazzi* following his every move, and the politicians discussing the international relations of one of the few Asian countries to escape European colonisation. The king's visit was particularly delicate because of recent armed clashes between the Siamese and the French in Southeast Asia and because of the ambition of some to make Siam a French colony or protectorate. The visit was important for the Siamese king in ensuring that this did not happen, and in portraying himself as a strong, competent and modernising monarch able to hold his own with royal peers in Europe as well as republicans in France.[2]

Chulalongkorn returned to Europe for a second tour in 1907 and other Asian, African and Middle Eastern royals came to Paris as well. They still remained less common than the many European monarchs who journeyed to France for official or private visits, to winter on the Côte d'Azur, take the waters at spa towns or enjoy the pleasures of Paris.[3] This chapter examines tours by two Southeast Asian monarchs: King Sisowath of Cambodia in 1906, and Emperor Khai Dinh of Annam in 1922. Unlike the Siamese king, they were monarchs of countries that had been taken over as French protectorates in the late 1800s; though nominally sovereigns of independent kingdoms in international law, they came in fact as vassals of the French colonial state. Welcoming them with the pageantry and deference due to royal heads of state, French authorities were nevertheless determined to affirm colonial paramountcy over their domains. The visitors from the East obligingly pledged loyalty to France, and the public was treated to the spectacle of Oriental potentates and their colourful entourages. Both visited at the times of *expositions coloniales* in Marseille, two in a series of grand displays of the empire designed to show off the might of France and the commercial and cultural wealth of its empire.[4] Such fairs often included groups of native people brought in for the occasion, performing 'traditional' activities in reconstructed settings. In a sense, the royals, too, were displays of France's imperium in Indochina.

France claimed an extensive empire in Southeast Asia, acquired from the end of the 1850s until the mid-1890s. Determined to establish a foothold in the region for commercial and geopolitical purposes, the French gradually secured control of what is today Vietnam. They first forced the emperor of Annam, who ruled from Hué, to cede the southern region of his kingdom, around Saigon, which they turned into the fully-fledged colony of Cochinchina. Then they made central Vietnam, or Annam, into a protectorate though leaving the emperor on the throne in Hué; Tonkin, or northern Vietnam, centred on Hanoi, technically also became a protectorate (except for Hanoi itself and the port of Haiphong, which were placed under full French control), but effectively came under French administration. In 1863, the French had also proclaimed a protectorate over Cambodia, leaving in power the king as ruler in the capital of Phnom Penh. In the 1890s, the colonisers acquired a set of polities that they moulded into the protectorate of Laos, eventually promoting the ruler of Luang Prabang to be its king. The five territories were administered, under the authority of a governor-general in Hanoi, as Indochine Française, and remained under French overlordship until the early 1950s. Production of rice, coal and eventually rubber made Vietnam one of the most profitable of French possessions, Cambodia provided the mystique of the Angkorian ruins, and Laos remained a quiet backwater of the empire.[5]

Kingship differed in Annam and Cambodia.[6] Confucian principles provided the foundation for the monarchy of Annam, which owed much to imperial China; indeed, before the arrival of the French, the emperor of Annam received his seal of office from the Chinese emperor.[7] The emperor resided in a 'forbidden city' within a citadel along the banks of the Perfume River in Hué, and elaborate and punctilious ceremonial marked the life of the court. The prime duty of the emperor, who seldom emerged from the citadel, was performance of the rites in honour of gods and ancestors considered crucial to the well-being of his people. Mandarins, selected by rigorous examinations on the Confucian classics in the manner of the Chinese, served as administrators and tax collectors.[8] In largely Buddhist Cambodia, the king was the *devaraja*, a semi-divine figure whose duties were both religious and secular, and whose power, in principle, was absolute. Members of the royal family and the Buddhist clergy played key roles in national life.[9] In neither Vietnam nor Cambodia was succession to the throne governed by primogeniture, and the practice of taking multiple wives and concubines meant continuing struggles for power among potential heirs, alongside intense intrigues among mandarins, courtiers and, after the institution of the protectorates, the French colonisers.

The French objective was to ensure that docile rulers occupied the thrones and confined themselves to sacerdotal and cultural duties, leaving real authority with the French proconsuls, the Résidents Supérieurs, in Hué and Phnom Penh and their superiors in Hanoi and Paris. This did not always prove easy because of the competition for succession to the thrones and, in Vietnam, persistent resistance against the foreign occupiers. A revolt against the French in Vietnam in 1885, in which the youthful emperor was implicated, led to the deposition of the ruler and his exile to Algeria, and the French subsequently dethroned and banished (to Réunion Island in the Indian Ocean) two other emperors, one in 1907 on the basis of what they considered his madness, the other in 1916 following a further revolt.[10] The French steadily whittled away the prerogatives and powers of the emperor, making him, for many critics – both contemporary nationalists and later historians – into little more than a puppet by the time of Khai Dinh, who reigned from 1916 to 1925. With Khai Dinh, colonial authorities hoped, however, that they had finally found a Francophile emperor who would not only remain loyal but who would serve as an active collaborator in their projects; to French disappointment, his reign was cut short by ill health.[11] Somewhat paradoxically, the French had tended to strengthen the powers of the Cambodian king, at least by buttressing his status and ceremonial role, especially since they found King Sisowath, who ruled from 1904 to 1927, to be accommodating and widely respected.

The French rewarded fealty on the part of their feudatories, and a visit to France counted as one of the greatest acknowledgements of loyalty. Both Sisowath and the reigning Vietnamese emperor in 1900, Thanh Thai, had expressed a desire to visit Paris in that year for the *exposition universelle*, but the tours did not eventuate. Sisowath demurred on the grounds of poor health, and the French decided that it would be imprudent for the Vietnamese ruler – probably because of the unbalanced mental state that would later see his ouster – to travel to Europe. A senior Cambodian prince did visit Paris for the exposition in 1900, though Prince Yukanthor issued a strong condemnation of French colonial rule in Cambodia; he then fled to Brussels and spent the rest of his life in exile.[12] Yukanthor's actions provided a warning about the dangers to colonisers of overseas travel by native royals and a reminder of the potential influence subject dynasties might still exercise. In 1906, coinciding with a colonial exposition in Marseille, they nonetheless organised a tour for King Sisowath.[13] A Vietnamese monarch was brought to Paris only sixteen years after the Cambodian's visit.[14] Neither, however, travelled to European countries other than France, in marked contrast to the peregrinations of the Siamese king and the crown prince of Japan during their European sojourns.

Asian kings in the colonial metropole

The European tours offered recognition for the loyalty of Sisowath and Khai Dinh, but also provided opportunities for them to familiarise themselves with France, meet its leaders, witness its political and military power and make pilgrimages to its cultural sites. The tours showed off to the French people and to an international audience the nominally sovereign rulers of France's protectorates, while popularising Asian culture within France and garnering support (never unanimously enthusiastic) for France's colonial enterprise. The visitors, it was hoped, would depart with enduring impressions of the grandeur of France, and the beneficence of French overrule in their realms.

Tours, in addition to being major political events, represented complex logistical operations, demanding careful planning, punctilious adherence to protocol and considerable expense. Most of the documents in the French colonial archives about the king's and emperor's visits indeed pertain to the minutiae of the tours. Lodgings had to be arranged for the royal parties, generally stately residences for which furnishing had to be rented from the 'Mobilier national', the French national furniture collection. One list of the furnishings procured for Sisowath's temporary residence in Paris runs to fourteen pages, with thirty items per page. Folders also contain bills from private suppliers for such articles as a washbasin, shower and mattress. Expenditures for a banquet held in the Bois de Vincennes for Khai Dinh included improvements to the garden, renovation of the pavilion where eighty guests were seated, the food itself, flowers and other table decorations, and the clean-up after the event; clearly concerned about the cost, an administrator has neatly crossed through the original outlays on the budget to indicate reduced allocations. Food, not surprisingly, was a major concern, and for the Cambodians, the French decided that the king and senior members of his family, as well as the visiting ministers and mandarins, would be served French cuisine, while the women and servants in his entourage would have Cambodian fare. Bureaucrats also had to book passage on French steamships from Asia to Europe – for Sisowath's visit twenty-three 'hors classe' prestige cabins, plus fifteen first-class, forty-three second-class and sixty third-class cabins. Once arrived in France, trains had to be provided with suitably regal carriages for the conveyance of visitors from Marseille to Paris and back, and there was local transport around the city and excursions to the provinces. Another matter was the provision of ceremonial guards and mounted escorts, and the question of appropriate military salutes, always calculated to reflect the precise rank of a visitor. Timetables were formulated for a series of busy engagements, including the customary if brief courtesy calls on senior officials and the rather tedious leaving of visiting-cards at the residences of other important administrators, as well as receptions and tourist visits, not forgetting free time for the royals to rest and do their shopping. The organisers also considered requests from private persons who wished to solicit favours or patronage from the visitors or advertise their wares. Before Sisowath's arrival, the authorities received petitions from several who claimed an interest in Cambodia, a proposal from the Aéro-Club de France to demonstrate hot-air balloons (which was declined), an invitation from the Théâtre Sarah Bernhardt to a performance (which was accepted), and a memo from the Baccarat crystal firm hoping that the Cambodian king would honour their showrooms with a visit, as had an earlier visiting Persian shah. Officials planning the tours in 1906 took their cue from the precedents followed on the visit to Paris in 1904 of the bey of Tunis, another ruler of a French protectorate, and they reviewed arrangements for the shah in 1900 and a Bulgarian prince in 1905.[15]

Arrival of the royals in France began with the docking of the ships in Marseille and ceremonial greetings by national, colonial and local officials. Both the Cambodians and the Vietnamese proceeded by rail to Paris for meetings and dinners at the presidential palace and ministries, many other receptions, visits to such tourist sites as the Eiffel Tower, excursions to the provinces, displays of French military might (an unsubtle reminder of who was really in charge in the colonies), and recreation and shopping. Other visits seemed tailored to the perceived interests of the visitors, such as a stop at the École Coloniale (originally established for Cambodian students) for Sisowath, and at the library of the Société de Géographie and at Vietnamese student hostels for Khai Dinh.[16] Both Sisowath and Khai Dinh also dutifully visited the colonial exhibitions in Marseille.

Cambodia attracted attention at the fairs and during the royal visit not only for its archaeological wonders, but also its dancers. Dances with intricate choreography and graceful hand movements by young women arrayed in colourful silk costumes represented an esteemed art form practised in the Khmer royal court, imbued with great symbolic and spiritual significance. King Sisowath came to France accompanied by several dozen Khmer dancers and musicians, and their performances in Marseille and Paris enchanted spectators with their beauty and gentle sensuality. Auguste Rodin, confessing that 'I contemplated them with ecstasy', was so taken after a show in Paris that he spent days making sketches of the nubile young women, and he spontaneously followed the troupe back to Marseille so he could continue drawing them.[17]

The Cambodian king made predictable speeches (in Khmer) acknowledging his welcome and thanking his hosts for the 'protection' accorded Cambodia, but in a faux pas at a banquet, he ventured to make not only political comments but incendiary ones. He called for France to 'give me back my Alsace-Lorraine', a pointed but well-chosen comparison between the two frontier provinces annexed by Germany after its defeat of France in the war of 1870–1871 and the provinces of Battambang and Siem Reap that had been taken by the Siamese. He also called for France to join him in declaring war on Britain for alleged designs on border regions of Cambodia. The band hurriedly struck up the 'Marseillaise' after the translation of his words.[18] (Diplomats presumably smoothed any ruffled British feelings, and in 1907 they indeed engineered the return of the 'lost provinces' from Siam to Cambodia, a move that managed not to derail King Chulalongkorn's second trip to France.[19]) Other than that contretemps, Sisowath's comments were warm, banal and well received.

If Sisowath's tour, and the charming Khmer dancers, seemed to fit perfectly into the ambience of Belle Époque Paris, Emperor Khai Dinh travelled to France in the wake of the First World War. He proved carefully discreet, making only the blandest and most fervently loyal public remarks. Khai Dinh lauded French business at a reception at the chamber of commerce in Marseille, and praised the 'great idea' that France represented at the city hall in Paris. Only once did he broach more overtly political issues, when he commented that since the war 'a certain movement of ideas has been produced' – a veiled reference, no doubt, to Wilsonian ideas of self-determination, budding nationalism and Bolshevism – and he followed that statement with a proclamation that 'I, and my people with me, firmly count on France, the great protecting power, to maintain order in my country. Not that I formulate this wish in a dynastic interest, but in the interest of my people, of the peace to which we are firmly attached, and in the interest even of the France that we love'.[20] The comment was undoubtedly music to French ears.

The French had recruited Vietnamese as soldiers for the European theatre (the recruitment campaigns not without a connection to the 1916 revolt) and as labourers in munitions factories and other wartime industries in the metropole. To memorialise the Vietnamese deaths in the war, a traditional Vietnamese communal house, or *dinh*, faced by an elaborate decorated screen and massive incense urn, had been erected on the grounds of the Jardin Botanique Colonial in the Bois de Vincennes.[21] There was also a French-style stele in honour of Christian soldiers '*morts pour la France*'. A rescript from the emperor of Annam had been placed in the *dinh*, and in 1922, two of the visiting emperor's most important engagements were to visit the memorial site and to lay a wreath at the Tomb of the Unknown Soldier under the Arc de Triomphe. Accompanied by his young son (the future, and last, emperor of Vietnam, Bao Dai) and a bevy of military brass and colonial officials, Khai Dinh paid his respects to the French and Vietnamese soldiers who had fallen in the Great War, his gestures hailed as signs of the firm fealty of the colonised Indochinese comrades-in-arms.

8.1 'Visite de Khaï-Dinh', antique postcard of visit of Emperor Khai Dinh to Paris, 1922

Reactions to the Asian royal tours

Sisowath's and Khai Dinh's tours were widely covered in French newspapers at a time when the pageantry and celebrity of monarchy evoked enormous public fascination and provided many column inches for the large number of periodicals published in France. (The visit also attracted interest from *littérateurs* and even composers.[22]) Coverage was generally favourable, though hardly devoid of stereotypical and racially inflected comments about the Asian monarchs and their countries, and occasional depreciation of their status. Sisowath was particularly popular, and his donation of 5,000 gold francs, just before he set out for France, for relief of families of a thousand people killed in a mine disaster in France, was much applauded. Khai Dinh attracted the attention of writers and photographers who underlined the brave wartime service of the Vietnamese. Press reports and images served as information and propaganda for empire, and also provided a chance for ordinary French people to participate vicariously in the glamour and exoticism of the Cambodian and Vietnamese tours.

Illustrated periodicals featured many images of the royal visits, complemented by pictures of the rulers at home that showed them in regal and informal activities – Khai Dinh on his throne, alighting from a palanquin to visit the Résident Supérieur in Hué, going for a fishing trip. A full page of pictures in one issue of *Le Monde illustré* showed the emperor in Paris in his carriage, at the Arc de Triomphe, at the Longchamp races and at the Jardin Botanique Colonial. The front page of *Le Petit Journal*, which claimed the highest circulation of any French newspaper, was a full-page sketch of some notable event of the week, generally rendered in colour and with a rather sensationalistic tone. (Crime provided regular subjects for cover images.) *Le Petit Journal* dedicated three covers to King Sisowath's visit. The first showed the Khmer dancers and musicians performing at the colonial fair in Marseille, an Angkorian-style tower in the background and King Sisowath in the audience. A week later, the cover again showed the king, this time riding in a horse-drawn carriage escorted by the helmeted soldiers of the Garde Républicaine, in front of the Paris Opera; elegantly gowned women and men doffing their hats crowd the footpath, with the king raising his top-hat to acknowledge the spectators. Finally, and somewhat curiously, a third cover shows a performance at the open-air theatre, the Pré-Catalan, in the Bois de Boulogne, though the dancers are French men and women in eighteenth-century dress and powdered wigs swirling in a quadrille, the Cambodians almost invisible in the audience – a presumably intentional mirror to the earlier illustration of the Khmer dancers in Marseille.[23]

France's conservative newspaper of record, *Le Figaro*, published some seventy articles (though many only brief descriptive notes) about Sisowath's 1906 tour. The paper offered relatively little editorialising, though even before Sisowath set foot on French soil, it reassured readers that 'we certainly have no reason to doubt his loyalty, and even less to fear that he harbours hopes of absolute independence'. It hoped that he would leave with 'a good memory, a durable and useful impression for the future and for our interests and his own'. The paper followed the king's activities closely, and when he had himself measured for a French uniform noted that he wanted to don such apparel 'thus to indicate to his subjects how much he is proud of feeling himself under our protection'. A critical comment on his opium-smoking was one of the few negative statements. The paper defended the cost of the tour, paid out of the protectorate budget, and celebrated the dancers.[24] (Jean Jaurès' socialist *L'Humanité* reported on the visit as well, though devoting more attention to the Khmer dancers than the king.) *Le Figaro* in 1922 similarly reported the visit of Khai Dinh – 'representative of one of the oldest and most illustrious races in the world, the living sign of a thousand-year old tradition' – and interpreted this first-ever overseas tour by a Vietnamese emperor as a unique gesture of respect for France. Human interest anecdotes filled out reports, such as the emperor's poetry-writing and supposed interest in football. It congratulated the emperor on deciding to leave his young son Bao Dai in France for his education, and it quoted his platitudes about the greatness and beneficence of France. Such coverage paralleled the words and images presented in the popular press and the illustrated periodicals.

The most extraordinary representation of Sisowath's tour appeared in *L'Assiette au beurre*, a satirical magazine that devoted an entire sixteen-page issue to caricatures of the king's visit by Tomás Leal de Camâra, a republican Portuguese artist born in India.[25] Viewed today, many are racist (with Sisowath in one instance portrayed as a chimpanzee), though the leftist journal was equally unbridled in lampooning European figures. The front cover picture shows Sisowath, barefooted but wearing a frockcoat and medals, sitting atop a very large elephant, below which is a far smaller French president sitting atop a Gallic rooster. However, the drawing on the rear cover neatly inverts the image; this time, a tiny Sisowath kneels before a huge and rather menacing elephant, which is caparisoned with a revolutionary Phrygian cap and the sash of the Legion of Honour; he says: 'Now I understand why Cambodians should love France.'

Several cartoons in the issue wittily send up both the Cambodians and the French. On being presented to the portly and bearded French

8.2 'Sisowath à Paris', caricature of King Sisowath of Cambodia in Paris, cover of *L'Assiette au beurre*, 30 June 1906

president, the newly elected Armand Fallières, the king is told, 'Sire, this is our Sisowath'. In an Élysée drawing-room, Fallières offers: 'I will introduce you to Madame la Présidente'; to which Sisowath politely responds, 'I will be very happy indeed, Monsieur le Président, to make the acquaintance of your favourite' – a sly reference to the large number of wives and concubines in the Cambodian's court. Receiving the Cambodian, the grandly moustachioed Colonial Minister, Georges Leygues, stands in front of a cohort of rather androgynous Cambodian dancers: 'But no, Sire, don't surprise us with your dancers. The true Parisian has as many as you ...', a playful comment, most likely, on the popularity of can-can dancers and on the Lothario reputation of French men. A reference to dancers appears in another cartoon with a more political cast. An obese, cigarette-smoking French president sits in a salon, one arm around a veiled Tunisian woman, the other around a bare-breasted Algerian dancer, as Tonkinese, Cambodian, Congolese and Malagasy women lounge on the sidelines: 'Me, too, I have dancers – they are my fine colonies.'

Politics pointedly shows up in Leal de Camâra's other illustrations. Sisowath is shown chatting with the socialist leader Jules Guede, who says: 'Yes, Citizen Sisowath, your happiness depends on that of France, and France will only be happy in four years, when the radical socialists, the unified collectivists, the internationalists and the antimilitarists will be in power – all patriotic but never nationalist', to which a puzzled king replies, in English, 'What is it?' In a sketch of a diplomatic reception, the Japanese minister to France remarks: 'Cambodia! Just another backwater (*patelin*) that will come to Japan by the Force ... [*sic*] of our Diplomacy'.

In yet another, a bemused Sisowath looks at an overweight priest kneeling before a crucifix (with a sword hanging beside it): 'If that's civilisation, I would just as much remain a savage!' 'L'Idole' is the title of a cartoon of a plutocrat with bursting bags of coins: 'Rockefeller (king of gold and oil) – "Don't think, Sire, that only Orientals are idolatrous; we are, too, and our idol is MONEY"'.

A unique and very different commentary on Sisowath's visit comes from an account written by his Minister of the Palace (effectively, prime minister), Okna Veang Thiounn, who accompanied the king to France. A volume of two hundred pages (though inexplicably it does not cover the last two weeks of the tour), the memoir was seemingly written with a view to being circulated in Cambodia.[26] It opens with Sisowath's proclamation about his forthcoming voyage 'so that His Majesty may know, in order to imitate them, the virtues of the great government in Paris, so that the bridge of friendship between

Cambodia and France may be solidly reinforced, and so that the French government will continue in its intention to aid the Khmer monarch and people to develop magnificently in all ways'. The remainder is chronological and factual, with Thiounn only occasionally allowing a personal aside or detailed opinions about conditions in France or Franco-Cambodian relations. It reads as a travelogue, the first half recording the voyage from Cambodia through Vietnam, Singapore and Ceylon, across the Indian Ocean, via the Suez Canal and on to France. There are, however, some random editorial comments: Thiounn characterises Singaporean merchants as rapacious, finds the Ceylonese landscape beautiful, and notes that inhabitants of the Horn of Africa are or were cannibals. Parts of the French section read as a tour guide, perhaps intended for future Cambodian visitors, with lists of hotels (giving addresses and room prices), restaurants, shops and their specialities. There are indeed endless lists: of those who accompanied the monarch and those whom he met, the dimensions of ships and distances crossed, the clothing the king wore. Details are given of each reception and meeting, and the perfunctory and predictable chitchat in which the king engaged. The volume also records gifts the king presented to French officials, such as silver or gold boxes, cigarette trays or pieces of jewellery.

There is much of interest in Thiounn's work, apart from the chronicle of the king's tour. Readers notice passing mention of aspects of French life that appeared different to the Cambodians: the paved roads and windows with glass panes, the new motorised transport and mechanical lifts, the French habit of embracing each other in greeting. When he speaks about the Christian religion, Thiounn carefully notes whether the ministers of each denomination were allowed to marry. Institutions such as banks – to which the minister was dispatched to withdraw cash for the king – were almost unknown in Cambodia, and thus inspire descriptions. Thiounn was clearly on the lookout for institutions and practices that might be adopted in his homeland; he found, for example, that the work of philanthropic societies might be advantageously introduced into the kingdom. Thiounn's respect for his king is manifest, and he notes that the French also turned out in gratifyingly large numbers to cheer the monarch. (He adds that there were also pleas for help, as well, from indigent people, who assumed that the visiting royal, hailed for his donation to the mine disaster victims, was wealthy and munificent.) He portrays the visit as apolitical and uncontentious, omitting any reference to the contretemps occasioned by Sisowath's banquet comments, and concludes that it was a triumph for the king that boded well for Franco-Cambodian relations in general.

COLONIAL KINGS IN THE METROPOLE

It is difficult to know exactly what the Cambodian king and the Vietnamese emperor thought about their experiences in France. Sisowath, often beamingly jovial in photographs, appears to have enjoyed himself a great deal (though it is unknown whether the caricatures that appeared in *L'Assiette au beurre* discomfited him). He seems relaxed in both Cambodian and European clothing, or sometimes a combination of the two, usually sporting a derby hat topped with a diamond-studded finial – Thiounn remarked that the French spectators preferred seeing him in 'native' costume. He generously handed out medals to those who provided services, including the director of the Grands Magasins du Louvre, where he shopped; he enquired at the Sèvres porcelain factory about having a monogrammed dinner service produced, and he bought souvenirs at the shop at the Eiffel Tower. He threw bread to animals at the zoo, and poked at some with his cane; the royal party had a good laugh when a Cambodian elephant sprayed a young prince with water. He enjoyed listening to gramophone records and seeing a new-fangled film after a dinner at the Élysée Palace, and he sat in the courtyard of his residence in Paris when military bands came to serenade the royals. He won one bet, but lost another, at the races in Argenteuil. He had an excursion to Fontainebleau (whose chateau Thiounn remarked could only be compared with Angkor Wat) and, while in Marseille, to the Provençal countryside. Sisowath had such fun at a circus one evening that he returned the following night with his daughter; according to Thiounn's account, jugglers in Marseille delighted the ruler's young children and the dancers. He even requested that his stay in France be prolonged, though the French were not amenable to the suggestion. Sisowath nevertheless delayed the departure of his ship in Marseille for several hours in order to take a last jaunt around the city.

Khai Dinh's sentiments are less easy to discern; in photographs, always dressed in a Vietnamese silk gown and turban and never in Western clothing, he looks impassive. He does seem to have enjoyed visits to the Arc de Triomphe, the Longchamp racecourse, the colonial botanical garden and the presidential retreat at Rambouillet. He had an outing to the countryside for several days of rest at the Renaissance chateau of the Duc de Valençay, in the company of the colonial minister and a bevy of French aristocrats. (With memories of his dethroned predecessors in mind, Khai Dinh may have learned that the chateau had served for the detention for King Ferdinand VII after his deposition following Napoleon's invasion of Spain). He was reported to appreciate French food to the extent that the bags of rice he had brought along remained unopened.

Khai Dinh's reserve may have been in keeping with his notions of imperial gravitas, but it could also reflect his knowledge of the criticism he and his tour had provoked from Vietnamese nationalists. By the 1920s, several strands of Vietnamese nationalism, both monarchist and anti-monarchist, had gained currency at home and abroad. Among more radical writers, opposition to the throne as a symbol of pre-colonial feudalism and colonial subjection had emerged. Phan Chau Trinh, one of the most articulate of Vietnamese nationalists, was living in exile in France at the time of Khai Dinh's visit.[27] Phan composed a long open letter (eleven pages in an English translation) and had it delivered to Khai Dinh in Marseille. The emperor, rather than the French, was his primary target, as Phan believed that the tenets of the French Revolution, constitutionalism and parliamentarianism provided strategic bases for the regeneration of Vietnam. He charged that the emperor had sustained and entrenched a 'barbaric autocratic monarchy': 'During the last eighty years, the emperors ... have been despotic, the ministers below deceitful, the laws severe, the punishments ruthless.' Quoting from Confucius and Mencius, he lambasted recent emperors for failing to rule according to hallowed principles. He castigated the emperor for expecting Vietnamese to perform the anachronistic and humiliating practice of prostration before the monarch, even in France, and for even arranging for a statue of kowtowing mandarins and courtiers to feature at the centre of the Vietnamese pavilion at the Marseille colonial exhibition. Phan spoke of the emperor's 'reckless extravagance', including great consumption of champagne during his trip, and the wearing of ostentatious gowns with heavy brocade, gold epaulettes and jewels. He added that the emperor engaged in 'excessive pleasure outings' when 'the people are suffering under your rule', and accused him of 'shady deals' during his stay in Europe. The emperor claimed the voyage was, in part, a study trip, yet Phan thundered, not entirely correctly: 'You have not stepped into a museum, a university, a chamber of commerce, a manufacturing plant, a monument of French civilisation.' He concluded that 'Your present visit, therefore, will end in failure', and he called on the emperor to abdicate.[28]

A second negative response to the emperor's visit came from another Vietnamese in France, Nguyen Ai Quoc, who later took the name Ho Chi Minh. Ho had condemned colonialism at the inaugural conference of the French Communist Party in 1920, to the communists' resounding approval, and he contributed articles to an anti-colonial leftist newspaper published under communist auspices, *Le Paria*. Ho wrote a short play about the emperor, 'Le Dragon de bambou', which satirised the grandeur and pomposity of the emperor and his court, depicting him as only a puppet monarch. The play, which was performed in Paris but has now been lost, showed antique collectors whittling twisted bamboo into the shape of a dragon, the symbol of the monarchy:[29]

'It is just a toy. It is a dragon but indeed it is still a bamboo stick ... proud of its name and its dragon shape. Yet it is only a useless monster.' The metaphor of a lifeless ruler later appeared in a poem by Ngo Duc Ke, a prominent nationalist with a background in the scholar-gentry; it was addressed to Emperor Gia Long, the founder of the Nguyen dynasty to which Khai Dinh was heir: 'Whoever goes to Hell should ask of Gia Long / Whether this guy Khai Dinh was really his grandson? ... / Last year he went to France and dishonoured our country / The Protectorate has carved a wood-statue / That is the king all right; but where is our country?'[30]

Ho wrote another short piece with regards to Khai Dinh, published in *L'Humanité* (by now the organ of the Communist Party), 'The Lamentations of Trung Trac'. Showing historical allusions common in Vietnamese writing, the title referred to the Trung sisters, heroines who led resistance to a Chinese invasion of Vietnam in 39 CE. The monologue is cast as a late-night dream of the emperor in which Trung Trac appears to him, reciting the exploits of his forbears who opposed conquest and struggled for the independence of the Vietnamese people. 'What a cruel shame, what terrible disillusion, what a painful bitterness would your ancestors feel, beyond the clouds, seeing a people you [the ancient emperors] left free now enslaved, a country that they emancipated in servitude, with the weakness of the successor to their throne.' The spectre accuses the emperor of defaulting on his duties, failing even to perform the rites appropriately, and going to France 'to sing the virtues of those who exploit and oppress your people'. Other peoples were awakening, but the Vietnamese slumbered in their misery; now the spirits of the ancestors were summoning them to action.[31]

The visiting emperor may or may not have been aware of these works, and praise rather than criticism for his tour came from some other Vietnamese quarters,[32] but he was clearly aware of the tides of nationalism that threatened to engulf both the old imperial order and the colonial order in Vietnam. Such a situation illustrated the difference between Vietnam and Cambodia, where an anti-colonial movement was much slower to develop; it also marked the changes that had occurred in the colonial world in the years between Sisowath's pre-war tour and that of Khai Dinh in the 1920s.

Asia in Paris: the spectacle of empire

The French tours of Sisowath and Khai Dinh were part of the spectacle of empire, the colonies and protectorates brought home to *la mère-patrie*. They constituted *mises-en-scène* of colonial kings and Oriental pageantry on show to the citizens of the republic. The photographs, sketches and cartoons in the press testified to journalistic and popular fascination with monarchy even in republican France, especially with the visits of romantic sovereigns from afar. Okna Thiounn's comments on French life mirror the fascination that visiting Asians had for Europe, the sights of Paris perhaps as intriguing for the Cambodians as the Khmer dancers presented for Rodin or Angkorian temples appeared for tourists at colonial expositions or those who made the long journey to the East. Yet politics was never far from pageantry. Official responses to royal tours abound with fine sentiments pronounced on all sides about loyalty, progress and the unbreakable bonds between metropole and colony – the rhetoric that justified French colonialism and mandated the allegiance of native peoples. Yet during Khai Dinh's tour, the more discordant views of Phan Chau Trinh and Ho Chi Minh provided contrary perspectives, and underlined the very real stakes that could not be entirely masked behind glittering receptions and fine words.

Their words also focused attention on a key issue: what was the role and responsibility of a monarch who represented his people and their culture, and who embodied a lineage of honoured ancestral rulers, but who was now subjected to colonial overrule? Camâra de Leal's cartoons pointed up the paradoxes and hypocrisies of colonialism as only a satirist could do, the images poignantly reducing the king from a monarch triumphantly astride an elephant to one making obseisance to a Gallicised 'king of the jungle'. The dazzle of the tours, the deference of officials in their addresses to 'Votre Majesté', and the cheers of the crowds could hardly obscure the fact that Sisowath and especially Khai Dinh were hardly masters even of their own houses under colonial dominion, and that critics of colonialism, both in France and in the colonies, were raising louder and louder voices of opposition to the foreign overlordship, especially by the 1920s in Vietnam.

For the French, the tours were great successes, and some of the Cambodians and Vietnamese shared that satisfaction. Sisowath returned to Cambodia to reign for another two decades and died at the advanced age of eighty-seven in 1927. Khai Dinh, already of uncertain health when he journeyed to France, lived for only three years after he arrived back home and died, in 1925, at the age of only forty. Neither visited France again. Sisowath's and Khai Dinh's reputations since their reign have been mixed. A gilded French-sculpted statue of Sisowath was erected in Phnom Penh in 1909 in honour of the king, and of the retrocession of the 'lost provinces' to Cambodia, a mark of celebration during the monarch's lifetime.[33] The later King Sihanouk, however, thought of his predecessor as little more than a 'parrot' ready to say yes to what the French demanded. Milton Osborne, a distinguished scholar of Cambodia, makes an astute judgement: 'Sisowath was a classic Herodian, a man and king ready to cooperate with the colonial power in a relationship that he saw as suiting his interests.' He adds that for Cambodians 'Sisowath continued to be revered as their monarch, a figure who, with his semi-divine status, was someone and something more than a man'.[34]

Khai Dinh constructed a remarkable mausoleum for himself, a grandiose part-Vietnamese part-European edifice where he sits in 'statuified' majesty.[35] Though the tomb in Hué remains a major tourist attraction (for Vietnamese as well as foreigners), Khai Dinh has fared less well in post-colonial Vietnam and among historians of that country. Truong Buu Lan, who teaches in the United States, characterises the emperor as a 'pallid figure, subservient in every sense to the colonial master'; if he distinguished himself in any way, she says, it would be only for three things: his trip to France, the mausoleum he constructed, and the opportune nature of his dying to leave a young son on the throne.[36] The French-based historian Nguyen The Anh entitles his chapter on the reign 'Khai Dinh and the Definitive Putting to Death of the Confucian Order' and traces the erosion of the emperor's remaining powers, which he was unable to staunch.[37] Patrice Morlat advances a somewhat different interpretation, suggesting that Khai Dinh's loyalty preserved a dynasty that the French had considered abolishing after the 1916 revolt. Morlat argues that Khai Dinh was trying to free himself from mandarin courtiers and their antiquated beliefs, and recreate the monarchy. He saw collaboration with the French as a way to achieve the modernisation of his country; caught between the court and the colonists, however, he could not succeed.[38] One current Vietnamese government website dismisses Khai Dinh as a 'powerless emperor' who 'adulated the French' and earned little affection from his subjects; an English-language Vietnamese work states that he 'contributed nothing to the cause of establishing the nation'.[39] For the respected contemporary historian Nguyen Dac Xuan, an authority on the Nguyen dynasty and the history of Hué, Khai Dinh falls into the category of those emperors – unlike the three 'patriotic' monarchs dethroned and exiled by the French – who were little more than puppets of the colonial regime.[40] Of course, historical and political opinions about past rulers vary from period to period, especially in countries with such complex colonial and post-colonial histories as Cambodia and Vietnam.[41]

After an eleven-year reign by Sisowath's son, his throne passed in 1941 to Sisowath's grandson Sihanouk, who would be on and off the throne of the Khmer kingdom, but a constant actor in its politics, during its troubled and often tragic history for the next sixty years. Sihanouk's son Norodom Sihamoni – who spent almost his entire early life overseas, in Paris and Prague – now reigns in Phnom Penh, though real power lies with the strongman prime minister, Hung Sen. As for the Vietnamese dynasty, Khai Dinh's son Bao Dai remained in France as a student after the 1922 tour, and returned to Paris after a trip to Hué for his coronation in 1926. Bao Dai indeed spent much of his later life in France, and lived there after the overthrow of the Vietnamese dynasty.[42] He died in Paris in 1997 and is buried there.[43]

When Sisowath travelled to France in 1906, monarchs reigned in most of the countries of Europe and Asia – France a notable exception – and crowned heads inspired respect and awe. By the time of Khai Dinh's tour in 1922, thrones had toppled in Europe and Asia, and anti-colonial nationalists were clamouring for emancipation, though France and other countries could still hold expositions that celebrated colonialism and confidently proclaim the enduring attachment of their distant possessions. The early twentieth-century tours of Sisowath and Khai Dinh were intended to show off France to the royal vassals of the republic, and to show off the Oriental potentates to the French public, to present a spectacle of enchanting exoticism brought under the power of *la plus grande France*. The visits of Sisowath in his Cambodian apparel or European uniform, and Khai Dinh in his elaborate brocaded gowns, both men decorated with the insignia of the Legion of Honour, paraded traditional rulers in attire cut to French colonial design. However, the spectacle could not but reveal the naked realities of French colonial rule and the contradictions that would eventually challenge both monarchies and empires.

Notes

1 Ottoman and Persian rulers, however, did travel to Western European capitals. See, e.g., David Motadel, 'Qajar Shahs in Imperial Germany', *Past and Present*, 213 (2011), 191–235. Visits of Asian ambassadorial delegations took on the character of royal tours; see, e.g., L.E. Bagshawe, *The Kinwun Min-Gyi's London Diary: The First Mission of a Burmese Minister to Britain, 1872* (Bangkok: Orchid Press, 2006), pp. 60–65, 246–288, 295–298 on the embassy's stays in France, and Kume Kunitake, *Japan Rising: The Iwakura Embassy to the United States of America and Europe, 1871–1873*, ed. Chushichi Tsuzuki and R. Jules Young (Cambridge: Cambridge University Press, 2009), pp. 211–257, 453–460 on the Japanese in France.
2 Robert Aldrich, 'France and the King of Siam: An Asian King's Visits to the Republican Capital', in Julie Kalman (ed.), *French History and Society: Papers from the 2014 George Rudé Seminar*, Vol. 6 (2015), pp. 225–239; online at H-France, www.h-france.net/rude/rudevolvi/AldrichVol6.pdf, accessed 1 June 2016.
3 See Michael Nelson, *Queen Victoria and the Discovery of the Riviera* (London: Tauris Parke, 2007) and Stephen Clarke, *Dirty Bertie: An English King Made in France* (London: Arrow, 2015).
4 See Alexander C.T. Geppert, *Fleeting Cities: Imperial Expositions in Fin-de-siècle Europe* (New York: Palgrave Macmillan, 2010).

COLONIAL KINGS IN THE METROPOLE

5 A good overview is Pierre Brocheux and Daniel Hémery, *Indochina: An Ambiguous Colonization, 1858–1954* (Berkeley: University of California Press, 2009). On Vietnam, see Christopher Goscha, *The Penguin History of Modern Vietnam* (London: Allen Lane, 2016). On Cambodia, John Tully, *A Short History of Cambodia: From Empire to Survival* (Crows Nest, NSW: Allen & Unwin, 2005); Alain Forest, *Le Cambodge et la colonisation française: Histoire d'une colonisation sans heurts (1897–1920)* (Paris: L'Harmattan, 1993); and Penny Edwards, *Cambodge: The Cultivation of a Nation, 1860–1945* (Honolulu: University of Hawai'i Press, 2007).
6 On the monarchy of Laos, which is not covered in this chapter, see Grant Evans, *The Last Century of Lao Royalty: A Documentary History* (Chiang Mai: Silkworm Books, 2009).
7 The Vietnamese title for the ruler was translated as both 'king' and 'emperor'; the French preferred the former title until the 1920s. They also avoided use of the name 'Vietnam' so as not to encourage feelings of national unity among the residents of Tonkin, Annam and Cochinchina, and thus always referred to the sovereign in Hué as 'Emperor of Annam', though I have followed customary usage and occasionally refer to him as the emperor of Vietnam.
8 Nguyen The Anh, *Monarchie et fait colonial au Viet-Nam (1875–1925): le crépuscule d'un ordre traditionnel* (Paris: L'Harmattan, 1992), is the most comprehensive study of the Nguyen dynasty and the French. See also Oscar Chapuis, *The Last Emperors of Vietnam: From Tu Duc to Bao Dai* (Westport: Praeger, 2000), and Bruce McFarland Lockhart, *The End of the Vietnamese Monarchy* (New Haven: Yale University Press, 1993), as well as, for Khai Dinh, Patrice Morlat, *Indochine années vingt: Le rendez-vous manqué (1918–1928)* (Paris: Les Indes savantes, 2005), esp. pp. 278–292.
9 Milton Osborne, 'King-Making in Cambodia: From Sisowath to Sihanouk', *Journal of Southeast Asian Studies*, 4:2 (1973), 169–185.
10 Robert Aldrich, *Banished Potentates: Dethroning and Exiling Indigenous Monarchs under British and French Colonial Rule, 1815–1955* (Manchester: Manchester University Press, 2018), and 'Imperial Banishment: French Colonizers and the Exile of Vietnamese Emperors', in Joseph Zizek and Kirsty Carpenter (eds), *French History and Civilization*, Vol. 5 (Papers from the 2012 George Rudé Seminar), H-France (www.h-france.net/rude/rudevolv/12%20Aldrich%20Imperial%20Banishment%20 Vietnam%20final.pdf, accessed 1 June 2016).
11 Dang-Ngoc-Oanh, 'L'Intronisation de l'empereur Khai-Dinh', *Bulletin des Amis du Vieux Hué*, No. 1, 1916, pp. 1–24, shows the pageantry and reveals French hopes. On French attempts to gain the favour and fealty of the monarch, see Nguyen Thi Dieu, 'Ritual, Power, and Pageantry: French Ritual Politics in Monarchical Vietnam', *French Historical Studies*, 39:4 (2016), 717–748.
12 Pierre L. Lamant, *L'Affaire Yukanthor: Autopsie d'un scandale colonial* (Paris: Société française d'histoire d'Outre-Mer, 1989).
13 Discussion of Sisowath's tour is interleaved with commentary on present-day Cambodia in Amitav Ghosh's splendid essay 'Dancing in Cambodia', in his *Dancing in Cambodia, at Large in Burma* (Delhi: Ravi Dayal, 1998), pp. 1–53.
14 This was not the first time a Vietnamese royal had visited France; in 1787, a French missionary bishop brought Prince Canh, son of the emperor of Annam, for a visit to Paris, where he was fêted by the court of Louis XVI. Delegations of Vietnamese mandarins also visited France in 1841, 1863–1864 and later in the century; see Ta Trong Hiep, 'Le Journal de l'ambassade de Phan Thanh Gian en France (4 juillet 1863– 18 avril 1864)', and Christiane Pasquel Rageau, 'Récits de voyages de "mandarins" vietnamiens et cambogiens en France (1906–07)', in Claudine Salmon (ed.), *Récits de voyages asiatiques: Genres, mentalités, conceptions de l'espace* (Paris: Ecole française d'Extrême-Orient, 2005), pp. 335–366 and 385–406.
15 Fond ministeriels, INDO / AF / 26, Fond ministerial, A73, 74 and 75, Archives nationales d'Outre-Mer, Aix-en-Provence, contains relevant documents, almost all concerning questions of protocol, budgets and programmes for the tours.

Comparative documents for the emperor's tour are contained in Fonds Ministériel 1 AffPol / 1343, AOM.
16 'Visite de S.M. l'Empereur d'Annam à la Société de Géographie, le 10 juillet 1922', *Bulletin des Amis du Vieux Hué*, No. 4, 1922, pp. 321–335.
17 *Rodin et les danseuses cambodgiennes: sa dernière passion* (catalogue of an exhibition at the Musée Rodin) (Paris: Éditions du Musée Rodin, 2006).
18 John Tully, *Cambodia under the Tricolour: King Sisowath and the 'Mission Civilisatrice' 1904–1927* (Clayton: Monash Asia Insitute, 1996), pp. 10–11. Tully provides details of the king's activities during his sojourn in France.
19 See Nigel J. Brailey, *Imperial Amnesia: Britain, France and 'The Question of Siam'* (Dordrecht: Republic of Letters, 2009), and Christopher E. Goscha, *Thailand and the Southeast Asian Networks of the Vietnamese Revolution, 1885–1954* (Richmond: Curzon, 1999).
20 Quoted in *Le Figaro*, 10 August 1922.
21 Eric T. Jennings, 'Representing Indochinese Sacrifice: The Temple du Souvenir Indochinois of Nogent-sur-Marne', in Kathryn Robson and Jennifer Yee (eds), *France and 'Indochina': Cultural Representations* (Lanham: Lexington Books, 2005), pp. 29–48.
22 The first play written by Jean Cocteau – a short end-of-year comic revue authored with fellow students – was 'Sisowath en balade'. The king, tired of official engagements, goes for a walk-about in Paris, in the company of a pianist who carries a sign labelling him the 'accompanist'. One scene is included in Jean Cocteau, *Théâtre complet* (Paris: La Pléiade, 2003), pp. 1373–1379, and 1828–1829. Meanwhile, 'La Radadah, polka-danse' was dedicated to King Sisowath, the sheet-music cover featuring a caricatured Cambodian dancing with an idealised Frenchwoman.
23 *Le Petit Journal*, issues of 24 June, 1 and 22 July 1906.
24 *Le Figaro*, especially 19, 21, 22, 25, 27 June, 23 July and 5, 8, 11 August 1906.
25 *L'Assiette au beurre*, 30 June 1906.
26 Okna Veang Thiounn, *Voyage du Roi Sisowath en France*, trans. and ed. Olivier de Bernon (Paris: Mercure de France, 2006), which also contains several documents, including a French official's report of the trip, in the appendices. Born in the early 1860s into a Sino-Cambodian family, Thiounn was a former interpreter for French officials who had become secretary to the Cambodian council of ministers in 1863. With French support, in 1902, he became Minister of the Palace, a powerful position he held until the beginning of the 1930s. Thiounn remained one of the most influential figures in Phnom Penh until his death in 1946.
27 The mandarin Phan Chau Trinh (1872–1926) retired from the imperial administration in 1904. He made contact with a number of rebels and reformers, such as Phan Boi Chau, and was implicated in tax revolts in 1908, for which he was arrested and imprisoned. Released through the intervention of French supporters, he left Vietnam for France in 1911. During the First World War, he was again arrested for refusing conscription and allegedly asking for German assistance to Vietnam. With Ho Chi Minh, he attempted to present a set of demands on behalf of the Vietnamese to the Versailles Peace Conference. In 1925, he returned to Vietnam, where he died from tuberculosis the following year.
28 Phan Chau Trinh, 'Letter to Emperor Khai Dinh', in *Phan Chau Trinh and His Political Writings*, ed. Vinh Sinh (Ithaca, NY: Cornell University, 2009), pp. 87–102.
29 Pierre Baptiste (ed.), *L'Envol du dragon: Art royal du Vietnam* (Paris: Snoeck and Musée nation des arts asiatiques – Guimet, 2014).
30 Quoted in Truong Buu Lan, *Colonialism Experienced: Vietnamese Writings on Colonialism, 1900–1931* (Ann Arbor: University of Michigan Press, 2000), p. 35.
31 Nguyen Ai Quoc, 'Les Lamentations de Trung Trac', *L'Humanité*, 24 June 1922.
32 For instance, in an account by Pham Quynh, Director of the Imperial Cabinet, see Christopher E. Goscha, 'Récits de voyage vietnamiens et prise de conscience indochinoise (c. 1920–c. 1945)', in Salmon, *Récits de voyages asiatiques*, pp. 253–279.
33 Steven Boswell, *King Norodom's Head: Phnom Penh Sights beyond the Guidebook* (Copenhagen: NIAS Press, 2016), pp. 80–81.

34 Milton Osborne, *Phnom Penh: A Cultural History* (Oxford: Oxford University Press, 2008), p. 81.
35 Vietnamese emperors traditionally constructed grand mausoleums for themselves, in the midst of landscaped gardens with temples, pavilions and lakes to which they often repaired during their lifetimes.
36 Truong Buu Lan, *Colonialism Experienced*, pp. 18–19.
37 Nguyen The Anh, *Monarchie et fait colonial au Viet-Nam*, pp. 274–275.
38 Morlat, *Indochine années vingt*, esp. pp. 278–292.
39 www.lichsuvietnam.vn/home.php?option=com_content&task=view&id=1676&Itemid=34, accessed 1 June 2016; my thanks to Linh Do for summarising the observations on this Vietnamese-language website; Nguyen Viet Ke, *Stories of The Nguyen Dynasty's Kings* (Danang, Vietnam: Danang Publishing House, 2008), pp. 98–99.
40 Personal communication, Hue, 4 April 2015. I would like to thank Mr Nguyen for his long and very informative conversation with me, and his daughter for arranging for an interpreter.
41 On recent official approaches to the Nguyen dynasty in Vietnam, see Marina Marouda, 'Potent Rituals and the Royal Dead: Historical Transformations in Vietnamese Ritual Practice', *Journal of Southeast Asian Studies*, 45: 3 (2014), 338–362.
42 Bao Dai abdicated in 1945 and the dynasty was abolished under the government of Ho Chi Minh, but the former emperor returned to Vietnam as 'head of state', under the aegis of the French, in 1949. He maintained that position in the Republic of Vietnam (South Vietnam) following the independence of the Democratic Republic of Vietnam in 1954, but was overthrown in a coup in 1955.
43 For an insightful comparison of the two monarchs, see Christopher Goscha, 'Bao Dai et Sihanouk: la fabrique indochinoise des rois coloniaux', in François Guillemot and Agathe Larcher-Goscha (eds), *La Colonisation des corps: De l'Indochine au Viet Nam* (Paris: Éditions Vendémiaire, 2014), pp. 127–175. The emperor's autobiography is Bao Dai, *Le Dragon d'Annam* (Paris: Plon, 1980).

CHAPTER NINE

Tensions of empire and monarchy: the African tour of the Portuguese crown prince in 1907

Filipa Lowndes Vicente and Inês Vieira Gomes

In 1907 Prince Luís Filipe departed Lisbon for a tour of the Portuguese colonies in Africa, as well as South Africa and Rhodesia.[1] As the future king, the twenty-year-old prince was undertaking his first political mission (Figure 9.1). The primary goal was clear: to reinforce Portugal's position in Mozambique, Angola, Cape Verde, and São Tomé and Principe. (Guinea-Bissau was not included on the tour.) A second objective was to improve Portugal's relationship with Britain through a visit to Britain's major colonies in southern Africa. A particular catalyst was British accusations that slavery was practised in some of Portugal's territories, and that its authorities did not fight slavery strongly enough and officials even profited from it. These accusations transcended humanitarian and commercial interests. One of the strongest denunciations came from William Cadbury, the chocolate manufacturer, who depended for supplies on cocoa plantations, some of the largest located in São Tomé. A 1905 trip by Cadbury to São Tomé and Angola to investigate labour recruitment created considerable negative international publicity. The royal tour was intended to challenge these findings; the conflict was one of the 'tensions of empire'.[2]

The tour took place at a moment of intense rivalry between two European nations with interest in African resources. The background was the aftermath of the 1885 Berlin Conference on the partition of Africa. When Lisbon envisaged connecting its west coast colony of Angola to the east coast colony of Mozambique, London counter-attacked with the 'British Ultimatum' of 1890.[3] This rejected Portuguese occupation of further territory – claimed on the basis of historical rights – and worsened an already tense relationship. In Portugal, the ultimatum was viewed as a national humiliation that also aggravated existing resentment towards the monarchy. The dynasty saw its legitimacy threatened by the charge that Portugal was

TENSIONS OF EMPIRE AND MONARCHY

9.1 Crown Prince Luís Filipe, photographed in Africa, 1907

losing both African territory and national dignity, and the growing fragility of the crown affected how the 1907 tour was perceived.

The tour took place within several contexts. The first was national politics, dominated by tensions between the monarchy and the proponents of a republic. The second was international: British and Portuguese colliding attitudes, projects and experiences of empire. The third was colonial Africa, where the Portuguese territories presented specific challenges, including continued armed resistance in Angola and debates surrounding migration of labour from Angola to São Tomé, and from Mozambique to South Africa. At issue in these national, international and colonial conflicts were the survival of the monarchy in

Portugal – the form of government since the twelfth century – and the change from a model of colonial exploitation associated with slavery to a new one based on wage labour.

Only a year after his African tour, on 1 February 1908, Prince Luís Filipe was assassinated, along with his father, King Carlos, in an attack in Lisbon. The two perpetrators were acting individually, but were part of a widespread movement of opposition to the monarchy. Luís Filipe's younger brother, Manuel, who was injured but survived, was crowned as the new king. But the murders proved the key step in mounting antagonism to the crown that finally resulted in the monarchy's overthrow, and the establishment of the Portuguese Republic, in 1910.[4] The profound transformations of the political landscape, however, did not diminish the relevance of African colonies for the project of an 'Overseas Portugal'.

From Europe to Africa: the colonial grand tour

Luís Filipe's sojourn in Africa was meant to reinforce and unify the colonies under Portuguese rule, while also sending a message to European countries, mainly Britain, about which territories belonged to which colonial power. Yet the message was also a domestic one, directed at the king's subjects who should feel empowered by the prince's colonial experience. As with any undertaking that necessitated extra expenditures, royal tours could also be subject to criticism and opposition. This had occurred with earlier royal travellers, as when the young brothers, Princes Pedro and Luis – later King Pedro V and Luis I (who succeeded him) – set out on a European Grand Tour in 1854, and it was so again when Luis's grandson departed for Africa.[5]

The choice of destination is significant. In the mid-nineteenth century, the locations chosen for the princes' travels were mainly in northern Europe. By the beginning of the twentieth century, experience of colonial Africa was considered a more meaningful rite of passage for the future king. The Minister of the Colonies, Aires de Ornelas, recalled that he spent many hours on the voyage from Lisbon to Africa teaching the prince about colonial history and politics, and confessed surprise that 'everything was new to him'.[6] Moving from the fifteenth-century Prince Henry the Navigator and Vasco da Gama to the recent African campaigns, the minister described how he discussed Portuguese colonial politics, and also his own experience as a high-ranking officer and governor in Mozambique. The prince's lessons then focused on British colonial history, concluding with the trans-colonial relations between Portugal and Britain.

Luís Filipe's voyage represented the first tour of a colony by a future Portuguese king, but not by a prince. Two had earlier travelled to Goa, the major territory in Portuguese India: Prince Augusto in 1871–1872, and Prince Afonso in 1895. Afonso's tour came in the aftermath of a local revolt,[7] and was intended to reinforce Portuguese sovereignty at a time when memories of the 1857 revolts in British India were still alive and Portugal was concerned about British hegemony in South Asia.

The idea of an African royal tour was not new. Almost twenty years earlier, Luís Filipe's mother, Queen Amélia, invoking the success of the Prince of Wales's Indian tour of 1875–1876,[8] had unsuccessfully proposed that the entire Portuguese royal family travel to Africa.[9] A new opportunity arose in 1907, when Ornelas, colonial minister in the government of Franco, planned an official tour of Africa. According to Ornelas, the Portuguese ambassador to London sought his opinion on accusations that thousands of women, men and children were being forced to leave Angola to work on cocoa plantations in São Tomé. The 'pseudo-anti-slavery campaigns led by the chocolatiers', as Ornelas put it, were becoming diplomatic and political questions.[10] When the minister revealed his intention to go to Angola and São Tomé to investigate the allegations, the ambassador suggested that the prince accompany him. Luís Filipe's presence, it was also hoped, would counter strong antagonism towards the monarchy exacerbated by King Carlos's support for the 'dictatorship' of Franco. Through censorship, imprisonment of opponents and concentration of power in his own hands, Franco had managed to strengthen the republican cause.[11]

By 1907, an extremely diverse and aggressively politicised press existed in Portugal, and the royal tour elicited an immediate reaction from newspapers, their political allegiances influencing the ways in which the tour was portrayed.[12] One newspaper, for example, criticised the prince for travelling on a commercial ship instead of a navy vessel.[13] Others concentrated on more explicitly political points; the royal tour was condemned for staging a gala ball in the Angolan capital of Luanda when, not far away, an armed conflict was taking place. 'In Angola one dances and one dies!' cried a newspaper, though remaining cautious enough to state that the gala was the colonial minister's and not the prince's responsibility.[14] It was never colonialism per se, nor the Portuguese right to *own* an empire, that was at stake in the criticism. Instead, repudiation of the monarchy dominated the negative commentary. As a result of the tour, the prince became a scapegoat used to promote republican ideals. Newspapers were not mere reflections of politics, but political actors, their pages a privileged forum for debate by the intelligentsia.[15]

Politicisation of the tour within the context of domestic tensions between a weakened monarchy and a rising republican movement helps explain why the metropolitan press paid little attention to the international and colonial issues that had precipitated the tour.[16] It is as if accusations about Portuguese slavery in São Tomé and the tour's effort to answer such allegations were not so important as domestic politics. In the national press the tour was primarily used to criticise the crown and Franco's dictatorship. By contrast, in the Portuguese colonial newspapers and the South African press, criticism was mostly replaced by an enthusiastic official narrative praising the success of the Portuguese colonial enterprise and consolidation of Portuguese–British colonial relations.[17]

Opposition to the monarchy was revealed in more subtle ways in the colonies than at home. In Luanda, for example, the Commercial Association did not join in official celebrations because it was 'red', meaning 'Republican'.[18] Opposition was not expressed openly by colonised African subjects, but it was manifested by Portuguese colonists. However, as Ornelas ironically stated, a few colonists who sympathised with republican ideals put aside their antagonism to participate in the celebrations.[19] Thus, the tour represented a public enactment of the alliance between monarchy and government: the crown prince who would be the next king and the minister in charge of overseas territories.

Words and images: narrating the journey

Ornelas also wrote the major narrative of the tour, though it was published only in 1928. Ornelas had amassed a wide variety of sources: letters sent to his wife from aboard ship and from the African territories, excerpts of official documents, telegrams, Portuguese and British colonial newspapers, letters from the Queen Mother thanking him for fatherly support of her son, and letters by the prince to his younger brother Manuel. As was common practice when travel was perceived as an educational and transformative experience, the prince also kept a diary, although it has never been found.[20] The prince's travel writings and photographs remained within the private sphere, only coming to light through the minister's volume. Twenty years after the journey, Ornelas's account was marked by bitterness at criticism he and the prince had received from much of the press, and, of course, the overall antagonism to the monarchy that had led to the politically motivated shooting of the prince and the king.[21]

Photography provided a major way of documenting the prince's tour. Photographic processes were cheaper and simpler than in the past, and this democratisation of picture-taking meant that non-professionals, including the prince, had access to the medium.

Ornelas refers to the prince taking photographs with his own camera, an interest inherited from his mother.[22] Before his African tour, the prince had travelled with his family around the Mediterranean, where photography had been an avocation for the whole family.[23] While in Africa, Luís Filipe wrote to Manuel about how he had taken photographs of São Tomé, 'which thankfully came out well', and said that he might send some photographs as postcards.[24] Ornelas reproduced one of the prince's photographs, an image of the minister surrounded by three uniformed men, but lamented that another of his pictures, showing the group crossing a lake in Angola, had not turned out well.[25]

Other photographers also recorded the trip, including J.A. Benedy,[26] Arnold Borel[27] and J. Wexelsen.[28] The prolific Lazarus brothers became the best-known image-makers of the journey.[29] From the 1880s, images of specific events were reproduced and sold as souvenirs, and the day after the prince left Mozambique, the Lazarus brothers placed almost ninety prints on display at their studio.[30] Several months later, the company's advertisements still referred to the sale of 'Photographs of the Visit of His Royal Highness, o Senhor D. Luis Filipe'.[31] To promote royal *reportage* and reinforce their role as the leading photographers in Mozambique, the Lazarus studio prepared for Luís Filipe two photograph albums carefully documenting the tour's highlights. A newspaper congratulated the 'distinguished *atelier*' of the 'well-known brothers' on the gift.[32] The first album focused on the Swaziland railway, whose line connected Mozambique with the British protectorate. The second concentrated on the 'celebrations at Lourenço Marques', which the prince had greatly appreciated. Apart from photographs of the 'batuque', the impressive indigenous drumming and dance performance that, as we shall see, became the most striking Mozambican festivity, most images showed the colonial imprint in the landscape of the Mozambican capital: the customs house, governor's residence, cathedral, military club, captaincy buildings and English club ('an excellent picture', stated the English-language local newspaper, the *Guardian*).[33] The album also careful depicted the ways the city had been beautifed for the illustrious guest with triumphal arches on the main avenue and temporary kiosks and exhibits. In these urban, modernised spaces, what was also being displayed was the civilising impact of colonialism (which Hilary Sapire also found in the Prince of Wales's 1920s West African tour[34]). The leisurely, manly practice of hunting – African big-game hunting being the pinnacle of this sport – was also on show in the album, with one photograph depicting the prince and his party hunting near the Swaziland Railway – railway lines facilitated access to hunting territories.

Indigenous migrant labour

Central to the São Tomé trip were visits to the *roças*, village-type estates where thousands of labourers worked on cocoa plantations. Other than for public buildings in port cities, they constituted the major types of European construction (and were built on the initiative of the plantation owners). The *roças* encompassed the owners' lodgings, the quarters of the *serviçais* (workers), and medical and religious facilities. The royal party admired the 'order, method, quietness' of the Valle Flor Plantation, its owner a humble tradesman ennobled as a marquis.[35] The smaller Roça da Boa Entrada, according to Ornelas, was 'spotlessly arranged'.[36] The beauty of the landscape indeed made Ornelas wonder why São Tomé was not a tourist destination. Seeing the colonial use of resources and 'the education and civilisation of the indigenous people through work' impressed the prince, who stated he had never felt so patriotic as when he observed 'Portuguese modern colonization'.[37]

In stark contrast to international accusations of slavery-like recruitment and labour conditions, the official narrative was thus one about the civilising nature of work and the exemplary conditions in which it took place among an estimated 66,000 people transferred from Angola to São Tomé between 1876 and 1904.[38] Work, like religion – which was invoked in other contexts – embodied the transforming nature of the colonial presence. Through work, the racialised, colonised subject was able to transition from savagery to civilisation.[39] In Angola and São Tomé, the 'indigenous peoples were being civilised and nationalised through work, one being able to find perfect skilled workers in a variety of occupations'.[40] A common argument was that work, and the Portuguese, were saving Africans from the oppressive slave-like social structures of indigenous societies and chiefs who subjected them with 'fierce savagery'. Inaccessible locations in the uncolonised African interior, where the workforce was recruited, were as yet untouched by the 'civilizing action of progress and humanity'.[41]

Many speeches, books and newspaper articles refuted accusations against the Portuguese and reiterated that British motivations were neither humanitarian nor innocent, but the result of complex commercial and economic interests.[42] A documentary film was produced in 1909 to counter Cadbury's allegations, and it may even have included footage of the tour; though the film's whereabouts are unknown, it is considered the first example of 'Portuguese colonial cinema' and the 'first colonial film' ever made.[43]

The 'slavery question' is fundamental to understanding the tour, since it provided a continuous backdrop. Ornelas's aim was to investigate the source of the polemic, though debates continued to rage even after the tour was completed. The argument that the Portuguese saved labourers from African slavery still appeared, for instance, in a 1911 speech in Lisbon by the plantation owner Francisco Mantero.[44] The 'slave-stained' Africans, he said, were the real practitioners of slavery. Paid work, namely in the *roças* of São Tomé, opened the path to salvation. One of the strongest arguments against labour recruitment practices was that labourers' mobility was restricted, as Angolan labourers were not allowed to leave São Tomé. Mantero stated that the transformative experience of plantation labour went beyond work itself, involving the promotion of nuclear families among other civilising practices.[45] Denying workers this redemptive experience by returning them to the Angolan hinterland would be a violent act.[46] Halfway through his Lisbon speech, Mantero brandished a book to his audience illustrated with a print showing Cadbury's plantation in Trinidad, proof, he argued, of a hidden British interest in ruining the Portuguese development of São Tomé.[47] To legitimise his argument, Mantero used a British counter-narrative to contest the British accusations. In his recent *The Negro in the New World*, Sir Harry Johnston had proposed a graduated list of European colonisers' 'treatment' of 'blacks', and the Portuguese, stated Mantero, were placed first (with the British in fifth place).[48]

A silenced revolt in São Tomé and a pacification campaign in Angola

A revolt by plantation workers in São Tomé, a few days before the arrival of the royal party, remains one of the most striking incidents from the tour, as revealed in a collection of contemporary telegrams.[49] Despite their staccato language, the documents are clear that the worst possible scenario for the tour had taken place. While international attention was focused on the visit to São Tomé, the 'civilised' workforce of model plantations had revolted and killed white men, and were 'planning' to 'assassinate all Europeans'. This force consisted of not one or two, but five hundred people. (It is not stated whether they included women.) The fear of a general rebellion expressed in the first telegram reveals the tense, threatening climate, and the underlying discontent that led to violent action. It stands in stark contrast to the official documentation, and even non-official documents such as private family letters. This silence in the archive other than through these telegrams may reflect desire to conceal the uprising. Nothing would have gratified the British more than knowledge of a massive revolt by the enslaved. Apparently, and surprisingly, Portuguese officials did manage to silence the news, as evidenced by our difficulty in finding references to the incident. This concealment also reveals the 'nervousness' that Nancy Rose Hunt has described as the permanent mood traversing colonial policy-making.[50]

Events in São Tomé focused attention on the Angolan origin of plantation workers, and Angola was the prince's next stop. His itinerary included a Catholic secondary school, an exhibition of Angolan products – 'coffee, cotton, cacao, sugar, rubber, and some indigenous artifacts'[51] – a small zoo and a museum renamed in his honour, as well as official sites.[52] By the time Luís Filipe returned to Angola for a second visit after his trip to South Africa, the Portuguese were gaining the upper hand in the armed conflict in the Cuamato region – rebels there were still challenging Portuguese rule[53] – and that gave the reception at Mossamedes a 'patriotic meaning'.[54]

The batuque *as the performance of subjugation in Mozambique*

In Ornelas's 1928 book only one photograph directly relates to the African location. It is also the only one in which African people are visible. The caption reads 'Review of indigenous troops' (in Lourenço Marques). In contemporary documents, the most cited event of the Mozambican tour was the *batuque*, the 'drumming', in reference to the action of many hands playing drums and the impressive sound they made. Drumming, along with dance performances, is a familiar trope of European travel narratives about Africa, and a common feature of colonial encounters in which indigenous people perform for visitors.[55] As Jessie Mitchell notes, performances 'were one of the most common and iconic ways indigenous people and colonists related to each other in public life'.[56] There was much public symbolism in these encounters, in which some were observing (and listening), while others were being observed, and embodying what was expected within the colonial order: controlled bodies even during a performance that included movement, vocalisation and the playing of instruments. What took place in Lourenço Marques should be located within this tradition but also compared to events such as the Indian durbars.[57]

As many as 25,000 men took part in the *batuque*. It is important to note that the local government brought a large number from outside the city to create an impressive military and musical spectacle for the royal party and five hundred guests, among them representatives of South Africa and Prince Henry of Prussia. The first stage of the two-hour performance began when a 'group of blacks from Inhambane played the Portuguese national anthem on marimbas'.[58] Writing to his brother, the prince was exultant:

9.2 African performance for Crown Prince Luís Filipe, Lourenço Marques, Mozambique, 1907

The reception in Lourenço Marques was one of the most beautiful things one could – I can't say see – dream of. 20,000 blacks with their weapons were posted on both sides of the road as I went by, [and they were] yelling *Bahete InKosso*, which means *Salve Senhor*. It was most impressive. And the *batuque* with 25,000 people – the final greeting was fantastic.[59]

The almost complete absence of a controlling white presence at the event was repeatedly noted in contemporary sources as proof of Portugal's colonial strength, considered to be consolidated enough not to require such a demonstration of force. 'All foreigners were impressed with our power, mainly upon learning that 23,000 black men wandering freely in Lourenço Marques only led to the imprisonment of five men', stated the Marquis of Lavradio.[60] The performance of men dressed as warriors, carrying weapons of war, embodied a fundamental tension. While in principle the men could revolt, fight and rebel, here they contained their bodies and weapons within the performative dimension of dance, music and voice while 'seeming perfectly content'.[61] They were here to be seen and heard by the colonial elites and to praise the sovereign power symbolised by the prince.

A photograph in Ornelas's book shows hundreds of men with spears and shields forming a serpentine line. Only one element refers to the presence of colonial authority: a man with a white helmet, his back

9.3 Africans and Portuguese officials, Lourenço Marques, Mozambique, 1907

to the photographer and the viewer, stands still, displaying his quiet authority with the performance unfolding before his eyes. We do not see his body, only his coat and helmet, but we recognise the role he plays in representing the colonial presence. In the background, imposing colonial buildings are punctuated by palm trees rising towards the skies. This image contrasts with other photographs taken by professional photographers. While one depicts the performance seen from afar – a panoramic gaze eager to include as much as possible within the frame – two other images seem to capture a moment before or afterwards (Figure 9.2). People are waiting for something to happen and the photographers are much closer to their subjects (Figure 9.3). On one side, officials appear unaware of the photographer's presence. On the other, stand African men who were about to participate or have already performed. (Such tensions appeared in an indigenous performance elsewhere.[62]) This was the same kind of tension evident, as well, in European exhibitions where peoples of colour performed.

The tantalising controlled risk suggested by the *batuque* becomes more striking when considered in light of the events that had taken place in Mozambique earlier, when a local chief, Gungunhana, led armed resistance against the Portuguese until his defeat in 1895. The military reprisals captured Gungunhana, who was taken first to Lisbon, where he was publicly humiliated, and then exiled to the Azores, where he died in 1906. His downfall was regularly cited as the final, definitive victory over Mozambican resistance. To transform warriors into performers before a visiting prince twelve years after the confrontations thus took on symbolic meaning as the ultimate form of control. 'Only the Portuguese could do this in Africa!', admitted Admiral Sir Edmund Poe to Ornelas, who claimed that this conclusion was also reached by the Mozambican Anglophone press.[63]

The *Guardian*, an English-language publication in Mozambique, highlighted the contrast between 'the total freedom of action' of the Africans and their decision to 'show obedience and discipline' and 'to demonstrate loyalty to the Portuguese Crown'.[64] It located this colonised display of subjugation within a wider discussion of the 'nature' of natives. First, native chiefs had been defeated and replaced by Portuguese authorities. Second, 'generally speaking, the indigenous [people] were docile'. This observation relates to another argument put forward, that of the natives' suitability for the workforce. No longer involved in fighting against colonial sovereignty, they now could and should become paid labourers.[65]

A few days after the *batuque* in Lourenço Marques, the prince witnessed a similar, if much smaller, event in the region of Quelimane. After disembarking in the morning, the royal party went to Mass, as they did upon arrival in any colonial location. Attendance at Mass provided a demonstration of how Portuguese colonialism entangled with religion; Catholicism was part of both Portuguese culture and the 'civilising' mission. In the afternoon, the party used a railway line built by the Company of Zambezia, a major enterprise, to reach the interior. There they attended another performance, a 'simulacrum of a combat', a realistic re-enactment of a battle between Portuguese and indigenous people with an attack on an *aringa*, a fortified field and stronghold of the *sobas* or chiefs.[66] The attackers were African native troops, who represented the ultimate alliance between the colonial government and indigenous interests. The 'highly interesting and lively' performance took place after a visit to a factory to see rice-threshing machines. It was as if the industrial activity of the present, symbolising colonial economic profit, was made possible by the fact that local resistance was far enough removed in time to be dramatised and observed in a performance.

A few documents indicate that the earlier *batuque* inspired some dissonant voices. The 'indigenous people of Maputo' had refused to participate, apparently unhappy with new government regulations. The journalist who mentions this dissenting indigenous voice does so to contradict the British author Dudley Kidd, author of *The Essential*

Kafir, who accused the 'Portuguese native' of being 'a shy and degraded creature, completely under white subjugation'.[67] Furthermore, would these 'children of the bush' – referring to the African men who participated in the *batuque* – have shown such authentic joy had Kidd's claims been true? The royal tour illuminates how contemporary British and Portuguese colonial projects were continuously clashing in words, theory and ambitions. The frontiers the British and Portuguese shared on both sides of the African continent produced various kinds of rivalry, encounters and competition; one front in the conflict was the printed accusation.

The criticism was also domestic. Ornelas contrasts the positive coverage of the tour in the colonial African press with the 'political' coverage in the metropolitan Portuguese press, which, eager to deprecate the tour, reduced the Mozambican event to a *'batuque* of drunk blacks'.[68] The Africans' behaviour also evoked negative commentary. The logistics of bringing more than 20,000 men into the city over four days created many problems. The authority in charge of organising the ceremonies prepared a campground near the port, and provided food and firewood.[69] Several days after the event, a few complaints were made to the Office of Indigenous Affairs by Portuguese settlers in Lourenço Marques who demanded compensation for goods they believed had been stolen after the 'arrival of the *pretos* to the city'.[70] The *pretos* (the word used in official documents to designate the local black people, very often in a derogatory way) were accused of stealing livestock, wire and wood. White witnesses were asked to testify against the supposed thieves, though no proof of theft was ever produced.

The prince's journey through British Africa

In Portugal some critics condemned the expense of feeding and hosting thousands of men in Lourenço Marques for the *batuque*,[71] even if the costs had been paid by the 'Native Labour Association', and not the government.[72] This fact, never mentioned in Ornelas's account, deserves attention. The association must have been the Witwatersrand Native Labour Association (WNLA), popularly known as 'Wenela', a very powerful agency that recruited workers in Mozambique for South African goldfields. Given that these mines depended heavily on the Mozambican workforce, the decision of the WNLA to cover the expenses was certainly not coincidental. Was paying the costs of the *batuque* a way of compensating the Portuguese government for facilitating recruitment of native peoples? Or did the WNLA pay for the event because the gathering of a large number of men could become the first stage of their recruitment as labourers?

An 1897 Transvaal–Portuguese agreement, the first of its kind, had led to systematic recruitment by the Native Labour Association (NLA) of Mozambicans to work in the South African mines.[73] Instead of payment for specific licences, the Portuguese authorities demanded a lump sum.[74] The negotiations were not straightforward, as they were affected by many aspects of local Portuguese–British relations, from the building of railways to the attitudes of local Portuguese recruiters who resented foreign interference in their own labour markets.[75] By 1907 Winston Churchill, British Under-Secretary of State for the Colonies, stated that the 'immense influence' of the NLA over local politics 'has woven itself into all the apparatus of economic and social life of Johannesburg'.[76] Lord Harris, head of the Consolidated Gold Fields of South Africa, which controlled 'one of the biggest groups of companies on the Rand',[77] agreed that the NLA had a monopoly on labour recruitment, but added, 'only as regards Portuguese territory'. In South Africa and Mozambique, the NLA directly controlled the migration of thousands of labourers – 154,047 between 1903 and 1906 alone.[78] This labour trade has been the subject of extensive research in the context of global racialised labour migrations, past and present.[79]

Labour migration could take place *within* colonial empires, as happened with the movement of workers from Angola to São Tomé, and *between* empires, as occurred between Mozambique and South Africa, or between territories that did not yet have clear boundaries. Railways were central to labour mobility, just as they proved central to the royal journeys. Ornelas hoped that one day soon the prince, whom he said could by now be considered one of our 'colonials', would inaugurate the first transcontinental train, uniting Portuguese port cities on different sides of the African continent.[80]

Proximity to a major British colony had direct repercussions for urban life in Mozambique. English was visible on street signs, and English was the 'language which can be most heard'. The Portuguese saw this hegemony as a threat and proof of British interest in the colony.[81] Two other significant communities were also of consequence in Lourenço Marques; Chinese and Indians. Like the British, the Chinese and the Indian communities also paid for some of the royal tour festivities, and when financial constraints were severe, a Portuguese republican newspaper praised their gesture.[82] It is not clear if the diasporic communities paid on their own initiative and why they did so, but this must have been part of the consolidation of their public presence within the colony.

As the major British possession neighbouring Mozambique, South Africa became a natural extension of the prince's African tour. Ornelas's version, and the newspaper articles he reprinted, omitted any mention of conflict between Portugal and Britain, while reinforcing everything positive about the prince's arrival in Pretoria. Ornelas described the excitement of hunting from a motor-car driven at full speed,[83] as well as more sedate meetings with British authorities, including the High Commisioner Lord Selbourne and Louis Botha and Jan Smuts, future prime ministers of South Africa. The recruitment of Mozambicans for South Africa provided the main topic for their discussions, and, according to Ornelas, the 'Portuguese Government' managed to impose its position, though he does not state what this was. The South African leg of the tour was also seen as an important diplomatic opportunity within the context of Portuguese–British relations. Ornelas's description is enthusiastic, underscoring the triumphal receptions the royal party were given. Some of the more delicate situations that he omits, however, appear in the press.[84]

Lord Selbourne did not receive his guests with the dignity they thought they deserved. For instance, accommodations in Pretoria were not considered dignified enough for the royal party.[85] British authorities justified the lodgings by saying that Government House was not big enough for the fourteen members of the party, 'plus servants'; therefore, the junior members had slept in a 'very comfortable' train. Another complaint was that the reception on Luís Filipe's arrival in Pretoria was too low-key and private. The South African justification was that because the prince had spent the day hunting, the formal public reception was postponed until the following day. A private letter between two brothers, which alludes to these misunderstandings, was more colourful. Francisco de Melo Breyner, who served on the board of the local Association of Landlords, wrote to his brother that the Chamber of Mines, which represented wealthy mineowners, had organised a festive lunch in honour of the prince, and had invited Selbourne. 'Do you know what that son of a bitch answered?' wrote Breyner. 'That he would only accept if he were given first place, the prince coming second.'[86] When the Chamber of Mines confirmed that Luís Filipe was the principal guest of honour, Selbourne did not attend. News of the High Commisioner's impoliteness reached London, and the British demanded an explanation, while the Portuguese ambassador in London reported back to Lisbon.[87] Selbourne not only refuted allegations of discourtesy, but asserted that he was never intentionally unfriendly.

Johannesburg, which came next on the tour, was the site of a 'triumphal' reception. The considerable Portuguese immigrant community greeted the royal party, who also received an official representative from the Portuguese island of Madeira and the head of the Ferreira

Mine, in which a huge number of Mozambican natives worked.[88] The *Transvaal Leader* stated that the experience enabled the prince 'to learn from British colonial methods'.[89] Finally, the visitors went to Kimberley, where the director of the De Beers mine offered the prince and the minister a raw diamond each. Ornelas wrote to his wife that 'the trip to British Africa has been in all respects an extraordinary success', and that the 'colonial press' had been unanimous in recognising the significance of the prince's tour in strengthening Portuguese–British relations.[90]

More seen than heard: African voices

In all the territories traversed during the royal tour, African people were more seen than heard. The writings of the Portuguese party and journalists refer to Africans performing, enthusiastically applauding the arrival of the prince, and working in mines or *roças*. Africans are almost always anonymous characters in a narrative in which only the local white Portuguese authorities, European diplomats and British officials are identified by name or rank. Only rarely was the status of 'natives' identified, as when hundreds of *sobas* greeted the prince in the Angolan region of Lucalla.[91] In a few cases, though, mostly unnamed men described as 'indigenous' spoke in official events. On the prince's arrival in Benguela, for example, messages from local groups, including a 'Deputation of the Indigenous', were read aloud.[92]

There is evidence of two public interventions by Africans in São Tomé. The first took place at the governor's palace, where a 'commission of blacks' read a message that the minister eagerly sent to a Portuguese newspaper.[93] The second 'voice' was heard at the Town Hall. The prince and colonial authorities were gathered for the unveiling of a portrait of a well-known local plantation owner when 'a black appeared' to give a speech.[94] Ornelas immediately recognised him as ex-Sergeant Gamboa, whom he had met when the minister was head of the armed forces in Mozambique many years earlier. Gamboa, who had been an amanuensis in the Mozambican military headquarters, now made a 'nativist discourse'. In the local context, 'nativist' usually meant the point of view of the 'natives', who sought empowerment, and who wanted not to disrupt the colonial order, but to have more rights or voice within it. So much was being written about the São Tomé cocoa plantation workers, without their having a say, that it is striking that Gamboa spoke out, even if we cannot know what he said.

Many endings: returning home to a tragic conclusion

Returning to Portugal meant a return to the climate of opposition that had accompanied the departure of the royal party. The perception of public acclamation the travellers had enjoyed during the tour turned into bitter disillusionment with the cold welcome home.[95] The mind of the nation was focused more on local politics than overseas empire, which seemed so distant and irrelevant to the general discontent in Portugal. The death, a few months later, of the prince and king spelled the tragic climax of the conflict that played out during the tour.

In most royal tours in the colonial world in the first decades of the twentieth century, indigenous opposition, or 'unloyalty', was a major issue.[96] Hilary Sapire analyses how a major aim of the Prince of Wales's tour in India, in 1921–1922, and in Africa, in 1925, was to reinforce loyalism among subjugated peoples and local Western-educated elites. While this idea of loyalism, in a broad sense, underlies Luís Filipe's tour, there is a striking difference.[97] In the Portuguese case, the main manifestations of disloyalty were found among the Portuguese-born, white republicans, who questioned the monarchy and envisioned a change of government. There was no reference yet to a strong black Portuguese elite in colonial Africa. Most positions in the civil service were held by Portuguese men, largely military officers, many of whom transitioned directly from involvement in the armed conflict with Africans to positions governing them.

African subjects' loyalty to the Portuguese was a contested issue, and was not resolved at the time of the tour; indeed, in certain regions loyalty had never even been attained. In Mozambique the *batuque* emerged as the best proof of loyalism. The black men, 'twenty-three thousand, armed with their weapons of war, dressed in warrior attire and declaring "Bahete InKosso" to the son of the King of Portugal' were 'the same who in 1894 did not allow us to leave the city, the same who were fighting us ten years ago; the same who obeyed Gungunhana'.[98] They were 'the ones who today obey, respect and fear us', concluded the Marquis of Lavradio. The same could not be said of these warriors' Angolan equivalents, still fighting the Portuguese in Cuamato during the months of the tour. The same tension between the warrior as performer and the warrior as soldier was embedded in the São Tomé plantations. Here order as a synonym for organised labour was a paradigm being disrupted both by the workers themselves, five hundred of whom had staged a revolt shortly before the prince's arrival, and by the foreign accusations that condemned the Portuguese colonial workforce by placing it within the framework of slavery.

Implicit in these debates – independent of the complex motives behind them – is the questioning of colonial legitimacy itself. If workers were being forced into slavery-like conditions, their loyalty was determined by dependency, and therefore, was not loyalty but submission. Loyalism was still being negotiated on various battlegrounds: in the interior of Angola, where armed conflict was taking place, on the plantations of São Tomé, in the printed public culture, and within the national sphere, where monarchy itself was at risk.

The official thinking that led to the prince and minister's African tour placed hope in its capacity to serve as a unifying platform to counter domestic dissent. The 'immense colonial future of the nation is indissolubly linked to the Portuguese monarchy', stated Ornelas, who believed that reinforcing the overseas colonies as a national project – via the future king's passage through the empire – would soothe national conflicts.[99] However, far from calming the tense political climate at home, the royal tour only seemed to worsen it. On Luís Filipe's return, many newspapers continued their harsh criticism of the tour. One commentator was especially sarcastic when discussing the official idea of travel as a rite of passage from youth to adulthood, from prince to potential king, from 'child' to someone 'truly colonial'.[100] How could travel effect such a transformation in the prince, when the royal tour consisted of 'lunch in São Tomé', dinner in Angola that same day and, after 'hardly having finished dessert', a visit to Lourenço Marques, where 'tea and a comfortable feather bed' awaited?

As would soon become evident, the Portuguese colonial project as a whole did not depend on the crown at all. Rather, it became a vital aspect of both the First Republican Regime (1910–1926) and the right-wing dictatorship known as *Estado Novo* which only ended with the April Revolution of 1974, and had António de Oliveira Salazar as its major figure, and 'Overseas Portugal' as a major ideological canvas of its political project. The next official governmental tour of the colonies, thirty years after that of the prince, would not be royal but presidential. Óscar Carmona, a prominent figure in the 1926 *coup d'état* that overthrew the First Republic and led to the Salazar dictatorship, was president of Portugal from 1926 until 1951. In 1938, he went on a colonial tour which turned out to be much more popular and better received than the royal tour of 1907. Salazar's policy of economic and political isolation meant that while the rest of the world would soon be living through the Second World War, Portugal was poor but peaceful, its 'empire' being celebrated in all possible ways at home and abroad. In 1934 a major colonial exhibition and congress was held in Porto, and in 1938, the presidential colonial tour and, not by coincidence, an Angolan exposition, the Exposiçao-Feira de Angola, took place in Luanda. In 1940, two historical dates – the nation's birth in 1140 and its independence, in 1640, from a brief period of Spanish domination – were the *leitmotiv* for a celebration of Portuguese imperial culture at an ambitious event in Lisbon. The Exhibition of the Portuguese World, as it was known, occupied a large expanse of Belém, Lisbon's seafront monumental neighbourhood. The narratives presented by exhibitions and conferences asserted that the stable dimension of Portuguese identity was its colonial destiny and legitimacy, anchored by overseas dominions since the sixteenth century. Whether the government was a monarchy, republic or dictatorship, the imperial dimension remained a defining feature of national identity. Here was the ongoing official narrative in which the royal tour should be placed, though one that did not acknowledge the constant tensions, conflicts and disruptions that were also a part of the Portuguese colonial project.

Notes

1 We thank Naomi Parker for the invaluable contribution in editing this chapter and Miguel Bandeira Jerónimo and Ricardo Roque for their bibliographical suggestions.
2 Frederick Cooper and Ann Laura Stoler (eds), *Tensions of Empire: Colonial Cultures in a Bourgeois World* (Berkeley: University of California Press, 1997).
3 The bibliography in Portuguese is vast; in English see, for example, William Clarence-Smith, *The Third Portuguese Empire, 1825–1975: A Study in Economic Imperialism* (Manchester: Manchester University Press, 1985).
4 Douglas Wheeler, 'The Portuguese Revolution of 1910', *The Journal of Modern History*, 44:2 (1972), 172–194.
5 Filipa Lowndes Vicente, *Viagens e Exposições: D. Pedro V na Europa do século XIX* (Lisbon: Gótica, 2003), and '"The Future is a Foreign Country": The Visit of the Portuguese King D. Pedro V to the Parisian Exposition Universelle of 1855', Journal of Romance Studies, 3:2 (2003), 31–48.
6 Aires de Ornelas, *Viagem do Príncipe Real: Julho-Setembro de 1907* (Lisbon: [n.p.], 1928), pp. 24–25.
7 Ricardo Roque, *Antropologia e Império: Fonseca Cardoso e a expedição à Índia em 1895* (Lisbon: Imprensa de Ciências Sociais, 2001).
8 Leitão de Barros, *Duas visitas a Versalhes, 1938–1951* (Lisbon: Neogravura, 1951), p. 29, quoted by Ana Vicente and António Pedro Vicente, *O Príncipe Real Luis Filipe de Bragança, 1887–1908* (Lisbon: Inapa, 1998), p. 51. This book is a useful compilation of primary sources on the prince's life and we have used it extensively in this chapter.
9 Ornelas, *Viagem do Príncipe Real*, p. 15.
10 *Ibid.*; P.L. Marques, *O Marquês de Soveral: seu tempo e seu modo* (Alfragide: Texto D.L., 2009).
11 Wheeler, 'The Portuguese Revolution of 1910', p. 177.
12 Miguel Ribeiro Pedras, 'A Viagem do Príncipe: o périplo de D. Luís Filipe em África visto através da imprensa' (MA dissertation, Lisbon Polytechnic Institute, 2012); M.R. Pedras, 'A Imprensa e o Império na viagem do príncipe D. Luís Filipe a África', *Revista Brasileira de História da Mídia (RBHM)*, 5:1 (2016), 33–43.
13 *O Dia*, 9 July 1907, quoted by Pedras, 'A Imprensa e o Império na viagem do príncipe D. Luís Filipe a África', p. 37.
14 *Ibid.*
15 José Miguel Sardica, 'O poder visível: D. Carlos, a imprensa e a opinião pública no final da monarquia constitucional', *Análise Social*, XLVII:2 (2012), 344–368, pp.

348, 349; António Costa Pinto and Pedro Tavares de Almeida, 'On Liberalism and the Emergence of Civil Society in Portugal', in Nancy Bermeo and Philip Nord (eds), *Civil Society before Democracy: Lessons from Nineteenth-Century Europe* (Boston: Rowman & Littlefield, 2000), pp. 3–21; José Tengarrinha, *História da Imprensa Periódica Portuguesa* (Lisbon: Caminho, 1989); Rui Ramos, 'A Segunda Fundação (1890–1926)', in José Mattoso, *História de Portugal* (Lisbon: Círculo de Leitores, 1994), Vol. VI.

16 Pedras, 'A Imprensa', p. 41.
17 Ornelas certainly only chose to reproduce the positive coverage in his book. Ornelas, *Viagem do Príncipe Real*, pp. 102–114; M.R. Pedras, 'O Príncipe D. Luís Filipe e os escravos de São Tomé', *O Ideário Patrimonial*, 3 (2014), 73–86.
18 Ornelas, *Viagem do Príncipe Real*, p. 34; *A Luta*, 15 July 1907; José Luís de Almeida (Lavradio), *Memórias do Sexto Marquês de Lavradio* (Lisbon: Ediçõe Ática, 1947), pp. 67–69, quoted by Vicente and Vicente, *O Príncipe Real*, p. 65. This book is a useful compilation of primary sources on the prince's life and we have used it extensively in this chapter.
19 Ornelas, *Viagem do Príncipe Real*, p. 26.
20 Vicente and Vicente, *O Príncipe Real*, p. 65.
21 Ornelas, *Viagem do Príncipe Real*, p. 10.
22 *Tirée par ... A Rainha D. Amélia e a fotografia* (Lisbon: Documenta, 2016).
23 Vicente and Vicente, *O Príncipe Real*, pp. 49–93. There are, at least, six photographic albums from the trip to the Mediterranean: *Tirée par*, p. 124.
24 A.N.T.T., Cartório da Extinta Casa Real, Caixa 42-A, Maço 775, doc. 12.
25 Ornelas, *Viagem do Príncipe Real*, p. 35.
26 Photograph by J.A. Benedy, 'Viagem do Principe Real. Em Luanda. Sobas e as suas Comitivas', *Revista Brazil-Portugal*, no. 207, 1 September 1907, p. 237, in Vicente and Vicente, *O Príncipe Real*, p. 90.
27 The photographs of Arnold Borel are from DM-Échange et Mission, Lausanne, Switzerland.
28 Jill R. Dias, 'Photographic Sources for the History of Portuguese-Speaking Africa, 1870–1914', *History in Africa*, 18 (1991), 67–82; Beatrix Heintze, 'In Pursuit of a Chameleon: Early Ethnographic Photography from Angola in Context', *History in Africa*, 17 (1990), 131–156.
29 Paulo Azevedo, *Joseph e Maurice Lazarus: photographos pioneiros de Moçambique, 1899–1908, Cronologia* ([n.p.]: Arquivo Fotográfico Moçambicano José de Azevedo, 2016); Noeme Santana, 'Olhares Britânicos: Visualizar Lourenço Marques na ótica de J. and M Lazarus, 1899–1908', in F.L. Vicente (ed.), *O Império da Visão: fotografia no contexto colonial português (1860–1960)* (Lisbon: Edições 70, 2014), pp. 211–222.
30 *O Progresso de Lourenço Marques*, 1 August 1907, p. 4.
31 *A Tribuna*, 21 August 1907, p. 1; *A Tribuna*, 11 October 1907, p. 3.
32 *A Tribuna*, 21 August 1907, p. 1; PT/FCB-MBCB/AF/1/UI5601.
33 *Lourenço Marques Guardian*, 19 August 1907. Quoted by Azevedo, *Joseph e Maurice Lazarus*, p. 52.
34 Hilary Sapire, 'Ambiguities of Loyalism: The Prince of Wales in India and Africa, 1921-2 and 25', *History Workshop Journal*, 73 (2011), 50.
35 Ornelas, *Viagem do Príncipe Real*, p. 29.
36 *Ibid.*, p. 30.
37 *Ibid.*, pp. 30, 56.
38 M.B. Jerónimo, 'The "Civilisation Guild": Race and Labour in the Third Portuguese Empire, c. 1870–1930', *Proceedings of the British Academy*, 179 (2012), 173–199, p. 193.
39 The bibliography on this subject is vast. Among recent works are Catherine Higgs, *Chocolate Islands: Cocoa, Slavery, and Colonial Africa* (Athens, OH: Ohio University Press, 2012); Diogo Ramada Curto, 'Políticas coloniais e novas formas de escravatura', in Miguel Bandeira Jerónimo, *Livros Brancos, Almas Negras: a 'missão civilizadora' do colonialismo português (c. 1870–1930)* (Lisbon: Imprensa de Ciências Sociais, 2010), pp. 9–47; M.B. Jerónimo, *The 'Civilising Mission' of Portuguese Colonialism,*

1870–1930 (Basingstoke, Hampshire and New York: Palgrave Macmillan, 2015); Lowell J. Satre, *Chocolate on Trial: Slavery, Politics, and the Ethics of Business* (Athens, OH: Ohio University Press, 2005); and Douglas Wheeler, 'The Galvão Report on Forced Labor (1947) in Historical Context and Perspective: Trouble-Shooter Who Was "Trouble"', *Portuguese Studies Review*, 16:1 (2009), 115–152.
40 Ornelas, *Viagem do Príncipe Real*, p. 61.
41 *Revista Brasil-Portugal*, 1 September 1907, pp. 235–236, quoted by Vicente and Vicente, *O Príncipe Real*, p. 63.
42 A. Gomes dos Santos, 'Acusações Infundadas', *Portugal em África*, June–September 1907, pp. 505–507, quoted by Vicente and Vicente, *O Príncipe Real*, p. 56.
43 Joana Pimentel, 'La collection coloniale de la Cinemateca Portuguesa – Museu do Cinema: 1908–1935', *Journal of Film Preservation*, 64 (2002), 22–30, p. 23, 30; Maria do Carmo Piçarra, 'CINEMA IMPÉRIO: a projeção colonial do Estado Novo português nos filmes das exposições entre guerras mundiais', *Outros tempos*, 13:22 (2016), 126–151, p. 128; Patrícia Ferraz de Matos, 'Images of Africa? Portuguese Films and Documentaries related to the Former Colonies in Africa (First Half of the 20th Century)', *Comunicação e Sociedade*, 29 (2016), 175–196, pp. 177–178.
44 Francisco Mantero, *Portuguese Planters and British Humanitarians: The Case for S. Thomé* (Lisbon: Reforma, 1911), pp. 1, 6, 13; F. Mantero, *La Main d'oeuvre à S. Thomé et à L'île du Prince: extrait de a conférence* (Lisbon: Typ. do Anuário Commercial, 1911). See also F. Mantero, *Manual Labour in S. Thomé and Principe* (Lisbon: Francisco Mantero, 1910).
45 Mantero, *Portuguese Planters*, p. 18. See also *Occidente*, 30 August 1907, quoted by Vicente and Vicente, *O Príncipe Real*, p. 67.
46 Mantero, *Portuguese Planters*, p. 20.
47 *Ibid.*, p. 29.
48 *Ibid.*, p. 50; Harry H. Johnston, *The Negro in The New World* (London: Methuen & Co., 1910).
49 A.H.U, Copiador de S. Tomé, Livro 345, pp. 74–74 v. 1907, quoted by Vicente and Vicente, *O Príncipe Real*, p. 61.
50 Nancy Rose Hunt, *A Nervous State: Violence, Remedies and Reverie in Colonial Congo* (Durban: Duke University Press, 2016).
51 *Occidente*, 30 August 1907, quoted by Vicente and Vicente, *O Príncipe Real*, p. 55.
52 Ornelas, *Viagem do Príncipe Real*, p. 33.
53 Filipa Lowndes Vicente and Inês Vieira Gomes, 'Inequalities on Trial: Conflict, Violence and Dissent in the Making of Colonial Angola (1907–1920)', in Francisco Bethencourt (ed.), *Inequality in the Portuguese-Speaking World* (Eastbourne: Sussex Academic Press, 2018), pp. 217–242; René Pélissier, *História das Campanhas de Angola: resistência e revoltas, 1845–1941* (Lisbon: Editorial Estampa, 1986); R. Pélissier, 'Campagnes Militaires au Sud-Angola (1885–1915)', *Cahiers d'Études Africaines*, 9:33 (1969), 54–123.
54 Ornelas, *Viagem do Príncipe Real*, p. 89.
55 Matheus Serva Pereira, 'Em Busca dos "Grandiosos Batuques": Notas de uma pesquisa em História sobre as experiências dos classificados como "Indígenas" em Lourenço Marques (1890–1930)', *Transversos: Revista de História*, 8 (2016), 235–249; M.S. Pereira, *'Grandiosos Batuques': Identidades e experiências dos trabalhadores urbanos africanos em Lourenço Marques (1890–1930)* (PhD dissertation, Universidade Estadual de Campinas, 2016); Jeff Guy, '"A Paralysis of Perspective": Image and Text in the Creation of an African Chief', *South African Historical Journal*, 47:1 (2002), 51–74.
56 Jessie Mitchell, '"It Will Enlarge the Ideas of the Natives": Indigenous Australians and the Tour of Prince Alfred, Duke of Edinburgh', *Aboriginal History*, 34 (2010), 197–216, pp. 198, 201.
57 Charles V. Reed, *Royal Tourists, Colonial Subjects and the Making of a British World, 1860–1911* (Manchester: Manchester University Press, 2016), p. 191.
58 Ornelas, *Viagem do Príncipe Real*, p. 46; Lavradio, *Memórias do Sexto Marquês de Lavradio*, pp. 69–75, quoted by Vicente and Vicente, *O Príncipe Real*, p. 70.

TENSIONS OF EMPIRE AND MONARCHY

59 Luis Filipe to his brother Manuel, 3 August 1907, A.N.T.T., Cartório da Extinta Casa Real, Caixa 42–A, Maço 775, doc.3, Vicente and Vicente, *O Príncipe Real*, pp. 70–71.
60 Lavradio, *Memórias do Sexto Marquês de Lavradio*, pp. 69–75, quoted by Vicente and Vicente, *O Príncipe Real*, p. 70.
61 *Guardian*, 1 August 1907, quoted by Ornelas, *Viagem do Príncipe Real*, p. 106.
62 Mitchell, ' "It Will Enlarge the Ideas of the Natives" ', p. 209.
63 Ornelas, *Viagem do Príncipe Real*, p. 106.
64 *Guardian*, 1 August 1907, quoted by Ornelas, *Viagem do Príncipe Real*, p. 106.
65 Ibid.
66 Ornelas, *Viagem do Príncipe Real*, p. 71.
67 Dudley Kidd, *The Essential Kafir* (London: Adam and Charles Black, 1904), quoted by Ornelas, *Viagem do Príncipe Real*, p. 107.
68 Ornelas, *Viagem do Príncipe Real*, p. 109.
69 Esmeralda Simões Martinez, 'Uma pesada indemnização', *Revista de África e Africanidades*, 3:12 (February 2011), www.africaeafricanidades.com.br/documentos/12022011_12.pdf, accessed 8 May 2017.
70 Correspondência protocolada na Secretaria Geral do Governo, no. 710, 8 August 1907, quoted by Martinez, 'Uma pesada indemnização'.
71 *O Paiz*, 13 September 1907, quoted by Vicente and Vicente, *O Príncipe Real*, p. 90.
72 Lavradio, *Memórias do Sexto Marquês de Lavradio*, pp. 62–85, quoted by Vicente and Vicente, *O Príncipe Real*, p. 88.
73 Alan H. Jeeves, *Migrant Labour in South Africa's Mining Economy: The Struggle for the Gold Mines' Labour Supply, 1890–1920* (Kingston: McGill-Queen's University Press, 1985), p. 189. For a general history, Malyn D. Newitt, *The History of Mozambique* (London: C. Hurst & Co., 1995).
74 *Chamber of Mines of the South African Republic*, 11th Annual Report, 1899 (Cape Town: Argus, 1900), pp. 59–60.
75 Simon E. Katzenellenbogen, *South Africa and Southern Mozambique: Labour, Railways, and Trade in the Making of a Relationship* (Manchester: Manchester University Press, 1992), pp. 71–74.
76 *The Parliamentary Debates*, Vol. CLXIX (London: Wyman and Sons, 1907), 19 February 1907, p. 678; Katzenellenbogen, *South Africa and Southern Mozambique*, p. 71.
77 Walter H. Wills and R.J. Barrett (eds), *The Anglo-African Who's Who and Biographical Sketch-Book* (London: Routledge, 1905), p. 269.
78 Katzenellenbogen, *South Africa and Southern Mozambique*, p. 74.
79 For example, Cristiana Bastos, *The Colour of Labour: The Racialized Lives of Migrants* (European Research Council Advanced Grant) and hosted by Institute of Social Sciences, University of Lisbon (Grant number: ERC-2015-AdG-695573, 2016–2021).
80 Ornelas, *Viagem do Príncipe Real*, p. 92.
81 *Occidente*, 20 August 1907, quoted by Vicente and Vicente, *O Príncipe Real*, p. 73.
82 *O Paiz*, 13 September 1907, quoted by Vicente and Vicente, *O Príncipe Real*, p. 90.
83 Ornelas, *Viagem do Príncipe Real*, p. 47.
84 *A Lucta*, 30 September 1907, quoted by Vicente and Vicente, *O Príncipe Real*, p. 80.
85 Correspondência para o Príncipe D. Luís Filipe, 1907, Secretaria d'Estado dos Negócios da Marinha e Ultramar, Direcção Geral do Ultramar, MBCB, AHCB, NNG 3468/1; *A Luta*, 30 September 1907; Lavradio, *Memórias do Sexto Marquês de Lavradio*, pp. 75–78, 80, quoted by Vicente and Vicente, *O Príncipe Real*, p. 80.
86 Letter from Francisco de Melo Breyner to Thomaz de Melo Breyner, Lourenço Marques, 31 August 1907. A.P.N.A. 4.2.2, quoted by Vicente and Vicente, *O Príncipe Real*, p. 79.
87 Telegram signed by Soveral, 30 October 1907, A.H.D. Caixa 1089, 1907, quoted by Vicente and Vicente, *O Príncipe Real*, p. 80
88 Ornelas, *Viagem do Príncipe Real*, pp. 79–80.
89 Ibid., pp. 110–111, quoting an article in the *Transwaal Leader*, 19 August 1907.
90 Ibid., p. 51.
91 Ibid., p. 92.

92 *Ibid.*, p. 90.
93 Ornelas mentions sending the message to the *Diário Ilustrado*, but it has not yet been found.
94 Ornelas, *Viagem do Príncipe Real*, pp. 27–28; Augusto Nascimento, 'Conflitos raciais durante a República (1910–1926). Um campo de luta: a Imprensa dos Naturais', África. Rivista do Centro de Estudos Africanos, USP, S. Paulo, 16–17 (1994), pp. 165–176; Isadora de Ataide Fonseca, 'A imprensa e o império na África Portuguesa, 1842–1974' (PhD dissertation, University of Lisbon, 2014).
95 *Ibid.*, p. 12.
96 Sapire, 'Ambiguities of Loyalism', p. 50.
97 Reed, *Royal Tourists*, p. 192.
98 'Bahete InKosso' meaning 'Salvé Senhor'. Lavradio, *Memórias do Sexto Marquês de Lavradio*, pp. 69–75, quoted by Vicente and Vicente, *O Príncipe Real*, pp. 70–71.
99 Ornelas, *Viagem do Príncipe Real*, p. 97.
100 *A Luta*, 28 September 1907, quoted by Vicente and Vicente, *O Príncipe Real*, p. 92.

CHAPTER TEN

Belgian royals on tour in the Congo, 1909–1960

Guy Vanthemsche

Many know that King Leopold II played a decisive role in the creation of the Belgian empire in Central Africa. The king was driven by a life-long and obsessional quest for profitable overseas territories, in spite of the original indifference, reticence or even hostility of most of Belgium's leading politicians and businessmen.[1] His tenacity finally led to the establishment of the Congo Free State in 1885. Leopold's 'personal colony', based on ruthless exploitation and violence, was annexed by the Belgian State in 1908, after years of heavy criticism both in the country and abroad. Foreign opinion saw Leopold as a greedy monarch, exploiting and even butchering the Congolese population – a reputation that still lingers. But he was also confronted with growing unpopularity at home, in part due to his colonial endeavours. Nevertheless, after Leopold's death on 17 December 1909, no *damnatio memoriae* was inflicted upon him. On the contrary, Belgian political, economic and cultural elites immediately established a profane 'cult' of the deceased sovereign, praising his 'genius' and farsightedness in establishing the Belgian colony.[2] Successive Belgian kings invariably stressed the unbreakable bond, created by their predecessor, between monarchy and colony. The physical presence of royals in the Congo was an ideal way to express this close, almost unique, relationship.

Given this peculiarity, Belgian royal and princely voyages in the Congo cannot be considered as mere side stories. This chapter tries to unravel the multi-layered significance of these tours, both on the symbolic level and in the field of concrete politics: for the monarchy, for the colony and its inhabitants, for Belgium's domestic and foreign policy, and for the Congo's image abroad. Some of these trips have already been analysed in specialised monographs, but no general overview has been written to date. Although, because of space, many details concerning specific voyages cannot be mentioned here, a bird's-eye view reveals some characteristics that remain unnoticed when focusing on particular trips.

Setting the stage (the Congo) and presenting the main actor (the Belgian dynasty)

Belgian authorities faced three daunting challenges in 1908. First, the Congo's internal governance had to be reformed after years of maladministration. Second, plunder had to give way to a more 'sustainable' economic and social policy. Third, disastrous foreign perceptions had to be corrected. Belgium was a small and neutral country with limited experience overseas. Foreign powers were also secretly, sometimes even openly, questioning Belgium's sovereignty in Central Africa. Nonetheless, it took only a few years to radically change this ominous start to Belgian colonial rule. International developments, especially the First World War, confirmed Belgium as an established colonial power. The successful campaigns of the *Force publique* (the Congolese armed forces) against German colonial troops even increased the Belgian presence in Black Africa, as the small territories of Ruanda and Urundi were entrusted to 'small brave Belgium' as League of Nations mandates. This confirmation of the country's abilities did not end all foreign appetites and the Belgian African possessions remained the object of diplomatic or propagandistic intrigue, most notably revolving around interwar German colonial claims and British appeasement policy. After the Second World War, Belgian rule in Africa was increasingly questioned by anti-colonial opinion, for example, in the United Nations. These recurrent 'threats' to Belgian sovereignty in Africa led the authorities continually to reaffirm the legitimacy and the 'positive effects' of their overseas rule. By the same logic, they also tried to isolate the Belgian Congo, as much of possible, from external influences.[3]

In the Congo itself, the Free State's rudimentary bureaucracy was replaced by a more efficient colonial apparatus, which maintained 'law and order' over this vast territory, despite recurrent episodes of Congolese unrest and even uprisings. The new authorities eliminated the extreme forms of violence and extortion prevalent in Leopoldian Congo, but coercive practices remained, including forced recruitment of labourers. This insatiable hunger for an indigenous workforce resulted from the spectacular inflow of (mainly Belgian) capital after the First World War. Big enterprises in mining and plantation agriculture prospered – a growth made possible by huge investments in transport infrastructure and by State support of private companies. The Belgian Congo became a leading producer of commodities like copper, uranium, diamonds, tin and palm oil. In the 1920s, this process sparked a debate within the Belgian colonial establishment over excessive capitalist growth and the need for a 'smoother' way of ruling the Congolese populations.

Despite the heavy blow struck by the crisis of the 1930s, especially on the Congolese population, the export economy survived and developed further. New labour-saving methods boosted productivity and allowed for paternalistic 'protection' of the Congolese wage labourers. In the mid-1950s, the Belgian Congo reached its zenith. Its rulers presented it as a 'model colony': the economy thrived as never before; an ambitious Ten-Year Plan of Economic and Social Development (1949–1959) helped to 'modernise' the colony; and a network of primary schools and dispensaries, spanning most of the territory and mostly run by Catholic missions, provided basic educational and medical services.

In the second half of the 1950s, Congolese nationalism took form, developing in only a few years' time (1956–1959) into a mass movement that shattered Belgian illusions of long-lasting white rule. Political tensions led to a Round Table Conference held in January–February 1960 at which the main Belgian and Congolese parties decided to grant independence to the Congo on 30 June of that same year.

Of course, this setting moulded the royal tours in the Congo; conversely, the voyages themselves exercised *some* influence on the colony. But in order to understand this complex relationship, we also have to present some peculiarities of the Belgian dynasty.[4] When Belgium became independent in 1830, a German prince, Leopold of Saxe-Coburg, was chosen as head of state. Royal power was curtailed by the constitution: in Belgium, the king 'reigns, but does not govern'. Political power is in the hands of the Cabinet ministers, supported by a parliamentary majority; in theory, the king can take no personal political initiatives. Despite this, Leopold I (1790–1865, r. 1831–1865) maximised his influence, both formally and informally, founding a tradition continued by his successors. His son Leopold II (1835–1909, r. 1865–1909), for instance, waged a 'personal' foreign policy leading to the creation of the Congo Free State. Leopold II's nephew and successor Albert I (1875–1934, r. 1909–1934) was more respectful of the constitutional spirit. He nevertheless took personal command of the Belgian army during the First World War and influenced diplomatic talks with both Allies and enemies. While his role brought him immense prestige as *le Roi chevalier*, the same stance, taken by his son Leopold III (1901–1983, r. 1934–1951), triggered a major political crisis. When Belgium was invaded in May 1940 (and even before, during the 'Phoney War'), the monarch followed in his father's footsteps and acted as commander-in-chief of the army. But this time, the Belgian troops suffered utter and quick defeat. Leopold unilaterally surrendered to the Germans and refused to follow his government into exile to continue the struggle against the Nazis. Moreover, although technically a 'prisoner of war', he also tried to strike a deal with Hitler to establish an authoritarian regime in Belgium under German aegis. When the Allies liberated Belgium in 1944, the Germans abducted Leopold and kept him in captivity. The Belgian Parliament therefore appointed the king's younger brother, Prince Charles (1903–1983, regent 1944–1950), as the regent. Even after Leopold's liberation, he could not return to Belgium to resume his constitutional duties because important political forces opposed this move, judging Leopold's wartime attitude unacceptable. The resulting *Question royale* ('Royal issue') dominated Belgian politics for years. After a referendum in 1950 the king returned on 22 July that year, and protests set Belgium on the brink of a civil war. To avoid disaster, Leopold III abdicated in favour of his twenty-year-old son Baudouin (1930–1993, r. 1951–1993). Traumatised by his father's abdication, Baudouin had difficulty fully assuming his role. Yet he gradually became a respected and even popular monarch, far less prone to personal political initiatives than his predecessors. As we shall see, these crucial episodes in Belgian dynastic history had some influence on royal travels in the Congo.

An inventory of royal and princely voyages in the Congo (1909–1960)

The paradox has often been noted: Leopold II, the founder of the Congo Free State, never set foot in his African territories. Although other nineteenth-century monarchs never visited their own empire, most notably Queen Victoria, this abstention is somewhat surprising in Leopold's case, since he had undertaken several voyages outside Europe before his accession to the throne. One of his closest collaborators, Colonel Charles Liebrechts, told a newspaper in 1928 that Leopold 'often thought' of travelling to the Congo, even raising the question explicitly on two different occasions. Liebrechts and Henry Morton Stanley (who worked for the Free State) advised him against travelling to Central Africa. Transport infrastructure was still almost non-existent; logistics were rudimentary, and tropical sicknesses omnipresent. Moreover, the king was getting older when the Free State was founded.[5] Thus Leopold died without having seen the region he so profoundly transformed.

All of Leopold's successors, however, did visit the Congo, some of them several times, as Table 10.1 shows.

Table 10.1 Belgian royal tours in the Congo

Royal figure	Date	Duration (in days)	Type of voyage
Crown Prince Albert	2 April–15 August 1909	136	Exploratory voyage
Crown Prince Leopold	21 April–21 January 1926	175	Exploratory voyage
King Albert I and Queen Elisabeth	5 June–31 August 1928	87	Official visit
King Albert I	23 March–24 April 1932	33	Private trip
Crown Prince Leopold and his wife Princess Astrid	30 December 1932–17 April 1933	109	Official mission
Regent Charles	29 June–12 August 1947	45	Official visit
King Baudouin	15 May–12 June 1955	28	Official visit
Former King Leopold III and his morganatic wife Princess Lilian de Réthy	21 February–14 April 1957	53	Private trip
Queen-Mother Elisabeth	19 January–2 February 1958	15	Official mission (coupled with touristic visit)
King Baudouin	16 December 1959–2 January 1960	18	Personal political visit
King Baudouin	29 June–30 June 1960	2	Official visit (attendance at the independence ceremony)

'Royal' or 'princely' voyages included official visits of the Belgian heads of State to their colony (1928, 1947 and 1955). King Baudouin's brief presence at the independence ceremony on 30 June 1960, of course, also belongs to this type of tour, but it took on a special symbolism, since it marked at once the closure of the colonial era and the opening of a new chapter in the Congo's history. There were also 'official missions', that is, visits by a member of the royal family executing a specific government assignment (1933, 1958).[6] In other cases, members of the royal family travelled in the Congo more or less incognito, essentially for leisure and (theoretically) without executing public tasks.[7] Finally, two sojourns (1909 and 1925) can be labelled as 'exploratory voyages'. Conceived as a sort of colonial Grand Tour, these long trips (lasting respectively 136 and 175 days) were intended to 'initiate' the crown prince into colonial matters. In 1909, during the final days of Leopold II's reign, his dynamic nephew Albert was eager to discover Belgium's new colony. At first, the monarch opposed the crown prince's desire, probably because of the risks involved and the fact Albert was the only heir to the throne. But Leopold finally gave in, since the government supported Albert's plan.[8] The latter's eldest son Leopold shared a similar 'initiatory' experience, undertaking a voyage in the Congo in 1925. Leopold III's own son and successor Baudouin might also have been sent on a similar tour, but circumstances decided otherwise, breaking what might have become a dynastic 'tradition'. When the Second World War broke out, Prince Baudouin was only ten years old; and when peace returned, the pending *Question royale* prevented the princely 'initiation' tour.

Ways and means: transport modes and places visited

The twentieth-century transport revolution transformed travel to and within distant and immense territories such as the Congo. The three first royal and princely voyages to and from the Belgian colony (1909, 1925 and 1928) were still made by ship; all the following ones used aircraft. A direct air link between Brussels and the colonial capital Léopoldville was established only in 1935; consequently, in 1932 and 1933 the royals flew to and from Central Africa with the British company Imperial Airways – a choice not especially conducive to the strengthening of Belgian patriotic feelings. But this travel option remained almost unnoticed by the larger public given the private and discreet character of both trips. All the following voyages were carried out with Belgian military or civilian air transport (especially with flag carrier Sabena).

Travelling *within* the colony also changed drastically over the years. Crown Prince Albert's first voyage in 1909 was still exhausting, even adventurous: for many days, he walked, cycled or rode on horseback along many kilometres of rudimentary dirt 'roads'. He also travelled by boat and train although railway networks were still under construction. On two occasions, the prince's boat got stuck in sandbanks on the Congo River. Parts of Prince Leopold's trip in 1925 also were 'expedition'-like, including long marches in the jungle and the absence of comfort during many days. These details reveal one of the essential features of the Belgian colony as of all others: the gradual development of transport networks. Infrastructure developed quickly from the 1920s. King

Albert's visit in 1928 was officially motivated by the inauguration of the so-called BCK railway (*Chemin de fer du Bas-Congo au Katanga*), linking the mining province of Katanga to the Kasai region. Albert and Elisabeth's 1928 voyage was marked by another transport feat: they took an airplane. As mentioned, the direct air link between Belgium and the colony was established relatively late; but in the 1920s, the national airline Sabena already ran an extensive network between the main centres of colonial activity.[9] The royal flight from Léopoldville to Tshikapa (in the Kasai) was presented and perceived as a proof of modernity. Air travel eventually became commonplace. Still, the two most important post-war official visits (1947 and 1955) included a mix of transportation: aeroplane, train, boat and even some long-distance (and exhausting) car rides.

Official visits followed a fairly standardised pattern, a sort of classic Grand Tour also performed by the many other officials who visited the colony, especially in the 1950s (such as ministers and MPs). The 1928, 1933, 1947 and 1955 trips all started in the westernmost part of the Congo. The ports of Boma and Matadi acted as evident starting points when the sovereign reached the Congo by ship (1928); once the monarchs arrived by plane (1947 and 1955), the journey started in the capital Léopoldville. From there, officials visited the different key regions of the colony (not necessarily in the following order): the diamond-rich Kasai province; the mining province Katanga, including its capital city Élisabethville and other important mining centres like Kolwezi; then the Great Lakes region, generally coupled with a short visit to the mandate territories of Ruanda and Urundi;[10] finally the northeastern (Stanleyville) and northwestern part of the colony (Coquilhatville). In other words, thousands of kilometres were covered within a short space of time, but the royals indeed succeeded in visiting all the key regions of the colony, without neglecting any of them. The two 'exploratory voyages' (1909 and 1925), which lasted much longer than the official visits, also covered most of the colonial territory,[11] but things were different for the official missions and the private trips. They privileged the eastern part of the Congo, especially the Kivu region and the national parks that were a tourist attraction.

Ways and means: the media setting

The transport revolution went hand in hand with a communications revolution. The development of photography and film had important effects on the staging and impact of royal and princely voyages. Organisers initially had some difficulties in managing these 'new' media. Some photos were taken during Crown Prince Albert's 1909 exploratory voyage, but they were not really destined for public circulation.[12] Media coverage (through long newspaper articles) was mainly limited to the prince's homecoming, which was celebrated with grand ceremonies. Public resonance of the trip within the Congo was limited, as the colonial press was still in its infancy.

During the interwar period, royal and princely voyages gradually opened up to propaganda through press articles and images, but distrust of or lack of interest by the media persisted. In the 1920s, the press was still clearly held off. When the editor-in-chief of *Le Soir*, one of the Belgium's main newspapers, asked for an interview with Crown Prince Leopold before his departure, the king himself declined, because 'He feared that this interview could create susceptibilities in the other newspapers'.[13] The Association cinématographique de Belgique, the professional organisation of filmmakers, proposed that a cameraman accompany the crown prince on his trip. Alas, the palace declined this proposal also as 'the Prince wants to travel completely incognito'.[14] As a result, few publicly circulated photographic accounts exist of Leopold's first voyage to the Congo.[15]

The Court later began to realise that press reports and publicly distributed images were key elements to successful colonial tours. Albert and Elisabeth's official visit in 1928 was better covered, and several professional photographers were commissioned to create a photographic album that was widely circulated.[16] Some episodes of this voyage were also filmed, but the cinema was not yet fully exploited to record the royal trip. Once again, journalists complained about this 'missed opportunity': 'Cinematographic reports had not been foreseen in the program – just as press reports ... The great "documentary" has not been shot; the animated and graphic testimony of our Sovereign's visit to the colony does not exist'.[17] Even the newspaper press was considered more as a nuisance than as a propagandistic instrument. South African reporters who asked for some facilities to cover the king's passage through Élisabethville were rebuffed. According to the Belgian authorities, all arrangements had already been made: 'Knowing all the difficulties that the organisers have experienced *in order to satisfy the Belgian press* [my emphasis]', the South African journalists were informed that they should ask some third persons to get information concerning the royal stay in Katanga.[18] By the time of the princely mission of 1933, the Royal Palace was clearly preoccupied by the way Leopold's voyage was covered in the press.[19]

After the Second World War, the attitude towards press, photos and films changed drastically. Nevertheless, the prince regent's voyage of 1947 was, once again, a missed propagandistic opportunity. Jef Van Bilsen, a journalist appointed by the official Belgian press agency

Belga, accompanied Regent Charles during his forty-five-day tour of the colony.[20] His reports were sent to the Belgian newspapers, but the Belgian authorities never published a memorial album.[21] Only a modest brochure containing photos of the trip was produced by the colonial administration, namely as a special issue of *La Voix du Congolais*, the magazine written by and for *évolués* (Congolese subjects who were more or less 'educated' and 'Europeanised').[22] Some newsreels were of course shot during Charles's visit, but an official (or unofficial) propaganda film was not made – in spite of an offer made by André Cauvin, a Belgian filmmaker who had made propaganda films on the Congo during the Second World War and whose film *Congo* had even been nominated for an Oscar in 1944.[23] The domestic political tensions relating to the *Question royale* might explain the relative discretion of the Belgian authorities.

By contrast, King Baudouin's 1955 trip was fully reported. For the first time, the palace and the Belgian authorities spared no effort to stage and publicise the royal presence in the Congo. Consequently, this visit also left a lasting imprint in popular and political memory (and in historiography). Dozens of journalists were authorised to cover this voyage. Minister of the Colonies Auguste Buisseret declared that this would be 'the occasion of a particular effort to draw the attention of the Belgian public to the Colony, to show the natives the interest that the authorities of the Metropole have for them and to affirm Belgian authority and sovereignty over our territories in Africa'.[24] Day by day, Belgian newspapers published articles describing the royal stay. Thousands of photos were taken, some widely circulated. Several lavishly illustrated books and brochures were afterwards published to commemorate Baudouin's 'triumphant' visit to the colony.[25] This time, the filmmaker André Cauvin was commissioned by the Ministry of the Colonies to direct a full-length feature film in Technicolor. The result, *Bwana Kitoko*, was shown on many screens in Belgium, in the Congo and abroad, greatly contributing to the propagandistic success of Baudouin's first visit to the colony.[26] We will come back on the political and ideological dimension of this media strategy during the 1955 tour. On the other hand, Baudouin's impromptu visit of 1959 – a personal initiative of the monarch discussed below – was deliberately organised without press facilities.[27]

What the visits meant for the outside world

What exactly did these trips to the Congo mean – starting from the global political scene, down to the modest inhabitants of the country? During the colonial period, most visits were undertaken to emphasise the 'unbreakable' bond between Belgium and its overseas territories. Given the disastrous international image of the Free State and persistent doubts concerning Belgium's ability to run such a huge colony, this was of crucial importance. Albert's 1909 Grand Tour sent a clear message to the outside world: Belgium and its monarchy took their colonial duties seriously.[28] This established a baseline for all subsequent voyages. Before air travel took the royals to the Congo in only a few days' or hours' time, the journey by ship to and from the colony also confirmed Belgium's status as a colonial power. Stopovers on the way – for example in the Spanish Canary Islands, Portuguese Madeira, French Morocco, French Senegal or British South Africa, as was the case for Albert's 1909 voyage – resulted in local ceremonies and newspaper articles echoing Belgium's colonial involvement in Central Africa.[29] Once the royals were on the ground, notables from adjacent colonies traditionally paid their respects – a formal but symbolic confirmation of the Belgian character of the Congo.

The post-war voyages of 1947 and 1955 also sent a clear message to the outside world: more than ever, Belgium was attached to its overseas territories, and vice versa. But this time, a special emphasis was also put on 'social progress' and 'modernisation'. In his 1947 arrival speech in Léopoldville, the prince regent thanked the colony for its crucial contribution to the war effort and recognised the mother country's 'war debt' towards the Congo. This was to be 'repaid', among other initiatives, by the launching of a social welfare programme. Baudouin's 1955 visit portrayed the Belgian colony as a paradise of social and economic progress, with joyous masses of Congolese subjects enthusiastically welcoming their sovereign. As we have seen, the media were carefully mobilised to convey this image globally. This showcase strategy was meant to silence the widespread and growing criticism of Belgian colonialism.

From 1960, the international significance of royal visits to the Congo of course changed drastically. The royal presence during the independence ceremony of 30 June 1960 would show the international community that the colonial bond was severed in full mutual agreement and respect. Unfortunately, things turned out differently. In reaction to Baudouin's speech, a blatant apologia for Belgian colonial rule, the Congolese Prime Minister Patrice Lumumba gave his own unannounced speech, in which he highlighted the sufferings of the Congolese population. In the eyes of many Belgians, these anti-colonialist words were a clear 'insult' to the king (who himself was outraged).

What the visits meant for Belgian politics ... and for the royals themselves

Royal and princely visits to the Congo of course conveyed to the Belgian public the same proud message as to foreign audiences: Belgium was firmly attached to its overseas possession. But these voyages also connected to specific colonial and domestic policy. Both components were, moreover, closely intertwined with the royal and princely personalities. Some recurrent patterns can thus be identified throughout the years. Travelling in the Congo enabled the monarchs and crown princes to gain first-hand knowledge of this huge territory, meaning successive monarchs were often better acquainted with Congolese matters than were most Ministers of the Colonies. Direct contact with men on the spot sometimes led to enduring personal relationships that influenced colonial policy and administration. The most striking example is Prince Leopold's encounter with Pierre Ryckmans, a young colonial civil servant, during his 1925 travels in Urundi. In 1934, Ryckmans became Congo's governor-general thanks to Leopold III's personal intervention.[30] One should also emphasise that princes and kings visited the colony 'alone': politicians did not accompany ('chaperone') them. Sometimes the royals *met* the Minister of the Colonies or some other member of the Cabinet during their tour, but as a rule they travelled with a personal entourage of their own choice – a tradition that stressed dynastic autonomy.[31]

This interdependence of personal and political elements had already begun with Albert's 1909 'exploratory voyage', which the crown prince planned carefully.[32] In his personal travel diary, Albert criticised painful aspects of the colony's situation and had some harsh words for the Leopoldian heritage.[33] Albert's voyage added to his personal prestige: the press praised the young, amiable and athletic prince, returning safely from his 'dangerous expedition' in the heart of Africa. His image contrasted sharply with Leopold's, and when the old and unpopular king died a few months later, the 'public relations bonus' attached to Albert's Congo trip facilitated the monarchical succession and helped to restore dynastic prestige. In addition, the new king was convinced that things had to change in the Congo – notwithstanding all the official praise given to Leopold II, even in his own speeches. Although the constitution prohibited the king from *making* colonial policy, he could (and did) influence it in ways that by definition were discreet (and, hence, often still remain unclear).

King Albert's concern for the social dimension of colonisation was also apparent during his second voyage, in 1928. This time, unaffected and spontaneous contact with the colonial reality was more difficult, given the visit's formal nature. Nevertheless, critical thoughts concerning the Congo's situation once again appear in Albert's travel diary: although he was struck by the 'progress' made since his previous stay, he was not blind to enduring social problems.[34] Ministers and diplomats alike knew that the king had returned with an 'unfavourable impression'.[35] The shortcomings of medical and sanitary infrastructure, in particular, attracted both his and Queen Elisabeth's attention. It was no surprise then that the Fonds Reine Élisabeth pour l'Assistance médicale aux Indigènes (FOREAMI) was created soon after, in 1930.[36]

A similar pattern emerges when Prince Leopold, heir to the throne, was sent to the Congo in 1933 to study the agricultural situation. This mission, defined by Royal Decree (14 December 1932), did not come out of the blue. It reflected the ongoing polemic concerning the 'excessive' industrialisation of the colony. Octave Louwers, a specialist in Congolese matters, briefed the crown prince before his departure. This high-ranking civil servant belonged to the Catholic current criticising the capitalist activities in the Congo, which had devastating effects on the local population. His note to Leopold stated: 'In the capitalist exploitation system, the social and material improvement of the natives (*indigènes*) is not the essential goal of the country's development, as our Colonial Charter prescribes ... The main goal is the profit of the capitalist enterprises ... The natives only receive the crumbs falling off the table.'[37] In his private correspondence with his father, Prince Leopold criticised the state of things in the Congo. 'Dare I say that those who have exploited the agricultural riches of the Congo so far, merit the severe punishment they are undergoing for the moment [that is, the economic crisis]?' Furthermore, he noted, 'The beautiful principles of colonisation and the interesting scientific methods applied to agriculture that I have seen at work in the Dutch Indies are not applied in the Congo of this day'.[38] After his return home, the crown prince made a resounding speech in the Senate in which he pleaded for a new agricultural, more peasant-oriented policy in the colony – a statement not especially welcomed by colonial business elites. One of the expressions of this policy change, facilitated and prepared by the princely mission, was the foundation, in 1933, of the Institut national pour l'Étude agronomique du Congo (INEAC), charged with the promotion of colonial agricultural development.

Because of several historical accidents, it took fourteen years before a Belgian royal again set foot on Congolese soil. After King Albert's sudden death in a climbing accident in 1934, Leopold III had no time to visit the Congo: his attention was entirely monopolised by domestic and international problems. After the Second World War, the royal question had an undeniable impact on the organisation and significance of royal voyages to the colony. The anti-Leopoldist and leftist government coalition wanted to stress the legitimacy of Charles, the prince regent. Visiting the colony was an excellent way to convey this message to both the international and domestic public. The governor-general of the Congo wanted to give 'all the pomp possible' to Charles's voyage, and 'to render him the same honours as for the King himself'.[39] Pro-Leopoldists openly criticised this project. Given the explosive political atmosphere, it took some time before the voyage materialised. Apparently, Charles himself even thought of abandoning the idea. In March 1947 a new coalition came to power, consisting of both socialists and Catholics (who, in principle, were in favour of Leopold III's return). According to rumours, this change of government would lead to the postponement of the princely voyage; but in fact, it happened anyway.[40] Given this context, everything was done in order to avoid undue passion on either side, pro- or anti-Leopoldist. No album or commemorative book was published, no documentary movie made.[41] As we have seen, this voyage was also used to announce a new inflexion of Belgian colonial policy: the foundation of the Fonds du Bien-Être indigène (FBEI), a social welfare fund for the indigenous population.

As we have also seen, Baudouin's accession to the throne in 1950 was a decisive turn in the *Question royale*, yet did not end all controversy regarding the former King Leopold III, and persisting tensions marked royal travel in the colony. In 1952, Baudouin was already preparing his own official visit to the Congo.[42] But it took three more years before this plan came to fruition. Traditionally, every new Belgian sovereign visits in turn all provincial capitals shortly after his coronation, to establish a festive contact with the population of his realm (the 'Joyeuses Entrées'). Before Baudouin, this tradition had always been limited to Belgium itself. By presenting the 1955 visit as a (somewhat belated) 'Joyeuse Entrée', the authorities and the monarchy stressed that the Congo was an integral part of the national territory (the so-called 'tenth Province'). Moreover, the voyage was framed and staged as a major turn in Belgian colonial policy. The idea of 'Communauté belgo-congolaise', launched after the trip, promoted a more 'cordial' and 'open' relationship between the white colonists and the black population. In the eyes of its advocates, this new approach to race relations would avoid decolonisation: in some undefined future, the Congolese would be associated with the Belgians to administer the country *together*. During the 1955 visit, many direct encounters were organised between the monarch and his Congolese subjects – local indigenous rulers as well as modest employees or workers. In Stanleyville, for instance, Baudouin talked for a while to an unknown post office clerk named Patrice Lumumba, the future icon of African independence struggle.[43] All these carefully staged contacts (including the many handshakes) were eagerly captured in photo or film, and widely circulated throughout the world.

All observers stressed the enormous enthusiasm of the black population on every public appearance of the young monarch, always impeccably dressed in khaki Belgian military or in white colonial uniform. This was of course a most welcome development for the Belgian authorities, but even more so for the Court. Indeed, for some time, royal circles were developing their own strategy, separate from the Cabinet's policy. They wanted to establish a special relationship between dynasty and colony, possibly under the form of a vice-royalty or a diarchy (a member of the royal family would become the viceroy of the Congo, or even the king of an 'independent' Congo, in some future time).[44] This 'triumphant' tour also had important repercussions on Baudouin's personality and aura. The shy and rather bad-tempered young man who had left Belgium immediately transformed, during his

10.1 King Baudouin in Kamina, Congo, 1955

Congo visit, into a smiling, open and amiable man who now apparently was pleased to be a sovereign 'loved by his subjects'. In a certain sense, this voyage thus marks a turn in Baudouin's relationship with his domineering father, the abdicated King Leopold III, and with his stepmother Princess Lilian, who both were very close to the young monarch. On one occasion, rumours of a sudden journey of Leopold and Lilian to the northeastern part of the Congo, where they would meet young Baudouin, cast a dark cloud over the latter's successful sojourn. This plan – if it ever existed – was never realised, luckily for Baudouin's image. Once back in Belgium, his prestige increased steadily; his successful Congo voyage undoubtedly contributed to his growing domestic popularity.[45]

However, due to the inaccessibility of Baudouin's private archives, it is still impossible to know how matters evolved exactly. It is nevertheless clear that former King Leopold III indeed pursued personal political objectives, in which the Congo played some part. His strong character created some difficulty for the former monarch to admit that his public role had come to an end. His physical presence in the Royal Palace in Brussels symbolised his persistent will to influence political life – much to the displeasure of the vast majority of Belgian politicians. To help settle this problem, Leopold was made honorary president of a newly created institution, the Fondation internationale scientifique (FIS, created by a Royal Decree of 28 February 1956). Officially, this foundation was charged with the promotion of scientific research, essentially concerning overseas territories. This suited Leopold perfectly. Since his youth, he was keen on travelling in tropical regions – an interest aroused by his 1925 'exploratory' voyage to the Congo. This trip had been followed by many other far-off travels, and in the course of these 'expeditions', he had also developed a passion for photography, for wildlife and ethnographic observation, and for contact with 'primitive' people – a passion that would last until his death in 1983.[46]

In 1957, an important documentary film was made under the aegis of the FIS, *Les Seigneurs de la forêt*, set in the northeastern part of the Congo and showing its wildlife, its natural riches and the daily life of its indigenous inhabitants.[47] Leopold and Lilian 'privately' travelled to this region early that year, in part to attend the shooting of the movie, which the former king officially supported in his capacity as honorary president of FIS. However, this voyage also had a dimension that exceeded the purely scientific (or touristic) aspects. On coming home, Leopold made it clear, in a private letter to his mother Queen Elisabeth (Albert I's widow), that he also had some public ambitions in the Congo. 'As far as I am concerned, I am and will always be obliged to keep the most strict reserve in view of the office that Baudouin is now fulfilling. As for Lilian, you know that there is no role she can play here [in Belgium] ... In the Congo, the situation is entirely different. I notice that a vast field of action is offered to us there, which will allow us to play a useful, necessary and beneficial role.' According to Leopold, his son Baudouin 'shares our joy at the perspectives that are offered to us there and he is well decided to give us free rein'. Leopold therefore also asked his mother Elisabeth to give up a trip to the Congo she was planning in the near future. This voyage would thwart his own plans in the Congo, so the former king said.[48] Unfortunately, we do not know what these plans entailed; but one thing is sure: Leopold's wish was not fulfilled. On the request of the government, Queen Elisabeth went to the Congo in January 1958 to unveil a statue of her late husband in the Congolese city that bore his name (Albertville, now Kalemie, on the eastern border of the Congo).[49] These issues clearly demonstrate that royal voyages in the colony were significant moves in broader political (and personal) strategies.

It is also clear that the rapid decolonisation of the Congo, in the late 1950s, completely changed the context of these strategies. By the end of 1959, it was evident that Belgian colonial rule was nearing its end. After violent incidents and bloodshed in Léopoldville (January) and in Stanleyville (October), followed by the arrest of the nationalist leader Patrice Lumumba, the threat of further violence loomed over the country. King Baudouin then took a remarkable personal initiative: he would travel to the Congo, in the first place to Stanleyville, the city where severe trouble had just broken out. Although originally opposed, the ministers finally agreed to the royal plan, despite the high political risks involved.[50] During his eighteen-day stay, Baudouin held many talks – with both Belgian and Congolese personalities – about the Congo's future; but his journey did not yield any concrete results. At best, it somewhat improved the general atmosphere. But despite the great tensions in black public opinion, the trip also showed that the king was still popular among the Congolese. Excited crowds greeted the monarch during his public appearances – although observers noted that the enthusiasm had somewhat receded in comparison to 1955. One of the possible reasons of this enduring popularity will be mentioned in the following and final section. From the perspective of domestic (and dynastic) politics, this peculiar 1959 voyage was possibly related to the Court's strategy to maintain some role for the royal family in the future, independent Congo; lack of access to the post-1950 royal archives makes it impossible to know whether King Baudouin still hoped (or not) to become the head of state of this new African country. Maybe his sudden and impromptu sojourn in the Congo was a way to gauge this possibility.

Whatever it may be, the dynastic bond was well and truly severed when the Congo became independent: the country became a republic, and not a monarchy headed by some member of the Coburg dynasty. The king's presence in Léopoldville on 30 June 1960, at the independence ceremony, signified the irrevocable end of the dynastic link with this huge Central African country. A famous picture most symbolically captured this event: when driving in an open car, from the airport to the location where power would officially be transferred, a Congolese succeeded in grabbing King Baudouin's sword.

What the voyages meant for the Congolese people

The effects royal voyages had on the Congolese themselves are extremely difficult to assess. Nevertheless, some indications lift a tip of the veil covering their perceptions and reactions. King Albert's official visit in 1928 was deliberately organised 'with great ceremonial, in order to impress the natives, who had only kept very little memory of the all too discreet voyage of [Crown Prince Leopold] in 1925'.[51] On his arrival in Boma, the sovereign was struck by the enthusiasm of the native population (and the rather cool welcome of the white people); but some days later he also noted the distant attitude of the Congolese workers he came across.[52] Far more revealing are the following incidents. One day, a Congolese mechanic serving on the royal boat audaciously managed to talk to the king when the latter was strolling, alone with his wife Queen Elisabeth, on the shore of the Congo River. He complained about the bad treatment that he and his fellow men had to suffer from the white rulers. 'C'est la grande misère au Congo, le nègre fait tout le travail, il n'est pas payé, on lui donne des coups ... Le Roi Albert et la Reine Élisabeth sont venus, quand ils sont là, on nous laisse tranquilles, mais quand ils seront partis, ce sera la même chose. Le Roi ne sait pas tout, on lui cache tout. C'est la grande misère ici.'[53] These words, reported in Albert's private diary, are one of the rare subaltern voices reaching us through the thick layers of time. A letter handed over to the sovereigns by a few Congolese also belongs to this exceptional category of sources. The authors of this document complained about the hardships of colonial rule: 'Au Congo que nous sommes [sic], nous sommes dans le malheur! Les blancs nous maltraitent comme ils veulent, sur tout [sic] les blancs de [sic] Gouvernement'. They asked the king and the queen to send some representatives (preferably 'quelques noirs civilisés') to the Congo to redress all these evils. They also asked for good schools where the people would be educated, and concluded with a wish: 'Que le Royaume de Belgique Reigne [sic] au Congo à Jamais.'[54] On yet another occasion, a soldier stopped the royal car and handed over to the bewildered king a small sum – apparently, he gave back his (too low) wages in a sign of protest.[55] As Albert had learned a few words in the African languages, he may sometimes have spoken directly to Congolese men or women; this may have contributed to the image of an 'accessible' monarch, concerned with the well-being of his subjects.[56]

These few anecdotes indicate that the impact of royal tours on the Congolese people should not be underestimated. Apparently, the king was considered (at least by some of his colonial subjects) as a formidable and benevolent figure, a righter of wrongs, who would terminate the injustices perpetrated by the other white people. The following official visits show similar patterns. Prince Regent Charles's 1947 trip aroused great enthusiasm in the Congolese population.[57] We have already mentioned the enthusiasm of the Congolese during Baudouin's visits in 1955 and 1959. Some of Baudouin's (broadcasted) speeches also contained a passage in Lingala or Swahili, when he directly addressed the native crowds or a specific audience.[58] It is not clear whether or not this was the king's personal initiative (did he want to perpetuate his grandfather's example?); but these vernacular messages always aroused enthusiastic reactions in the Congolese population.

All observers of course abundantly emphasised the popular joy accompanying the royal appearances. Yet, another aspect of Congolese reactions was hardly noted – if at all. In 1947, a confidential report of the Congolese Secret Police (Sûreté) observed that the imminent arrival of the prince regent had triggered several petitions in the native neighbourhood of Léopoldville, 'in order to hand over diverse complaints to the Prince Regent, amongst others that they have to work too hard, that they don't earn enough, etc.'.[59] Likewise, Baudouin's 1955 visit generated wild rumours and great expectations among the Congolese: the king would change everything, suppress taxes, distribute presents, punish bad officials, etc. On his next trip, in 1959, Congolese crowds carried banners proclaiming at once 'Vive le Roi' and 'Vive Lumumba', or shouted 'Vive le Roi' as well as 'Vive l'indépendance'.[60] When Baudouin arrived in Stanleyville, the masses hoped that he would liberate Lumumba, who was imprisoned pending his trial.[61]

In the eyes of many Congolese, the king was seemingly endowed with almost supernatural power capable of altering the life of the ordinary people. In a note preparing for the 1955 voyage, former Vice-Governor-General Gaston Heenen wrote that 'for the mass of the natives, Royal Authority is of quasi-divine essence; the King's person has a sacred character; it must not be too accessible'. This is why 'such visits must not be too frequent' but also why 'the King's presence has to be surrounded with an imposing ceremonial. The natives are very sensitive to external appearance, to decorum'.[62] Recent eyewitness accounts of Congolese having seen Baudouin's triumphant tour show the lasting impact of this event on their minds. According to one spectator, 'When King Baudouin arrived, the white people stopped using the word "monkey" (*macaque*) when talking to black people ... The King explained that the Blacks and the Europeans should eat and drink together and that a black man could marry a European woman'. Another interviewee said: 'We hoped that he would bring a solution to all the problems we were confronted with.'[63] This final remark reminds us of the fact that royal tours clearly were a multi-layered phenomenon connecting the global scene, through domestic political strategy, down to the most modest perceptions and acts of ordinary people.

Notes

1 Many thanks to my colleague Matthew Stanard (Berry College) for having revised an earlier version of this chapter.
2 Matthew G. Stanard, *Selling the Congo: A History of European Pro-Empire Propaganda and the Making of Belgian Imperialism* (Lincoln: University of Nebraska Press, 2012), pp. 262–265.
3 Guy Vanthemsche, *Belgium and the Congo, 1885–1980* (Cambridge: Cambridge University Press, 2012).
4 Jean Stengers, *L'action du Roi en Belgique depuis 1831* (Brussels: Duculot, 1996).
5 'Pourquoi Léopold II n'alla pas au Congo', *L'Illustration congolaise*, October 1928, 82, 2015.
6 Respectively, a study of Congolese agriculture entrusted to Crown Prince Leopold by Royal Decree of 14 December 1932; the inauguration of a monument dedicated to the memory of the former king Albert I, entrusted to his widow, Queen Mother Elisabeth (1958).
7 King Albert visited the wildlife reserve park carrying his name, in 1932; former King Leopold III toured the Congo with his second wife in 1957.
8 Émile Vandewoude, *Le voyage du Prince Albert au Congo en 1909* (Brussels: ARSOM, 1990), pp. 8–9.
9 Guy Vanthemsche, *La Sabena et l'aviation commerciale belge 1923–2001* (Brussels: De Boeck, 2001).
10 The mandate territories were not visited in 1928.
11 In 1909, Prince Albert did not visit the Kasai. Prince Leopold's 1925 journey was more exhaustive.

12 Some have been published in Raymond Buren, *Journal de route du prince Albert en 1909 au Congo* (Brussels: Mols, 2008).
13 Archives of the Royal Palace, Brussels (ARP), Secretariat of King Albert, IV.B.58, the King's Secretary to E. Patris, editor-in-chief of *Le Soir*, 18 April 1925.
14 ARP, Great Marshal of the Court of Albert I (GMCA), 296, Jules Jourdain, president of the Association cinématographique de Belgique, to Maurice de Patoul, Chancelor at the Court, 30 January 1925; and vice versa, 9 February 1925.
15 Prince Leopold himself took more than a thousand private wildlife and ethnographic photographs (François Muhashy Habiyaremye and Jackie Van Goethem, 'Valeur environnementale, culturelle, historique et éducative des photos prises par le prince Léopold lors de son voyage au Congo belge en 1925', *Museum Dynasticum*, 1 (2008), 13–19).
16 *Le voyage au Congo de leurs Majestés le Roi et le Reine des Belges 5 juin – 31 août 1928. Album commémoratif ...*, Brussels, 1928. Queen Elisabeth's private photographs are analysed in Élodie Stroobants, *Le voyage du Roi Albert et de la Reine Élisabeth au Congo en 1928 au miroir de l'album photographique de la Reine* (MA dissertation, Louvain-la-Neuve, 2011); Anne Cornet and Florence Gillet, 'De reis van Albert en Elisabeth naar Congo', in Chantal Kesteloot (ed.), *Albert en Elisabeth. De film van een koninklijk leven* (S.l.: Mardaga, 2014), pp. 109–123.
17 Isi Colin, 'La Féerie congolaise et le Cinéma', *Le Soir*, 1928.
18 Archives of the Belgian Ministry of Foreign Affairs, Brussels (ABMFA), AN 13.433, G. Stadler, consul general in Southern Africa, to Paul Hymans, Minister of Foreign Affairs, 8 June 1928.
19 ARP, Secretariat of King Albert, IV.B.75, 'Note', 2 February 1933.
20 Jef Van Bilsen, *Kongo 1945–1965* (Leuven: Davidsfonds, 1993), pp. 77–85.
21 ABMFA, AN 13.433, Chief of Cabinet of the Minister of the Colonies to the Minister of Foreign Affairs, 22 December 1947.
22 *La Voix du Congolais. Voyage de son Altesse Royale le Prince Régent au Congo Belge, 29 juin 1947–12 août 1947* (Léopoldville: La Voix du Congolais, 1947).
23 ARP, Secretariat of the Prince Regent, 14, André Cauvin to André De Staercke, Chief of Cabinet of the Prince Regent, 13 February 1947.
24 Stanard, *Selling the Congo*, pp. 224–225.
25 Bernard Henry, *Sa Majesté le Roi Baudouin au Congo belge* (Antwerp: Sheed & Ward, 1955); M. Struye, *Reportage du voyage du Roi au Congo* (Brussels: n.p., 1955); Pol Walheer, *Le grand chef blanc* (Liège: Desoer, 1956); *Le voyage du Roi au Congo* (Brussels: Éditions des Artistes, 1955); André Cauvin, *Bwana Kitoko* (Brussels: Elsevier, 1956); Louis De Lentdecker, *Wapi Kongo?* (Bruges: Lode Zielens, 1955).
26 Mathieu Zana Aziza Etambala, ' "Bwana Kitoko" (1955), un film d'André Cauvin', in Patricia Van Schuylenbergh and Mathieu Zana Aziza Etambala (eds), *Patrimoine d'Afrique centrale. Archives films Congo, Rwanda, Burundi, 1912–1960* (Tervuren: MRAC, 2010), pp. 141–156.
27 Stéphanie Hocq, *'Bwana Kitoko' et les visites d'État au Congo* (MA dissertation, Louvain-la-Neuve, 2010), p. 103; and *Museum Dynasticum*, 24 (2012), 1, 3–48.
28 *The Standard Union* (New York), 8 September 1909.
29 ABMFA, AN 13.433 and B 63.
30 Jacques Vanderlinden, 'Le Prince Léopold au Ruanda-Urundi en 1925', *Museum Dynasticum*, 2 & 3 (1989), 19–23 and 30–39; J. Vanderlinden, *Pierre Ryckmans 1891–1959* (Brussels: De Boeck, 1994), pp. 124–126, 135, 191.
31 Belgian State Archives, Minutes of the Cabinet Meetings, 6 April 1955 (available on www.arch.be). There was one exception to this rule: during his impromptu voyage of 1959, Baudouin was accompanied by the Minister of the Belgian Congo Auguste De Schryver.
32 ARP, Private Secretariat of Albert and Elisabeth (PSAE), 326d and 330, personal note books.
33 Buren, *Journal*, passim.

34 Piet Clement, 'Het bezoek van Koning Albert aan Belgisch Congo, 1928', *Revue belge d'Histoire contemporaine*, 37:1–2 (2007), 175–221; Sofie Dammekens, *Een Belgische koning in de kolonie: De Congoreis van Albert I in 1928* (MA dissertation, Leuven, 2008); Gustaaf Janssens, 'De officiële bezoeken van koning Albert I aan de Verenigde Staten, Brazilië en Belgisch Congo', *Museum Dynasticum*, 21:2 (2009), 89–93.
35 Archives of the French Ministry of Foreign Affairs (AFMFA), Série Z – Europe 1918–1929, Sous-série Belgique, 139, file 'Colonies 1920–1929', 'Extrait du rapport ... 14 février 1929'.
36 Evrard Raskin, *Elisabeth van België* (Antwerp: Houtekiet, 2005), p. 239; Jozef Joris, 'Albert en Elisabeth in Belgisch Congo in 1928', *Museum Dynasticum*, 1 (1991), 32–37, at 36.
37 Cited in Julien Dufour, *Pour une autre colonisation: Le discours du prince Léopold au Sénat, le 25 juillet 1933* (MA dissertation, Louvain-la-Neuve, 2007), annex II, p. VIII.
38 *Ibid.*, pp. 45–46.
39 AFMFA, Série Z – Europe 1944–1949, Sous-série Belgique, 49, file 'Colonies 1944–1949', letter of de Saint-Martin, consul general of France in Léopoldville, to the French Ministry of Foreign Affairs, 24 June 1947.
40 *La Dernière Heure*, 18 April 1947.
41 For all of these elements, see, for example, ARP, PSPR, 13 and 14; Ruben Boon, 'De Prins-Regent naar Belgisch-Congo en Ruanda-Urundi (1947)', *Museum Dynasticum*, 24:1 (2012), 49–62; Rien Emmery, *Charles de Belgique 1903–1983* (Brussels: Racine, 2007), pp. 177–185.
42 ARP, Great Marshall of the Court of Baudouin (GMCB), Congo '55/1, Simone Sohier to the Great Marshall (?), 14 July 1952.
43 Jean Omasombo Tshonda and Benoît Verhaegen, *Patrice Lumumba (...) 1925–1956* (Tervuren-Paris: L'Harmattan and MRAC, 1998), pp. 181, 235.
44 Vanthemsche, *Belgium and the Congo*, pp. 84–89.
45 Mathieu Zana Aziza Etambala, *Congo '55–'65* (Tielt: Lannoo, 1999), pp. 18–39; Hocq, 'Bwana Kitoko'.
46 Léopold III, *Carnets de voyages 1918–1983* (Brussels: Racine, 2004); Esmeralda de Belgique, *Léopold III photographe* (Brussels: Racine, 2006).
47 Patricia Van Schuylenbergh, 'Entre science et spectacle: 'Les Seigneurs de la Forêt', le film initié par Léopold III', *Museum Dynasticum*, 2 (2002), 17–23.
48 ARP, Private Secretariat of Leopold III ('Argenteuil'), 55/1, former King Leopold III to Queen-Mother Elisabeth, 28 April 1957.
49 ARP, PSAE, 1073.
50 Godfried Kwanten, *A.-E. De Schryver 1898–1991* (Leuven: Universitaire Pers Leuven, 2001), pp. 533–534.
51 AFMFA, Série Z – Europe 1918–1929, Sous-série Belgique, 139, file 'Colonies 1920–1929', Jean Herbette, French ambassador in Brussels, to the French Ministry of Foreign Affairs, 24 April 1928.
52 Clement, 'Het bezoek van Koning Albert I', 192; Dammekens, *Een Belgische koning*, 58. Ms. of Albert's diary in ARP, PSAE, 320.
53 Albert's travel diary, 9 August 1928, edited by S. Dammekens, pp. 256–257 ('It is the great misery in the Congo, the negro does all the work, he is not payed, he is being beaten ... King Albert and Queen Elisabeth have come, when they are here, the whites do not harm us, but when they will leave, it will be the same as before. The King does not know everything, everything is hidden from him. It is the great misery here').
54 ARP, PSAE, 466, undated letter ('Confidentielle') by 'Vos serviteurs Congolais' ('In the Congo where we are, we are unhappy! The white people mistreat us as they want, most of all the whites of Government'; 'May the Kingdom of Belgium rule the Congo forever').
55 Clement, 'Het bezoek van Koning Albert I', 192.
56 ARP, PSAE, 319c: Albert's annotation books, containing twenty-one pages with words, sentences and expressions in local African languages.

57 Cited by Emmery, *Charles de Belgique*, p. 182.
58 Etambala, *Congo '55–'65*, p. 35.
59 ABMFA, AA, AE/II/3204, file 1188, letter of the Vice Governor General to the Minister of the Colonies, 29 April 1947.
60 Etambala, *Congo '55–'65*, p. 124; Hocq, *Bwana Kitoko*, p. 100.
61 Pierre Leroy, *Journal de la Province orientale* (Mons: Éditions des Cendres, 1965), p. 116.
62 ARP, GMCB, Congo '55/1, 'Remarques et suggestions à propos du programme de la visite du Roi au Congo', G. Heenen, undated note.
63 François Ryckmans, *Mémoires noires. Les Congolais racontent le Congo belge 1940–1960* (Brussels: Racine, 2010), pp. 83–84 and 88.

CHAPTER ELEVEN

Royal symbolism: Crown Prince Hirohito's tour to Europe in 1921

Elise K. Tipton

At the age of nineteen, Crown Prince Hirohito departed Tokyo in March 1921 for a six-month tour of Britain and the European continent. Later, several times, Hirohito fondly recollected this trip as the happiest time of his long, eventful life. The tour thus meant a lot to him personally, and his nostalgia suggests the restrictions on behaviour like a 'bird in a cage' that he would later feel when he became emperor. From a broader perspective, the fact that it was a historic event for the heir of the Japanese throne to travel to the West indicates that the tour took place during a pivotal period in Japan's modern history.

Two months after his return from Europe, Hirohito became regent, and in 1926 emperor. He would reign for nearly sixty-four years (1926–1989) as the Shōwa Emperor, 124th in a 'line unbroken for ages past' descended from the Sun Goddess Amaterasu according to the pre-1945 national ideology. His reign extended over the tumultuous pre-war and war years, defeat and occupation by a foreign power for the first time in Japanese history, and Japan's post-occupation rise to become the second largest economy in the world. The question of the European tour's influence on the future emperor's conception of his role as sovereign becomes significant because although Hirohito was not forced to abdicate or stand trial as a war criminal, his war responsibility has been and remains a matter of controversy among politicians, intellectuals, political commentators and activists as well as historians in both Japan and the West.[1]

Given the focus here on the tour itself, this chapter cannot and does not seek to resolve the controversy. Instead, an examination of the European tour – its inception, itinerary and reception in Europe and at home in Japan – acts as a lens for viewing radically changing social and political developments of the late 1910s and early 1920s and the role of the imperial throne in this contested setting. Moreover, study of the tour enables us to view the interaction between domestic politics and foreign policy in the new international environment following the end of the Great War and to draw attention to the use of royal symbolism[2] in both the domestic and international arenas. A brief comparison of Hirohito's visit to Taiwan in 1923 with his earlier European tour will also highlight the role of the throne as Japan reaffirmed its hold on an empire in the post-war environment where the rhetoric seemed to foreshadow the end of empires.

The decision for the tour

The decision to send the crown prince on a European tour was not made easily or quickly. It took nearly two years after presentation of the idea in 1919 to gain approval. But understanding the obstacles to inaugurating the tour first requires some description of Japan's political system and the emperor's role within it.

Emperors (or empresses) have reigned in Japan since the beginning of Japan's recorded history in the sixth century. As Ben-Ami Shillony points out, the Japanese imperial family is the oldest dynasty in the world, and the emperor was 'so sacred, that no one dared to overthrow it in recorded history'.[3] But ironically, the Japanese emperor was weaker than royals in other countries. Since the ninth century there was rarely a Japanese emperor who initiated policies, carried out governmental administration or commanded armed forces. However, the weakness of the emperor was counterbalanced by the fact that until the 1947 constitution only the emperor could confer legitimacy upon governments.[4]

Such was the historical role played by Japanese emperors, but the political system of Hirohito's time dated only to the late nineteenth century. The overthrow of the Tokugawa shogunate in 1868, known as the Meiji Restoration, ushered in modernisation policies based on Western models in all areas of Japanese political, economic, social and cultural life. This included a constitution in 1889 that established a Prussian-style parliamentary system. Incorporating Shinto myths, the constitution was presented as a gift from the emperor with the authority of an absolute monarch by virtue of his divine ancestry, but who delegated all executive, legislative and military powers to those who actually governed and commanded military forces. In practice, then, even the vigorous Meiji emperor *reigned*, but did not rule. The actual decision-makers were the oligarchs who had led the Restoration movement, and two key institutions, the Privy Council and Cabinet, were not even mentioned in the constitution. The emperor might influence a policy through his questioning of ministers, as Meiji sometimes did, but once a collective decision was made, the emperor was expected to sanction it. The Parliament, or Diet, had to approve laws, but it did not initiate them. Two parties emerged in the elected lower house, and it became difficult to govern without their support. Nevertheless, until 1918 so-called 'transcendental cabinets' above partisan politics were appointed through negotiations among the oligarchs and their protégés rather than formed by the leader of the majority party in the House of Representatives. Consensus decision-making among the oligarchs and the separation of the court from government became both the ideal and the norm.

This system worked relatively well as long as the original leaders of the Meiji Restoration lived, even though at times they strongly disagreed on policies. However, Itō Hirobumi, 'father of the constitution', was assassinated in 1908, and by 1918 the only remaining oligarch and supporter of transcendental cabinets was Yamagata Aritomo, 'father of the Japanese military'. That year, the parties in the Diet could no longer be ignored, resulting in appointment of Hara Takashi, the first prime minister from the elected lower house. Hara's ascendance reflected changes in the balance of power among the ruling elites – the bureaucracy, the military and the parties – in the aftermath of the First World War and a wave of 'democracy' advocated by labour and social reformers as well as politicians in the wake of nation-wide rice riots that had brought down the previous Cabinet.

Domestic politics developed within the context of the changed international environment. The victory of the Western allies over Germany stimulated the rise of democracy over absolute monarchy, as the Hapsburg, Hohenzollern and Ottoman empires collapsed. In addition, the emergence of the United States as the new dominant international power reinforced the impact of President Woodrow Wilson's Fourteen Points that supported both liberal democratic principles and future decolonisation, while popular discourse speculated on future war with Japan.[5] Meanwhile, the Russian Revolution of 1917 and the German revolution the following year encouraged labour and socialist movements around the world, including Japan. Hara was not in fact an advocate of democracy, exemplified by his lack of support for the universal male suffrage movement.[6] In addition, his appointment did not represent the institutionalisation of party governments or predominance of civilian governments over the military. For example, when Japan participated in the Allies' Siberian Intervention against Bolsheviks,[7] his party government was unable to control the army general staff, which remained constitutionally under the direct responsibility of the emperor rather than the Cabinet minister.

Nevertheless, it was a party government in charge when Japan emerged at the end of the war as one of the victorious allies. This entitled Japan to a seat on the Council of Ten at the Versailles Peace Conference, where it pursued its territorial demands as spoils of war. Still, while seeking to retain control of the German territories in China and the South Pacific that Japan had occupied during the war, the leaders of Japan's delegation were members of a faction who favoured the peaceful internationalist policies that would characterise Japanese foreign policy throughout the next decade. They supported the League of Nations and disarmament as part of cooperative diplomacy and accommodation with the major Western powers to assure Japan's position in the new world order.

Chief plenipotentiary and leader of the faction, Prince Saionji Kinmochi, was an urbane aristocrat and protégé of Itō Hirobumi who had lived in France for many years and was an old friend of Prime Minister Georges Clemenceau.[8] After Yamagata's death in 1922 he would become 'the last *genrō*' or 'elder statesman', responsible for negotiating behind-the-scenes transfers of power among the various elites in the formation of governments during the 1920s, 1930s and early 1940s. He is particularly significant in this chapter because of his support for Hirohito's European tour and his influence over Hirohito's education and conceptualisation of the emperor's role.

It was Hara and Saionji who first proposed the European tour for Hirohito. Hirohito's father Yoshihito, the Taishō Emperor (1912–1926), was not as strong mentally or physically as the 'great' Meiji. In 1917 and 1918 illnesses kept him from attending to many of his official duties, including consultation about involvement in the Siberian Intervention and opening of the Diet in December 1918. In addition, there were stories about Taishō's erratic behaviour, such as rolling up a paper and peering through it like a telescope during a Diet session. This particular incident was not based on fact, but in a new era of mass circulation newspapers and magazines, rumours of strange behaviour by the emperor undermined the dignity of the throne. Moreover, Hara and other leaders feared that Taishō's poor health and weak will made him susceptible to manipulation by the army and navy general staffs based on their direct access to the emperor. Consequently, when in 1919 Taishō suffered a series of debilitating strokes that impaired his speech and concentration as well as ability to walk, Hara began to forge a consensus in favour of a regency. Yamagata did not oppose it for he had never considered Taishō up to the high standard set by Meiji. Sending Hirohito on a tour of Europe would prepare him for becoming regent by giving him first-hand experience of the wider world, and travelling on a battleship to visit Japan's wartime allies would demonstrate the nation's status as a major power. Saionji and his ally Makino Nobuaki, de facto head of the delegation at Versailles and imperial household minister from February 1921, agreed that Taishō could no longer carry out his duties and that the tour would complete Hirohito's education.[9]

Until this time Hirohito's education was very isolated. He completed the elementary curriculum at the Peers' School, where the principal, Russo-Japanese War hero General Nogi Maresuke, instilled in the crown prince the samurai values of frugality, self-discipline, endurance through hardships and a strong sense of duty. Nogi himself exemplified loyalty by committing ritual suicide upon the death of his lord, the Meiji emperor, in 1912, an act both lauded and criticised at the time.

Hirohito then studied with only five other students at a special school in the Tōgū Palace grounds, headed by another Russo-Japanese War hero, Admiral Tōgō Heihachirō. Besides academic subjects, he studied military strategy and tactics to prepare him for being commander-in-chief, and he received training in Shinto rituals that he would perform as emperor. Critics of Hirohito have blamed his ethics teacher Sugiura Shigetake and history lecturer Shiratori Kurakichi for inculcating 'ultranationalist Confucianism', 'jingoist' nationalism and belief in Shintoist 'superstitions' in the crown prince,[10] but Stephen Large disagrees. While acknowledging his ethical conservatism and nationalism, Large argues that Sugiura taught that national power depended on the spiritual or moral power of the emperor, not primarily military or economic power, and that this would be gained through knowledge in the broadest sense, hence the broad curriculum designed for the future emperor. Having studied in the United States and Germany, Shiratori similarly emphasised the importance of interpreting history based on evidence and of distinguishing the difference between myth and history, specifically related to the Sun Goddess and the emperor's being a 'manifest deity'. Dr Hattori Hirotarō reinforced the need for evidence when nurturing Hirohito's study and what became a life-long passion for biology, despite military objections that it was too frivolous for the future commander-in-chief.[11]

The European tour's purpose of broadening the crown prince's education and perspective on the world echoed the objectives of many Meiji leaders' visits to Western countries. The most famous was the 1871–1873 diplomatic and study mission led by the court noble Iwakura Tomomi and including virtually all the top government leaders. However, sending the crown prince to the West was a different matter. Traditionalists believed that the crown prince of a 'divine country' should not travel to 'barbarian lands'. When he was crown prince, Taishō had left the home islands to visit Korea, then a Japanese protectorate before becoming a colony in 1910, but no crown prince had travelled to Western countries. Other opponents of the European tour expressed anxiety for Japan's and the throne's future since Hirohito would come into direct contact with Western democracy. Many considered it inappropriate because of the emperor's poor health, particularly if he should die while Hirohito was away and unable to perform the succession rites as required. The empress and others also feared for Hirohito's safety. The First of March Movement for independence in Korea in 1919 had been repressed, but the situation in Korea remained unstable and Korean nationalists might attack the crown prince during the tour. Taking up various objections, radical right-wing groups at home threatened to block the departure, and a group attacked Prince Saionji's son, court chamberlain Saionji Hachiro, in his home for supporting his father's promotion of the tour.[12]

The opposition voiced by some newspapers linked the European tour with another court issue of the time, namely Hirohito's engagement to Nagako, daughter of Prince Kuni Kunihiko of Satsuma. The engagement had been announced in January 1918, but became a 'Serious Court Incident' in 1920 with the discovery of colour-blindness in her mother's family. Yamagata was among those opposing the marriage for fear of the trait being transmitted to a future heir to the throne, but the emperor and empress as well as the crown prince supported Nagako. The dispute took on political dimensions because Yamagata represented the former Tokugawa domain of Chōshū, Satsuma's ally, but also political rival since the Restoration, and the opposition parties in the Diet tried to use the controversy to embarrass the Hara government. Newspaper stories about the incident elicited editorials' and readers' sympathy for Nagako, some even suggesting that Yamagata wanted to break up the engagement by sending Hirohito to Europe. In the end, the court reconfirmed the engagement to avoid compromising the honour and dignity of the imperial family.[13]

Yamagata offered his resignation as president of the Privy Council after opposing the engagement, and although this was refused, criticism of his position in the incident contributed to increasing the influence of Saionji's group of internationalists and constitutional monarchists. Members of Saionji's group, such as Makino, moved into important court positions, and at Hara's behest Saionji assuaged the empress's fears about the tour. Presenting the trip as a matter of state and therefore a Cabinet decision, not a private court decision, he argued that it would promote good relations between Japan and the West. This was of paramount importance for Japan's sake, and what was good for Japan was good for the imperial family, regardless of any risk to the crown prince.[14]

From this discussion, we can see how the decision that Hirohito tour Europe intertwined domestic political issues and competition among elites – the parties, bureaucracy, the military – with foreign policy and diplomacy in a post-war international environment where pre-war assumptions and balance of power strategies no longer prevailed.[15] Examining the process of the decision and its context reveals that the years after the end of the First World War were a turning point in the modern history of both the nation and the imperial throne.

To Europe and back

Obstacles finally overcome, Hirohito proceeded to Yokohama to board the battleship *Katori* on 3 March 1921. No protestors barred the way. Rather, thousands of people flocked to farewell Hirohito, as they would at every destination on his itinerary. Key members of Hirohito's thirty-four-person entourage included his American-educated political adviser Grand Chamberlain Count Chinda Sutemi, who had served as ambassador to Great Britain from 1916 to 1920; aide-de-camp General Nara Takeji, who was in charge of liaising with the army; and Hirohito's uncle, Prince Kan'in Kotohito, a graduate of French military academies and veteran of the Sino-Japanese (1894–1895) and Russo-Japanese (1904–1905) wars. All would continue to act as advisers and hold significant civilian, military and/or court positions during Hirohito's reign. Count Futara Yoshinori handled public relations, including publication of his official diary of the tour.[16]

Futara's role was important for both domestic and foreign audiences. At home, it would enhance the standing of the throne with images of a young, vigorous and healthy heir to distract from that of his sick father. In Europe, it would strengthen friendship between the imperial family and the rulers and people of the countries the future emperor would visit, as well as give 'a better idea of the Japan of to-day' in order to counter positive, but misleading, impressions due to 'exaggerated ideas of our "picturesqueness" and "orientalness" '.[17] Through Hirohito, tour leaders sought to project an image of Japan as a modern industrialised and civilised (i.e. Westernised) country, not only as a producer of beautiful exotic crafts and art.

Futara's efforts began well, judging from Hirohito's send-off from Tokyo and from the London *Times*'s report of the departure: 'Never before in the annals of Japan has the Heir to the Throne left his native shores and the precedent thus created, therefore, marks an epoch in the history of the most ancient dynasty in the world almost equal in importance to the Restoration in 1867 [sic].'[18] The article described Hirohito's interests and, notably, regarded one of Hirohito's greatest assets as his 'striking resemblance "both in person and character" to his grandfather',[19] thus linking Hirohito to strong Meiji rather than sickly Taishō. In fact, the slender, bespectacled Hirohito did not resemble his grandfather,[20] but *The Times*'s depiction represented the positive reception accorded the crown prince. In the United States the press also began extensive coverage of the tour, with the *New York Times* positioning Hirohito as the peer of European royalty.[21]

With the cruiser *Kashima* as escort, the *Katori* first stopped in Okinawa Prefecture. Formerly the Ryukyu Kingdom, Okinawa had only been incorporated into Japan in the early Meiji period and suffered from discriminatory economic, social and cultural policies. Perhaps this explains the lack of elaborate welcoming decorations and why the crowds were quiet, or 'reverential' according to the diary writers. Considering the discriminatory treatment, it is surprising that Captain Kanna of the *Katori* was an Okinawan and member of Hirohito's escort during his visit. Similarly, in light of assimilation policies, it is notable that Hirohito visited a museum displaying traditional Okinawan art and crafts. He also watched a demonstration of students 'exhibiting the art of self protection known as *Karate*'. The diary writers felt that *karate* needed explanation as 'resembling boxing',[22] which suggests the lack of familiarity and sense of difference that mainland Japanese felt towards Okinawa. Their tone remained positive, however, especially in surmising the pride of Captain Kanna's mother in seeing her distinguished son.

Still more positive was their comment on passing the colony of Taiwan. The diary writers noted that it was 'blessed with advantages of civilization not inferior to those in Japan proper'.[23] Acquired as Japan's first colony after defeating China in 1895, colonial administrators aimed to create Taiwan as a model colony that could be shown off to other world powers. Given the European destination of the tour, Hirohito did not make a stop, but would later visit the colony as regent in 1923.

British colonies were the designated stops on the way to Europe. Britain had been the only destination in original plans for the tour, not surprising since the Anglo-Japanese Alliance had been the core of Japanese foreign policy since its establishment in 1902 and was due for renewal in 1922. Later the itinerary expanded to include wartime allies on the continent, plus the Vatican and the Netherlands, which had the longest historical contact with Japan among European countries. Lack of time in light of Taishō's poor health prevented extension of the tour to the United States.

In Hong Kong security concerns about Korean nationalists limited Hirohito's onshore activities, and he even wore a bulletproof vest while sightseeing, but British officials entertained him lavishly. There and in Singapore thousands of Japanese residents came out on boats to welcome and farewell him, and he hosted 250 or so local dignitaries and Japanese residents on his ship. His Colombo stopover in Ceylon was meant to be an informal visit like others before reaching Britain, but the governor requested that it be a formal state visit. Hirohito was therefore welcomed with a twenty-one gun salute and escorted along an elaborately decorated passageway lined with Sikh guards and soldiers. Dinner at the governor's villa culminated in a procession of forty silk-apparelled elephants, and one knelt down in homage to the crown prince. Futara describes the scene as 'weird, fantastic and impressive at the same time'[24] – a bit of Orientalism in reverse. Hirohito also played golf, which was reported in Britain by journalists sent to cover his stay. The *Sunday Herald* referred to his popularity in Japan 'just as our Prince of Wales is here', an allusion that pleased Futara.[25]

During stops in Suez, Port Said, Cairo, Malta and Gibraltar, there were salutes by British warships decorated with Japanese flags and the usual official banquets, large parties, visits to museums and reviews of guards of honour, but also a tour of the Pyramids and Sphinx, reciprocal visits with the sultan of Egypt, his first visit to a theatre for an opera performance, and a meeting with Prince George (the future King George VI) on the flagship of the British Mediterranean fleet. In Malta he paid respects to the Japanese men who had died during the war when Japanese ships fought alongside the British in the Mediterranean.

At sea Hirohito continued activities like daily exercises, swimming in a pool improvised on deck or playing deck-golf, listening to lectures or reading about European history and political conditions, and practising French and the speeches he would be giving in Europe and learning the names and backgrounds of the numerous people he would meet. He also took lessons on Western deportment and etiquette to avoid faux pas, fear of which had been another objection to the tour.[26] As examples of the unusual relaxed protocol enjoyed on ship, Hirohito invited off-duty sailors to watch cinema entertainments or listen to lectures with him, and asked his suite to include sailors in the programme celebrating his twentieth birthday.[27]

Hirohito's advisers need not have worried about the crown prince making faux pas. Although reserved in temperament, Hirohito was young and relished the relative freedom of the tour, but he also displayed an unexpected ability to handle new situations. After the Prince of Wales formally welcomed him in Portsmouth on 7 May, Hirohito proceeded to Victoria Station in London, where King George V himself met the crown prince to inspect the guard of honour. Hirohito's attendants had not prepared him for the king's invitation to take the seat of honour in the State Carriage, so they were relieved and pleased that he acted in a 'natural and easy manner' (and thereafter no longer subjected him to etiquette lessons).[28] Throughout the tour Hirohito impressed both Japanese and foreigners alike with his behaviour and performance, mixing freely, exhibiting composure in many different circumstances and delivering his speeches without a hitch (and doing so in French while in France). Colonel F.S.G. Piggott, a Japanese speaker and interpreter in Hirohito's British suite, describes the tour as 'triumphal',[29] as did Japanese embassy officials' reports and private letters.[30] Prime Minister Hara noted in his diary his pleasure at the tour's success for the benefit of both the nation and the imperial throne.[31]

Hirohito remained three days in Buckingham Palace as a guest of the royal family, then five days as guest of the British government. King George bestowed prestigious honours upon him, such as making him an Honorary Field Marshal and admitting him to the Order of the Garter. Personally memorable to him, Hirohito would later recall the warm treatment by the royal family 'as if he were their own son', informal conversations about British politics with the king, and a visit by a half-dressed king to his rooms. Because Britain was in the middle of a coal strike and generally still suffering from the after-effects of

11.1 Crown Prince Hirohito and King George V in the state carriage on the way to Buckingham Palace, 1921

the war, Japanese officials were surprised at the grandeur of receptions and honours accorded by political leaders such as Lord Curzon, who was both Foreign Minister and leader of the House of Lords, and Prime Minister David Lloyd George.

As would also typify his stays on the continent, Hirohito paid homage to war dead, visited museums and factories, Parliament, the Bank of England, public and private receptions, the theatre (where the orchestra played Japan's national anthem to a standing audience), and Boy Scout exercises. Everywhere large crowds lined the streets and bridges and pressed to see and hear him when he went to Windsor for a lunch hosted by the Prince of Wales. At the Stock Exchange Hirohito had the 'entirely new experience' of having 'almost to force his way through the throng of people'.[32] Newspapers and magazines carried photographs of Hirohito in military uniform or Western civilian clothing and wrote articles about 'the young prince from Japan', a reference taken up by newspapers and magazines in Japan. *The Times* published a special Japan edition on the last day of his stay. Welcoming speeches all emphasised the friendship and alliance between Britain and Japan, and when he visited army barracks and military staff colleges, Hirohito wore his uniform as an honorary British field marshal.

After his period as guest of the government concluded, Hirohito left for Scotland. He stopped in Cambridge, where he received an honorary doctorate and met Japanese students. He also attended a lecture given by Professor R.J. Tanner, a constitutional law specialist who had tutored George V when he was crown prince. Tanner, explaining how constitutional monarchy functioned in Britain, emphasised the limited governing powers of the monarch, whose primary function was to symbolise the unity of the people.

Hirohito's stay at the Duke of Atholl's castle in Scotland was intended to be a rest and recreation visit, but although enjoying motor excursions through the countryside and fishing expeditions, Hirohito could not avoid military reviews, visits to churches, hospitals and a naval arsenal, the award of another honorary doctorate (from the University of Edinburgh), and welcoming messages by villagers who were seeing a Japanese person for the first time. Unexpectedly, he also saw 'genuine democracy' first-hand. The duchess had explained that she and the duke normally lived in a small building with only a few servants, but at the farewell banquet Hirohito was still surprised to see the duke and duchess join in dancing with villagers who had volunteered to act as extra servants for his visit. This stimulated a wish for more direct contact with the people on his return to Japan.[33]

After twenty days filled with engagements, including hosting a reception for all Japanese residents of London, as well as the other

11.2 Crown Prince Hirohito at Cambridge University on receiving an honorary doctorate, 1921

activities mentioned earlier, Hirohito departed for France with a formal farewell by the king and Prince of Wales. Halfway across the English Channel a French flotilla of five destroyers took over from the British escort, despite Hirohito's visit being designated as an informal one. Hirohito's treatment as a head of state contrasts with that of King Sisowath and Emperor Khai Dinh, described in Chapter 8 in this volume. And although the informal designation of his stay reduced the number of meetings with government officials, Hirohito did make an official visit to President Alexandre Millerand's official residence for an inspection of the guard of honour and a luncheon in his honour. Millerand's welcoming remarks referred to a long relationship of French friendship with Japan and their partnership as wartime allies. Hirohito's speech reiterated similar sentiments and added his appreciation of French cultural as well as scientific and military influences on Japan and the world more generally. The French government announced that the former commander-in-chief of French forces, Marshal of France Joseph Joffre, would make a courtesy return visit to Japan and that Marshal of France Philippe Pétain, the hero of Verdun, would act as Hirohito's guide to battlefields. Futara and Sawada welcomed the announcements as expressions of the government's appreciation for wartime support.[34]

Hirohito made two stays in France, divided by state visits to Belgium and the Netherlands. Considering Hirohito's keen interest in military history, it is not too surprising that battlefield tours, as well as visits to war memorials and military schools and observations of military manoeuvres, dominated both stays, notably a whole day at Verdun and viewing devastation still evident in surrounding towns. But there were also days packed with sightseeing tours of the city (including going up the Eiffel Tower, which a Japanese flag festooned on that day) and Versailles, visits to historical and cultural sites (such as the Louvre and Napoleon's tomb), factory and university visits and receptions with other French government officials. In addition, there were entertainments such as an opera, a couple of days of golf and a day at a horse race as well as social gatherings with Japanese residents and others who had flocked to Europe in hopes of meeting Hirohito. One evening Hirohito graciously offered to forego after-dinner entertainments to accompany President Millerand and his wife to a war relief fundraising performance of *Macbeth* by a noted American actor after hearing that Millerand had chosen to attend dinner with the crown prince over the performance despite its significance for cross-Atlantic cultural diplomacy. And on one day with no engagements, Hirohito walked through the streets in a lounge suit and for the first time in his life shopped for gifts for family and friends, and for himself bought a bust of Napoleon that he would keep in his study.[35]

Between the two French stays, Hirohito made official visits to Belgium and the Netherlands. According to an agreement with the Belgian government, Hirohito and his attendants wore full dress uniforms, and Hirohito stayed in the palace as guest of King Albert I and the queen. The war was still fresh in memories, as exemplified by Hirohito's praise for the king's heroism as an aviator and visits to Ypres (as had been recommended by King George V) and other battlefields. Hirohito also visited Waterloo, the battlefield of Napoleon's defeat. A tour of the Congo Museum and Antwerp harbour and numerous official and unofficial gatherings with members of the royal family, prominent individuals and high government officials filled out the five-day stay.

The Netherlands had been neutral during the war, but Japan had a long history of relations with the Dutch, being the only Europeans allowed to trade during the Tokugawa period through the Deshima port in Nagasaki. This was behind the country's early request to be included on Hirohito's itinerary.[36] Both Queen Wilhelmina and Hirohito referred to that long history in their speeches during the official banquet at the palace where Hirohito was staying. Cultural and economic activities characterised this stay, such as a visit to a diamond factory, a stop at the Rijksmuseum, where Hirohito lingered in admiration over Rembrandt's *Night Watch* painting, and visits to the Stock Exchange and Rotterdam shipbuilding yard. He also showed interest in the Palace of the Woods where collections of curios and art treasures from Holland's trade with Asian countries were held, and the Palace of Peace to which Japan had contributed three pieces of brocade with a design of flowers and birds. In both the Netherlands and Belgium Hirohito attracted large crowds, including a Dutch woman dressed in a kimono shouting *'banzai'*.

Hirohito's last official state visit was to Italy and the Vatican, following his second stay in France. According to the official diary, Hirohito was welcomed by the mayor of Rome 'in the ancient Roman manner' when the royal cortege reached Esedra square, and King Victor Emmanuel III had decided to treat the crown prince as a chief of state throughout his visit.[37] Consequently, in addition to gun salutes and guards of honour in Naples, soldiers lined the railway line between Naples and Rome every fifty steps and along the route of the royal carriage from the train station to the palace. The king's welcome speech referred to the Japanese imperial line 'unbroken for thousands of years', Japan's artistic creativity, its ability to adopt modern civilisation and its wartime support.[38] Hirohito as usual filled his stay with tours of historical and cultural sites, military reviews and numerous receptions and banquets. However, he also visited Pope Pius XI at the Vatican, wearing his military uniform but without the Italian medals he had received in consideration of unfriendly relations between the papacy and Italian Royal House. On his last day in Rome he waived protocol in order to accept the request for a meeting from President Tomas Masaryk of Czechoslovakia, making a total of seven heads of state and the Pope met on the tour.[39]

With Italian destroyers escorting the *Katori* out of port, Hirohito began the voyage home on 18 July and arrived at Yokohama on 3 September to an enthusiastic welcome and special festivities. Authorities encouraged crowds to applaud and shout *'banzai'* instead of greeting the crown prince with the customary reverential silence.[40] By all accounts, the tour could not have been more successful at home or in Europe. The Home Ministry had relaxed restrictions on printing photographs of the imperial family. Consequently, the Japanese media had been able to show Hirohito in situations other than riding in an official motorcade, for example, in a frock coat with a high collar and walking stick and walking on the street in civilian attire.[41] They also followed the tour extensively with maps and detailed articles, and a special issue of the popular magazine *Fujin gahō* (Women's Graphic) even reported the themes of Professor Tanner's lecture. In addition to fulfilling the tour's objectives of completing his education and preparing him for becoming regent, Hirohito's 'media star' performance had achieved another important objective of enhancing the image of the throne and Japan's international status even more than tour advocates had hoped.

Hirohito the regent and Taiwan

The experiences with Western democracy and lifestyles led to expressions by both Hirohito and the press of a desire to become a 'modern monarch' upon his return and appointment as regent in November 1921. Besides Westernised personal dress and daily habits, Hirohito introduced reforms in the palace that allowed commoners to become ladies-in-waiting and eliminated the previous hierarchy of ranks. He also encouraged use of standard Japanese language instead of special court language.[42] The debonair regent continued to attract media attention, and on one occasion Hirohito approached photographers within less than the prescribed twenty metres and posed jauntily with his riding crop by his side.[43] His association with the sociable Prince of Wales was reinforced during the British crown prince's reciprocal visit to Japan in 1922. They played golf as well as competed in traditional Japanese archery, but behind the public relations success the Prince of Wales privately expressed relief at escaping from the formality of the Japanese court at the end of his stay.[44] Hirohito and Nagako also appeared as a modern couple in European dress during their wedding procession in January 1924.[45]

However, Hirohito's hope for more contact with the people was not to be. Even in his close circle of friends his waiver of protocol at a homecoming party met with a reprimand from his mentor, the elder statesman Prince Saionji. Saionji favoured Western European-style constitutional monarchy, but not American-style democracy. Moreover, mixing with the public declined after Hirohito became regent, especially after the onset of political violence. Only a few weeks before Hirohito became regent, Prime Minister Hara was assassinated. Protests and assassination attempts by radical leftists, rightists and

Korean nationalists disturbed the domestic political scene during the rest of the decade.

Consequently, even before a communist sympathiser shot at Hirohito's car in December 1923, security was tight for Hirohito's two-week visit to Taiwan in April. Travelling as regent, the de facto human symbol of the emperor-system, to a colony differed from his European tour, when he was visiting among equals or superiors. Nevertheless, its purpose and timing similarly reflected the earlier discussed post-war domestic and international developments of democratic movements and anti-colonialism as well as competing civilian and military elites and the Taishō emperor's mental and physical infirmity. Resistance to Japanese colonial rule by the Han Chinese majority and smaller number of indigenous people in Taiwan had been suppressed by the end of the Meiji period, and there was no independence rebellion as occurred in Korea in 1919. However, Taiwanese returning from stays in Japan or China displayed a new democratic spirit and national consciousness. Some formed the League for the Establishment of a Taiwanese Parliament and the Taiwan Culture Society.[46] In this context Hirohito's visit may be seen as a symbolic 'recolonisation' of Taiwan.[47]

Reaffirmation of colonisation was highlighted by Hirohito's first stop being the site where Japanese invasion forces had landed in 1895 during the Sino-Japanese War and their commander, Imperial Prince Kita Shirakawa, had died from malaria. Visits to Shinto shrines, military facilities and Japanese-built factories and schools reaffirmed Japan's possession of Taiwan while also emphasising the modernising benefits of Japanese colonialism. Hirohito's dignified behaviour, praised and extensively covered in the local press, reinforced the Confucian image of the monarch as 'the model of morality for the common people' and moral source of Taiwan's achievements.[48] He openly expressed satisfaction with educational reforms that increased emphasis on arts and humanities.

These reforms actually reflected changes in colonial policy aimed at stemming Taiwanese nationalism and were also linked to the domestic political changes discussed earlier. Long an opponent of autocratic colonial rule, Prime Minister Hara had appointed the first civilian governor-general, Den Kenjirō, in late 1919 to effect localisation and incorporation of Taiwanese as loyal imperial subjects. Then, in 1922 an edict of integration and equality introduced relatively liberalising reforms designed to tame the Taiwanese.[49] The government in Tokyo hoped that providing an opportunity for both Japanese resident settlers and the colonised Taiwanese to see the regent, embodying the focus of their loyalty, would not only reinforce belief in the monarchy, but also give them a sense of being linked to the centre even from the periphery of the empire. Like the European tour, royal symbolism thus served political ends.

Conclusion

The European tour had prepared Hirohito well for his role as regent and accomplished the goal of elevating the image of the throne at home and of Japan abroad. It thus exemplifies the power of royal symbolism in both domestic and foreign politics. Regarding conceptions of his role, direct encounters with constitutional monarchies during the tour reinforced views of limited monarchy from Hirohito's previous education and advocated by Saionji and other close advisers. When Tokyo University professor Minobe Tatsukichi was vilified in 1935 for his theory of the emperor as an 'organ' of the state, not a god, Hirohito defended him. However, such support was expressed privately.

As emperor under the Meiji constitution, Hirohito intervened in political controversies only three times: in 1928 to reprimand Prime Minister Tanaka Giichi for his inability to force a court martial of officers who assassinated the Manchurian warlord Chang Tso-lin; in 1936 to put down a military insurrection in Tokyo by one faction of the army against the party government; and in 1945 to end the war by surrender. In 1928 he felt he had gone too far, so that the only other interventions occurred when government and military leaders were at an impasse. Hirohito agreed with Saionji that regardless of personal preferences and imperial sovereignty, the emperor should not be involved in decision-making in order to maintain the transcendence of the throne.[50]

Only after 1945 did a new constitution overcome the tension between constitutional monarchy and imperial sovereignty by declaring the emperor a 'symbol of the state and the unity of the people'. It also aligned Hirohito's role with the personal preferences for limited monarchy that had been shaped during his European tour. But despite now being merely a 'symbol emperor', when Hirohito travelled again to Europe in 1971, his fond memories of the 1921 tour would be marred by the different reception. This time protests against the tour at home came from the left rather than the right. Despite the tour being billed as strictly ceremonial, leftists regarded his travel as a head of state to be a subversion of the constitution. In the seven countries he visited, heads of state received him graciously. For example, Queen Elizabeth II restored Hirohito to the rank of field marshal and membership in the Order of the Garter, honours that had been retracted during the war.

However, protestors in the crowds greeted him with anger and insults rather than cheers.[51] The war and his 'war responsibility' were still not issues of the past.

It was the same individual – Hirohito – and the same country – Japan – that he represented, but both the domestic and international contexts for the 1971 tour differed greatly from the 1921 tour. Rather than the heir to the throne of a rising power, he was now the elderly figurehead of a defeated nation, whom many still blamed for the deaths of their loved ones. We can see here that instead of royal symbolism being a means to ameliorate tension and communicate goodwill, it revived bitter memories and hostility against a wartime enemy.

Notes

Note: Japanese names are in Japanese name order, surname first, unless as authors publishing in English using Western name order.

1 For summaries of the debate over Hirohito's 'war responsibility' and the lack of reliable sources, see Stephen S. Large, *Emperor Hirohito and Shōwa Japan: A Political Biography* (London and New York: Routledge, 1992), pp. 2–3; Ikuhito Hata, *Hirohito: The Shōwa Emperor in War and Peace* (Folkestone: Global Oriental, 2007), Editor's and Author's prefaces.
2 Antony Best argues for the importance of royal symbolism and royal diplomacy for easing tensions and communicating goodwill in British–Japanese relations in 'A Royal Alliance: Court Diplomacy and Anglo-Japanese Relations, 1900–41' ResearchGate (November 2006), pp. 18–28. www.researchgate.net/publication/4809028, accessed 2 December 2016.
3 Ben-Ami Shillony, 'Introduction', in Ben-Ami Shillony (ed.), *The Emperors of Modern Japan* (Leiden and Boston: Brill, 2008), p. 1.
4 *Ibid.*, p. 2; Large, *Hirohito*, p. 12.
5 Frederick Dickinson and Paul Dunscomb emphasise the impact of the First World War on Japanese domestic politics and foreign policy. Frederick Dickinson, *War and National Reinvention: Japan in the Great War, 1914–1919* (Cambridge, MA: Harvard University Asia Center, 1999); Paul Dunscomb, *Japan's Siberian Intervention, 1918–1922: 'A Great Disobedience Against the People'* (Lanham: Rowman & Littlefield, 2011). On the popular discourse about war with Japan, see Jabez T. Sunderland, *Rising Japan: Is She a Menace or a Comrade to be Welcomed in the Fraternity of Nations?* (New York and London: G.P. Putnam's Sons, 1918).
6 Dickinson, *War and National Reinvention*, pp. 219–21.
7 Dunscomb, *Japan's Siberian Intervention*, 'Introduction'.
8 Lesley Connors, *The Emperor's Adviser: Saionji Kinmochi and Pre-War Japanese Politics* (London: Croom Helm and Nissan Institute for Japanese Studies, 1987), p. 65.
9 Stephen S. Large, *Emperors of the Rising Sun: Three Biographies* (Tokyo, New York and London: Kodansha International, 1997), pp. 100–103.
10 For example, David Bergamini, *Japan's Imperial Conspiracy* (London: Heinemann, 1971); Edward Behr, *Hirohito: Behind the Myth* (London: Hamish Hamilton, 1989); and Herbert Bix, *Hirohito and the Making of Modern Japan* (New York: HarperCollins, 2000).
11 Large, *Hirohito*, pp. 17–19; for a similar assessment of Sugiura, see Toshiaki Kawahara, *Hirohito and His Times: A Japanese Perspective* (Tokyo and New York: Kodansha, 1990), p. 24. On overcoming military objections to study of biology, see Osanaga Kanroji, *Hirohito: An Intimate Portrait of the Japanese Emperor* (Los Angeles: Gateway Publishers, 1975), p. 58.

ROYAL SYMBOLISM

12 Kanroji, *Hirohito*, pp. 79–80. For another version of the attack, see Bergamini, *Japan's Imperial Conspiracy*, p. 313. On objections to the tour, see also Kawahara, *Hirohito*, pp. 28–29.
13 Kawahara, *Hirohito*, pp. 26–27; Bergamini, *Japan's Imperial Conspiracy*, p. 312; Large, *Emperors of the Rising Sun*, pp. 103–104.
14 Connors, *The Emperor's Adviser*, pp. 89–90.
15 Kenneth Pyle puts greater emphasis on the influence of the international system on domestic politics. Kenneth B. Pyle, *Japan Rising: The Resurgence of Japanese Power and Purpose* (New York: Public Affairs, 2007), chapter 5.
16 Count Yoshinori Futara and Setsuzo Sawada, *The Crown Prince's European Tour* (Osaka: The Osaka Mainichi Publishing Co., 1925).
17 *Ibid.*, pp. 6–8.
18 Quoted in *ibid.*, pp. 13–14. The supposed unprecedented, hence historic nature of the heir apparent leaving the islands was often repeated during the tour. Large, *Emperors*, p. 78.
19 Futara and Sawada, *European Tour*, p. 14.
20 See photographs of Meiji and Hirohito in Large, *Emperors*, pp. 121, 130.
21 Sally Hastings, 'Empress Nagako and the Family State', in Shillony, *Emperors*, p. 246.
22 Futara and Sawada, *European Tour*, pp. 16–17.
23 *Ibid.*, p. 17.
24 *Ibid.*, p. 30.
25 *Ibid.*, p. 31.
26 Kanroji, *Hirohito*, p. 85.
27 Futara and Sawada, *European Tour*, pp. 42–43.
28 Kanroji, *Hirohito*, pp. 85–86; Futara and Sawada, *European Tour*, p. 57.
29 Piggott renewed his close relationship with Hirohito, enjoying a private audience while military attaché at the British embassy in Tokyo in 1922 and again in 1936. F.S.G. Piggott, *Broken Thread: An Autobiography* (Aldershot: Gale & Polden, 1950), pp. 128, 160, 207, 271.
30 Kanroji, *Hirohito*, p. 85.
31 Quoted in Bix, *Hirohito*, p. 113.
32 Futara and Sawada, *European Tour*, p. 72.
33 *Ibid.*, pp. 84–85.
34 *Ibid.*, p. 94.
35 Later joined by heads of Darwin and Abraham Lincoln. *Ibid.*, pp. 104–106.
36 *Ibid.*, p. 125.
37 *Ibid.*, pp. 141–142.
38 *Ibid.*, p. 145.
39 *Ibid.*, p. 153. The Spanish king Alfonso XIII gave a lunch in Hirohito's honour at the Spanish Embassy in Paris.
40 Hastings, 'Empress Nagako', p. 247.
41 Bix, *Hirohito*, p. 110.
42 Kanroji, *Hirohito*, p. 99; Kawahara, *Hirohito*, p. 41.
43 Julia Adeney Thomas, 'The Unreciprocated Gaze: Emperors and Photography', in Shillony, *Emperors*, p. 185.
44 Best, 'A Royal Alliance', pp. 24–25.
45 Hastings, 'Empress Nagako', pp. 248–249.
46 Komagome Takeshi, 'Colonial Modernity for an Elite Taiwanese, Lim Bo-seng: The Labyrinth of Cosmopolitanism', in Liao Ping-hui and David Der-Wei Wang (eds), *Taiwan Under Japanese Colonial Rule, 1895–1945: History, Culture, Memory* (New York: Columbia University Press, 2006), p. 148; Masahiro Wakabayashi, 'The Imperial Visit of the Crown Prince to Taiwan in 1923', *Journal of the Japan-Netherlands Institute*, 2 (1990), 235–245, at 236.
47 Wakabayashi Masahiro, 'A Perspective on Studies of Taiwanese Political History: Reconsidering the Postwar Japanese Historiography of Japanese Colonial Rule in Taiwan', in Liao and Wang, *Taiwan Under Japanese Colonial Rule*, p. 33.
48 Bix, *Hirohito*, pp. 137–139; Wakabayashi, 'Imperial Visit', pp. 238–239.

49 Liao Ping-hui, 'Taiwan under Japanese Colonial Rule, 1895–1945: History, Culture, Memory', in Liao and Wang, *Taiwan Under Japanese Colonial Rule*, p. 8; Mark Peattie, 'Japanese Attitudes toward Colonialism, 1895–1945', in Ramon Myers and Mark Peattie (eds), *The Japanese Colonial Empire, 1895–1945* (Princeton: Princeton University Press, 1984), pp. 104–109.
50 Large, *Emperor Hirohito*, pp. 30, 60–61; David Titus, *Palace and Politics in Prewar Japan* (New York: Columbia University Press, 1974), pp. 326–327.
51 Kawahara, *Hirohito*, pp. 193–196; Large, *Emperor Hirohito*, pp. 182–185. The protests during the European tour made Japanese leaders reluctant to send Hirohito on a tour to the United States, despite invitations from presidents Richard Nixon and Gerald Ford. When he did visit in 1975 journalists again brought up questions about the war and his responsibility, but Hirohito's answers satisfied most people, and he appeared 'human' and at ease in a variety of situations, so that, on the whole, the tour went smoothly and was deemed a success. Large, *Emperor Hirohito*, pp. 186–190.

CHAPTER TWELVE

The throne behind the power? Royal tours of 'Africa Italiana' under fascism

Mark Seymour

Compared with some of the royal domains covered by this volume, Italy was a latecomer to nationhood, a latecomer to colonial possessions, and a latecomer to royal tours of overseas colonies.[1] The Italian nation officially came into being in March 1861, when Piedmont's King Victor Emmanuel II inaugurated a new constitutional monarchy, created from several disparate principalities during the decades of the 'Risorgimento'. That term, meaning 'resurgence', rhetorically linked Italy's national unification with the glories of the Roman empire. Although conquering a new empire was not among the nascent government's early priorities, the foundations for one were laid in the Horn of Africa from the early 1880s, reaching a pre-1914 plateau with Italy's acquisition of 'Libia' after a war with the Ottoman incumbents in 1911–1912.[2] However, emblematic of the colonies' relatively low priority for the new Italy, no head of state or prime minister was to visit any of these possessions until well into the 1920s.[3]

The First World War left Italy in a state of disarray that gave rise to Mussolini's fascist regime in 1922. In contrast to the previous era, the re-creation of a Roman empire quickly became a central fascist aspiration.[4] This new priority was symbolically indicated by Mussolini's visit to Tripoli in 1926, the first-ever colonial visit by an Italian government head.[5] The fascist regime reached its apotheosis in 1936 with victory in a war against Ethiopia and the declaration of an Italian empire. Diminutive Victor Emmanuel III, Italy's king since 1900 and still head of state though overshadowed by Mussolini, became 'Emperor of Ethiopia'. Despite the king's new title, Mussolini had from the outset positioned himself as the heir-apparent to ancient Rome's imperial tradition, and Victor Emmanuel seemed to perch only awkwardly on the throne behind the power.

Nevertheless, the king ultimately made more tours of the Italian colonies than did Mussolini. Indeed, all royal tours of Italian foreign possessions took place within the fascist period. The first, to Tripolitania (the northwestern region of what would become modern Libya), took place in 1928. This was followed by journeys to Eritrea in 1932, Cirenaica (the eastern region of Libya) in 1933, Somalia in 1934, and finally, as emperor, to Libya again in 1938. The king also made a state visit to Egypt in 1933, and, though not to an Italian colony, the journey consolidated the fascist regime's image as a Mediterranean power. That these royal tours all took place during the fascist period gives them a unique historical complexity, because of the ambiguous political position of the king vis-à-vis the Duce, as Mussolini became known.

These ambiguities have long been grist to the historiographical mills of Italian fascism, though almost entirely from a domestic perspective.[6] While the king assumed an apparently subaltern position, his constitutional power to appoint or dismiss the head of government was never diminished, and ultimately he used it to end Mussolini's regime. Accordingly, the two figures have often been portrayed as a 'diarchy', despite the Duce's apparent dominance. Questions about the role of the monarchy during fascism have so far received their most exhaustive treatment in Paolo Colombo's subtle study of 'the fascist monarchy'.[7] Colombo highlights the symbolic importance of the king's voyages to Africa, but the topic is not a central theme.[8] Indeed, with the notable exception of a recent contribution by Alessandro Pes, there has been surprisingly little research analysing the diarchy's power dynamics as they played out in fascist Italy's increasingly important African colonies.[9]

Few historians would disagree with Pes's claim that the regime's propaganda represented 'Africa Italiana' as a fascist achievement.[10] Indeed, Mussolini's post-1936 official title as 'Founder of the Empire' suggested that Italian Africa was virtually the Duce's personal achievement. By implication, the king took the title of emperor simply as a result of Mussolini's triumph. A 1937 cover illustration of the popular weekly magazine, *Domenica del Corriere*, perhaps inadvertently captured the way imperial expansion exacerbated ambiguities at the heart of the diarchy (Figure 12.1).

Even if the power to govern was Mussolini's, the fact that the king made five official visits to Italy's colonies while the Duce made only two raises a question over Pes's secondary argument, that the king was 'only a subsidiary actor in the process'.[11] In practical terms this is undoubtedly true, but what about the symbolic terms that are so crucial to the political role of a royal personage? The question is made more pressing by any examination of illustrated magazines such as the

12.1 King Victor Emmanuel III and Mussolini: 'The King-Emperor and the Founder of the Empire', *La Domenica del Corriere*, 16 March 1937

Domenica del Corriere[12] or the newsreels made by the regime's cinema institute, the Istituto Luce. These portrayed the royal tours to a wide audience, and they certainly foregrounded the king, and then the 'king emperor', in their accounts and images.

Through such media, Italians were regularly exposed to rousing accounts and vibrant portraits of their royals on tour. In an examination of those tours, this chapter develops a new perspective on the perennial question of how far Victor Emmanuel's imperial throne lay behind the Duce's authoritarian power. First, though, background on the king's appointment of Mussolini is essential to both grasping the ambiguities of the political relationship and considering the significance of royal pageantry within a fascist regime. Reconstruction of the tours can then focus on the way they were represented to the Italian public.

A king and a Duce?

As head of state, Victor Emmanuel III appointed Mussolini as prime minister, despite the fascist party's poor electoral polling, in October 1922. He did this much as President Paul von Hindenburg was to appoint Adolf Hitler, more notoriously, a decade later: it was a way out of an electoral impasse resulting from a divided political centre, threats of revolution from the left, and loud sabre-rattling on the right. Mussolini lost no time in reversing the previous century's constitutional gains and by early 1925 had established himself as Duce – the nation's authoritarian leader. Despite claims of fascist 'totalitarianism', Mussolini's power was less total than other dictators, since his regime made notable accommodations with established power structures such as the Catholic Church and the royal House of Savoy. Nevertheless, Mussolini successfully built around himself a powerful personality cult, and he remains the towering figure in much historiography of Italy's fascist period.[13]

By contrast, once the narrative reaches the point where the king commits the fatal error of appointing Mussolini, most historians consign Victor Emmanuel to the role of a small cork bobbing passively on inexorable fascist currents.[14] One author describes the king as reduced to an infernal round of meaningless pageantry, 'endlessly laying foundation stones and cutting ceremonial ribbons'.[15] Of course, the king also signed, apparently willingly, the legislation generated by the fascist government. More recently, research influenced by cultural history has suggested that while Victor Emmanuel was relegated to pageant performer and signatory, such ceremonial roles did not necessarily denote a second tier of political power.

Indeed, under fascism public ceremonies rose to unprecedented levels of importance, and they built on earlier ceremonial forms pioneered by royalty and religion. Such rituals provided ideal templates for the spectacles that both constructed and displayed the power of interwar dictators. It is worth noting, too, that Victor Emmanuel's public appearance in Milan after an assassination attempt against him in 1928 resulted in an 'unforgettable demonstration of over 100,000 Milanese', and similar expressions of public sentiment also occurred in Rome.[16] This reminds us that it was not only Mussolini who drew vast crowds under fascism. Even though Mussolini's pageantry has attracted far more attention from historians, the king clearly had more influence over the public than we usually assume.

This extends to royal tours: when the king travelled, both nationally and in the colonies, the crowds assembled. Catherine Brice has argued that the king was particularly important to fascist ritual after the conquest of Ethiopia, and she cannot put to rest a sense that the monarchy also retained its character as an autonomous institution.[17] Augmenting the suggestive crowd scenes just mentioned, royal tours of Italy's colonies support the notion that the monarchy continued to operate in a realm at least partially its own. At the very least, earlier dismissive portrayals of the king as little more than the regime's pageant-puppet are ripe for rethinking. But it can also be argued that the royal tours in Africa helped the monarchy to shore up whatever autonomy it possessed, and that this was ultimately crucial for the Duce's demise.

The First Tour: Tripoli, 1928

Whether the Italian monarch on tour in the colonies appears puppet-like or autonomous partly depends on the sources consulted. Archival records of the king's colonial tours reveal a strong sense of continuity with a long royal tradition of domestic travel. The very title of the rubric under which the official records are found denotes continuity rather than rupture: 'Civil House of His Majesty the King and Ministry of the Royal House: Tours Office'.[18] The physical quality and substance of the documents are just what a historian would expect from a European monarchy: high-quality paper with coats of arms; much concern with hierarchy, protocol, timetables, largesse to staff and subjects, and so on. Collectively the documents bespeak attentive service to the monarch, smacking more of long-standing royal traditions than of a king making the rounds on behalf of an upstart regime.

The way the journeys were carried out also continued established traditions of royal tours within Italy.[19] Although the regime embraced aircraft as symbols of modernity, the king always travelled by royal train and yacht. On his first colonial tour, instead of embarking at a port near Rome, he took the opportunity to visit southern Italy first, only boarding the yacht in Sicily.[20] The royal train and yacht were institutions in themselves. Recurrent among the archival material are meticulous diagrams showing the layout of the train's carriages, depending on the entourage, which changed from tour to tour.[21] On the journey to Tripoli, the party included the king and Queen Elena, the princesses Giovanna and Maria, the Minister of Colonies, 'and others'.[22] Images of the early train's interior are not readily available, but in 1930 a new one was commissioned. The *Domenica del Corriere* published images of its surprisingly Baroque-looking interior, which showed no hint of the modern style favoured by fascism. The article described the train as a 'small mobile palace', decorated with 'gold, silks, brocades, rugs and precious woods'.[23] The style was 'royal', and it staked a clear claim to aesthetic independence from the regime.

The yacht also connoted 'royalty' rather than 'regime'. An elegant vessel of 135 metres in length, it carried the dynastic name *Savoia*. Launched five years before the voyage to Tripoli, it was quite new, but like the train, its design eschewed modernity.[24] Indeed, with its concave prow, long bowsprit, and twin rearward sloping masts, the *Savoia* had more in common with the sailing ships of the previous century than with the powerful, modern warships on which Mussolini liked to travel. For all the king's military obsession, his vessel represented the luxurious, leisured aspects of aristocracy more than its military roots. Perhaps to make up for this, on the voyage across the Mediterranean, the *Savoia* was accompanied by two battleships and no fewer than fourteen torpedo-boats of the Italian Royal Navy. Underlining connections to an earlier historical epoch, many of these vessels were named after the great battles of the Risorgimento.[25]

The king's modes of travel may suggest that he occupied a realm above and beyond the regime, but once on colonial soil it is clear that he was there to serve the state's ends. Of all Italy's colonies, Libya was geographically the closest, and the area in which the fascist regime invested most ambition. Fascists dubbed the Libyan coastline Italy's 'fourth shore', and ultimately planned to settle thousands of Italian peasants there. The 1928 visit to Tripoli marked the conclusion of a long process of 'pacification' of the Libyan hinterlands, begun soon after Mussolini came to power. This had involved the controversial use of modern weapons, including gas, to subdue tribes and peasants.[26] If the Duce's own visit to the colony in 1926 indicated its new importance to the regime, the king's visit two years later signalled the triumph of the planned 'riconquista'. Fascism was a bellicose regime, dubbing even its domestic policies a series of 'battles', and it is no coincidence that this first royal tour was headlined 'The Triumphal Voyage of the Sovereigns in Tripolitania'.[27]

Accounts designed to propagandise this element of conquest foreground the 'triumphal' aspect of the tour, without losing the sense that the king and his family inhabited a semi-autonomous sphere. Key events of the arrival day were a formal procession through Tripoli, dinner at the governor's house, and an evening performance of, appropriately, Verdi's masterpiece of orientalism, *Aida*.[28] Activities over ensuing days included a lengthy railway journey to visit various oases. At one of these, the king, queen and princesses received 'beautiful presents of gold and jewelry', presumably in fairly structured encounters with indigenous notables. At the oasis of Zuara Marina, a deputation of Italians living in Tunisia came to meet their sovereign. On another day, the royal family visited the classical ruins of Leptis Magna, once the Roman empire's most distant outpost. A celebrated archaeological site for tourists royal and otherwise, this visit symbolically underlined the historic 'depth' of Italian claims to Libya. *The Times* newspaper expressed the cumulative results of all these activities by quoting the words of an Arab chieftain: 'Now that the King has been here in person we know that the country really belongs to him.'[29]

Italian readers were treated to quite sumptuous illustrations that conveyed the same message. The *Domenica del Corriere*'s cover on 9 May 1928 featured a conventionally colonial scene: swords, sashes, feathers, flags, tropical whites, Roman columns and pith helmets. The king, standing with the queen atop ceremonial steps, hands out medals to indigenous soldiers who fought for Italy during the 'pacification'. Though fascist symbolism normally saturated public ceremonies in this period, this scene is devoid of obvious traces of the regime. It would be going too far to argue that the image presents the 'pacification' as the king's personal achievement, but it certainly encourages the public to associate colonial triumph with the monarchy. In this vein, contemporary international observers such as *The Times* interpreted the tour as a great success for the Italian king, and commentators as far away as Los Angeles perceived the tour as a clear sign of the monarchy's self-assertion in the context of the fascist regime.[30]

The regime's newspapers regaled the reading public with details of royal tours, and Pes has argued that they placed emphasis on demonstrating the monarch's subservience to fascism. This may be the case later on, but it is not obvious in the early tours. By 1925 Italian journalism had fully lost its freedom, treating the regime with anything from polite servility to outright fawning, so it is unsurprising if the press tended to portray the king as a sort of pageant puppet. This is very much the way Pes interprets the Rome newspaper *Il Messaggero*'s accounts of the king's 1938 tour, noting that the 'stars' of its reports were the fascist projects, which the king simply unveiled.[31] But in most reports of the 1920s and even later, the king still outranks individual fascist projects. Just as the illustration in the weekly *Domenica del Corriere* made no reference to fascism, an editorial in Italy's most-read daily, the *Corriere della Sera*, interpreted the first royal tour as a 'substantial contribution to the maturation of colonial feelings among Italians'.[32] What is remarkable about this prominent article is the focus on the monarchy and the absence of the regime.

Press accounts of the royal tour nevertheless lost some of their grandiose momentum after a few foundation stones had been laid or a few ribbons had been cut. Daily appointments and continued 'fervid homage' from subjects or colonisers may well have worn down the king and anaesthetised readers.[33] But under the regime, newspapers were not the only way that 'triumphs', royal or fascist, were kept in the public view. As part of its totalitarian quest, Mussolini's government pioneered the use of visual and aural media, with the Istituto Luce's celluloid newsreels' obligatory projection in commercial cinemas from 1927 preceding widespread radio transmission.[34] Africa provided a setting that was as novel as the new visual medium itself, and the Istituto Luce made many short 'cine-news' episodes of the royal tours, as well as documentaries.[35]

One of the earliest documentaries on Italian colonialism ostensibly starred Mussolini. Made during his visit to Tripoli in 1926, the thirty-one-minute silent documentary fuzzily advertises the colony as a desert now yielding harvests and raising livestock through Italian know-how and industry. The Duce in fact features minimally, only appearing for brief stints, wielding a pickaxe to turn a first sod, or leading a tour of the archaeological excavations of Leptis Magna.[36] These are symbolic activities very similar to those undertaken by the king. Two years later the monarch's own journey was also the subject of a Luce documentary, though unfortunately the film is not accessible.[37] Some hint of what might be seen is provided by footage created by British Pathé, which shows the king also touring Leptis Magna. Both examples portray Mussolini and the king as equal endpoints of an unbroken line between imperial Rome and the new Italy.[38]

So far, it seems the regime was content for its emerging colonies to appear as an achievement shared between the diarchy. A popular paperback published in 1934 reinforces this sense. The introduction to Mirko Ardemagni's *Il re in Africa* places the king at the cutting edge of Italy's new colonial mission: 'If today Italy can now boast its own colonies ... it is due to the able guidance of a monarchy rich with historical experience and secular wisdom.'[39] Fascist endorsement of the book appears in a foreword by Italo Balbo, governor-general of Libya from January 1934.[40] Balbo's words lay glory at Mussolini's feet, but as a whole the book suggests that even as the regime neared its apogee, 'Africa Italiana' owed as much to the ancient wisdom of the House of Savoy as to the youthful energy of fascism.

Italy's first royal colonial tour concluded after five intense days on 22 April 1928. Turin's newspaper *La Stampa* (published in the Savoy dynasty's ancestral city), waxed lyrical about the 'delirious, enthusiastic, imposing' crowd that farewelled the king. The public refused to disperse from the governor's house even after the *Savoia* headed north towards the *'madre patria'* on 'waters shimmering in the sunset'.[41] The governor of Libya told the gathered crowds that the king, taking his leave, had said 'I have spent in Tripolitania five of the most beautiful days of my life'.[42] Was the king in fact caught in the special infernal circle reserved for royal figures condemned to perform eternal pageants? Or was he still dignified by a genuine symbolic role? And would the diarchy's power dynamics become clearer in subsequent royal tours?

Eritrea, Cirenaica and Somalia, 1932, 1933 and 1934

The first tour to Tripolitania was either triumphant enough for the regime to send the king on similar tours, or sufficiently to the king's taste to prompt him to undertake more – or perhaps both. Well before the regime's high point at the conquest of Ethiopia in May 1936, the king made four journeys to the African continent in quick succession: to Eritrea (on the Red Sea) in autumn 1932; to Egypt in February 1933; to Cirenaica (east of Tripolitania) in spring 1933; and, the most distant of his reign, to Somalia, in autumn 1934 – an arduous trip of almost six weeks. In many ways these royal tours followed templates established by the first, though the king travelled without consort or family on all but the visit to Egypt. But six years separated 1928 and 1934, and within an ambitious regime, other differences might well be expected as time progressed.

One striking difference is immediately clear in the Istituto Luce's documentary of the king's 1932 tour of Eritrea.[43] Unlike those films made about Mussolini's 1926 journey and the king's in 1928, this documentary had sound – a combination of the soundscape captured while filming and a superimposed musical score. This adds a distinct dimension and encourages a new level of emotional engagement. While for the historian the 1926 and 1928 documentaries might represent silent, spasmodic footnotes to the evocative prose of well-written journalism and lively artists' impressions, the 1932 film makes the daily newspaper reports seem belaboured and repetitive. It is no wonder that film technology is regarded as a fascist primacy, though the newspaper accounts do remain extremely useful for details and context.

The same is true for Ardemagni's book, which spells out how the 1932 tour fitted into the regime's grandiose vision in a way that film does not. Of all Italy's colonies, Eritrea was the oldest, but also, the author surmises, the least familiar. It had the highest levels of commerce with Italy, and although 'Eritrea is not California', the territory presented 'vast possibilities that have until now been undervalued'.[44] The king's tour in 1932, 'fifty years after the initial conquest', ostensibly celebrated an agreement for preferential access made by Italy's Rubattino Steamship Company in 1882, but the tour also foreshadowed the new energy to be injected into Eritrea.[45] The piecemeal process of colonisation from the late 1860s was also punctuated by 1887's battle of Dogali and the Treaty of Wichale (Uccialli) in 1889.[46]

This royal tour did in fact celebrate achievements and commemorate losses. Ardemagni wrote that along the king's journey, 'displays of jubilation came in the form of fantasias executed by indigenous Arabs and Eritreans'.[47] The documentary corroborates this, showing not only formal Western ceremonies and military bands, but vibrant indigenous dancing to rhythmic music, accompanied by presumably jubilant ululations – though how orchestrated or spontaneous, we cannot know. Throughout the royal tours, film footage and illustrations of natives generally portray them as an indistinguishable mass, often performing for the king. What is clear is that both viewers and readers see the king as a prime-mover and an object of veneration. In the Eritrean documentary, a sense of the king's historic gravitas is reinforced during the film's strikingly silent moments: a formal visit to the monument for 500 Italian soldiers who lost their lives in battle against natives at Dogali, and another to the monument to 5,000 who fell during Italy's famously ignominious defeat at Adua in 1896 – the first time in history that an indigenous army had defeated a European power.[48]

After the poignant silence, the soundtrack resumes, interweaving African music with Italian opera, as if to convey a vision of a more harmonious future. Signs of that future come with the king opening schools in Adi-Ugri, then visiting sites dedicated to what a title screen proclaims is the 'Rational Production of Agave for the Making of Ropes'. Much as the indigenous music intertwined with the opera, the film shows hundreds of Eritreans working both traditionally and with the benefit of Italian machinery, making the desert plant into a commodity useful for a modern maritime power. The available footage of the Eritrean tour (which may not have been the complete documentary) concludes with a farewell scene of tribal dancing in front of the king and his entourage.[49]

Apart from occasional Roman salutes, again, visual indications of the regime are surprisingly minimal. Instead, the atmosphere of the live footage appears remarkably similar to that captured by the image on the front cover of the *Domenica del Corriere* (Figure 12.2). The king and fellow dignitaries are hailed by Africans performing 'devozioni', as the caption claims. A keen eye might spot the typically fascist 'rational' style of the buildings in the background, but this is clearly a royal tour in the monarch's own right, and the regime was not thrust forward to claim credit for all the colonial achievements. It could be suggested, conversely, that in return for the legitimacy the king's assent gave the regime, he was permitted to bask in the reflected glow of its achievements.[50]

In any case, the tours were clearly mutually agreeable. After the tour of Eritrea, it was only four months before the king set off again, in February 1933, this time taking the queen and their two daughters to visit King Fuad of Egypt, who had by then enjoyed eleven years of independence from Britain. Though not to an Italian colony, the journey reinforced Italy's rising status as a power in the 'Near East', where over the last few years, as London's *Times* noted on the occasion, 'she has produced a marked impression'.[51] The king's tours were undoubtedly an important element of this impression, and as earlier, the visit occasioned great Italian media interest. Egypt's evocative sites made ideal film sets, and there are several 'cine-news' accounts of the royal family's activities, including the princesses riding camels.[52] Journalists made much of the way Italian merchants and technicians contributed to the Egyptian economy, triumphantly tracing direct lines between the civilising mission of imperial Rome and that of contemporary Italy.[53]

The king may well have taken a liking to the relative autonomy afforded him in Africa, because his next tour took place only two months after his return from Egypt. In April–May 1933 Victor Emmanuel visited Cirenaica, the future Libya's eastern province, for about eight days. On this occasion he did not take the queen or his family, but he did have an official entourage. As with the 1928 visit to Tripolitania, he arrived on the *Savoia* from Sicily, and toured key archaeological and public-works sites. The image on a cover of the *Domenica del Corriere* recalls an earlier illustration in the same publication: the king travels through the desert in an imposing open car, followed by tribesmen on horseback.[54] In common with earlier images, the king is placed at the centre, and his motor-car figures as a potent symbol of progress and

12.2 King Victor Emmanuel III in Eritrea, *La Domenica del Corriere*, 16 October 1932

power. But generally within this tour, a greater proportion of the press accounts foreground the 'achievements of the regime', and the king appears as a pretext for their display more than he had done in the earlier travels.

Among the four 'cine-news' reels available, two titles make direct reference to fascist projects: one is 'H. M. the King on the Seafront of Victory in Benghazi', the 'seafront' being a fascist-built road; the other has 'H. M. the King visiting hospitals, schools and fascist headquarters of Benghazi'. The shift is subtle, but it is reinforced by other reportage. The *Corriere della Sera* titled one article 'The Victory King in Fascist Cirenaica', mentioning that 'blackshirts and young fascists were among the first to congregate under the windows of the king's residence'.[55] Another daily report bore the title 'The Sovereign visits Benghazi and the imposing works of the regime', and included photographs of orderly streets and new buildings.[56] The text underlined the 'very great benefits' brought by the work of fascism 'in the colonies too', claiming that the king had come to witness that progress personally.[57]

It may be that an apparent shift towards foregrounding the regime's achievements was a result of the individual correspondent's personal loyalties, because it did not become the rule. That colonial tour was followed about eighteen months later by the longest journey the king was ever to make: an absence from Italy of almost six weeks on a tour of Somalia, Italy's 'second-born Italian colony, the most distant of all, facing the Indian Ocean, traversed by the equator'.[58] The king travelled without the queen or their daughters, probably because of the journey's duration and arduous nature. The distance of Somalia from Italy clearly fascinated the press, but it also resulted in scantier reporting. Internationally, *The Times* announced before the journey that the king was to visit the only one of his colonies he had not yet seen, but its subsequent accounts were cursory.[59] Surprisingly, the Istituto Luce lists only two newsreels, and both are about the voyage, through the Suez Canal and Red Sea, not Somalia itself. A documentary about the king's journey is also listed, but alas it is as yet inaccessible.[60]

The press thus provides the only readily accessible contemporary accounts of this tour. While glances at the pages of both *La Stampa* and the *Corriere della Sera* give the impression that by late 1934 more and more articles on the national context centred upon the Duce and the regime's achievements, those seem less dominant in accounts of the king in Somalia than they were for Cirenaica. This could also be because the achievements themselves were less concrete. The newspapers provided similar accounts throughout the tour, though

Turin's daily, perhaps more sensitive to royal matters, published two articles even before the king arrived, describing the collective emotion in anticipation of his arrival: after years of hard work, the colonists yearned for the blessing of a figure they saw as 'Victor Emmanuel III the Victorious, the Head of Heads [Capo dei Capi], the basis of oaths in court'.[61]

Nine illustrations making up a two-page feature in the *Domenica del Corriere* showed Mogadishu's cathedral and urban projects, but others were of a rather ramshackle sugar refinery, and three indigenous figures – a man (in local military uniform), a woman and a child (both in local costume).[62] The following week's cover was a striking return to the traditional trope of dignitaries and natives in the colonies: the king and his entourage in brilliant colonial whites watch indigenous people dancing. A sense of the fascist regime is no more prominent here than it was in similar images of 1928 and 1932, which is to say, there are no signs of the regime at all.

La Stampa had emphasised that the king was 'the head of heads', but the *Corriere della Sera* went further, suggested that for the locals, although the king carried out such earthly duties as opening a museum, he was viewed as almost god-like. Natives, the paper claimed, were saying 'King like Allah. Never saw Allah. Want to see King'.[63] To many locals of the hinterlands, Victor Emmanuel would literally have appeared as a *deus ex machina*: a unique feature of the Somalian tour was a motor safari of over 2,500 km, in a 'caravan' made up of some sixty-six Fiat vehicles. As roads were virtually non-existent, this would have been arduous for both vehicles and passengers. Reported proudly by Turin's newspaper (owned by Giovanni Agnelli, one of Fiat's founders), the motorcade maintained 'an average speed of 50km/h in temperatures reaching 45 degrees, with minimal incident'.[64] In this account, the tour's stars were in fact neither the king nor fascist achievements, but the products of Italian industrial capitalism.

In all three Italian newspapers considered, fascism's achievements do appear, but by no means to the exclusion of the king or other interests. Underlining the regime's achievements, *La Stampa* wrote about the agriculture of Genale, where 20,000 hectares had been divided into ninety-eight concessions for Italian settlers. These were now Italy's main source of bananas, coconuts and peanuts. The king's presence honoured the colonisers and concession-holders during another long motorcade, 'an interminable parade of over 140 tractors'.[65] The *Corriere della Sera* opined that it was not necessary to have visited Somalia twelve years ago (when Mussolini came to power) to recognise 'how much fascism had done economically and politically for the colony'.[66]

Ultimately, though, the king's last day in Somalia suggested that his colonial tours were more royal than they were fascist. Before leaving Africa the king went hunting. According to the *Domenica del Corriere*, after 'hours of walking through a forest so thick it had to be opened up with machetes', the hunting party came across a large elephant 'not 15 metres away'. The king shot it, and the elephant fell, 'raising its trunk menacingly' as it did so.[67] An illustration of this dramatic encounter featured on the newspaper's cover, conveying to the Italian public not an image of the colonies as beneficiaries of fascism's modernising vision, but as the timeless locus of a historic European and royal prerogative: hunting big game (Figure 12.3).

Four years elapsed before the king's next – and final – colonial tour. During those four years, Italy's fascist regime had taken on something of the Somalian elephant's proportions on the world stage, and behaved much more menacingly. It had waged war on Ethiopia and, with much fanfare after victory in May 1936, proclaimed its African possessions to constitute an empire – to the renowned horror of deposed emperor Haile Selassie. Historians tend to agree that this achievement represented both the regime's and Mussolini's popular apogee.[68] The Duce took as his new title 'Founder of the Empire', and Victor Emmanuel became the emperor, or *Re-Imperatore* (king-emperor), to be precise. With a successful war in Ethiopia behind it and an imperial future, would the final royal tour be distinctive, now that its protagonist was also an emperor?

The first and last imperial tour: 1938

The destination of the tour was not Ethiopia, which had to make do with the appointment of the king's cousin, Duke Amedeo D'Aosta, as viceroy.[69] As Richard Bosworth points out, despite the military victory, two-thirds of the Ethiopian 'empire' were yet to be occupied, and 'the rest was scarcely pacified'.[70] Probably because of this, neither the empire's founder nor the new emperor himself ever visited Ethiopia. Instead, both made important visits to the much more secure imperial holding represented by Libya. Mussolini went there in March 1937, and Victor Emmanuel, without his consort, followed in May 1938. These tours were clearly linked to the increasingly tense international situation, with Mussolini in particular seeking to position Italy as friend and protector of the Arab and Muslim world.[71] Despite the theme of friendship, the Istituto Luce's documentary, *Il Duce in Libia* (sporting the novelty of a voiceover, in the martial, staccato style typical of the regime's later films), projects the bellicosity of the late 1930s from the moment the Duce arrives on board 'one of our fastest and most powerful battleships', the *Pola*.[72]

12.3 King Victor Emmanuel III elephant-hunting in Somalia, *La Domenica del Corriere*, 2 December 1934

The documentary made during the royal tour the following year is similar, but nevertheless different. As Pes has argued in relation to this tour, we do see the king spending a great deal of time anointing fascist projects. His itinerary seems to follow in the footsteps left by Mussolini the previous year, but that probably reflects the limited number of sites and monuments available to visit. Nevertheless, the two documentaries present notable differences. The tenor of that on the king is much softer than that documenting Mussolini's visit. Its voice-over is less martial, indeed almost mellifluous. The music is soft, orchestral, at times cloyingly sentimental, with high-pitched violins – the music used by Hollywood to denote less earthly realms.[73] If this tonal difference warrants interpretation, Mussolini comes across as the martial body of the empire, while the king appears as something more akin to a spirit.

The spirit of the times was bellicose though, and this is evident from the outset in newspaper coverage of the royal tour, which could not use music to manipulate the readers' emotions. *The Times* noted that Victor Emmanuel, embarking according to custom on the *Savoia* in Sicily, was to be attended throughout the tour by General Pariani, 'the Under-Secretary for War'.[74] The absence of the queen reinforced the image of the tour as one undertaken by military men. The *Manchester Guardian* used the occasion to explain the strategic importance of Libya to Italy as the reason for the area's 'constant state of military preparedness'.[75] The *Corriere della Sera*'s reports develop in the same vein, displaying a decidedly more military flavour than on previous visits. Its first article reports that the king's main activity was to observe military manoeuvres, announcing that on the anniversary day of Italy's entry into the First World War, the king would review the armed forces in action, 'with aviation playing an important role'.[76] The next day's article was headlined 'Military Effectiveness of the Fourth Shore'.[77] The king was known for his interest in things military, but his previous tours had not presented him with the same opportunities to indulge his martial passions.

After an initial flurry of extravagant military exercises, the tour settled down to the more familiar civic tasks of giving royal approval to economic, social and cultural undertakings. The *Corriere*'s correspondent made much of the progress achieved during the ten-year interval since the king's first visit in 1928. To the monarch's 'attentive and delighted eyes appeared inspiring visions of fields undulating with grain, florid vineyards, proud almond groves, and hills covered with olive trees in endless lines'.[78] The *Domenica del Corriere*, in a photo-spread, also portrayed the king at work in colonial civic duties. The seven different scenes tell a story similar to that of the first royal tour, ten years earlier, but with one exception: in a close-up of the king, in repose on a chair in a tent, he looks old and tired, indicating that he found this tour more fatiguing than those 'most beautiful days' in Tripoli in 1928.[79]

Sunset: on empire, fascism and the Italian monarchy

The last royal tour of Italy's foreign possessions concluded, as usual, with a sea voyage back to the *'madre patria'* aboard the royal yacht. The final scenes of Luce's documentary capture something poignant as the king leaves the wharf on a small boat that would take him out to the *Savoia*. The tender passes beneath a row of vast, state-of-the-art battleships, just like the one on which Mussolini had arrived in Libya the previous year. As the *Savoia* comes into view, elegant and aristocratic as it was, it looks decidedly quaint and meek compared to the imposing modern warships in the previous frames.[80] In 1938, with the king clearly ageing, a similar contrast could be drawn between the imposing 'Founder of the Empire' and the diminutive emperor himself. At that moment, there could be little doubt that in practical terms, the throne stood in the shadows of the Duce's power.

Ultimately though, the king's symbolic (and constitutional) power outstripped that of the Duce, even if not for long. The king may have been meek, but unlike Mussolini he had the benefit of a long royal tradition behind him. In the context of his reign during the years of fascism, the colonial tours suggest that that tradition provided the king with a realm in some way separate from a regime that gained power as the result of his own decisions. Indeed, during tours of fascist Italy's overseas colonies, the king was to be seen at his most autonomous from that regime. It may well be that, aided by those royal tours, the king was able to preserve the monarchy's prestige at a level just sufficient to avoid being completely 'swallowed' by the regime, allowing the institution to take a final, crucial step to topple Mussolini from power.

Entry into the Second World War proved a disaster for Italy, and the conflict soon destroyed the empire that had been the jewel of fascism's crown. By July 1943 'Africa Italiana' had been swept off the map by Allied action, and it was clear that the regime was not nearly so strong in war as it had claimed to be in peace. Victor Emmanuel had little choice but to dismiss the Duce. After the war, tainted by association with fascism, the king, in an attempt to preserve the monarchy, abdicated in favour of his son Umberto, on 9 May 1946. But there was to be no saving the Italian crown after fascism. On 2 June 1946, the Italian people voted in the first broad election since 1924 (including women voters for the first time) by a safe margin to abolish the monarchy and make Italy a republic.[81] Victor Emmanuel exiled himself to Egypt, where he was welcomed by a friend he had last visited triumphantly in 1933, King Fuad.

The reign of Victor Emmanuel III thus concluded as it had begun: on a ship. In 1900 the young prince, while on a private voyage with his wife to Corfu, had heard of the death of his father, Umberto I. Out of telegraph range, officials on an Italian torpedo-boat had tracked the prince's vessel down, informed Victor Emmanuel of his father's death, and told him that he was now king.[82] Forty-six years later, he left Italy, for Africa, one last time, not on the erstwhile royal yacht *Savoia*, but on a modern cruiser of the Italian navy.[83] It was the last feeble echo of Italy's 'royals on tour', for halfway through his reign, Victor Emmanuel had fatally tied his throne to fascism. By doing so, he unwittingly set the Italian monarchy itself on course for oblivion.

Notes

1 I acknowledge the permission of Rome's Biblioteca di Storia Moderna e Contemporanea to reproduce images from its digitised collection of *La Domenica del Corriere*, and thank dott. Eugenio Semboloni for his kind assistance. Thanks to Jane McCabe, who helped me in the early stages of this research, and also to Paolo Colombo, Giacomo Lichtner and Marjan Schwegman for their helpful comments on earlier versions of this chapter.
2 Collectively known to Italians as 'Libia' even in the nineteenth century, the provinces of Tripolitania, Fezzan and Cyrenaica were only formally amalgamated under that name in 1929. R.B. St John, *Libya: Continuity and Change*, 2nd edn (Oxford: Routledge, 2015), p. 1.
3 M. Ardemagni, in *Il re in Africa* (Milan: Mondadori, 1934), p. 13, claims that the House of Savoy had long been 'tenacious advocates of the civilizing mission in Africa', referring to King Victor Emmanuel III's cousin Prince Luigi Amedeo di Savoia's explorations of the Somalian coast in 1893 and east Africa in 1906 as examples.
4 E. Ryan, 'Violence and the Politics of Prestige: The Fascist Turn in Colonial Libya', *Modern Italy*, 20:2 (2015), 123–135.
5 D. Mack Smith, *Mussolini's Roman Empire* (London: Longman, 1976); N. Labanca, *Oltremare: Storia dell'espansione coloniale italiana* (Bologna: Il Mulino, 2002), p. 168.
6 A. Pes, 'An Empire for a Kingdom: Monarchy and Fascism in the Italian Colonies', in R. Aldrich and C. McCreery (eds), *Crowns and Colonies: European Monarchies and Overseas Empires* (Manchester: Manchester University Press, 2016), pp. 245–261, here p. 245.
7 P. Colombo, *La monarchia fascista 1922–1940* (Bologna: Il Mulino, 2010).
8 Ibid., pp. 176–178.
9 Exemplifying the paucity is Labanca's *Oltremare*, in which Victor Emmanuel III receives but one mention in 569 pages.

10 Pes, 'An Empire for a Kingdom', p. 246.
11 *Ibid.*, p. 246. Strictly speaking, Mussolini made a third trip to Libya in 1942, but since 1939 the former colony had been an integral part of Italy. See St John, *Libya*, p. 18.
12 The *Domenica del Corriere*, an important source for this study, was a popular and influential illustrated Sunday supplement to Italy's most widely-circulated newspaper during fascism, Milan's *Corriere della Sera*. See M. Forno, *Informazione e potere. Storia del giornalismo italiano* (Rome-Bari: Laterza, 2012), p. 105.
13 Essays by C. Duggan contextualise the 'cult of the Duce' within Italian history from 1861, including precedents from the royal family and the Pope: C. Duggan, 'Political Cults in Liberal Italy, 1861–1922' and 'The Propagation of the Cult of the Duce, 1925–26', in S. Gundle, C. Duggan and G. Pieri (eds), *The Cult of the Duce: Mussolini and the Italians* (Manchester: Manchester University Press, 2013), pp. 11–26 and 27–40. In the same volume, see G. Finaldi, 'Mussolini and the Italian Empire, 1935–1941', pp. 144–158, on the Duce's cult in the empire.
14 See, for example, D. Mack Smith, *Italy and its Monarchy* (New Haven: Yale University Press, 1989), pp. 254–267.
15 S. Bertoldi, *Vittorio Emanuele III. Un re tra le due guerre e fascismo*, 2nd edn (Turin: UTET, 2002), p. 280. Translations from the Italian are my own throughout the chapter.
16 *Domenica del Corriere*, no. 18, 29 April 1928; 'Dopo l'infame attentato a Milano', p. 7; and 'La grandiosa dimostrazione di Roma al sovrano', p. 8. The scale of the crowds is made clear by photographs.
17 C. Brice, 'Riti della corona, riti del fascio', in E. Gentile (ed.), *Modernità totalitaria. Il fascismo italiano* (Rome-Bari: Laterza, 2008), pp. 189–190.
18 Archivio Centrale dello Stato, Casa Civile di S. M. Il Re e Ministero della Real Casa. Ufficio viaggi (henceforth ACS, RC, UV), busta (b.) 39 fascicolo (f.) 2, and b. 44, f. 1.
19 A recent facsimile reproduction of the king's travel journal shows that Victor Emmanuel III was an assiduous visitor to all parts of Italy throughout his reign: *Sì, è il re. Le memorie private di un sovrano*, ed. V. De Buzzaccarini and P. Mello (Padua: Edizioni Nuova Charta, 2013). The facsimile is only partial, and alas the years in which the king visited Africa are not reproduced.
20 Ardemagni, *Il re in Africa*, pp. 16–17.
21 For example, ACS, RC, UV, b. 44, f. 1, s.f. 54.
22 'I sovrani sbarcano stamane a Tripoli', *Corriere della Sera*, 18 April 1928, p. 1.
23 O. Cerquiglini, 'Come viaggiano i Sovrani d'Italia', *Domenica del Corriere*, 23 May 1937, pp. 5–6.
24 www.culturanavale.it/documentazione.php?id=267, accessed 9 January 2017.
25 'I sovrani sbarcano stamane a Tripoli', *Corriere della Sera*, 18 April 1928, p. 1.
26 A. Abdullatif Ahmida, 'When the Subaltern Speak: Memory of Genocide in Colonial Libya 1929 to 1933', *Italian Studies*, 61:2 (2006), 175–190.
27 'Il trionfale viaggio dei sovrani in Tripolitania', *Domenica del Corriere*, 6 May 1928, p. 7.
28 R. Cantalupo, 'La monarchia e l'Africa', *Corriere della Sera*, 19 April 1928, p. 1.
29 'The King of Italy in Libya: A Successful Visit', *The Times*, 21 April 1928, p. 11.
30 Eugene J. Young, 'Mussolini between Fire of Throne and Pontiff', *Los Angeles Times*, 13 May 1928, p. 6.
31 Pes, 'An Empire for a Kingdom', p. 253.
32 R. Cantalupo, 'La monarchia e l'Africa', *Corriere della Sera*, 19 April 1928, p. 1.
33 'La seconda giornata dei Reali in Tripolitania', *Corriere della Sera*, 20 April 1928, p. 1, makes much of the 'fervid homage' paid to the king by Italians resident in Tunisia, who came to meet him.
34 R. Ben-Ghiat, *Italian Fascism's Empire Cinema* (Bloomington: Indiana University Press, 2015), p. 27.
35 The archive at www.archivioluce.com/archivio is fully and freely searchable. On 10 January 2017 the online catalogue listed at least four documentaries and twelve short 'cine-news' items about Victor Emmanuel's five colonial tours.

36 *Il trionfale viaggio di S. E. Mussolini in Tripolitania*, www.archivioluce.com, accessed 10 January 2017.
37 The relevant page at www.archivioluce.com/archivio/indice indicates that the documentary, *Nelle oasi. Viaggio dei Sovrani nella colonia d'oltre mare*, is either missing or currently being digitised. Accessed 10 January 2017.
38 *With the King of Italy in Tripolitania*, British Pathé, www.youtube.com/watch?v=kZpGqwhkjC8, accessed 10 January 2017.
39 Ardemagni, *Il re in Africa*, p. 16.
40 Ibid., p. 9.
41 Mario Bassi, 'Il trionfale saluto della Tripolitania ai sovrani che ripartono per l'Italia', *La Stampa*, 23 April 1928, p. 3.
42 Ibid.
43 *Il Viaggio di S. M. il Re in Eritrea* (1932), www.archivioluce.com/archivio, accessed 13 January 2017.
44 Ardemagni, *Il re in Africa*, pp. 64–65.
45 Ibid.
46 M. Clark, *Modern Italy, 1871–1995*, 2nd edn (Harlow: Longman, 1996).
47 Ardemagni, *Il re in Africa*, pp. 79–81.
48 *Il Viaggio di S. M. il re in Eritrea*, www.archivioluce.com/archivio, accessed 13 January 2017.
49 Ibid.
50 I thank Giacomo Lichtner for suggesting this interpretation.
51 'Italy in the Near East', *The Times*, 22 February 1933, p. 13.
52 Eight such films are listed at www.archivioluce.com/archivio, accessed 14 January 2017.
53 O. Vergani, 'I Sovrani visitano la diga di Assuan' [an Italian-sponsored dam project], *Corriere della Sera*, 26 February, 1933, p. 3.
54 *Domenica del Corriere*, 14 May 1933, cover page.
55 C. Tomaselli, 'Il Re della Vittoria nella Cirenaica fascista', *Corriere della Sera*, 28 April 1933, p. 1.
56 C. Tomaselli, 'Il Sovrano visita a Bengasi e le imponenti opera del regime', *Corriere della Sera*, 30 April 1933, p. 5.
57 B. Maineri, 'La Cirenaica visitata dal Re', *Domenica del Corriere*, 7 May 1933, p. 5.
58 O. Cerquiglini, 'Il Re in Somalia', *Domenica del Corriere*, 11 November 1934, pp. 8–9.
59 'Telegrams in Brief', *The Times*, 5 October 1934, p. 13.
60 Archivio Istituto Luce, www.archivioluce.com, accessed 14 December 2016.
61 'L'attesa della Somalia nell'imminenza dell'arrivo del Re', *La Stampa*, 1 November 1934, p. 1.
62 O. Cerquiglini, 'Il Re in Somalia', *Domenica del Corriere*, 11 November 1934, pp. 8–9.
63 S. Aponte, 'Fastose e ardenti manifestazioni al Re nella visita alla capitale della Somalia', *Corriere della Sera*, 5 November 1934, p. 7.
64 'Brillante affermazione della carovana FIAT', *La Stampa*, 26 November 1934, p. 1.
65 G. Calderini, 'I concessionari di Genale', *La Stampa*, 13 November 1934, p. 1.
66 S. Aponte, 'L'ultima giornata del Re in Somalia', *Corriere della Sera*, 16 November, p. 8.
67 *Domenica del Corriere*, 2 December 1934. The quotations are from the caption beneath the cover image.
68 R. Bosworth, *Mussolini* (London: Arnold, 2002), p. 308.
69 Pes, 'An Empire for a Kingdom', pp. 255–256.
70 Bosworth, *Mussolini*, p. 308.
71 Ibid., p. 336.
72 *Il Duce in Libia* (1937), www.archivioluce.com, accessed 16 January 2017.
73 *Viaggio di S. M il Re Imperatore in Libia* (1938), www.archivioluce.com, accessed 16 January 2017.
74 'King of Italy's Visit to Libya', *The Times*, 21 May 1938, p. 13.
75 'Italy in Libya', *The Manchester Guardian*, 24 May 1938, p. 12.

76 S. Aponte, 'Il Re Imperatore arriverà oggi a Tripoli', *Corriere della Sera*, 21 May 1938, p. 1.
77 S. Aponte, 'Efficienza guerriera della Quarta Sponda', *Corriere della Sera*, 23 May 1938, p. 1.
78 S. Aponte, 'Il Re a Misurata lungo la Litoranea', *Corriere della Sera*, 28 May 1938, p. 1.
79 'Il Re-Imperatore in Libia', *Domenica del Corriere*, 5 June 1938, p. 5.
80 *Viaggio di S. M il Re Imperatore in Libia* (1938), www.archivioluce.com, accessed 16 January 2017. The departure appears in the last minute of the film.
81 Mack Smith, *Italy and its Monarchy*, pp. 337–339.
82 R. Bracalini, *Vittorio Emanuele III. Il re 'vittorioso'* (Milan: Mondadori, 1987), p. 7.
83 Mack Smith, *Italy and its Monarchy*, p. 338.

CHAPTER THIRTEEN

Strained encounters: royal Indonesian visits to the Dutch court in the early twentieth century

Susie Protschky

On 28 December 1936, Gusti Raden Ajeng Siti Nuruh Kusumawa Rhdani, a daughter of Prince Mangkunegoro VII, danced at the Noordeinde Palace in The Hague accompanied by a gamelan orchestra. The musicians were not in the room. Instead, the music was broadcast live on radio from the Mangkunegaran (the prince's palace in Surakarta, Central Java), where three other women from the royal household danced their parts in time to the orchestra's strains. Together, the four women were performing a *serimpi*. The American art historian Claire Holt, who observed the dance at the Mangkunegaran during her training in the 1930s, noted its origins as a 'stylised and inconclusive duel' between two pairs of female warrior opponents.[1] In its display of 'controlled languour, a collected inwardness, and subtlety', the *serimpi* celebrated the triumph of refinement over the baser human passions, and was thus a favoured entertainment for Javanese royalty.[2] At celebrations for the Dutch monarchy in the Netherlands East Indies (colonial Indonesia), such courtly dances were frequent at the gala performances sponsored by Dutch officials and Javanese aristocrats during the festivities they were obliged to host.[3]

However, the December 1936 performance was the first of its kind at a Dutch court. It was given in honour of Crown Princess Juliana of the Netherlands' engagement to a German nobleman, Prince Bernhard of Lippe-Biestefeld. In this most unusual live recital, radio dramatically bridged the distance between the Netherlands and its oldest and most important overseas possession, the jewel in the modern Dutch empire. Juliana and her mother, Queen Wilhelmina (1880–1962), were so taken with the spectacle that they had it repeated at the wedding ball on 7 January 1937.[4]

This spectacular, carefully orchestrated courtly encounter between Dutch and Javanese royal women on Dutch soil was widely reported in metropolitan and colonial newspapers, but only in the briefest terms. With very few exceptions,[5] press accounts of the Indonesian royals who travelled to the Netherlands for the wedding focused on Prince Mangkunegoro and on the other male delegates from the royal houses of Central Java and Sumatra who attended the festivities. Present-day knowledge of the *serimpi* performance comes mainly from a recent account by a Dutch scholar, Rita Wassing-Visser, in her important book on gifts from Indonesian royals to the House of Orange over some three and a half centuries of Dutch colonial rule.[6] Wassing-Visser's description uses sources from the Dutch Royal Archive (*Koninklijk Huisarchief*) to revive an encounter that has been almost forgotten, perhaps because it took place for a closed audience of Dutch royals and their most distinguished guests, rather than a larger public observing the festivities outside the palace gates or reading in newspapers what journalists were permitted to observe. Indeed, the princess's dance has been subsumed into a relatively short list of encounters between Queen Wilhelmina's household and Indonesian royals in the Netherlands that took place over the monarch's long reign, from 1898 to 1948. Within this time, the Dutch monarchy's meetings with Indonesian nobility were invariably reported-in exotic and salubrious terms by Dutch sources from the Indies and the Netherlands. Historians reflecting on Wilhelmina's reign, and writing after Indonesia achieved its independence from the Dutch in 1949, have maintained this image of congenial relations. Studies have certainly shown that Indonesian royals bristled (discreetly) at the indignity of cooperating with the colonial officials who represented the Dutch monarchy on Indies soil.[7] However, where the limited scholarship turns to encounters in the Dutch court, the assumption that Indonesian royals relished their exclusive fraternity with an international royal elite holds sway.[8]

    This chapter inspects that assumption more closely from the perspective of both Dutch and Indonesian royal courts. Given that Queen Wilhelmina presided over her country's colonial possessions entirely *in absentia*, without ever gracing the East Indies, West Indies or Suriname with a personal tour for the duration of her half-century reign, such an examination is long overdue. Indeed, the only direct encounters between the Dutch monarch and Indonesian royals happened in the Netherlands, at her court. This chapter examines how such meetings were represented in Dutch print media, how they were privately assessed by the Dutch court, and how Indonesian royals negotiated their own status as aristocrats during these encounters, by conforming in person but asserting some agency in the gifts they presented to the queen and her household.

Sources on Indonesian–Dutch encounters

Dutch-language newspaper reports from the Netherlands and the Indies give relatively little information on the unfolding of such meetings apart from basic details such as who was present and what observable duties they performed. Commemorative books are richer sources. Produced for high occasions like births, weddings and jubilees, *gedenkboeken* – written in Dutch and frequently illustrated with photographs – provide more insight into royal encounters, but generally uphold the image of convivial meetings. As I shall demonstrate, reading these same accounts against the grain reveals rather more strained relations. On visits to the Dutch court, the pomp of indigenous royals was considerably reduced and constrained compared to the sumptuary privileges they enjoyed on their own soil. After all, Indonesian royal visits to the Netherlands were tours of duty, performed to pay homage to a Dutch queen who, according to the constitution, ruled them all.

A protocol specifically regulating the reception of visitors from the East Indies at Wilhelmina's court provides further evidence, from the Dutch monarchy's perspective, of the strained nature of such encounters. The document, which has not been examined before, dates from the latter half of Wilhelmina's reign (from or after 1926),[9] and is the only one of its kind that exists in her private archive. It pertains specifically to 'Native and Foreign Oriental' visitors. Following legal categories in the Netherlands Indies, the former referred to the autochthonous ethnic groups of what is now Indonesia, while the second signified groups that colonial authorities considered immigrants (despite the long history of their settlement in the Indies): Chinese, Arabs and South Asians.[10] The protocol divides these non-European visitors from the Indies into three categories to determine what level of access to the queen they were to be granted, where, and in what sort of company, among other details. The first category comprised 'sovereigns and native luminaries ... with an official commission'. These were the Indonesian royals who were invited to the Netherlands for high occasions, and were discussed and photographed in published accounts of celebrations for the House of Orange. The second category mentioned in the protocol pertained to very important persons,[11] and the third to students.[12] These were visitors whom Wilhelmina had not invited and wished to receive advance notice of if they requested an audience with her. For reasons that will be explained, Indonesian nobles were highly likely to be among both groups, but Wilhelmina's court extended very few of these visitors the courtesies that were given to visitors on an official commission. Indeed, the protocol reveals particular concerns for Wilhelmina when she faced encounters with the women of Indonesian royal households – precisely like the one that occurred at her daughter's engagement and wedding, when the court was entertained by a princess of the Mangkunegaran.

Delegations: Indonesian royals with an official commission to the Dutch court

The protocol governing the reception of 'Natives and Foreign Orientals' at Wilhelmina's court categorically described Indonesian royals visiting with an official commission as *'vassals* who come to bear tribute to their Sovereign or Suzereign'.[13] From 1898, all the so-called 'self-governing' royals of the Indonesian archipelago had been subjected to Dutch rule through a standard treaty (*korte verklaring*, or 'short statement').[14] In the Princely States (*vorstenlanden*) of Central Java, the kings and princes of Surakarta (the Pakubuwono and Mangkunegoro, respectively) and Yogyakarta (sultan Hamengkubuwono and the Pakualam) were nominally sovereign, allowed by the Dutch to keep their courts and many of their ceremonial privileges. Yet they had progressively, between 1757 and 1830, lost their real power. The Dutch proscribed access to the major sources of these rulers' revenue in the hinterland (*mancanegoro*) around their palaces, banned them from raising their own militias and conducting diplomacy, forbade them from independently naming their successors, and largely restricted these royals to the *kraton* (palace compound).[15] As the eminent Javanist, Stuart Robson, concisely observed:

> the Sultan 'ruled' only by the grace of the colonial government; each generation had to swear allegiance to the Dutch throne, and at each change the noose was twisted even tighter. The Sultan was only a 'Highness', whereas the Dutch Queen was a 'Royal Highness' and the Governor was a 'father' of the Sultan.[16]

When Indonesian royals visited Queen Wilhelmina in the Netherlands they were formally known as a 'delegation' (*delegatie*). Some made their visit during an annual round of court receptions. Most, however, came at the major milestones of her rule: her inauguration in 1898, marriage in 1901, silver jubilee in 1923, the crown princess's nuptials in 1936–1937, and Wilhelmina's fortieth regnal jubilee in 1938.[17] Because of the length and cost of the journey to the Netherlands, many Indies aristocrats made long visits extending up to a year, some taking the opportunity to settle a son or nephew into a Dutch secondary school or university. The formal purpose of these visits, however, was to offer the Dutch monarch tribute by appearing in her procession and at other public occasions, and by making speeches and offering gifts during a ceremonial audience.

Wilhelmina's court protocol explains that, except 'in very special circumstances', 'no more honour should be extended to these vassals than to ambassadors of foreign Heads of State'.[18] In general, then, Indonesian royals visiting Wilhelmina were to be treated *like* an embassy: a great irony since, unlike most other embassies (save those from the West Indies or Suriname), the head of state to whom they deferred and paid tribute was the same one that notionally represented them. Apart from vacillating on whether a 'podium or other elevation' should be offered to the most distinguished visitors – a standard custom in the Indies, but one that may have irked the short-statured Queen of the Netherlands – the protocol does not describe how these delegations were to be received. However, published photographs and accounts in the commemorative books issued for high occasions provide some insight on these details and how they were to be communicated to the public. These descriptions and images were made by Dutch journalists and court attendants, and focus on the procession and audience components of the delegation.

From the Dutch perspective, commemorative books celebrate the centripetal powers of the queen to command personal tribute from the Netherlands' chief colony by receiving sultans and princes from all over the archipelago. One of the most reproduced images in Dutch *gedenkboeken* shows the daughters of the Sultan of Langkat offering to Wilhelmina and her son-in-law, Prince Bernhard, orchids that had been flown by plane from the East Indies (Figure 13.1). The flowers were presented on 10 September 1938 during an audience at the Olympic Stadium in Amsterdam, before a live audience of tens of thousands of people. The ceremony was described in the caption of one book as the 'stunning climax' (*schitterende apotheose*) of events at the stadium.[19] The commentary in another book from that year used an Arab-Malay term with wide currency in the Indies to describe how the princesses showed the queen '*hormat*' (honour/reverence) in the local manner, by making a *sembah* (a genuflection that usually entails kneeling, placing the hands before the forehead and bowing to the ground). The book goes on to say how deeply impressed the queen and all who saw this display were: 'In this *hormat* given by both Princesses of the blood, the entire Indies bowed at the feet of the Netherlands' Queen.'[20]

Considering these same sources from an Indonesian perspective opens more ambiguous interpretations of these delegations. For a start, they were quite small, never exceeding the eight representatives who descended on Wilhelmina's court for her fortieth regnal jubilee in 1938.[21] That peak year's delegation fails to even approximate the

13.1 Tengku Latifah and Tengku Kalsun, daughters of the sultan of Langkat, offering orchids to Queen Wilhelmina on the occasion of the fortieth anniversary of her reign, Olympic Stadium, Amsterdam, 1938

hundreds of indigenous royal families of the East Indies at that time. In addition, very few retainers seem to have attended those delegates who were present. A photograph that circulated in commemorative books during the last decade of Wilhelmina's reign shows a single servant bearing a *payung* (ceremonial parasol) for a sultan attending an audience with the queen (Figure 13.2).[22] On another occasion, one *payung*-bearer was shared among four sultans and a crown prince attending a military parade.[23] Such parsimonious retinues were a drastic departure from how even lower nobility appeared in public at formal occasions

STRAINED ENCOUNTERS

13.2 Queen Wilhelmina receiving the sultan of Modjopait at Paleis Het Loo for the Scouts World Jamboree, 1937

in the Indies. When indigenous aristocrats displayed themselves in public on their home soil, small armies of servants trailed behind them or sat in clusters on the floor when their masters assumed a throne or podium. Many of these retainers had ceremonial roles consisting largely of bearing ornamental, sacred heirlooms (*pusaka*), objects like the parasol, betel (*sirih*) set and dagger (*kris*). In Indonesian courts, and more widely throughout Southeast Asia, these items were made of precious stones, metals and fabrics, and were thought to be instilled with magical qualities that heightened the ruler's power and mystique.[24] Ironically, these very objects that Indonesian royals were prevented from carrying on their official commissions to the Dutch court were the favoured gifts given as tribute to the Dutch royal family throughout Wilhelmina's reign.[25]

In the Indies, sumptuary laws regulating the public use of regalia for indigenous royals and government officials fluctuated according to the colonial government's pleasure.[26] Generally speaking, however, the paucity of regalia that necessarily attended the virtual absence of servants for Indonesian delegates to the Netherlands would, in the Indies, have been considered a scandalous constraint of royal entitlements. On Dutch soil, protocol demanded that Indonesian royals be accompanied by European translators or adjutants instead of their own servants in their audience with the queen.[27] These escorts tended to be Dutch officials, many of them commoners with only government ranks to their names.

The modest size of the Indonesian delegations to Wilhelmina seems to have been determined in large part, and on both the Indonesian and Dutch sides, by practical matters. Where would they all be accommodated and how were they to be funded? For Wilhelmina's inauguration in 1898, for example, the House of Orange outsourced the lodgings of their guests to aristocrats with bigger palaces. The complete royal delegation from the Indies was housed near Utrecht at the Huis ter Haar, the 'medieval' design of which dated from 1892. This, the largest castle in the Netherlands, stood on the private, ancestral lands of a Dutch baron, Étienne van Zuylen van Nyevelt van de Haar, whose rich wife, Hélène de Rothschild, had subsidised the lavish renovations to his thirteenth-century heirloom.[28] The prohibitive costs of receiving royal delegations to the Netherlands were felt by hosts and visitors alike. For Indonesian royals, whose court expenditures were limited by the colonial government, money was in not in endless supply; indeed, it dwindled throughout the last decades of Dutch rule.[29] Furthermore, from the outset of the queen's reign, the Dutch government indicated that it was not willing to spend a fortune to bring Indonesian royals to the Netherlands. For Wilhelmina's inauguration, for example, the Parliament directed the Ministry for the Colonies to support the travel of, as Wassing-Visser explains, 'only the most important princely courts and then only one per major island'.[30]

The decision to have the 'major islands' of the Indies represented signifies a characteristically Dutch, colonial conception of the archipelago that was in conflict with indigenous geopolitics. The Dutch had organised the Indies into administrative units by province (the larger islands generally constituted a whole province), subdivided into residencies and districts. However, the sultanates and princely realms of the archipelago, which were the remnants of older empires that preceded Dutch rule, frequently extended beyond these land and sea borders. To choose just one royal (when there were invariably many) per island therefore raised questions of hierarchy and precedence that would have been offensive to the prestige and honour of each ruler. In the Princely States of Central Java, for example, the titles of the major royal dynasties – Axis and Authority of the Cosmos for the *susuhunan* Pakubuwono and the sultan Hamengkubuwono, respectively – leaves no doubt as to each house's sense of eminence, and also hints at their long-standing rivalry with each other.

Aside from Mangkunegoro VII, no king or prince of Central Java ever went to the Netherlands to meet the queen in person, nor did the rajas of Bali. Susuhunan Pakubuwono X (r. 1893–1939) of Surakarta consistently sent proxies in his stead to the Netherlands, and apologies to Wilhelmina that were formulated in terms of his ill health.[31] Yet he participated heartily enough in celebrations for himself as well as the Dutch monarchy at his own *kraton*, and was an intrepid traveller within the Indies.[32] In addition, the Axis of the Cosmos energetically sent photographs and albums of himself in which he amply demonstrated the pomp of his court and his splendour as king.[33] Few indigenous royals appear to have been driven to travel halfway across the world to personally subordinate themselves as vassals to a foreign monarch, only to be constrained in the sumptuary privileges that displayed their own royalty in an Indonesian idiom.

Royals on tour: Indonesian aristocrats on the colonial circuit

Not all Indonesian royals whom Queen Wilhelmina received in the Netherlands were on an official commission. Many went to the Netherlands on other business, particularly in the 1920s and 1930s, when a growing number of socially and geographically mobile Indonesians travelled to the metropole, often to further their education. The sons (and, very occasionally, daughters) of the nobility attended elite Dutch secondary schools, military colleges and universities in growing numbers in response to the formalisation of requirements for specialised training to hold their increasingly bureaucratised, albeit more or less hereditary, offices.[34] These Indonesians were participating in the same 'colonial migration circuit' between the Netherlands and the Indies that benefited Europeans and Indo-Europeans in the colonies.[35]

In the latter part of Wilhelmina's reign, 'out of regard for the strong increase in this group', her court protocol explicitly recognised the need to address the impromptu visit of Indonesian royals on tour.[36] Indeed, a major problem for her private secretary appears to have been discerning, among the numerous indigenous aristocrat-officials who might be present in the Netherlands, which of them was royal enough to merit access to the queen. Her court protocol tackled this question by creating two groups apart from the royals on official commission: one that could loosely be understood as 'VIPs', and the other, students.

Individuals from the first group were conceived as 'people of merit; of learning; those who have been in a somewhat executive position'. None were to be received without counsel from the Minister for the Colonies. He advised on who should gain an introduction to the queen and who, of a very select few, would be permitted an additional 'special audience' or 'reception', which permitted a more extended conversation ('an explication of their thoughts') with the queen. The introduction was a short, ceremonial presentation modelled on the annual public audiences the queen gave at her courts in Amsterdam and The Hague and at the opening of the States General (the Dutch Parliament). Introductions were to be 'more circumscribed than the "ceremonial reception" of persons from group I [royals on official commission]'. The special audience, on the other hand, was intended as 'a distinction only for those who, through their development, position and achievement, are remarkable'.[37]

Regents were given special mention among those in the VIP group who were 'certainly to be considered' for presentation. On Java, these were the *bupati*, the counterparts of Dutch Assistant Residents and the top-ranking indigenous officials in the administrative hierarchy. They were appointed by the Governor-General, answered to the Resident, and governed the Javanese arm of the colonial civil service. As Heather Sutherland shows in her important studies of the *bupati* and their gradual co-optation, from the mid-nineteenth century onward, into the colonial bureaucracy, most were from the *priyayi* class of lower nobility who claimed descent from the subjugated or deposed sultans of Java.[38] These men were selected by a Dutch administration in thrall to the idea that the 'natural' rulers of the native population, and their best partners in a system of indirect rule, were the aristocrats who commanded the loyalty of the local population. By the turn of the century, regencies were still hereditary in practice, but the colonial government enforced the expectation that office-holders acquire a Dutch education and specialised qualifications. As a consequence, the sons of noble officials were required to speak and read fluent Dutch (and other European languages) and attend school and perhaps even university in the Netherlands. They were among the best travelled and most educated people in the Indies, indigenous or European.[39]

Wilhelmina's court protocol rightly recognised that these men were likely to constitute the third group, 'young persons who go to the Netherlands for their education'. The document outlined how the queen was ideally to receive such visitors as a group deputation, to do so infrequently ('now and then, in intervals of four or five years'), and to avoid distinguishing individual members. Student deputations were to be treated *like* Europeans (specifically, 'European corporate bodies').[40] In this sense, the Queen's court in the Netherlands ratified widespread practices in the Indies that made 'Europeanness' a flexible category which, as Bart Luttikhuis has shown, often accommodated educated, upwardly mobile Indonesians and Indo-Europeans.[41] However, the protocol was adamant that recognising such advancements should be

> achieved without it 'getting to the heads' of any of these young people. And in no circumstance shall those to whom the privilege of an audience falls have the boldness or brutality to try anything in the absence of a European intervening.[42]

Receptions were to be considered only for individuals 'of high birth', and 'AT THE WILL OF HIS FAMILY – more or less for political reasons', which suggests that some lobbying often preceded the meeting to which the queen acceded. 'So it could be', the protocol speculates, 'that the son of a Native Prince is sent to the Netherlands for his education, and HE ATTEMPTS to offer tribute to Her Majesty'. The document ruled that it would be 'difficult' and certainly 'not desirable' for the queen to grant an audience to such a person, since he 'would only in highly exceptional circumstances be sufficiently interesting'. He was to be met with briefly, before the commencement of an official soirée, and then to be subsumed within the general party. The protocol concedes the 'highly exceptional circumstance' in which a breakfast or tea at the Paleis Het Loo, in the forested heart of the Netherlands, might be offered instead, but points out that the prince would 'always be excluded from taking part at Her Majesty's or even the Marshal's table'. Importantly, only those aristocrats who also demonstrated some merit – for example, 'through very exceptional mastery of study' – were to be treated *like* a VIP (the second group) and given a special audience.

Claims to royal lineage, bumptiousness and a pushy family were therefore not sufficient for indigenous aristocrats in order for the queen to extend them a warm welcome. Indeed, the list of qualifications in the protocol erects barriers to access and elaborately buttresses an apparent disinclination on the queen's part to accommodate royals who were not on an official commission to her court. The final section of the protocol is worth quoting at length, for it reveals a particular source of anxiety for the queen in encountering Indonesian royals.

> [Native Princes] should NOT, AS A RULE, be accompanied by one [woman] or women or female family members. By the same token, no ladies of Her Majesty's court should be present at the presentation or audience.
>
> Should the concerned person – by way of exception – be accompanied by his wife or female family members, then Her Majesty shall receive these ladies in a completely private setting where, for example, the *Grootmeesteresse* [female Dutch courtier with a knighthood] shall be present and also, as a rule, a translator.
>
> These receptions of Native ladies (or other Eastern Nationalities) shall occur in an entirely 'European' fashion.[43]

While the polygamy of indigenous elites is referred to here obliquely ('one [woman] or women or female family members'), it surely underpins the queen's aversion to meeting the women of indigenous princely households. Wilhelmina was devoutly Christian, confessing in the autobiography published near the end of her life that, throughout her reign, she had often felt 'lonely but not alone', consoled by her faith in times of trial.[44] Some of those tribulations no doubt included her husband's infidelities, a proclivity she did not share: Wilhelmina was devoted to Prince Hendrik while they were married and (like her cousin, Queen Victoria), remained a pious widow long after he died. Wilhelmina thus epitomised the Christian feminine virtues of religious faith and (monogamous) wifely dedication. It is in this context that the protocol regulating her encounter with the ladies of polygamous, mostly Muslim Indonesian dynasties needs to be understood. To some extent, in striving to exclude such encounters from public spaces, the protocol defers to Indonesian sensibilities by arranging sex-segregated meetings, but within limits: the women were to adapt to Wilhelmina's European court.

The document ends with an order that the Ministry for the Colonies should recommend 'one or more topics of conversation ... to facilitate the discourse' at such meetings. Wilhelmina's private archive shows that staff of the ministry were regularly occupied with tasks of linguistic and cultural translation, which included translating letters from various indigenous kings and princes into Dutch and adding explanatory memoranda as to the ceremonial meaning of gifts from these rulers. Her protocol suggests that the ministry was also exercised in the matter of alleviating the queen's sense of distance and difference from, and perhaps discomfort with, the women of Indonesian royal households.

Negotiating status: gifts from Indonesian royals to the Dutch monarchy

In direct encounters at her own court, Wilhelmina was able to regulate aspects of her engagement with royal visitors from Indonesia. However, there were certain opportunities for the latter to express their status in an Indonesian idiom through the gifts they chose to give the Dutch queen. In portraits especially, Indonesian royals were able to exercise some agency as to how they were represented. The numerous portrait photographs that Indonesian royals sent of themselves instead of appearing in person at Wilhelmina's court might be interpreted as exercises in their right *not* to be present at all – just as the queen never deigned to visit the Indies in person, for reasons that include her reluctance to compromise her own singular authority as an imperial queen.[45]

Portraits given by Indonesian royals enabled them to defy the edicts and customs of Wilhelmina's court that constrained the use of regalia. For Wilhelmina's fortieth regnal anniversary in 1938, Mahmud Abdul Jalil Rahmad Shah (r. 1927–1948), the sultan of Langkat, personally attended for the first time celebrations for the queen in the Netherlands.[46] It was his daughters who made the spectacular presentation of orchids to the queen at the Olympic Stadium. Among the gifts the sultan presented on his visit was a family portrait, hand-drawn by a Dutch artist, and mounted in a silver-inlaid ebony frame. It showed, in triptych form, the sultan and his chief wife flanking four male relatives, all of whom bore the regalia of his court (Figure 13.3). From left to right, the portrait presented the sultan's brother, Tengku Kuding, with a golden betel box; another brother, Tengku Poetra, holding a golden parasol; the crown prince, Tengku Moesa, with a *tepong tawar* set (containing a ceremonial dish of holy water and yellow rice); and another son, Tengku Athar, holding a dagger. Since the *tepong tawar* was traditionally a gift for celebrating a monarch, Wassing-Visser has characterised this portrait gift as a symbolic offering of homage to the queen.[47] It might equally be argued, however, that the sultan was representing his own regalia and key members of his dynasty to Wilhelmina in a pictorial form that circumvented her restrictions on his regalia and compensated for his capacity to physically present these people and objects to the queen.

13.3 Th.M. Schipper, portraits of (from left to right) the sultan of Langkat, two of his brothers, his son the crown prince and another son, and his wife, 1938

Other Indonesian royals similarly used forms of portraiture to convey their status to the Dutch monarchy. In 1937 Prince Pakualam VII of Yogyakarta assembled an entire album of drawn and photographed portraits of his predecessors and children as a wedding gift to Crown Princess Juliana. I have argued elsewhere that this album, which represented a prince *in absentia*, constituted an assertion of dynasty equal to that of the House of Orange.[48] Where it conformed to Dutch expectations was in its depiction of the Pakualam as a monogamous ruler, and in this sense the portraits are broadly representative of works sent to Wilhelmina by Indonesian royals. There is one notable exception. Pakubuwono X, who was a prolific giver of photograph albums to the queen, departed from convention in 1923. For Wilhelmina's silver jubilee the *susuhunan* sent her a set of three paintings, an unjoined triptych, perhaps to give the queen the option of dismantling the set. It showed the Pakubuwono flanked by two of his wives, the eldest and youngest.[49] The gift is exceptional for its defiance of the usual representation of Indonesian kings as having just one queen.

The selection and composition of these gifts from Indonesian royals reveal how hand-drawn and photographic portraits provided means to restore, in representative forms if not in the flesh, some of the sumptuary status that was denied those who appeared at Wilhelmina's court in person.

Conclusion

Royal Indonesian visits to the court of Queen Wilhelmina in the early twentieth century represented an opportunity for the Dutch head of state to perform her centripetal powers as an imperial monarch on the domestic stage. For this reason perhaps, many Indonesian royals abstained from visiting her in person, preferring to assert what limited sovereignty they had on their home soil, in front of a subject population that continued to recognise their traditional authority. For those indigenous royals who did tour the Netherlands and submit to Wilhelmina's protocols, which constrained their usual sumptuary privileges and required their deference to her, such an audience was nonetheless an opportunity to assert their own elite status. A visit to the queen's court and participation in her public procession conferred on Indonesian royals membership of an exclusive global community – only royalty could have such privileged access to a monarch. Indonesian royals on tour also took prime position in the transnational circuit of travellers between the Indies in the Netherlands, one that trumped the rights and expectations of most Europeans on the route.

The opportunities and costs of encounters between Dutch and Indonesian royals were complex and required careful negotiation for both sides. Together, Wilhelmina's court protocol governing the reception of indigenous visitors from the Indies, my analysis of published photos and accounts of royal Indies delegations from the Indonesian perspective, and the portraits that Indonesian aristocrats presented to the queen reveal the tensions that beset such engagements on Dutch soil. The queen's protocol discloses her concerns about accommodating royals of a different religious and ethnic background while also retaining her sovereign status and asserting her cultural mores. Dutch commemorative books reveal how the retinue and regalia of Indonesian royals were constrained on visits to the queen's court in ways that would have been considered an affront in the Indies. Portrait gifts from Indonesian royals indicate one of the modes in which indigenous vassals could resist those constraints, even if only in pictorial form.

Notes

1 Claire Holt, *Art in Indonesia: Continuities and Change* (Ithaca and London: Cornell University Press, 1967), pp. 117–119. See also Miriam J. Morrison, 'The bedaya-serimpi dances of Java', *Dance Chronicle*, 2:3 (1978), 188–212 at 189, 203, 206–210.
2 Holt, *Art in Indonesia*, p. 103.

3 Pakubuwono X, the *susuhunan* of Surakarta, staged a *serimpi* performance danced by his granddaughters at his palace for Wilhelmina's silver jubilee in 1923: Koninklijk Huisarchief, The Hague (KHA) A50 FA/0772. He also attended a *serimpi* at the Dutch Governor's house in 1937: KHA A50 FA/0772. A year later, the Governor of Yogyakarta held a *serimpi* for the queen's fortieth regnal celebrations: Koninklijk Instituut voor Taal-, Land- en Volkenkunde (KITLV), Leiden, Album 289, J. Bijleveld-Visser, images 35243, 35262, 35263.
4 Rita Wassing-Visser, *Koninklijke geschenken uit Indonesië: Historische banden met het huis Oranje-Nassau (1600–1938)* (The Hague and Zwolle: Stichting Historische Verzamelingen van het Huis Oranje-Nassau and Waanders, 1995), pp. 219–220.
5 *Het prinseljk huwelijksfeest* (De Spaarnestad: Haarlem, 1937), pp. 22–23.
6 Wassing-Visser, *Koninklijke geschenken*.
7 John Pemberton, *On the Subject of 'Java'* (Ithaca and London: Cornell University Press, 1994).
8 Gert Oostindie, *De parels en de kroon: De koningshuis en de koloniën* (Amsterdam: De Bezige Bij, 2006), p. 91.
9 KHA A50, Xxa 355. The document was drafted by Wilhelmina's private secretary. It definitely dates after 1918, as it refers to the Council of the Indies, a colonial government advisory body with some elected indigenous members that was founded in that year. Wassing-Visser claims that the first female royal delegates from Indonesia came in 1926 (Wassing-Visser, *Koninklijke geschenken*, p. 211), and since the protocol mentions women, it is highly likely that it was drafted at or after that time.
10 Charles Coppel, 'The Indonesian Chinese as "Foreign Orientals" in the Netherlands Indies', in Timothy Lindsay (ed.), *Indonesian Law and Society* (Sydney: Federation Press, 1999), pp. 33–41.
11 'PERSONS WHO HAVE OBTAINED A CERTAIN SOCIAL POSITION IN THE INDIES (be it after study in the Netherlands, or only study in the Indies) AND THEY – as adults – COME TO THE NETHERLANDS TO BROADEN THEIR VIEWS OR THEIR STUDIES. ... [This group] shall include people of merit; of learning; those who have been in a somewhat executive position.': KHA A50, Xxa 355.
12 'YOUNG PERSONS WHO GO TO THE NETHERLANDS FOR THEIR EDUCATION OR TO COMPLETE THEIR EDUCATION': KHA A50, Xxa 355.
13 KHA A50, Xxa 355 (my emphasis).
14 M.C. Ricklefs, *A History of Modern Indonesia since c. 1200*, 4th edn (Stanford: Stanford University Press, 2008), p. 178.
15 Vincent J.H. Houben, *Kraton and Kumpeni: Surakarta and Yogyakarta, 1830–1870* (Leiden: KITLV Press, 1994), pp. 4, 7, 64, 77–78, 93, 138, 351, 354.
16 Stuart Robson, 'Introduction', in Stuart Robson (ed.), *The Kraton: Selected Essays on the Javanese Courts* (Leiden: KITLV Press, 2003), pp. ix–xxvi at xix. In fact, the queen would have been 'Majesty' rather than 'Highness'.
17 Wassing-Visser, *Koninklijke geschenken*, pp. 109, 194, 197, 203, 205–206, 211, 215, 220–222, 234–236.
18 KHA A50, Xxa 355.
19 *De veertigjarige regeering van H. M. Koningin Wilhelmina: 1898–6 September–1938 Oranje album* (Amsterdam: Holdert & Co, 1938).
20 David Kouwenaar, *Amsterdam tijdens het feestbetoon bij het 40-jarige regeeringsjubileum van H. M. Koningin Wilhelmina van 5 tot 12 september 1938* (Amsterdam: De Bussy, 1938), p. 210.
21 Wassing-Visser, *Koninklijke geschenken*, pp. 234–235.
22 The photograph was published in *Koningin Wilhelmina: Veertig jaren wijs beleid* (Amsterdam: 'De Telegraaf' and H.J.W. Becht, 1938), and *De gouden kroon: Gedenkboek bij gelegenheid van het gouden regeringsjubileum van H.M. Koningin Wilhelmina* (Haarlem: De Spaarnestad, 1948).
23 Wassing-Visser, *Koninklijke geschenken*, p. 235.
24 Irmawati Marwoto-Johan, 'Ritual Heirlooms in the Islamic Kingdoms of Indonesia' in James Bennett (ed.), *Crescent Moon: Islamic Art and Civilisation in Southeast*

Asia (Adelaide and Canberra: Art Gallery of South Australia and National Gallery of Australia, 2006), pp. 144–155.
25 Wassing-Visser, *Koninklijke geschenken*.
26 Pemberton, *On the Subject of 'Java'*, p. 191.
27 KHA A50 Xxa 355.
28 Wassing-Visser, *Koninklijke geschenken*, pp. 109, 111.
29 Pemberton, *On the Subject of 'Java'*, p. 146.
30 Wassing-Visser, *Koninklijke geschenken*, p. 108, see also p. 105.
31 *Ibid.*, p. 109.
32 Pemberton, *On the Subject of 'Java'*, pp. 28, 112–117, 121. In 1932, Pakubuwono X sent Wilhelmina a photo album he had made to celebrate his own fortieth regnal jubilee: KHA A50 FA/0695.
33 In 1923 Pakubuwono X sent Wilhelmina an album of the celebrations for her silver jubilee at his *kraton*: KHA A50 FA/0772. In 1937 he sent Crown Princess Juliana an album celebrating her wedding, showing his attendance at the gala event at the Governor of Surakarta's house: KHA A50 FA/0777/A.
34 Heather Sutherland, *The Making of a Bureaucratic Elite: The Colonial Transformation of the Javanese Priyayi* (Kuala Lumpur and Hong Kong: Heinemann Educational Books (Asia) Ltd, 1979), pp. 76, 130; Cees Fassuer, *De Indologen: Ambtenaren voor de Oost 1825–1950* (Amsterdam: Aula, 2003), pp. 291, 330.
35 Ulbe Bosma, 'Sailing through Suez from the South: The Emergence of an Indies-Dutch Migration Circuit 1815–1940', *International Migration Review*, 41:2 (2007), 511–536; Susan Legêne, 'Dwinegeri: Multiculturalism and the Colonial Past', in Benjamin Kaplan, Marybeth Carlson and Laura Cruz (eds), *Boundaries and their Meanings in the History of the Netherlands* (Leiden and Boston: Brill, 2009), pp. 223–242.
36 KHA A50 Xxa 355.
37 *Ibid.*
38 Heather Sutherland, 'Notes on Java's Regent Families: Part I', *Indonesia*, 16 (1973), 112–147; Sutherland, *The Making of a Bureaucratic Elite*.
39 Harry Poeze, *In het land van de overheerser: Indonesiërs in Nederland 1600–1950* (Dordrecht: Foris, 1986).
40 KHA A50 Xxa 355.
41 Bart Luttikhuis, 'Beyond Race: Constructions of "Europeanness" in Late-Colonial Legal Practice in the Dutch East Indies', *European Review of History*, 20:6 (2013), 539–558.
42 KHA A50 Xxa 355.
43 *Ibid.*
44 Wilhelmina, *Eenzaam maar niet alleen* ['Lonely but not alone'] (Amsterdam: Ten Have, 1959).
45 Pieter Eckhardt, 'Wij zullen handhaven! De symbolische betekenis van de Nederlandse monarchie in Nederlands-Indië 1918–1940' (Masters dissertation, University of Amsterdam, 2002), pp. 30–35.
46 Wassing-Visser, *Koninklijke geschenken*, p. 222.
47 *Ibid.*, p. 236.
48 Susie Protschky, 'Negotiating Princely Status Through the Photographic Gift: Paku Alam VII's Family Album for Crown Princess Juliana of the Netherlands, 1937', *Indonesia and the Malay World*, 40:118 (2012), 298–314.
49 Wassing-Visser, *Koninklijke geschenken*, pp. 195, 203.

CHAPTER FOURTEEN

The 1947 royal tour in Smuts's Raj: South African Indian responses

Hilary Sapire

As an entourage of Daimlers carrying the British royal family and Prime Minister Jan Smuts entered the Curries Fountain Sports Grounds in Durban on the morning of 22 March 1947, the visitors were greeted 'with one of the most overwhelming and emotional welcomes yet accorded the royal family in South Africa'.[1] A crowd of 65,000 cheered as the royal cavalcade, led by the Moslem Boys Brigade Band, drew up before a Taj Mahal-styled royal dais. Standing beneath its canopy, the veteran Indian 'moderate' politician, Hajee Ahmed Sadeck (A.I.) Kajee declared:

> Your South African Indian people of this City of Durban – the largest colony of Indians in the Southern Hemisphere outside India – extend with our homage and loyalty a warm and cordial welcome to Your Majesties. Our hearts are filled with joy that you are in our midst.[2]

Forty of the city's prominent Indian men and women were presented to the king as young girls wearing 'colourful saris' handed 'magnificent' bouquets of roses and carnations to the queen and princesses. Songs were sung by children in Tamil, 'traditional' music was performed while King George VI, Queen Elizabeth and Princesses Elizabeth and Margaret mingled informally with ex-servicemen, scouts and girl guides before leaving for their next engagement with Durban's African residents. While the mannered loyalism of Kajee's speech and ornamentalist pageantry were replicated in meetings between the British king and his Southern African subjects during a spectacular three-month royal tour, the size of this crowd is noteworthy. Taking place in the midst of the passive resistance campaign, the most sustained South African Indian protest against the government since Gandhi's departure from the country in 1914, and in defiance of the call by the Natal Indian Congress (NIC) to boycott all ceremonies of welcome for the royal family, the apparent enthusiasm for the rituals of king and empire seems somewhat anomalous.

Whilst both this incongruity and the 'contested ... nature of Indian political and social imaginations' epitomised by the turn-out in Durban have been remarked upon, the significance of the royal visit in its own right has yet to be examined.[3] Neither the reasons for the masses' 'refusal to give the royal visit a miss' nor the role of 'moderate' leaders in opposing the NIC's boycott call have been elucidated in the extensive writings on this mercurial period in South African Indian politics.[4] Addressing this gap, the present chapter considers the apparent resurgence of imperial royalism at a moment when a rhetoric of democratic rights and tone of defiance suffused South African Indian political discourse. It explores the deepening of political divisions within the leadership in early 1947, drawing attention to the 'moderates', a grouping marginalised in a dominant historical narrative of Indian politics that prioritises the emergence of progressive cross-racial and transnational alliances that would mobilise against apartheid in succeeding decades.[5] Focusing on positions taken by the moderate leadership during bitter disputes over the visit, this chapter sheds light on an alternative, if discredited, trajectory taken in South African Indian politics.[6]

The optic of the royal visit in the principal city of Natal, the most Anglophone province, also brings a historiography of post-war Indian politics and society into dialogue with an expanding literature on imperial monarchy, colonies and global British identity. A key vehicle for tracing the latter has been the transoceanic royal progresses that brought British monarchs or their close relatives into direct contact with their imperial subjects, and through which a shared ideology of rule that linked rulers and ruled was soldered.[7] By the 1920s in India, and the 1940s in Africa, monarchical ideology had run into the 'articulate opposition' of anti-colonial nationalism, and royal ceremonial was increasingly manipulated or challenged outright to express opposition to empire.[8] Neglected in this discussion of royal tours and the limits of loyalism have been the significant South Asian communities in eastern and southern Africa. Their attitudes towards the crown and British connection were complicated by their diasporic character, their intermediate position within colonial society and the existence of competing external sources of political and moral authority in the form of the Government of India and the Indian nationalist movement. Taking place at the same time as the king's cousin, Lord Mountbatten, was in India negotiating Britain's exit from the Asian subcontinent, and when Jawaharlal Nehru, as head of the transitional Indian government projected himself as global leader of a resurgent 'Asianism' and anti-colonialism, the 1947 visit posed unsettling questions about South African Indian identity, senses of belonging, and loyalty.[9]

ROYALS ON TOUR

South Asian loyalism and imperial monarchy in South Africa

After months of anxiety about the possibilities of an embarrassing boycott of the royal visit by Natal's 228,000 Indian inhabitants, the authorities and tour organisers could sigh with relief at the hearty reception at Curries Fountain, a venue more readily associated with militant protest meetings. Commenting on the tour's overall success, the *Economist* observed that while 'African royalist enthusiasm' could be relied upon and was 'always touching', the responses of Indians 'whose sympathies were still with India rather than with the land of their adoption was more doubtful'.[10] While reflecting contemporary white prejudices about both Africans and Indians, the *Economist* drew attention to a variegated South African Indian identity that had evolved since the first indentured migrants and 'passenger' Indians arrived in Natal in the 1860s and 1870s. South African 'Indianness' had emerged initially as an imposed category to distinguish the newcomers within a colonial racial hierarchy, but developed over time as a powerful form of self-ascription. It overlaid and partially disguised cleavages of caste, religion, language, places of origin, gender and occupation, and served as a means by which Indian-born elites distinguished themselves from other 'non-Europeans' with whom they shared legal disabilities and experiences of racial discrimination.

The Indian crowds which greeted the king in Durban were made up of the descendants of indentured labourers, primarily from the Hindi-speaking Gangetic plains and south Indian coast brought to work on the sugar plantations, mines and railways of Natal, and of 'passengers' who came voluntarily as traders and businessmen. The latter were largely Gujarati Muslims and their poorer kin, some of whom came via Mauritius.[11] From their base in Natal, a number of former indentured servants, traders and *dukawallahs* (small retailers) fanned out into the Transvaal and Cape Colony, but the most substantial communities developed in Natal and the Transvaal following the ending of the system of indenture in 1911. Moving from sugar fields to Durban and its fringes, former indentured labourers established themselves as fishermen, hawkers, craftsmen, traders and market gardeners with large numbers moving into factory labour in the interwar years. By mid-1949, there were 123,165 Indians in Durban, sandwiched between 129,683 white residents who jealously defended their economic privileges, and a rapidly urbanising isiZulu speaking African population of 109,543 with whom they lived and worked in close proximity.[12] Within distinctive enclaves – a mixed-race 'black belt' of shacks on the city's outskirts, slums, the business and trading area around Grey

Street – a profusion of political, religious, welfare and cultural associations sprang up to serve this diverse community. Most of the working poor were Hindu (74 per cent) – as opposed to 19 per cent Muslim and 5 per cent Christian – with Tamil as the most widely spoken home language. A small elite of traders, merchants, property-owners and professionals presided over Indian Durban's cultural and social life. They served as patrons of charity, educational, welfare and social organisations that crossed class, religious and language divides, and compensated for the wholesale neglect of the municipal authorities. Through merchant-dominated organisations such as the NIC, the elite led resistance to successive sets of restrictions on Indian access to the franchise, immigration, trading and residence rights.[13]

The separatist implications of 'Indianness' was reinforced by a civilisational discourse of Indian superiority over Africans, and by the exertions of political organisations such as the NIC to foster a distinct racial political identity. 'Indianness' also encompassed an imaginative engagement with 'Mother India'.[14] Along with family connections, and cultural ties with India, visits to South Africa by nationalist figures, from Gophal Krishan Gokhale in 1912 to Indira Nehru in 1941, played a signal role in reinforcing these affinities.

Identification with the nationalist aspirations of Indians on the Asian subcontinent and the turn to South Asian politics in local campaigns, especially from the 1920s, was complemented by a tendency to use the British imperial connection for the redress of grievances; thus 'Indianness' was intertwined with imperial discourses of citizenship, egalitarianism and equality under the law.[15] Indeed, the *Economist*'s observations about Indians' unexpectedly warm reactions to the royal visit belied a long-standing tradition of loyalism and royalism, albeit one discredited from the late 1930s following the radicalisation of Indian politics, and one contested and ambiguous from its inception. Indian loyalism had been articulated by the NIC when it was established in 1894 by Mohandas K. Gandhi as a means of expressing the aspirations of 'British Indians' in Natal, claiming the extension of the rights of British citizens and protections under the doctrine of imperial equality. The claim, based on the Queen's Proclamation of 1858 that 'all shall alike enjoy equal and impartial protection of the law' was raised repeatedly as a counter to the denial of these rights by the South African authorities and to whites' exclusivist claim to Britishness, and was supported by early nationalists and liberals in India.[16] The idea of an imperial monarch embodying personal rule and the implicit promise of constitutional remedy remained compelling for Indian elites despite repeated failures of appeals to the crown and British governments and participation in the empire's wars.[17] For

Indians throughout the empire, appeals to the crown were predicated on a conception of the monarchy as the source of citizens' civil and political rights.[18] Thus, in the face of periodic bouts of anti-Indianism, demands from whites for repatriation and segregation of Indians, South Africa's merchant dominated organisations continued to proclaim fidelity to crown and empire and to embrace a pragmatic politics of compromise well into the 1930s.

These expressions took place especially on royal occasions such as coronations, deaths and births of monarchs, jubilees and royal visits, events which generated discussion within the Indian press about imperial monarchy and the capacity of the monarch and the British government to intercede in South African affairs. Given the rarity of opportunities for Indians to represent themselves before white citizens and figures of authority, royal ceremonial also provided a stage for the performance of the civility and respectability of Indian elites and, thereby, their worthiness of meaningful political inclusion. Dignified protest couched in loyalist rhetoric, moreover, offered a means of highlighting the demeaning and unequal ways in which Indians were expected to participate in important civic events. Such opportunities included the visit of the Duke of Cornwall and York to South Africa during the South African War and his coronation as George V in 1911, occasions when resentment over the racially separated civil ceremonies was sublimated.[19] But during the tour by the Prince of Wales (the future Edward VIII) in 1925, both the ambiguities of Indian loyalism and internal dissension about Indian participation in segregated ceremonies came into the open.

The tour took place at a particularly intense moment of white anti-Indianism and demands for legislative measures against the 'Asiatic menace'.[20] The chief cause of contention for the NIC was that the Durban Corporation's plans for welcome celebrations for the prince precluded a common event for all the city's 'burgesses'.[21] They saw the insistence on a separate Indian event and the refusal to allow Indians to be present at a civic banquet and ball as emblematic of their inferior and unequal status. Pointing out that it was more than 'dinner party equality' that they were demanding, Manilal Gandhi, son of the Mahatma and editor of the *Indian Opinion*, said a 'principle of equality in the eye of the law' was at stake. Although disillusioned with British imperialism and captivated by developments in India, Gandhi couched Indian discontents within the framework of loyalism. Invoking the notion of British fairness and justice thwarted, and challenging white loyalists who were once 'helots' in Kruger's Transvaal, he wrote: 'Every freedom loving Britisher, due to his blood ... must appreciate our position and so must the Royal ambassador of the British Empire':

We are treated as helots and that is the status we are offered and special laws for the purpose have already been enacted in the name of His Majesty the King, and furthermore are under preparation. We have no voice to oppose these acts in this county. We were, however, hopeful that as loyal citizens of the British Empire the British Government would come to our aid, but to our utter disappointment we have failed even in that last straw.[22]

Notwithstanding authorities' fears of a boycott similar to that which disrupted the Prince of Wales's Indian tour in 1921 and 1922, 'there was not the faintest echo of a *hartal*'; a crowd of 18,000 Indian residents attended the event organised by the prominent businessmen E.M. Paruk.[23] Although the NIC absented itself from this function, officials met with the prince. Indian shops were bestrewn with lights, as was Gandhi Library and Rustomjee Hall, where flashing messages announced Durban Indians' divided loyalties: 'Long live the future Emperor of India' and 'Swaraj is our Birthright'.[24]

Participation in royal and civic ceremonial, albeit on terms consonant with 'honour' and 'self- respect', was integral to the strategies employed by the NIC in seeking imperial intercession and informal access to power.[25] The former aim was rewarded in 1927 with the Cape Town Agreement, which created a mediatory role for the Government of India through the appointment of a diplomatic representative from India to South Africa. Successively named 'agent', 'agent-general' and 'high commissioner', this official was expected to intercede between the South African government and Indian citizens in the interests of 'British dominion harmony'. Although highly esteemed, agents were often criticised at the time – and by historians – for encouraging a willingness to compromise, an over-reliance on the Government of India and top level deal-making that precluded cooperation with other 'non-Europeans'.[26] Certainly, agents promoted elite alliance-building and confirmed the loyalist and royalist stance adopted by elites. The first agent, Srinivasa Sastri, for example, encouraged the merchant leaders to cultivate alliances with white liberals who could lobby authorities and to entertain white political and public figures at the 'Orient Club'.[27] At a civic reception in Kimberley in 1929, Sastri's successor, Sir Kurma Venkata Reddi, assured his largely white audience of Indians' 'inextinguishable faith ... fidelity, reverence and love of the throne'.[28] These sentiments were repeated in 1934 by the royal-born Kunwar Maharaj Singh, who welcomed Prince George, a younger son of George V, to Durban with the guarantee 'that from no community and no race will your Highness receive a more cordial welcome than from South African Indians of all classes'.[29] The controversies that dogged the Prince of Wales's visit in 1925 were absent in 1934; Sorabjee

Rustomjee, who had opposed participation in the official ceremonies in 1925, decorated his own home with lights, read a loyal address from the NIC and presented the prince with an inscribed silver salver.[30] The NIC, moreover, and the rival break-away Colonial Born Settler Indian Association (CBSIA), vied for prominence and precedence in events associated with the visit.[31] Despite the political tensions between the two organisations – provoked by the NIC's cooperation with the government's investigations into a colonisation scheme to re-settle Indians outside of South Africa – Indian leaders participated fully in the king's silver jubilee celebrations of 1935 and the coronation of George VI in 1937, decisions that reflected the dominance of moderates and the robustness of the imperial framework in which they expressed their aspirations.[32]

This changed markedly from the late 1930s with the arrival on the political scene of a younger generation of 'colonial-borns' who drew inspiration from the Indian nationalist movement and the international left, as well as trade unionists galvanised by Indian working-class militancy and revitalisation of the Communist Party of South Africa. The expression of overt, rather than coded criticism of imperial monarchy and the British connection was indicative of this shift. At a meeting in Durban's 'Red Square' in 1941, for example, a radical young NIC member, Dawood Seedat, expressed exasperation with the language of duty to king and country:

> We have got no more time for kings and emperors. The King is not fit to be Emperor of India ... The British Empire is not an Empire but a Vampire. It drains all the wealth out of India and keeps millions of our people in suffering, starvation, sickness, illiteracy, and without homes.[33]

The Second World War posed a particular dilemma for the 'colonial-borns'. Some, inspired by the 'Quit India' campaign that convulsed India in 1942, endorsed Seedat's sentiments, and continued to oppose the moderates' decision to assist Britain's war effort. With the Nazi invasion of the Soviet Union in June 1941, however, most radicals had adopted a Popular Front position in favour of participation in the war, while retaining demands for the extension of democratic rights.[34] Yet a discernible transition in attitudes towards Britain and the crown had taken place, especially among younger coloured, African and Indian leaders; they increasingly depicted white rule as emanating from, and defended by, Britain, a stance that challenged their elders' faith in the imperial connection and crown. The watchwords of compromise and conciliation were replaced by 'equality' and 'democracy', with uncompromising demands for a common franchise, removal of the colour bar, a widening of the struggle to include all black South Africans.

Armed with a more egalitarian programme, younger radicals ousted the old guard from the NIC leadership in 1945.[35] Professionals like Drs Monty Naicker and Kesavaloo Goonam, and trade unionists such as Communist Party members H.A. Naidoo and George Ponnen, found receptive ears in a city transfigured by industrialisation and Indian and African urban immigration. By the mid-1940s, at 106,604 almost the same size as the European population, Durban's Indians were subjected to renewed assaults of white residents up in arms over 'Indian penetration' and intensified competition over space, trade and jobs with Africans.[36]

Inspired by diverse ideological currents, including Indian nationalism, communism and Gandhian strictures, the NIC, like the Transvaal Indian Congress (TIC), moved in new directions, championing working-class protest and the needs of the poor, cultivating a common 'Non-European' identity and forging transnational political alliances. Described by one observer as 'Durban's turbulent Indian tub-thumpers', the new leaders embraced a politics of confrontation that culminated in the passive resistance campaign of 1946 to 1948 with its own pageantry and street theatre.[37] When the royal family arrived in Cape Town in February 1947, passive resistance was in its eighth month, its leaders buoyed by the condemnation of South Africa in the inaugural meeting of the UN General Assembly.

Passive resistance, Smuts and the royal visit

The campaign had been launched in response to Prime Minister Smuts's notorious *Asiatic Land Tenure and Indian Representation Act* or 'ghetto act' of January 1946 which provided for compulsory segregation of Indians by placing restrictions on Indian acquisition and occupation of property in Natal for the first time. To make it more palatable, Smuts proposed to give Indians limited political representation through a communal parliamentary franchise.[38] The act caused widespread outrage; invoking the great *satyagraha* protests of the past, Monty Naicker, leader of the NIC, called for passive resistance, beginning with a *hartal* in Durban on 13 June.[39] The spectacle of processions, mass meetings, pamphleteering and the establishment of a 'camp' on vacant land in defiance of white hooliganism stirred many young African nationalists seeking to break away from the polite constitutionalism of the ANC old guard. 'In Durban, the Indians ... are experiencing rebirth' observed the writer and ANC Youth Leaguer Herbert Dhlomo, 'What of the Africans?'[40] In response to the 'ghetto act', the Government of India had recalled its representative and imposed a trade boycott on South Africa, and at the

NIC's request 'to uphold the honour and dignity of Indians abroad', the viceroy's council referred the matter to the UN.[41] Welcoming the opportunity to assume the mantle as global leader of anti-colonial resistance, Jawaharlal Nehru, now chief of the interim Indian government, requested his sister, Vijaya Lakshmi Pandit, to take up the South African issue in the General Assembly as head of the Indian delegation, and encouraged Indian activists in South Africa to make common cause with Africans.[42] By now, the split between moderates and radicals had deepened to the extent that two separate South African Indian delegations went to New York to advise the Indian delegation: the Passive Resistance Council deputation of radicals, H.A. Naidoo, Sorabjee Rustomjee (accompanied by the left-wing senator Hyman Basner and the ANC President, Dr Alfred B. Xuma) and the moderate representatives of the South African Indian Congress (SAIC), A.I. Kajee, P.R. Pather and Albert Christopher.[43]

The outcome at the General Assembly represented a moral victory for the Indians. South Africa's policies towards Indians were roundly condemned and the government was called upon to treat them in conformity with treaty obligations between India and South Africa, and the provisions in the UN charter. Despite much rejoicing at celebratory rallies in South Africa, however, it proved an anti-climax. Significantly, the British government had refused to support the Indian case, and rather than exacting concessions from the South African government, the latter was enjoined to enter Round Table discussions with the Government of India and report back to the UN on their progress in the following year. At home, Indian unemployment was rising, European anti-Indianism had been inflamed further, and fuelled a bitter white consumer boycott of Indian stores that had been originally called in response to India's trade sanctions. The Durban City Council had replaced large numbers of Indian employees with Africans, and there was renewed talk of repatriation.[44] South African Indians' champion, Nehru, moreover, seemed reassured by Smuts's commitment to address Indian grievances, stating that any further action by the Indian government would be premature.[45] Stung by the exposures at the UN and the withdrawal of the Indian high commissioner, however, Smuts delayed negotiations with the Government of India, preferring to explore the extension of limited forms of representation for Indians at the local level.[46] If the separate Indian delegations returned empty-handed, they brought back starkly opposed agendas for the coming year. The NIC deputation was determined to re-ignite passive resistance and capitalise on the international support for their cause. To this end, Monty Naicker and Yusuf Dadoo, his Transvaal counterpart, made plans to attend the All-Asia Conference in Delhi in March, an event intended by Nehru to galvanise 'Asianism' and anti-colonialism under India's leadership. The moderates, by contrast, declared their confidence that the two governments would comply with the UN resolution and enter negotiations, and argued that it was time to call off passive resistance.[47]

By the time the Indian deputations returned to South Africa, plans for a visit by the British royal family were well advanced. Proposed by Smuts in 1945 to provide the king with an opportunity to recover from the rigours of the war, hopes for a royal tour became both more ambitious and controversial. For the monarchy and British government, this first post-war royal tour assumed the status of an 'imperial mission' at a moment when the unity of the empire seemed to be unravelling – not least due to imminent Indian independence and the intra-imperial tensions between India and South Africa – while for the South African government, there were distinctly domestic agendas and expectations. Two were particularly pertinent to Natal, home to both an electorally significant loyalist, white Anglophone citizenry and the Union's largest Indian population. The first was to use the royal magic to galvanise electoral support for Smuts's United Party in the face of an ascendant Afrikaner nationalist movement. The fear was that a National Party victory in elections the following year could result in the loss of South Africa to the Commonwealth at a delicate moment of decolonisation in Asia. Second, the 'soft power' of a royal tour could help repair the country's reputational damage following the humiliation at the UN 'by countering the propaganda against South Africa overseas'.[48] Considering that white Natalians' insistence on protection from Indian 'penetration' had brought about the 'ghetto act', passive resistance and international opprobrium, there was a conviction that 'South Africa's relations with the outside world [would] largely depend on the attitude Natal adopts'.[49] And Durban, the 'unrepentant city of humiliation for the Indian community', would host the province's most significant civic ceremonial.[50]

Preparing for the royal visit in the midst of the passive resistance campaign and in the glare of international scrutiny necessitated meticulous planning and diplomacy. Although the sub-committee responsible for arranging 'Non-European' events in the Durban area was aware that racially separate ones would be controversial, the organisers justified the decision on the grounds that that it would be impossible to control vast racially mixed crowds.[51] Accordingly, the NIC was invited to appoint two representatives to assist in the organisation of events for the Indian community.[52] In a carefully phrased reply intended for the press, A.I. Meer, the NIC joint general secretary, declined, making it clear that in the circumstances it was 'most unreasonable to expect Indians to participate in any rejoicing or celebrations in honour of Royalty':

> We cannot but suggest that you advise Their Majesties to postpone their visit until such time as there is peace and goodwill in South Africa between the rulers and the ruled, the white and the non-white, the represented and the unrepresented, the privileged and the underprivileged, so that all who constitute the South African nation can equally share, not only its burdens, but also its rewards.[53]

In support of their stance, the NIC could draw on the authority of Gandhi who called for a postponement of the visit until 'a more propitious time when the colour bar has become a thing of the past'.[54] Unfazed, the Durban City Council continued planning, confident that Indians 'would wish to attend functions in their thousands'.[55] In a joint statement with the Transvaal Indian Congress, the NIC called for a boycott, pointing out that the government's denial of passports to Naicker and Dadoo, preventing them from travelling to India, represented yet another 'curtailment of the meagre civil liberties' of non-Europeans.[56] Over the next three months, extended public discussion took place in the press, pamphlets and rowdy public meetings. Whilst ostensibly about participation in the royal visit ceremonies, this debate represented an extended public dialogue about how Indians should campaign for wider political and economic rights after their 'victory' at the UN. As in the past, this royal visit served as an arena in which competing conceptions of identity, belonging, citizenship and governance were aired, along with alternative understandings of the place and significance of the imperial monarchy in the post-war world.

The NIC leaders were aware of the visit's propaganda value to the government. Leaders predicted that the government would use images of rapturous crowds to demonstrate that 'the exposures at the UNO were exaggerated and that ... South Africa is a country where racial problems have been amicably settled'.[57] Much was at stake, therefore, in how Indian opinion-makers and leaders projected their stance on the visit. Whilst the tour and hereditary monarchy were rejected as 'backward and undemocratic' anachronisms by left-wing organisations to which a handful of Indian leaders belonged, Indian newspapers and the NIC expressed the familiar loyalist refrain of disappointment and betrayed hopes.[58] Principled objections to participation in the celebrations were connected to the 'ghetto act' and the 'injury' done to Indians by the South African Union government. Overturning the loyalist trope of the monarch as the source of rights, some journalists and politicians claimed that both the king and British government were complicit in their 'legalised oppression'. The king had not only consented to the 'ghetto act', pointed out one speaker at a mass meeting, but represented the British government 'who double-crossed us at UNO'.[59]

Nonetheless, many pro-boycotters accepted that even if the king bore some responsibility for his government's 'misdeeds', he was not to blame for the 'racialism' that meant that even in celebrations in honour of royalty, Indians were 'faced with racial discrimination'.[60] 'When Indians can fight shoulder to shoulder with Europeans in war', it was asked, 'why cannot they stand side by side and watch their Majesties?'[61] Indian newspapers took care to emphasise that a proposed boycott was not intended to be disrespectful to the royal family and that it was a cause of 'profound grief' that participation in the celebrations was impossible.[62] Describing Indians as South Africa's 'stepchildren' debarred by skin colour from the enjoying God-given freedoms, Manilal Gandhi once again entered the discussion.[63] Consistent in opposition to imperialism, his stance reflected the Gandhian strand of the passive resisters; he urged restrained conduct, calling for 'mourning' rather than 'unseemly demonstrations' or 'harsh, unkind or disrespectful' words that would embarrass the royals or the authorities. Issuing a challenge to the government, he proposed that the historic opening of Parliament by the king be marked by an 'outstanding act'. There could be no greater honour to the royal family, he proclaimed, than the abolition of the Colour Bar, nor any greater cause of happiness 'to the hearts of millions of suppressed people.'[64]

Commentators understood that there would be uneasiness at the prospect of causing offence to the royal family. One letter-writer, otherwise sympathetic with the aims of passive resistance, wrote of his hopes that compromise could be reached with the council so that 'unpleasant scenes' during the visit could be avoided.[65] In recognition that support for passive resistance did not translate into endorsement of a boycott, at a meeting in March, Monty Naicker proposed deleting the word 'boycott' from speeches. It did not, he explained, 'fully reflect the intentions of the Indians'. He cited Gandhi's concept of abstention instead as 'national and dignified' and one that better conveyed the essentially peaceful nature of the protest.[66] Quite how Indians should protest, however, was debated. Opposition was expressed, for example, to involving children as 'futile politics'.[67] Confronting fears of employer reprisals against boycotting workers and storekeepers' anxieties about losing custom, the public was told that 'we have not called upon Indian merchants to close their shops, or workers to strike in protest or the Indian public to organise pickets or demonstrations to prevent anyone from attending celebrations'. All that was being asked of Indians was to refrain from celebrating, not leaving work or pulling children out of school.[68]

Moderates and monarchy

If much pro-boycott discourse contained a deferential tone, the moderate call for participation was inflected with the pragmatism of strategic loyalism. Thus, as Ahmed Ismail, the SAIC leader put it, notwithstanding the grief caused by discriminatory legislation the discourtesy of a boycott 'would not redound to our credit'.[69] Kajee and a fellow traveller on 'the conservative road', P.R. Pather, likewise called for suspension of passive resistance and cooperation with government reforms following the UN victory.[70] This stance was consistent with their positions since the 1920s. As paternalists, patrons and pragmatists, they intuitively shrank from militancy and mass politics, and preferred cooperation with white organisations and authorities as a modus operandi in campaigning for Indian rights. This approach, combined with a reluctance to work in partnership with African organisations and their acceptance of an element of 'self- segregation', earned them the sobriquets of 'reactionaries' and 'collaborators' in the 1940s and the bitterness of some of the invective during the royal visit.[71] With such figures, practical rather than dewy-eyed about the symbolism of monarchy, the visit presented an opportunity to reassert the primacy of a politics based on tact, diplomacy and elite negotiation. Appearing prominently alongside the royal family and the prime minister, they could reclaim the authority and prestige they had lost. Pather bluntly pointed out the futility of boycotting the visit. 'Nothing could be more stupid', he announced, 'for Their Majesties have no say in this matter at all and no benefit would be derived from such a boycott'.[72] Indeed, moderates insisted, the king was 'above' politics and should receive due deference. Such a view seems to have gained wider acceptance. At a debate organised by the Maritzburg Indian Technical Students Society, a majority of the audience voted for the motion that the king's position was 'entirely symbolic'.[73]

A key concern of many letter-writers was the danger of antagonising whites with whom 'we have got to live'.[74] Not only was it impolitic to provoke whites unfavourably disposed towards Indians, but a boycott could alienate liberals 'who are struggling with us, even today, to make this country a really democratic one'.[75] A boycott, moreover, could create a negative contrast with Africans and Coloureds who were expected to treat the royal family as 'honoured guests' and to relegate political grievances to the background during the visit. Indians likewise, it was urged, should 'rise above repression and colour domination ... and demonstrate their inherent qualities of courage and loyalty'.[76] Religion was also brought into play. The Moslem Volunteer Corps, for example, appealed to Muslims to 'show their usual greatness of heart by making the Royal Visit above and outside politics'. Muslims should attend the celebrations because the principle of loyalty to the sovereign had been laid down in the Quran.[77] Arguing that loyalty to the king commanded deeper significance for Indians than for people 'inhabiting regions west of Suez where it is only a sentiment of respect to the political head of the state', one letter-writer explained that for Hindus, too, religion commanded respect for the monarch as symbol and representative of political authority and power in the 'highest interests of humanity'.[78]

If a measured debate was conducted in the press, tensions surfaced in the streets and community halls. At a packed meeting in Pietermaritzburg called by the anti-boycott group within the SAIC in mid-February, a motion was proposed condemning use of the visit for 'ventilating grievances'. Before it could be voted on, a group of passive resistance leaders including Manilal Gandhi, Billy Peters, Monty Naidoo and Dr Goonam entered the hall and attempted to address the audience, prompting a mêlée in which a 'Gandhi cap' of one of the passive resisters was seized and burned. They were forced outside the hall but, watched over by the police, rallied some 500 supporters.[79] The NIC claimed that organised hooligans had prevented their leaders from speaking, and similar scenes of 'political rowdyism' and 'open gang warfare' elsewhere were reported.[80] Indian gangs from Natal were rumoured to be terrorising those campaigning for non-participation in Johannesburg.[81]

Feelings also boiled over the 'Nehru telegram' in March. While the pro-boycotters boasted Gandhi's endorsement of 'abstention as a national and dignified step', moderates claimed the backing of Nehru for participation.[82] Quoting a telegram addressed to the provincial congresses, but which ended up in the possession of the SAIC, moderates claimed that Nehru had advised against 'overt demonstrations' against the royal visit.[83] Nehru purportedly wrote that while the Government of India did not wish to dictate the decisions of South African Indians, he was personally opposed to a boycott. The danger existed that a boycott could complicate and cloud the main issue on which the UN had decided in Indians' favour.[84] The NIC officials initially claimed not to have received the telegram, casting doubt on its existence and on the reliability of the moderates' word.[85] Given Nehru's statement a few days earlier that the Indian government would not act whilst awaiting the South African government's initiatives in addressing Indian grievances, it is likely that he did counsel the South African organisations along these lines.[86] The *Indian Opinion* accepted the possibility that the telegram existed, though it deplored the uses to which it was being put. Going further, the newspaper pointed out that the South Africans were better placed to make a judgement: 'if we allow ourselves to be spoon-fed by leaders in India then we are fit for nothing'. Making their own stand was a matter of self-respect and 'national honour', even if it meant going against revered Indian leaders.[87]

The boycott collapses

In response to Dr Dadoo's claim that SAIC's participation in the royal celebrations would be 'unconstitutional', the SAIC president, Ahmed Ismail, averred that it was his prerogative and in the best interests of his people to 'submit myself to Their Majesties'.[88] By late February, the position had gained widespread support.[89] At a meeting of 100 Indian representatives presided over by the Durban mayor, a Royal Visit Indian Reception Committee Party was established to arrange details for the Indian event at Curries Fountain.[90] Within ten days, for the first time, Indians attended an official meeting of the Royal Visit Regional Committee where Kajee guaranteed that Indians would accord the visitors a 'right royal welcome'.[91] As the royal 'white train' drew closer to Natal's borders, more groups came out in favour of participation, including Indian employees of the liquor and catering trades, and representatives from madrassas, schools and religious associations, Girl Guides, sports clubs and ex-servicemen's groups.[92] The Natal Indian Teachers Society decided against participating, but individual teachers formed a committee to prepare children in the performances of Indian folk dances, national songs and national anthems. A coordinating committee was also set up in Northern Natal.[93] In Ladysmith in early March, after a meeting of some 500, the region's Indian Chamber of Commerce, noting the growing ill will between whites and Indians, dissociated its members from the NIC boycott decision and arranged a conference of 'representative Indians to discuss the critical position facing the Indian community'.[94] When the royal party approached the town, the king was greeted by a crowd of 3,000 – half Ladysmith's Indian population.[95] In Pietermaritzburg, the next major centre he visited, Indians 'turned out in their thousands'. The fervent singing of 'God Save the King' and the South African anthem, 'Die Stem', following an Indian dance 'of hieratic stateliness', led the tour's official chronicler to conclude that in the existing state of relations between Indians and the Union this 'was greater evidence of the healing power of the royal visit'.[96]

Conclusion

The *Manchester Guardian* correspondent accompanying the royal party was less sanguine in his appraisal of the royal visit's effects. Most striking was the 'complete split in the Indian community' that arose from the 'ill-advised' attempts of Congress to boycott the royal visit, giving the moderates an opportunity to challenge the radical leadership.[97] Echoing the *Guardian*'s analysis, the historian W.B. White argues that the weakening of the NIC as a consequence of the boycott's failure emboldened moderates to establish a rival organisation, the Natal Indian Organisation (NIO), and resume their time-honoured strategies of negotiation and suasion.[98] At that very moment, illustrating the divisions that had opened up, the leading 'radicals' Monty Naicker and Yusuf Dadoo, having eventually been furnished with travel documents, returned to South Africa from the All-Asia Conference with fresh resolve to contest the legitimacy of 'Smuts' Raj'.[99] In the aftermath of the royal visit, radicals questioned the reasons for the massive participation in the welcome ceremonies. Debi Singh, secretary of the NIC's Passive Resistance Council, claimed that it was the 'shallow attractions [of] the pageantry' that brought the crowds onto the streets, and that this in turn was due to the failure of the leaders to 'politicise' the tour sufficiently.[100] The government's intelligence agent who monitored Indian political activity came to the opposite conclusion. Natal's Indians were 'hopelessly' divided, he reported, and most people were 'heartily sick of the whole movement to oppose the Legislation passed by parliament last year'.[101] Whether fatigue with passive resistance was a factor, historians agree that the campaign had run out of steam by early 1947 and could not recover the momentum and élan of its opening months. After the UN decision, financial support from wealthy merchants drained away, and some criticised the campaign as damaging.[102] Many merchants were unnerved by the racist boycott by whites of Indian business, action that also negatively affected employees and patrons.[103] The cancellation of contracts caused unemployment and discontent, especially in Northern Natal where opposition to passive resistance was marked, and where merchants openly supported participation in the royal visit.[104] Indications are that workers' fears of intimidation and reprisals by employers might have been a factor behind their attendance at the celebrations; in one large factory, employees had been terrified into believing that non-participation would open them to the risk of losing jobs and 'being replaced by natives'.[105] In a labour market where striking Indian workers could be replaced from a huge pool of African work-seekers, this insecurity was surely significant.[106]

Individual motivations for attending the ceremonies undoubtedly varied. To be sure, curiosity and the desire to participate in an event of national significance which featured daily in the local and global media, the allure of pageantry and the distractions of mingling in crowds in a city *en fête* were compelling. Interviews among storekeepers in Ladysmith revealed that 'the visit had been good for trade', while a waiter observed that it was mistaken to confuse attitudes towards the royal tour with the passive resistance campaign. Far from wanting to keep away, Indians built their own welcome arches and travelled from all the towns in order to participate.[107] Biographical and anecdotal accounts suggest that affective loyalism had some residual purchase. Recalling how her grandmother's sitting room had been adorned with images of both Sarajoni Naidu and Queen Victoria, 'the heroine of the Indian indentured labourers', the writer Deverakshanan Govinden recalls that families such as hers saw themselves as a proud part of the British empire, 'even if they were treated as its step children'. In their rural outpost, deference to the British crown was accepted in her family as 'indisputable'.[108] It is notable how even those who later lost their imperial faith recalled the visit with nostalgia. The politician, lawyer and academic Kader Asmal, who founded the Irish Anti-Apartheid Movement and became a government minister in the 'new' South Africa, recalled his childhood pleasure at being been chosen to present a bouquet to Princess Margaret in 1947: 'I couldn't have been prouder', he wrote, 'even though, when the crucial moment arrived, I curtsied instead of bowing. I was a royalist to the core'.[109]

The royal visit of 1947 was the swansong of this brand of loyalism. The futility of the return to methods of conciliation and elite deal-making with which it was associated was cruelly exposed when the Nationalist Party which came to power in the following year proved more purposive than its predecessor in pushing through its radical segregationist programme of apartheid. As Goolam Vahed and Thembisa Waetjen put it, the 'imperial nods to inclusion' was giving way finally to 'a politics of purge'.[110] Coinciding with the final months of India's colonial existence and the emergence of the UN, as the new 'sovereign', the loyalist tradition established in Natal by Gandhi's NIC had come, with the royal visit, to a decisive close.

Notes

1 I thank Jeremy Krikler, Saul Dubow, Goolam Vahed and the editors for their close readings of this chapter and invaluable suggestions, and Gustav Hendrich for his research assistance.
2 *Indian Views*, 26 March 1947; *Inkundla ya Bantu*, 27 March 1947; *Natal Witness*, 24 March 1947.

3 Goolam Vahed, Ashwin Desai and Thembisa Waetjen, *Many Lives: 150 Years of being Indian in South Africa* (Pietermaritzburg: Shuter, 2010), pp. 182–183; Goolam Vahed, 'The Making of "Indianness": Indian Politics in South Africa in the 1930s and 1940s', *Journal of Natal and Zulu History*, 17 (1997), 34–35.
4 Uma Duphelia-Mesthrie, *Gandhi's Prisoner? The Life of Gandhi's Son Manilal* (Cape Town: Kwela Books, 2004), p. 314.
5 Uma Duphelia-Mesthrie, 'The Place of India in South African History: Academic Scholarship, Past, Present and Future', *South African Historical Journal*, 57 (2007), 12–34.
6 However, see Goolam Vahed and Thembisa Waetjen, 'Shifting Grounds: A.I. Kajee and the Political Quandary of "Moderates" in the Search for an Islamic School Site in Durban, 1943–1948', *South African Historical Journal*, 67:3 (2015), 316–334.
7 Miles Taylor, 'The British Royal Family and the Colonial Empire from the Georgians to Prince George', in Robert Aldrich and Cindy McCreery (eds), *Crowns and Colonies: European Monarchies and Overseas Empires* (Manchester: Manchester University Press, 2016), pp. 27–50.
8 David Cannadine, *Ornamentalism: How the British Saw their Empire* (London: Penguin, 2002), p. 143; Terence Ranger, 'Making Northern Rhodesia Imperial: Variations on a Royal Theme, 1924–1938', *African Affairs*, 79:316 (1980), 349–373, at 358; Chandrika Kaul, 'Monarchical Display and the Politics of Empire: Princes of Wales and India 1870–1920s', *Twentieth Century British History*, 17:4 (2006), 471–473.
9 See Mark Mazower, *No Enchanted Palace: The End of Empire and the Ideological Origins of the United Nations* (Princeton: Princeton University Press, 2009), chapter 4.
10 *Economist*, 10 May 1947.
11 Vahed, 'Making of "Indianness"', p. 3.
12 Maurice Webb and V. Sikhari Naidoo, *The Indian: Citizen or Subject?* (Johannesburg: South African Institute of Race Relations, 1947); Goolam Vahed, 'The Making of an Indian Identity in Durban, 1914–1949' (PhD dissertation, Indiana University, 1995), p. 72; John Soske, '"Wash Me Black Again": African Nationalism, the Indian Diaspora, and Kwa-Zulu Natal, 1944–1960' (PhD dissertation, University of Toronto, 2009), chapter 1, available at www.sahistory.org.za/archive/%E2%80%98wash-me-black-again%E2%80%99-african-nationalism-indian-diaspora-and-kwa-zulu-natal-1944-1960, accessed 5 May 2017.
13 Vahed et al., *Many Lives*, p. 168.
14 Vahed, 'Making of "Indianness"', pp. 3–5.
15 Parvathi Raman, 'Yusuf Dadoo: Transnational Politics, South African Belonging', *South African Historical Journal*, 50 (2004), 27–48, at 31.
16 Sukanya Banerjee, *Being Imperial Citizens: Indians in the Late Victorian Empire* (Durham, NC and London: Duke University Press, 2010), p. 22.
17 Under Gandhi's leadership, South African Indians volunteered in the South Africa War in support of the British, offered assistance to the Natal government in the suppression of the Bhambatha revolt of 1906, and many volunteered to serve the British in East Africa during the First World War. Ashwin Desai and Goolam Vahed, *The South African Gandhi: Stretcher-Bearer of Empire* (Stanford: Stanford University Press, 2015).
18 W.K. Hancock, *Smuts: The Field of Force, 1919–1950, Vol 2* (Cambridge: Cambridge University Press, 1968), pp. 148–149.
19 *Natal Mercury*, 14 August 1901; Surendra Bhana, *Gandhi's Legacy: The Natal Indian Congress 1994–1994* (Pietermaritzburg: University of Natal, 1997), chapter 1.
20 Surendra Bhana, 'Indianness Reconfigured, 1944–1960: The Natal Indian Congress in South Africa', www.nelsonmandela.org/omalley/index.php/site/q/03lv02424/04lv02730/05lv02914/06lv02917.htm, accessed 6 June 2015.
21 *Indian Opinion*, 8 May 1925.
22 *Indian Opinion*, 10 May 1925; Mesthrie, *Gandhi's Prisoner*, pp. 168–169.

23 Ralph Deakin, *Southward Ho! The Tour with the Prince of Wales to Africa and South America* (London: Methuen and Company, 1925), pp. 133–134.
24 *Cape Times*, 5 June 1925; Mesthrie, *Gandhi's Prisoner*, pp. 168–169.
25 *Indian Opinion*, 8 May 1925.
26 Bhana, *Gandhi's Legacy*, p. 19; Vahed et al., *Many Lives*, p. 100.
27 Vahed, 'Making of an Indian Identity', pp. 225–226.
28 Ismail C. Meer, *I Remember: Reminiscences of the Struggle for Liberation and the Role of Indian South Africans, 1924–1958*, ed. Enuga S. Reddy and Fatima Meer, South African History Online, www.sahistory.org.za/archive/i-remember-reminiscences-struggle-liberation-and-role-indian-south-africans-1924–1958-i-c, accessed 17 January 2015.
29 Archibald A. Frew, *Prince George's African Tour* (London: Blackie & Son Limited, 1934), chapter CVLL.
30 Ibid.; Mesthrie, *Gandhi's Prisoner*, p. 226.
31 Mesthrie, *Gandhi's Prisoner*, p. 225; Meer, *I Remember*.
32 Vahed, 'Making of "Indianness"', p. 8. Formed in 1933, the CBSIA championed the rights of all 'colonial-born' Indians who regarded South Africa as their permanent home. The NIC and CBSIA eventually merged giving rise to the Natal Indian Association (NIA) in 1939 which in turn combined with the NIC to form a reconstituted NIC. Mesthrie, *Gandhi's Prisoner*, pp. 224–225.
33 Ashwin Desai and Goolam H. Vahed, *Monty Naicker: Between Reason and Treason* (Pietermaritzburg: Shuter and Shooter, 2010), p. 106.
34 Essop Pahad, 'The Development of Indian Political Movements in South Africa, 1924–1946' (PhD dissertation, University of Sussex, 1972), pp. 169–170.
35 Uma Dhupelia-Mesthrie, 'Gandhi and Indian Nationalism in South Africa', *Historia*, 54:1 (2009), 13–33.
36 Vahed, 'Making of "Indianness"'; John Soske, 'Wash Me Black', pp. 67–73.
37 Durham University Library (DUL): Special Collections: Baring Papers, Baring to Machtig, 21 November 1944.
38 Doulat Ramdas Bagwandeen, 'The Question of "Indian Penetration" in the Durban Area and Indian Politics, 1940–1946' (PhD dissertation, University of Natal, 1983), chapter 7, p. 339.
39 *Satyagraha* means 'soul force' or 'firmness in Truth' and describes the strategy of resistance to unjust authority developed by Gandhi in South Africa in the early twentieth century.
40 *Ilanga*, 22 February 1947; Soske, 'Wash Me Black', p. 62.
41 Vahed, 'Making of "Indianness"', p. 26.
42 Jonathan Hyslop, 'Segregation has Fallen on Evil Days': Smuts' South Africa, Global War, and Transnational Politics', *Journal of Global History*, 7 (2012), 438–460.
43 *Inkululeko*, Second Issue, March 1947; Mesthrie, *Gandhi's Prisoner*, pp. 313–314.
44 DUL, Baring Papers, GRE 1/11/1–100, 'The Attitude of the Union Government to the UNO Resolutions of the Future Status of South West Africa and on the Treatment of Indians in the Union of South Africa', 17 March 1947.
45 *Sunday Statesman*, 22 February 1947.
46 *Leader*, 22 February 1947; *Rand Daily Mail*, 6 February 1947.
47 *Rand Daily Mail*, 11 February 1947.
48 National Archives (NA), Pretoria: Smuts Papers, 'Indian Boycott of the Royal Family', 21 February 1947; W.B. White, 'Passive Resistance in Natal, 1946–1948', *Journal of Natal and Zulu History*, 5 (1982), 1–28, at 14.
49 *Sunday Times*, 16 February 1942. In a referendum held during the royal visit, however, Durban's white citizens rejected the extension of a limited municipal franchise to Indians.
50 P.S. Joshi, *Struggle for Equality* (Bombay: Hind Kitabs, 1951), p. 18.
51 NA: Department of External Affairs (BTS) 22/2/1434 vol. 1, Mitchell to Forsyth, Prime Minister's Office, 2 September 1946.
52 NA:BTS 22/2/1434 vol. 1, A.N. Baker, Honorary Secretary, Regional Committee to the Joint Honorary Secretaries, Natal Indian Congress, Durban, 4 September 1946.

53 NA:BTS 22/2/1434 vol. 1, A.I. Meer, Joint General Secretary, Natal Indian Congress to Mayoral Secretary, Durban, 11 September 1946; *Indian Opinion*, 27 February 1946.
54 *Passive Resister*, 11 November 1946.
55 NA:BTS 22/2/1434 Vol. 1, A.N. Baker, Mayoral Secretary to Joint Honorary Secretary, Natal Indian Congress, 16 September 1946; NA: BTS 22/2/434 Vol. 1, Minutes of the Meeting between the representatives of the four provinces in the interdepartmental committee of the Royal Visit, Pretoria, 25 and 26 September 1946.
56 *Cape Standard*, 15 January 1947; *Indian Views*, 26 February 1947.
57 *Passive Resister*, 24 January 1947. In contemporary journalism the UN was referred to as 'UNO' (the United Nations Organisation).
58 *Ilanga*, 4 January 1946 [sic]; *Inkululeko*, First Issue, February 1947.
59 *Leader*, 15 February 1947; NA: Smuts Papers A1 167 Vol. CLXVll, AP Headquarters, Pretoria Confidential: Mass Meeting (Indian) Durban.
60 *Leader*, 8 February 1947; *Indian Views*, 26 February 1947; *Leader*, 1 March 1947; *Natal Mercury*, 19 February 1947; *Cape Standard*, 18 March 1947.
61 *Natal Mercury*, 19 February 1947.
62 *Leader*, 8 February 1947; *Indian Opinion*, 14 February 1947.
63 *Indian Opinion*, 14 February 1947.
64 Mesthrie, *Gandhi's Prisoner*, 313; *New York Times*, 4 February 1947.
65 *Rand Daily Mail*, 17 September 1946.
66 NA: Smuts Papers C6/2427/7 'Confidential: Indian, Communist and Native Boycott in Connection with the Royal Visit of Their Majesties the King and Queen and Princesses, South Africa, 1947'.
67 *Leader*, 8 February 1947.
68 *Leader*, 22 February 1947.
69 *Indian Views*, 26 February 1947.
70 *Rand Daily Mail*, 11 February 1947.
71 Vahed and Waetjen, 'Shifting Grounds'; Bhana, *Gandhi's Legacy*, pp. 48–51.
72 *Leader*, 15 February 1947.
73 *Leader*, 15 March 1947.
74 *Leader*, 15 February 1947.
75 *Natal Witness*, 25 February 1947; *Indian Views*, 26 February 1947.
76 *Natal Mercury*, 17 February 1947. Both Zulu traditionalists and the *amakholwa* (Christian Westernised elite) criticised the Indian boycott stance. *Sunday Times*, 9 March 1947; *Ilanga*, 1 March 1947.
77 *Natal Mercury*, 21 February 1947; *Natal Mercury*, 20 February 1947.
78 *Natal Mercury*, 19 February 1947.
79 *Guardian*, 20 February 1947; *Rand Daily Mail*, 17 February 1947.
80 *Natal Mercury*, 27 February 1947; *Natal Witness*, 20 February 1947.
81 *Sunday Times*, 16 February 1947.
82 *Passive Resister*, 7 March 1947; *Indian Views*, 26 February 1947.
83 *Indian Views*, 26 February 1947.
84 Ibid.
85 Ibid.; *Passive Resister*, 7 March 1947.
86 *Sunday Statesman*, 22 February 1947.
87 *Indian Opinion*, 28 February 1947.
88 *Indian Views*, 26 February 1947; *Leader*, 1 March 1947.
89 *Leader*, 1 March 1947.
90 *Natal Mercury*, 21 February and 23 February 1947.
91 The National Archives, Kew (TNA): Dominion Office (DO) 119/1429 Telegram from High Commissioner for the United Kingdom, Cape Town to the Secretary of State for Dominion Affairs, London, 5 March 1947.
92 *Natal Mercury*, 5 March 1947; *Leader*, 15 March 1947.
93 *Natal Mercury*, 17 February 1947.
94 *Times of India*, 4 March 1947.
95 Donal Morrah, *Royal Family in Africa* (London: Hutchinson, 1947), p. 86; *Times of India*, 15 March 1947.

96 Morrah, *Royal Family*, p. 86; *Leader*, 22 March 1947; *Leader*, 1 March 1947.
97 *Manchester Guardian*, 7 April 1947; *Natal Mercury*, 27 February 1947. Gandhi blamed Smuts, 'Europeans' and 'our "moderates"' for harming 'the greater cause of liberty for which the movement of *satyagraha* has stood'. *Indian Opinion*, 23 May 1947.
98 White, 'Passive Resistance', pp. 1–28.
99 A.I. Meer, 'Prison Horrors and Indignities in Smuts Raj', *Blitz*, cited in *The Indian in South Africa–Pamphlet* 4 (Durban: Durban Corporation, c. 1947).
100 *Torch*, 7 April 1947.
101 United Party Head Office, University of South Africa Files 28.9–28.12, 'Royal Visit, Cape Town 21 Feb, 1947'.
102 *Natal Mercury*, 6 March 1947.
103 *Rand Daily Mail*, 18 March 1947.
104 DUL, Baring Papers, GRE 1/11/1–100, 'The Attitude of the Union Government to the UNO Resolutions of the Future Status of South West Africa and on the Treatment of Indians', 17 March 1947; Maureen Swann, 'Ideology in Organised Indian Politics, 1891–1948', in Shula Marks and Stanley Trapido (eds), *The Politics of Race, Class and Nationalism in Twentieth Century South Africa* (Harlow: Longman, 1987), pp. 203–204.
105 *Indian Opinion*, 21 February 1947.
106 Desai and Vahed, *Monty*, p. 201.
107 *Spotlight*, 29 March 1947.
108 Deverakshanan Govinden, 'The Indentured Experience and Indian Women in Colonial Natal', in John C. Hawley (ed.), *India and Africa, Africa in India: Indian Ocean Cosmopolitanisms* (Bloomington: Indiana University Press, 2008), pp. 55–77, 69–70.
109 Kadar Asmal and Adrian Hadland with Moira Levy, *Politics is in My Blood: A Memoir* (Johannesburg: Jacana, 2011), pp. 34–35.
110 Vahed and Waetjen, 'Shifting Grounds', p. 334.

INDEX

Note: Page references followed by *tab* indicate tables; those in **bold** type indicate illustrations.

Abd el-Kader 42
Abdul Hamid 27, 29, 32, 35
Abdülhamid II, Sultan 110, 120
Aceh 23–25
Aceh embassy
   composition 27–28
   funeral of Abdul Hamid 29–30, 32
   presentation of envoys 30–33
   as royal tour by proxy 26, 29–34
   subsequent significance 34–36
   tour of Dutch provinces 33–34
   voyage to Europe 28–29
Acland, Henry Wentworth 101
Afghanistan 10
Africa Italiana 212–228
Afrikaners *see* Cape Dutch
air travel 18, 174–175
Alauddin Riayet, Sultan of Aceh 26–27, 34, 35
Albert, Prince Consort 64
Albert Edward, Prince *see* Edward VII, King
Albert I, King 171, 174, 176, 179–180, 203
Albert Victor, Prince 56, 59, **63**, 64–66, 68, 70, 73
Alexander I, King 13
Alfred, Prince (Duke of Edinburgh)
   assassination attempt 13, 80–81
   Australian visit 13, 56, 67, 80–81
   global tours 56, 59, 60–61*tab*, 62, 64, 68, 71–72
   sets precedent for princely tours 56–57, 59, 62, 64, 68, 70–72, 74
Algeria
   1871 insurrection 51
   as 'Arab kingdom' 45
   citizenship issues 47–48, 51

French dominion over 41–42
   Napoléon III's visits 44–51
Anglo-Boer Wars
   Cape Dutch and 87
   Irish and 83, 90
Anglo-Chinese War 41
Angola 152–154
Annam
   kingship in 127, 138
   see also Bao Dai, Emperor; Khai Dinh, Emperor
anti-colonialism 138–139, 171, 206, 251
Ardemagni, Mirko 118, 220
Armenian massacres 113
Asian royal tours
   Emperor Khai Dinh 130–132
   French reactions to 132–139
   Indonesian official delegations 236–241, 247
   King Chulalongkorn 125, 130
   King Sisowath 128–130
   Vietnamese nationalists' criticisms 138–139
   see also Aceh embassy
assassination attempts 13, 80–81, 114, 206, 215
assassinations 13, 148, 152, 205
L'Assiette au beurre 133, 134, **135**, 137
Australian visits
   1868 13, 56, 60*tab*, 67, 80–81
   1881 56, 60*tab*
   1901 61*tab*, 66–67
   1927 61*tab*

Bacchante HMS 60–61*tab*, 65, 68–69
Baghdad railway 117–118

[271]

INDEX

Balbo, Italo 219
banquets *see* food and banquets
Bao Dai, Emperor 131, 142
batuque (drum performance)
    154–158, **155**, **156**
Baudouin, King
    1955 visit to the Congo 177,
        181–183
    1959 visit to the Congo 184–185
    accession to throne 172, 181
    at Congo independence ceremony
        173, 178, 185
    portrait **182**
Bechuanaland 9–10
Belgian Congo *see* Congo
Belgium
    Hirohito's visit 203
    list of royal visits to the
        Congo 173*tab*
    royal dynasty 171–172
    royal influence on colonial policy
        169, 171, 179–180
    royal question 172, 181
    see also Congo; Congo Free State;
        names of Belgian royalty
Beresford, Lord Charles 71, 74
Berlin-to-Baghdad railway 117–118
Bhagvatsinh, Thakur Sahib
    education 96–99, 101
    European tour 104–105
    guided tour of Britain 98–104
    medical studies in Scotland
        102, 106
    portrait **97**
    progressive attitudes 106–107
    publications 106
    visits Queen Victoria 102, 106
Bhopal, Begum of 11
Boer Wars *see* Anglo-Boer Wars
Boers *see* Cape Dutch
Bonaparte, Charles-Louis Napoléon
    see Napoléon III, Emperor
Bonaparte, Eugène Louis Napoléon
    (French Prince Imperial) 52
British national identity / Britishness
    81–83, 253–255
    see also empire loyalism

British royal tours
    by royal couples 8, 57, 61*tab*, 66,
        74, 87–91, 250
    by royal princes
        dates and destinations 56, 59,
            60–61*tab*, 64, 65, 68
        entourages 65–67
        objectives 58–59
        precedents set by Prince Alfred
            56–57, 59, 62, 64, 68, 70–72, 74
        preparatory training for 64, 68
        role of Royal Navy 59, 62, 69–70
'British Ultimatum' (1890) 146
Bülow, Bernhard von 112, 118–120
Burma 10, 72
Burne, O.J. 100
Bwana Kitoko (film) 177

Cadbury, William 146, 153
Cambodia
    Khmer dancers 12, 130, 135
    kingship in 127
    see also Sisowath, King
Cape Dutch 83–88
Cape Town Agreement 255
Carlos I, King 148, 149
cartoons and caricatures 133, **134**,
    135, 137
Catholics and Catholicism
    German Catholics 115–116, 120
    Portugal's 'civilising mission' 157
    see also Irish Catholic imperial
        loyalty
Cauvin, André 177
ceremony, performance and spectacle
    Cannadine on 4
    French 125–126, 132, 139–140
    Indian durbars and investitures
        8, 13, 71
    under Italian fascism 215
    Khmer dancers 130, 135
    Mozambican *batuque* 154–158,
        155, **156**
    Wilhelmina's fortieth regnal
        anniversary 237, **238**
chaperones and guardians 65–67
Charles (Belgian prince regent) 172, 181

INDEX

Charles X, King 41
Christian IX, King 8
Christianity and European colonialism 46, 49, 157
Christie, John 66
Chulalongkorn, King 125, 130
Church of Christ the Redeemer (Jerusalem) 110, 114
Cirenaica 212, 221, 223
citizenship issues 51
Clanwilliam, Earl of 66, 73
Clearly, Henry William 88–91
commemorative books and albums 56, 68, 151, 171, 176, 235, 237, 239
Congo
  itinerary of royal tours 175
  list of Belgian royal visits 173*tab*
  reporting and filming royal visits 175–177
  significance of royal visits 177–186
  social and economic conditions 179–180
  as 'tenth province' 181
Congo Free State 169, 171
Congo Museum 203
Cornwall and York, Duke and Duchess of 57, 61*tab*, 87, 254
coronation oath 90–91
coronations 71, 95, 142, 254, 256
Corriere della Sera 218, 223–224, 227
costs of royal tours 58, 111, 128, 158, 236, 240
Cowell, Major John 66, 73
Crete 113–114

Dalton, John Neale 66, 73
decorations *see* triumphal arches
Décret Crémieux 51
Delhi durbar 8, 13
Devi, Sunity 96
diarchy, Italy as 211–212, 214–215, 217–219, 224, 225, 227–228
diplomatic aspects of tours 9–10, 68, 112, 117–118, 160
Domenica del Corriere 212, **213**, 214, 217, 224, 225, 227, 230n12

Duce *see* diarchy, Italy as; Mussolini, Benito
Durban 250, 252, 254, 255, 257, 259–260, 264–265
durbars 8, 13, 71
Dutch court
  Indonesian delegations to 236–241, 247
  serimpi performance at 233–234
  see also Wilhelmina, Queen

Edward, Prince of Wales (later Edward VIII) 67, 205, 254–256
Edward VII, King 4, 64, 67, 70–73, 90–91
Egypt 114, 212, 221
Elisabeth, Queen (of Belgium) 180, 184
embassies and delegations to Europe 10–11, 236–241, 247
  see also Aceh embassy
Emma, Queen 11
empire loyalism
  Cape Dutch 83–88
  Chinese in New Zealand 91
  in the Congo 186–187
  ethnic outsiders and 81–83, 91
  Irish Catholics 80, 85–91
  O'Farrell and 80–81
  in Portuguese African colonies 162–163
  South African Indians 250, 252–256, 264
entertainments (informal)
  hunting tigers and elephants 70–71, 151, 160, 225, **226**
  visiting brothels 67
entourages 7
  for Begum of Bhopal 11
  for Belgian royals 179
  for British princes 57, 65–67
  for Hirohito 197
  for Indonesian royalty 239–240
  for Sisowath 129
  for Victor Emanuel 216, 221
  women members 12

[273]

INDEX

Eritrea 212, 219–221
ethnic outsiders and empire
    loyalty 81–83
  Cape Dutch 83–88
  Chinese in New Zealand 91
  Irish Catholic Australians 80–81
  Irish Catholic New
    Zealanders 88–91
  South African Indians 250,
    252–256, 260
  Taiwanese under Japanese rule
    206–207
Eugénie, Empress (wife of
    Napoléon III)
  Asian art collection 41
  friendship with Queen Victoria 52
  marriage 39
  at opening of Suez Canal 43
  pilgrimage to South Africa 52–53
  visit to Algeria 11, 44
  voyages as widow 52
Europe: non-Western royal visitors
    1–2, 9–11
  see also Aceh embassy;
    Chulalongkorn, King;
    Hirohito, Prince; Indonesian
    royalty: official visitors to
    Dutch court; Kalakaua,
    King; Khai Dinh, Emperor;
    Sisowath, King
Euryalus HMS 60–61*tab*, 62, 65

Fallières, Armand 135
fascism, Italian
  colonisation in Africa 220,
    223–224
  position of monarchy under
    211–212, **213**, 214–215,
    217–219, 224, 225, 227–228
  use of film for propaganda 218,
    219–220, 227
  see also Mussolini, Benito
Fayrer, Joseph 71
female royals on tour 11
Fenians 80–81
Figaro, Le 133

filming of royal tours
  Congo 177
  in Italian Africa 218, 219–221, 223
food and banquets 9, 33, 47, 128–129
France
  Asian embassies to 10
  citizenship issues 51
  frequency of royal visits to 2
  non-Western royal visits to 11,
    125–131, 129, 135–137,
    202–203
  overseas colonies and
    empire 41–42
  press coverage of Asian royal visits
    to 132–133, **134**, 135
  protectorate rights in Palestine 115
  protectorates in Southeast Asia
    125–128
  reaction to Kaiser's Ottoman visit
    114–115
  see also Napoléon III, Emperor
Franco, João 149
Franz Ferdinand, Archduke 13
Fuad, King 221
Futara Yoshinori, Count 197, 203

Galatea HMS 60–61*tab*, 65, 68–69, 70
Gamboa (ex-Sergeant) 161
game hunting 70–71, 151, 160,
    225, **226**
Gandhi, Manilal 254, 261, 263
gender issues 11–12, 127, 244
George, Prince (Duke of Kent) 255–256
George, Prince (later Duke of
    Cornwall and York, then
    George V) 56, 59, 63–66,
    68–70, 73–74
  portrait **63**
  tours as Duke of Cornwall and
    York 87, 88–91
  tours as young prince 56, 59,
    60–61*tab*, 64, 65, 68, 70
  see also George V, King
George I, King of the Hellenes 68
George V, King 95, 199–200, **200**
George VI, King 13, 95, 250, 256, 259

[274]

INDEX

German Catholics 115–116, 120
German Protestants 114
German Templer colonists 118
Germany
  Armenian massacres and 113
  Berlin-to-Baghdad railway 117–118
  Kaiser's influence on foreign policy 112–113, 117–118, 119
  Kaiser's Ottoman visit
    commercial and colonial motives 116–120
    German public opinion on 112
    international context 113–114
    itinerary 110
    religious aspects 114–116, 119–121
gifts
  to Dutch monarch 234, 237, **238**, 240, 245–247, **246**
  from King Sisowath 136
  to Prince Luís Filipe 151
  to Queen Victoria 11
  of religious sites 111, 112, 120
  from Sultan of Aceh 25, 32, 72, 217
Glencross, Matthew 4
Goa 148–149
Gondal, Maharaja of *see* Bhagvatsinh, Thakur Sahib
Grey, Sir George 86
Gungunhana (Mozambican chief) 156–157

Hancock, George 98
Hara Takashi 193, 194, 200, 205, 206
Herzl, Theodor 112, 119–120
Hirohito, Prince (later Emperor)
  assassination attempt on 206
  education 195, 199
  engagement incident 196
  European tour (1921)
    entourage 197
    influence on his thinking 191, 201, 205
    itinerary in Britain 199–201
    itinerary in Europe 202–204
    opposition in Japan to 195–196
    passage to Europe 197–199
    purpose and planning 17, 194–197, 205
  intervention in political controversies 207
  portraits **200**, **202**
  as regent 206–207
  visit to Europe (1971) 207–208
  visit to Taiwan 206
historiography of royal tours 3–6
Ho Chi Minh 138–139
Hohenlohe-Schillingsfürst, Chlodwig 113, 116, 118–119
Holy Land
  exchange of holy sites 111, 112, 120
  French protectorate rights 114–115
  Templers' bids for territory 118
  Zionist bids for territory 112, 119–120
L'Humanité 133, 139

imperialism
  French, in Southeast Asia 125–128
  Hobson on 16
  new imperial history 5
  royal tours and 6–7, 15–17, 117
independence ceremonies 5, 8, 173, 175, 185
India
  British royal tours 70–73
  relations with South Africa 255, 257–259
Indian and Colonial Exhibition 95
Indian princes
  attendance at major imperial events 95
  education 94, 96–98
  progressive attitudes 103–104, 107
  Queen Victoria and 95, 103
  visits to Britain 98, 100
  see also Bhagvatsinh, Thakur Sahib
'Indianness' 252–253
Indians in South Africa *see* South African Indians

indigenous migrant labour 152–153, 158–159
Indochine Française 126
Indonesian royalty
  asserting own royal status 241, 245–247
  gifts to Queen Wilhelmina 237, **238**, 240, 245–247
  official visitors to Dutch court 236–241, 247
  role of pomp and regalia 239–240
  strained encounters with Dutch monarchy 235, 237–241
  as 'vassals' of Dutch monarch 236–237
Irish Catholic imperial loyalty
  in Australia 80–81
  during Boer Wars 83, 90
  limits to 90–91
  in New Zealand 88–91
Ismail, Ahmed 262, 264
Italy
  abolition of monarchy 229
  Bhagvatsinh's impressions 105
  Hirohito's visit 204
  monarchy's autonomy under fascism 211–212, **213**, 214–215, 217–219, 224, 225, 227–228
  proclamation of empire 225
  royal tours to Italian Africa 212–228
  see also Victor Emanuel III

Japan
  political system 192–194, 207
  recolonisation of Taiwan 206
  role of throne 192, 207
  royal symbolism 207
  see also Hirohito, Prince; Taishō Emperor
Jerusalem 110, 111, 115
Jewish communities, Algeria 47–48, 51

Kaiser's Ottoman tour
  comercial and colonial motives 116–120

German public opinion and 112
international context 113–114
itinerary 110
religious aspects 114–116, 119–121
Kajee, A.I. 250, 258, 262, 264
Kalakaua, King 57
Keppel, Sir Henry 65, 66, 67, 70, 73
Khai Dinh, Emperor
  critics of his French tour 138–139
  French press and 132–133, 139
  reign and reputation 127, 141
  visit to France 130–131, **131**, 137
Khmer dancers 130, 135
kingship
  in Annam and Cambodia 126–127, 140
  Vietnamese critics 138–139

labour, indigenous migrant 152–153, 158–159
Langkat, Sultan of **239**, 245, **246**
Laurenço Marques see batuque (drum performance)
Leal de Camâra, Tomás 133, 135
Leo XIII, Pope 105
Leopold I, King 171
Leopold II, King 11, 14–15, 169, 171, 172
Leopold III, King 171–172, 174, 179–180, 183–184
long-distance royal tours 14–15, 60–61tab, 174–175
Louis-Philippe, King 41–42
Louis XIV, King 10
Louwers, Octave 180
loyalism see empire loyalism
Luís Filipe, Prince
  assassination 148, 162
  lessons in colonial history 148
  portrait **147**
  visit to Portuguese Africa 17, 148–159
  visit to South Africa 159–161
Lumumba, Patrice 178, 182, 184, 186

McCracken, Donal 83
MacKenzie, John 83

INDEX

MacMahon, Patrice 46
Macnaughten, Chester 96–97
Maharaja of Gondal *see* Bhagvatsinh, Thakur Sahib
Malabari, Behramji 98, 101, 102, 105
Mangkunegoro VII (Javanese ruler) 233, 236, 241
married royals, tours by 38, 44, 57, 66, 176, 216, 250
Marschall von Bieberstein, Adolf 113, 118, 120
Masaryk, Tomas 204
Maurits (*stadhouder* of Orange-Nassau) 25, **31**
Maximilian, King 41
Meade, Richard (Earl of Clanwilliam) 66, 73
media reporting of tours *see* filming of royal tours; newspaper and magazine coverage; newsreels
Mehrkens, Heidi 5
Meiji Restoration 192–193
migrant labour 152–153, 158–159
Millerand, Alexandre 202
Milne, Alexander 65, 74
Milner, Alfred 88
Milner, John 67
Minobe Tatsukichi 207
Mir Hasan 27
Modjopait, Sultan of **239**
Mongkut, King 41
Morocco 10
Mozambique
  armed resistance to Portuguese 156–157
  batuque performance for royal visit 154–158
  source of labour for South African mines 158–159
Müller, Frank Lorenz 5
Murphy, Philip 5
Mussolini, Benito 211–212, **213**, 214–215, 225, 227, 228

Naoroji, Dadabhai 103
Napoléon III, Emperor
  expansion of French empire under 42
  foreign and colonial policy 40–43
  granting of amnesty by 48
  policies towards Algeria 43–45, 47–51
  political rise and fall 39–40, 43
  reputed Arabophilia 45
  Siamese embassy to 10
  visits to Algeria 8, 44–51
  see also Eugénie, Empress
Nasr Allah Khan 10
Natal Indian Congress (NIC) 250–251, 253, 254–260, 263, 265
nationalism 16, 87, 88–90, 138–139, 171, 206, 256
Native Labour Association 158–159
Nehru, Jawaharlal 251, 258–259, 263
Netherlands
  Hirohito's visit 204
  see also Aceh embassy; Wilhelmina, Queen
'new imperial history' 5
'new royal history' 4
New Zealand
  1901 royal visit 60–61*tab*, 67, 68, 88–89
  Irish Catholics in 88–91
newspaper and magazine coverage
  Asian kings' visits to France 132–135, 139
  Belgian tours of the Congo 175–177
  Hirohito's European tour 201
  Indonesian-Dutch royal encounters 235
  New Zealand royal visit (1901) 88–91
  South African royal visit (1901) 84–87
  Victor Emanuel's African tours 217, 219, 221–225, 227
newsreels 214, 218, 219–221, 223
Ngo Duc Ke 139
Nguyen Ai Quoc, 138–139
Nguyen Phuc Canh, Prince 2
NIC *see* Natal Indian Congress

[277]

INDEX

Nicholas II, Tsar 116, 121–124
non-Western royal visitors to Europe
   miscellaneous 1–2, 129
   see also Aceh embassy;
      Chulalongkorn, King;
      Hirohito, Prince; Indian
      princes; Indonesian royalty:
      official visitors to Dutch
      court; Kalakua, King; Khai
      Dinh, Emperor; Sisowath, King
Norodom Sihamoni, King 141–142
Norodom Sihanouk, King 141

O'Farrell, Henry James 80–81
Okinawa 198
Onslow, William Lake 66
Ornelas, Aires de 148–149, 150, 158, 160, 163
Ottoman empire: Kaiser's visit
   comercial and colonial motives 116–120
   German public opinion on 112
   international context 113–114
   itinerary 110
   religious aspects 114–116, 119–121
'Our Sailor Princes' (wood engraving) **63**

pageantry and pomp *see* ceremony, performance and spectacle
Pakualam VII, Prince 236, 246
Pakubuwono X (susuhunan of Surakarta) 236, 241, 246
Palestine 118–119
Parkes, Henry 80–81
Pather, P.R. 258, 262
performances
   Indonesian *serimpi* 233–234
   Khmer dance 130, 135
   Mozambican *batuque* 154–157
Pes, Alessandro 212, 217–218
Petit Journal, Le 132
Phan Chau Trinh 138
Phillips, A.M. 96
photography
   Belgian tours of the Congo 175–177
   British royal tourists 72
   Luís Filipe's African tour 150–151, 154–156
   photographic portraits as gifts 241, 245–246
Pius XI, Pope 204
planning and organisation 17–18
   of British princely tours 67–68
   Hirohito's tour 194–197, 205
   Kaiser's tour to the Levant 110–111
   Luís Filipe's African tour 150–151, 154–156
   royal visit to Durban 259–260
   Sisowath's visit to France 128–129
Pocahontas 2
polygamy 96, 127, 244
pomp and ceremony *see* ceremony, performance and spectacle
portraits, as official gifts 241
Portugal
   accusations of slavery against 146, 149
   assassination of king and crown prince 148, 162
   motives for African royal tour 146–147, 149
   presidential colonial tour (1938) 163
   republicanism 13, 147–148, 148–150, 149–150
   Salazar's colonial project 163–164
   slave-labour question 146, 149, 152–153
   tensions with Britain 146
press coverage *see* newspaper and magazine coverage
propaganda value of royal visits 16, 132, 176, 197–198, 205, 216–220, 260
protectorates 7, 114–115, 125–128

race and racism 133, **134**, 187
Rajkumar College 94, 96, 98–99, 101
Rama V *see* Chulalongkorn, King
Ranavalona III, Queen 11
regalia 240
regents *(bupati)* 242

[278]

INDEX

religion
  British coronation oath 90–91
  Christianity and European colonialism 46, 49, 157
  German Christians in Palestine 114–116, 120
  gift-giving of holy sites 111, 112, 120
  Islamic dietary laws 33
  as motive for Kaiser's Holy Land visit 114–116
  and Portugal's 'civilising mission' 157
  Wilhelmina's religiosity 244
  Zionist movement 112, 119–120
  see also Irish Catholic imperial loyalty
Renown HMS 60–61*tab*, 69, 70, 71
republicanism
  Bhagvatsinh on 104–10
  Irish 80–81
  Italy 229
  Portugal 13, 148–150
Repulse HMS 60–61*tab*, 69, 70
Rodin, Auguste 130
Royal Navy
  naval training for princes 62–65, 68
  role in royal tours 68–70
  see also warships
royal symbolism, Japan 207
royal trains 216
royal yachts 17, 110, 216, 228
Russell, William Howard 73
Russia 115, 116
Ryckmans, Pierre 179

SAIC *see* South African Indian Congress
sailor princes 59, 62, **63**
St Peter's Church (Middelburg) 29, 35
Saint-Simon, Claude Henri 44, 51
Saionji Kinmochi, Prince 194–196, 205
Salazar, António de Oliviera 163–164
São Tomé 152–153, 161
Scott, Lord Charles 66, 73

Seedat, Dawood 256
Selbourne, Lord 160
Serapis HMS 60–61*tab*, 71, 79
serimpi dance performance 233–234
Shiratori Kurakichi 195
Siam 10, 41, 125, 130
Sihanouk, King 141
Singh, Jagatjit 104
'Sisi', Empress 13
Sisowath, King
  French press and 132–133, **134**, 135
  reign and reputation 127, 140–141
  visit to France 127–130, 135–137
Smuts, Jan 250, 257–259
Somalia 212, 223–225
South Africa
  German immigration 86–87
  immigrant labour for gold fields 158–159
  imperial loyalty of Cape Boers 83–88
  imperial loyalty of Indian community 250, 252–256, 264
  Luís Filipe's visit 159–161
  passive resistance campaign 257–263
  relations with india 255, 257–259
  royal visits 60–61*tab*, 64, 86–87, 250, 252, 253–256
  United Nations condemnation 258
  see also South African Indians
South African Indian Congress (SAIC) 258, 262–264
South African Indians
  'Indianness' of 252–253
  leadership division 259–264
  loyalism and royalism among 250, 252–256, 264
  participation in royal events and tours 250, 252, 253, 254–256
  passive resistance campaign 257–263
  proposed boycott of royal tour 260–264
spectacle of empire *see* ceremony, performance and spectacle
Sri Muhammad 27, 32

INDEX

La Stampa 219, 223–224
Standish, Frederick 67
Sugiura Shigetake 195

Taishō Emperor 194–195, 206
Taiwan 198, 206–207
Tanner, R.J. 201, 205
Tarleton, John W. 65–66
Templer colonists 118
terrorism *see* assassination attempts; assassinations
Thakur Sahib Bhagvatsinh *see* Bhagvatsinh, Thakur Sahib
Thiounn, Okna Veang 135–137
Thomas Cook (travel agency) 110–111
tiger hunting 71
transport and modes of travel
  of Aceh's ambassadors to the Netherlands 28–29
  long-distance tours 14–15, 19, 67, 174–175
  royal trains and yachts 17, 110, 216, 228
  symbolic and ceremonial aspects 17–18
travel, educational value for princes 57, 68, 98
Tripolitania 212, 215–219
triumphal arches 46, **62**, 91, 151

United East India Company (VOC) 24, 26
United Nations 258
Urbain, Ismaÿl 44, 46, 48

van Meteren, Emanuel 30–32
van Vervou, Frederik 30, 33, 34
Vatican 115, 204
Verson, Bishop Michael 91
Victor Emanuel III, King
  abdication 228
  assassination attempt on 215
  autonomy under fascist regime 211–212, 214–215, 217–219, 224, 225, 227–228
  media coverage of royal tours 217–219
  portrait **213**
  royal tours
    to Cirenaica 212, 221, 223
    to Egypt 212, 221
    to Eritrea 212, 219–221
    to Libya 212, 225–228
    to Somalia 212, 223–225
    to Tripolitania 212, 215–219
Victoria, Queen
  attitude to princely tours 58, 65
  friendship with Eugénie 40, 52
  Queen's Proclamation (1858) 253
  receives non-Western royals 10–11, 57, 95, 103
  visit to France 40
Vietnam
  French dominion over 42, 126
  nationalism and anti-colonialism 138–139
  soldiers' deaths in First World War 131
VOC *see* United East India Company (VOC)

Wap, Johannes, Jacobus Franciscus 94
warships 7, 48, 66, 69, 71, 194, 197, 216, 225, 228
Werner, Leonard 28
West Indies 68
Wilhelm II, Kaiser
  affinity for Ottoman empire and Muslims 112, 120–121
  assassination plot against 114
  influence on foreign policy 112, 117–118, 119
  tour of Ottoman empire
    commercial and colonial motives 116–120
    German public opinion on 112
    international context 113–114
    itinerary 110
    religious aspects 114–116, 119–121
Wilhelmina, Queen
  aversion to polygamy 244

[280]

INDEX

categories of Indonesians received by 235–236, 241–242
gifts given to 237, **238**, 240, 245–247
portraits **238**, **239**
royal Indonesian delegations to 236–241, 247
serimpi performance for 233–234
William IV, King 59
women
    Bhagvatsinh on women's freedom 103–104
    female royals on tour 11–12, 38, 44, 57, 66, 216, 244, 250
    polygamous Indonesian royal wives 244

yachts, royal 17, 110, 216, 228
Yamagata, Aritomo 193, 194, 196
Yukanthor, Prince 128

Zionist movement 112, 119–120
Zuid Afrikaan, De 83–87

EU authorised representative for GPSR:
Easy Access System Europe, Mustamäe tee 50,
10621 Tallinn, Estonia
gpsr.requests@easproject.com

www.ingramcontent.com/pod-product-compliance
Lightning Source LLC
Chambersburg PA
CBHW050209240426
43671CB00013B/2274